THE
AMERICAN REVOLUTION
IN GEORGIA

THE
AMERICAN
REVOLUTION
IN GEORGIA
1763-1789

BY KENNETH COLEMAN

UNIVERSITY OF GEORGIA PRESS

ATHENS

CONTENTS

****

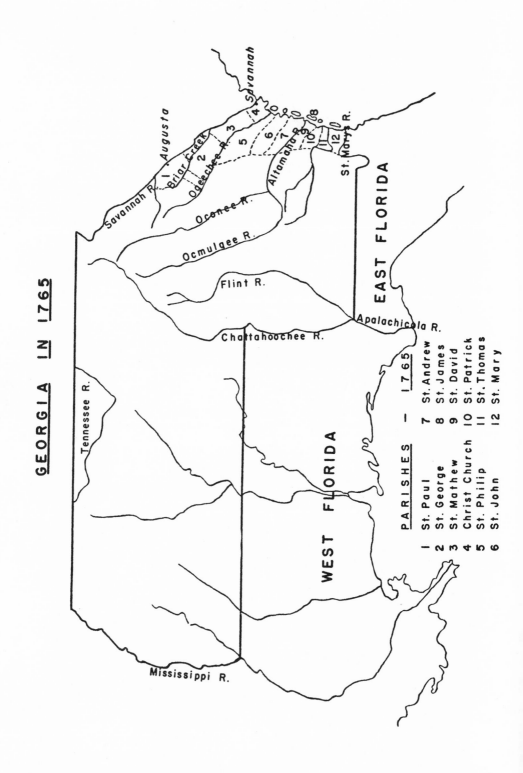

GEORGIA IN 1765

PARISHES — 1765

1 St. Paul 7 St. Andrew
2 St. George 8 St. James
3 St. Mathew 9 St. David
4 Christ Church 10 St. Patrick
5 St. Philip 11 St. Thomas
6 St. John 12 St. Mary

WEST FLORIDA

EAST FLORIDA

Mississippi R.

Tennessee R.

Chattahoochee R.

Apalachicola R.

Flint R.

Ocmulgee R.

Oconee R.

Savannah R.

Augusta

Briar Creek

Odeechee R.

Altamaha R.

Savannah

St. Marys R.

PREFACE

****

THIS study begins in 1763 because the ending of the French and Indian War in that year and the resulting new imperial policy were the immediate causes of the American War for Independence. The study aims at a general treatment—political, economic, social, and military—of the events leading up to the break with Britain, the fighting years, and the years of readjustment immediately after the fighting stopped and independence became a reality. An overall picture of political happenings is given, except for state government during 1779-1781 when the view is blurred and indistinct. Georgia's colonial history between 1779 and 1782 has been treated fully, as have state relations with the Continental Congress and with other states.

The text and conclusions of this study give more emphasis than has previously been given to the British and upcountry viewpoint and significance. However, the author has sought to give a fair treatment of Whig or Tory, coast or upcountry—to present the good and bad points of Sir James Wright and Elijah Clarke, Joseph Clay and George Walton, Button Gwinnett and Lachlan McIntosh.

Nobody undertakes a study of this type without a deep debt of gratitude to others who have labored in the same or related fields, to librarians and archivists who have made the task easier, and to teachers and friends who have encouraged the work. Two former teachers were responsible for my undertaking this study. Dr. E. Merton Coulter, the longtime dean of Georgia historians, helped to arouse my interest in Georgia's past in student days at the University of Georgia and later suggested this specific topic. Dr. Merrill Jensen of the University of Wisconsin taught me about the American Revolution, suggested source materials, and gave considerable help and encouragement throughout this study. Mrs. Louise B. Hays, the late director of the Georgia Department

vii

of Archives and History, offered suggestions from her knowledge of this period in Georgia's history; and Mrs. Mary G. Bryan, the present director, was of great help in my work in that Department. Mrs. Lilla M. Hawes, director of the Georgia Historical Society, was most helpful. The late Miss Grace Gardner Griffith at the Manuscripts Division of the Library of Congress introduced me to the study of British archives and was helpful in other ways, as were other staff members of that Division. Thanks are also due Mr. W. W. DeRenne, formerly at the University of Georgia Library, and the staff of the Wisconsin Historical Society Library, the staff of William L. Clements Library at the University of Michigan, the South Carolina Archives Department, the Charleston Library Society, Duke University Library, the New York Public Library, and to many others noted in the footnotes and the bibliography.

Dr. Merrill Jensen, Miss Nina Rusk, Mr. Andrew Sparks, and the staff of the University Press have read this manuscript at some stage and given considerable help. Dr. Richard K. Murdoch and Mr. J. David Griffin, University of Georgia, have helped with that necessary but tedious job of proofreading. Publication is made possible through funds from the Ford Foundation and from the University of Georgia.

To all these I offer by sincere thanks with the realization that without their help this study would have been much more difficult.

KENNETH COLEMAN

History Department
University of Georgia

GEORGIA
1763 - 1774

1

****

G ROWTH was the most obvious characteristic of His Britannic Majesty's Colony of Georgia during the decade and a half before the American colonies revolted in 1775. Until 1763 Georgia was the youngest and weakest of the British Southern colonies. But the Treaty of Paris, which ended the Seven Years' War in 1763, removed the Spanish, who had been unpleasant neighbors to the south ever since Georgia's founding. The two new British provinces, East and West Florida, were new friends who added considerably to Georgia's military security and general peace of mind. Spanish interference with the Creek Indians, Georgia's most belligerent red neighbors, was ended. The colony's frontiers were safer than they had ever been before. The royal proclamation of 1763 created for the first time a definite southern boundary, the St. Marys River. The removal of the Spanish from the Floridas made possible settlement south of the Altamaha River. Some of the older mainland colonies objected to the provisions of the proclamation of 1763 that restricted white settlement to the area east of the headwaters of streams flowing into the Atlantic. Georgia's settlement had not reached nearly this far west yet; so there was no dissatisfaction on this account.

Besides getting rid of her unpopular Spanish neighbors to the south, Georgia in 1763 more than doubled her land available for white settlement. A congress attended by British Indian Superintendent John Stuart, the Southern governors, and the Southern Indians was held in Augusta in November, 1763, at which the Indians were informed of the exit of the Spanish and French from

1

the area east of the Mississippi, a new basis for white-Indian trade and peace was laid, and a land cession was made by the Indians. The cession included lands between the Savannah and Ogeechee rivers from just above Ebenezer to Little River, above Augusta, and a strip of coastal land about thirty miles deep between the Altamaha and the St. Marys rivers.[1] Georgia had already expanded beyond the original Indian cession of 1733, but the 1763 cession gave her enough land to take care of the rush of new settlers for at least ten years. The lands between the Savannah and the Ogeechee were soon being settled by immigrants from the older colonies to the north and by Scotch-Irish direct from Northern Ireland.

Georgia's spirit of optimism and hopefulness for the future came from more than getting rid of her Spanish neighbors and the Indian cession of 1763. These changes were as much an indication of the colony's new attitude as they were a result. Both changes resulted from international political moves that Georgia could not possibly have brought about by her own efforts. Perhaps what really explained the new attitude was the fact that Georgia was at last fully over her unpleasant infancy of utopian idealism and had entered into a lusty adolescence of self-satisfied frontier realism. She had ceased to be the favorite charity of Englishmen and had become an ordinary American colony. She now had Negro slaves and strong drink, lawyers and plantations, a governor and a legislature; and she was pretty much left to work out her own destiny. She still got some financial help from Parliament and wanted more military help from the British army than she got. Economically and politically she was smaller and weaker than her neighbor, South Carolina, but time would bring maturity. The frontier has always been sure of a better day to come. And the majority of the white Georgians were frontiersmen.

Politically, Georgia looked like any other royal colony after the Trustees gave up their control and a royal government was instituted in 1754.[2] The executive head of the government was a governor and council appointed from England. The legislature was made up of two houses, the Upper House of Assembly, which was the governor's council sitting for legislative business, and the Commons House of Assembly, elected by residents who owned fifty acres of land. The main courts were a court of errors, the highest court in the colony, made up of the governor and his council; a general court, the court of general jurisdiction; and justice of the peace courts, called courts of conscience—it was said because the justices used conscience instead of legal training to arrive at decisions. The duties and powers of each part of the government were the usual ones in a royal colony.

Governors and other administrative officials were controlled by detailed instructions from England. But the fact that colonial assemblies could not be forced to carry out royal instructions was one of the weak points in British colonial administration which it never overcame. The more important colonial executive officials (including the governor, the attorney general, the chief justice, the secretary, the receiver general of quit rents, the surveyor general, the provost marshal, and customs officials) were always paid by a Georgia civil list provided by Parliament. Since a number of these officers were sent out from England, it was possible to keep officials close to the viewpoint of the British government, and it was impossible for the colonial assembly to use nonpayment of their salaries as a club to control them. All colonies founded after the middle of the eighteenth century (Nova Scotia, Georgia, East and West Florida) had their executive officials paid by Parliament, and in these younger colonies executive control was stronger than in the older colonies where salaries were voted by the local assembly.

One thing that made Georgia's government different from that in several other colonies was the ability of her last royal governor, James Wright (1761-1782). Wright had studied law at Grey's Inn and had been called to the bar there. He had resided in South Carolina, where his father was chief justice, and had been attorney general, colonial agent to London, lawyer, and planter. He knew the political and economic conditions in the Southern colonies, and his legal training and work as South Carolina's agent in London had given him a good acquaintance with the workings of the British government.[3] Wright was the only one of Georgia's three colonial governors who had any real qualifications for the office or any real interest in the development of the colony. He was above the average of colonial governors in his ability to get what he wanted out of his assembly and his colony. He worked hard at his job rather than ignoring it as did some nobles who took colonial offices to recoup their fortunes. He was popular with "the better sort of people"—the only kind he wanted popularity with— and he had the personal respect of his political enemies. He summed up his own character as governor when he said, "It has ever been my study to discharge my duty both to the King & People with integrity, & to the utmost of my power . . . ."[4] He was

a typical eighteenth century gentleman who considered government to be the concern of "the better sort of people" rather than
of the lower classes. Throughout his long term as governor, Wright
remained in Georgia except for one leave, 1771-1773, and the
period 1776-1779 when he was driven out by the revolutionary
government.

Wright had considerable personal interest in Georgia's economic development. The entire time that he was in Georgia he
was acquiring lands, plantation stock, and slaves and was one of
the largest planters in the colony by the 1770's. There is no evidence of his acquiring land for speculative purposes, something
that he opposed consistently as governor. All the evidence points
to the fact that he farmed the lands which he acquired and that
his lands were acquired legally under the headright system then
in effect.[5] Economically Wright and Georgia grew together, and
his personal interest in Georgia's economy made him concerned
with doing what he could to keep it healthy.

Wright's relationship with his executive council was always
harmonious, and the council almost always followed his leadership
and backed him in his arguments with the Commons House of
Assembly. The tendency towards the end of the colonial period
was to appoint the main executive officers of the colony to the council, a policy which gave Wright a council easy to work with but
which deprived him of the more disinterested opinion of the leading nonofficeholding colonials. Wright was a good executive leader
and seldom had any serious differences with his executive officers,
who usually followed his lead.

Wright's relationship with his assemblies was harmonious
throughout most of his period as governor. Of course there were
differences and protracted arguments between the governor and
the assembly, and there was certainly an opposition party after
1765. But for ordinary legislative matters, Wright and the assembly
got along quite well. Here again Wright was a leader, and the
assembly usually followed his suggestions as to needed legislation.
Besides his formal messages to the assembly, Wright tried to work
personally through his friends in the two houses to secure what he
wanted. Since the Commons House contained only twenty-nine
members at its largest, such close personal contact was easy. Wright
had a good entree into the proceedings of the Commons House
of Assembly in that he appointed its clerk, who received a part
of his pay from the parliamentary grant, and regularly read the

journal of the House daily when it was in session. As a rule Wright signed all bills passed by the assembly and urged their approval in London.

Strictly speaking, throughout the colonial period Georgia had but one government, that in Savannah. Parishes did exist (twelve after 1765) as subdivisions for religious organizations, militia, voting, and local justice; but they were administrative subdivisions rather than units of local governments. All real functions of government were carried out in Savannah by the provincial government. There was only one general court for the colony. All land was granted by the governor and council sitting in Savannah. Road building and maintenance, construction or repair of public buildings and churches, clearing of navigable streams and construction of dock facilities, and other such governmental duties were carried out by commissioners appointed by the assembly and under its supervision. Strictly local affairs such as the cleaning of the streets and squares of Savannah and Sunbury, the creation and payment of town watches, and other local law-enforcement activities were provided for by the assembly. There was little real need for government outside Savannah until the 1773 Indian cession was settled.

Virtually the only elected parish officials were the vestrymen and church wardens. Justices of the peace, constables, parish tax collectors, and other local officials were appointed from Savannah. Parish taxes were assessed by the vestrymen and church wardens for the support of the parish church and for the relief of the poor. Other than the vestrymen and church wardens, the most important parish officials were the justices of the peace, who held the local courts of conscience, and the militia officers. The militia was organized upon parish lines for convenience, but all officers were appointed by and responsible to the governor.

Indian relations were important to most of the American colonies, but to a frontier colony like Georgia they were of the utmost importance. The treaty and Indian cession of 1763 did not bring immediate peace to the southern back country. The Indians did not fully understand the change which had been made, and French agents continued to operate east of the Mississippi regardless of the fact that this was now British territory. The Creeks, the strongest Indian group in the South, were the last to accept the results of the peace, the 1763 cession, and British friendship. They delayed the surveying of the boundary line agreed

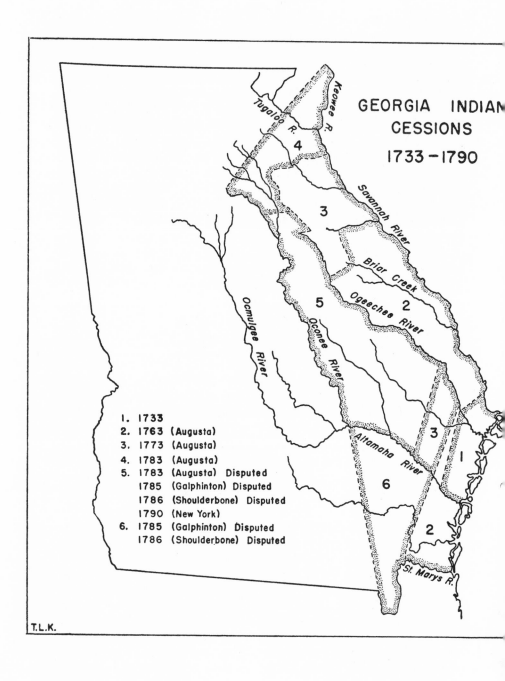

GEORGIA INDIAN
CESSIONS
1733 – 1790

1. 1733
2. 1763 (Augusta)
3. 1773 (Augusta)
4. 1783 (Augusta)
5. 1783 (Augusta) Disputed
   1785 (Galphinton) Disputed
   1786 (Shoulderbone) Disputed
   1790 (New York)
6. 1785 (Galphinton) Disputed
   1786 (Shoulderbone) Disputed

T.L.K.

upon in 1763, so that it was not finished until December, 1768.[6]
By 1765 the Creeks were generally peaceful, and Governor Wright
reported that there were no whites killed by Creeks in 1766.[7] This
was a most unusual record! Peace with the Creeks continued until
1768, but after that it deteriorated. By this time the best lands of
the 1763 cession had been granted, and frontiersmen began to
push against the frontier and to violate the Indian territory more
and more. Wright and his council tried to enforce literally the
treaty agreements, especially the boundary line between whites
and Indians and the punishments prescribed for violation by
either side. Justice to the Indians was difficult because the only
armed forces available to the colony consisted of militia, and
frontier militia was not noted for fairness in its ideas of Indian
justice. By 1771 and 1772 the Indian situation had become
serious again.

   In 1771 the traders to the Cherokees offered to cancel all Indian
debts, which were considerable, and to furnish the Cherokees
much more goods if they would cede a tract of territory about sixty
miles square north and west of Augusta. In February a treaty
of cession was actually signed between the Cherokees and the
traders, but the proclamation of 1763 required that all land cessions from the Indians be handled by the government. Wright,
favoring this cession because of the additional land that it would
open for settlement in Georgia, worked for approval of it while
he was in England on leave in 1771-1773. The situation was complicated by the fact that the Creeks claimed a part of this Cherokee
cession and it was doubtful if they would cede their claims. The
British government approved the proposed cession; instructions
were issued to Stuart, the Indian Superintendent, to try to get the
cession; and Wright returned to Georgia to help with the negotiations. At an Indian congress held in the summer of 1773 at Augusta
Indian traders worked hard to get the Creeks to approve the
cession so that their debts could be paid. The Creeks and Cherokees ceded jointly a tract of over 1,600,000 acres between the
Savannah and Oconee rivers north and west of the area ceded in
1763, and the Creeks ceded an additional tract of about 500,000
acres between the Ogeechee and Altamaha rivers just west of the
small strip ceded in 1763. Wright and the assembly wanted an
additional cession between the Ogeechee River on the east and the
Altamaha and Oconee rivers on the west extending north to the
fall line or the source of the Oconee. The Creeks and Superin-

tendent Stuart opposed this cession, and only the extreme southern part of it was made.[8]

Many of the Creeks opposed the 1773 cession, and the whites rushed into the new lands rapidly after the treaty was signed. There were renewed Creek troubles almost at once. Many Georgians feared a full scale Indian war and were sure that they could not defend themselves, as their militia was outnumbered by Creek warriors. An urgent appeal for British troops was made but was refused as had been other recent requests for frontier protection. The British commander-in-chief in America promised to send troops if hostilities actually broke out, but not before. This might be too late. A special session of the assembly met in the summer of 1774; and, at Wright's and Stuart's insistence, the British government issued instructions to all the Southern colonies to stop the Creek trade, instructions that could never be carried out completely. In the fall a Creek conference was called at Savannah at which both Indians and whites promised to live up to their former agreements and to respect the boundary line separating them.[9] But peace between whites and Indians was really impossible, for the whites were determined to have the rich lands reaching to the Oconee and the Indians were just as determined to keep their "favorite hunting grounds." Regardless of official agreements, whites would continue to cross into the Indian lands and the Indians would continue to murder the offending whites. Stuart realized the situation and pressed the British government to take a firmer stand, but signs of rebellion in America were too obvious for any action to be taken.

The desire of the whites for more Indian lands naturally led from political to economic affairs because the economic item of first importance in a frontier and agricultural society was land ownership and acquisition. Nobody in Georgia after 1760 could complain that land was hard to acquire. The colony granted lands upon a headright system that allowed 100 acres of land to every head of family and fifty additional acres for every member of the "family," black or white. Land was granted free (excepting survey and office fees) but for the 1773 cession, which was sold at one to five shillings per acre under the old headright restrictions. Grantees could purchase additional lands beyond what they were entitled to under the headright system.[10] Land speculation never became the mania in colonial Georgia that it did in some of the older colonies. Governor Wright opposed speculation because it caused large tracts of desirable lands to be held without settlement, and Wright was sure that Georgia needed all the settlers it could get for protection against the Creeks and also for economic advancement. All the evidence points to indications that lands granted in colonial Georgia were earned under the headright system, and that the majority of such granted lands were farmed, logged, or used in some way. Since all lands in Georgia, except the 1773 cession, were granted entirely by the governor and council, it was possible to prevent speculation and illegal acquisition of land easier than in colonies where local authorities made grants. Wright said in 1773 that 6,695,429 acres had been ceded by the Indians in Georgia since 1733, and less than a million acres had actually been granted, yet there was little ungranted plantable land in the colony exclusive of the 1773 Indian cession. Throughout the colonial period land continued to be granted in all parts of the colony, but more was granted after 1760 in the frontier parishes.

Before 1763 Georgia settlers had come from England, Germany, Scotland, Northern Ireland, and the colonies to the north. The Germans were mainly centered at Ebenezer, some twenty miles above Savannah, and in Savannah itself. Darien on the Altamaha was the seat of Highland Scots who had come over as members of Oglethorpe's regiment. New England Puritans, who had come to Georgia after temporary residence in South Carolina, were settled about forty miles below Savannah at Midway, St. John's Parish. Scotch-Irish usually settled on the upper frontier whether they came direct from Northern Ireland or from one of the colonies to the north. People from other colonies settled throughout Georgia, though there tended to be more of these on the upper frontier with the Scotch-Irish. Financial assistance was often given by the colony to the Scotch-Irish who were too poor to pay their passage money and establish themselves in their new homes. Most of the people who settled the 1763 and 1773 Indian cessions were Scotch-Irish or from the Northern colonies.

Settlement of the 1773 cession was especially rapid despite the fact that the land was sold instead of granted free. By 1773 this was the only good unsettled land available in the Southern colonies, and it was eagerly sought by frontiersmen from the Carolinas and Virginia and immigrants from Northern Ireland. Most of the settlers were young, had large families, and owned few slaves—

typical frontiersmen in every respect. Settlement was still going on rapidly at the time the fighting with Britain began, and settlement was not stopped, only slowed, during the war years.

The rapid growth of Georgia's frontier after 1763 helped the growth of the colony's few towns. Savannah, the metropolis of the colony, increased its population and business as is evidenced by the arrival of new artisans and by increased trade. But it was Augusta that grew most rapidly. Before 1763 it had been mainly a defense and Indian trading center. Indian trade continued, but after 1763 the town became more and more a trade center for the surrounding agricultural area. On the coast, the town of Sunbury on the Midway River in St. John's Parish had been created Georgia's second port of entry in 1762. Its trade was mainly local with Savannah except for the export of rice and lumber produced in the vicinity. In 1770 the town of Brunswick was officially created at Carr's Field on the Turtle River, and plans were laid for development of a considerable harbor in the river and on nearby Saint Simon's Island, but real growth there had to await the nineteenth century.[11] Besides Savannah, Augusta, and Sunbury, the only towns worthy of the name in colonial Georgia were Ebenezer, Midway, and Darien. Like the rest of the Southern colonies, Georgia was predominantly rural.

In a general report which Wright made to the London government in 1773, he showed that Georgia's population had grown from 6,000 whites and 3,500 Negroes in 1761 to 18,000 whites and 15,000 Negroes in 1773. Most of these inhabitants lived along the coast between the Altahama and the Savannah rivers, the lower area between the Ogeechee and Savannah rivers, and up the Savannah River to Augusta. As yet few lived beyond the Ogeechee, north or west of Augusta, or south of the Altamaha.[12]

The economic support of this constantly growing population was to a large extent agriculture, forest industries, and the Indian trade. Along the coast and tidal streams were the rice plantations, which produced the greatest agricultural wealth. High ground grew indigo and Indian corn. Frontier farms in the upcountry produced wheat, Indian corn, tobacco, and a little hemp. Throughout the province large quantities of livestock, especially cattle and hogs, were pastured. They were usually marketed in the form of salt meat sold to West Indian planters for slave food. Governor Wright, with eleven plantations of over 24,578 acres and 523 slaves, and Lieutenant Governor John Graham, with over

26,000 acres, were representative of some of Georgia's largest planters. Most of the large plantations were located on the coast, the coastal islands, or not very far upriver on the Savannah, Ogeechee, or Altamaha rivers. The upcountry was an area of small farms with few slaves and more emphasis upon subsistence farming, though practically everybody had at least one money crop.

In the coastal area live oak, cypress, and pine were the main timber cut, with pine and hardwoods in the upcountry. Most lumber and lumber products were produced along the coast or navigable streams because of the necessity of transportation. Lumber, shingles, pitch, tar, and turpentine were the main forest products; and the West Indies furnished their major market. Augusta early became an important center of the Southern Indian trade, replacing Charleston for much of this business. By 1768 Georgia was exporting yearly 306,510 pounds of deer skins secured through the Indian trade; but this amount declined to 284,840 pounds by 1770. An undetermined amount of skins bought by Augusta traders continued to be exported through Charleston. After the Floridas became British, some of the Indian trade shifted from Augusta to Pensacola because of easier entry into the Creek country from there.

There was no manufacturing, except household, in colonial Georgia. The people, as is usual in a frontier community, devoted themselves almost entirely to farming operations and imported their manufactured goods. A little cheap homespun cloth, a few cotton stockings, some plantation shoes, blacksmith products, and a little furniture made up Georgia manufactures. Despite the abundance of good timbers for shipbuilding, few ships were built.[13] Though Georgia had some direct trade with Britain, the great majority of her European trade went through Charleston because of better shipping connections, insurance rates, and naval convoy routes. Coasting vessels plying between the mainland colonies and the West Indies stopped at Savannah and were responsible for much trade and contact with the outside world. Trade was carried on with Charleston, the West Indies, New England, England, and the middle colonies. To the West Indies went rice, corn, peas, lumber, shingles and staves, a little livestock, and considerable barreled beef and pork. Georgia imported sugar and rum and got most of her hard money from this trade. Manufactures of all sorts came from Britain and from the continent through Britain. To Britain went deer skins, rice, indigo, naval stores, lumber, and lumber products. Imports from Britain amounted to about £76,-322 a year by 1773 and exports to £68,000. Food, especially fish and flour, was imported from the Northern colonies, who bought little in return, so that they secured the cash which Georgia derived from the West Indian trade. In 1772 there were 161 vessels cleared through the port at Savannah and 56 at Sunbury. In 1773, there were exported 11,276 tons of produce valued at £121,677. In value of both imports and exports Britain led, the West Indies came second, and the Northern colonies last.[14]

Savannah business was carried on mainly by merchants who acted as importers of European goods and factors for Georgia produce and who sold their goods for cash or country produce. Sometimes a Savannah merchant was in partnership with a London, Charleston, or Philadelphia merchant; but the more usual situation was for the Savannah merchants to act as agents for merchants in these cities. Most of the capital was local and business was done on credit. Sometimes a large planter, like James Habersham, was also a merchant. Most merchants dealt in all types of goods; an advertisement of newly-arrived stock might include slaves, hardware, sugar, fine Madeira wine, clothing, books, flour and other foods, farm implements, and medicines. There were numerous artisans advertising in the *Georgia Gazette* as "just from London" and offering their services as bakers, peruke makers, clothiers, milliners, cabinet-makers and carpenters, jewelers, printers, paperhangers, and so on. Often the situation in Savannah must have been as James Habersham found regarding tailors in 1767 when he said "all my clothes are miserably spoiled by the Bunglers here, and after repeatedly trying new Hands" he was forced to ask his friend William Knox to get him some suits made in London.

Georgians were concerned with provision for both this life and the next.[15] From its very inception the colony had been closely tied to the Church of England and had received considerable help from the Society for the Propagation of the Gospel in Foreign Parts. In 1758 Georgia was divided into eight parishes, and provision was made for the establishment of the church in each. Though the law nowhere stated that the Church of England was the established church in the colony, such was its obvious intent.[16] The lands south of the Altamaha were organized into four additional parishes after 1763. Despite the parish organization, before the 1770s there was little church activity and no church buildings or rectors except in Christ Church (Savannah) and St. Paul's (Augusta) parishes. A church was built in St. George's, St. John's, and St. Philip's parishes and each had rectors part time in the 1770s.[17] Parish vestries were both political and religious bodies and were elected by all freeholders of the parish, Anglican or nonconformist. Rectors were paid by Parliamentary grant, the Society for the Propagation of the Gospel in Foreign Parts, the local assembly, and the parishes themselves—usually by a combination of several of these sources. In the royal period there seemed little concern on the part of the Anglican church for missionary work in the parishes without rectors or among the Indians.

In regard to religion the majority of Georgians were dissenters by the time of the Revolution, and there were certainly more dissenting church organizations than Anglican. There were Presbyterians at Darien among the Highland Scots, in Savannah, and among the Scotch-Irish in the back country; but there was little Presbyterian church organization in the back country. Congregationalists in St. John's Parish maintained their own church and local government. The Germans at Ebenezer and Savannah were mainly Lutheran and maintained religious contact with Germany from whence they drew their clergy until after the Revolution. The vestry in St. Matthew's Parish, the site of Ebenezer, was composed of the deacons and elders of Jerusalem Church, a fact indicating that the Lutherans were not molested in religion or government and that a parish vestry did not have to be Anglican at all.[18] There were Quakers at Wrightsborough on the frontier, Baptists on the frontier by 1773, and a few Jews in Savannah who maintained worship at least part of the time. Certainly the strongest and probably the most religious body in colonial Georgia was the Lutheran organization at Ebenezer and the several surrounding churches, usually served by the same clergy. The Germans remained a close knit group, under the leadership of their clergy. Their substantial red brick church, built around 1770, still stands at Ebenezer, the oldest church building in Georgia.

Georgia dissenters usually got as good treatment as Anglicans. Several dissenting clergy were granted glebes as were Anglican rectors, and the Lutherans were sometimes considered a part of the church establishment in the colony. John Joachim Zubly, the minister of the Independent Meeting House (Presbyterian) and the German Calvinistic congregations in Savannah, was the outstanding dissenting Georgia clergyman and the guardian of dissenters' rights. Zubly, a native of St. Gall, Switzerland, was a man of considerable intellectual ability and broad religious beliefs. He often argued with Samuel Frink, the narrow and legalistic rector of Christ Church in Savannah, about clergymen's fees, rights, etc. Zubly was clerk of the vestry in Christ Church and carried on extensive planting operations.[19] Religious tolerance was the rule in colonial Georgia. There is only one record of arrest for religious reasons, and the Baptist preacher who was arrested for preaching without a license was freed and continued preaching.[20]

Education, like religion, was supposed to be controlled and supervised by the Church of England; but the Church was little concerned with it. Two schoolmasters were paid out of the Parliamentary grant, but otherwise schooling was a private affair. Most clergymen, Anglican and dissenters alike, kept schools to supplement their income; and a schoolmaster was generally maintained by Jerusalem Church at Ebenezer for the education of the young. The college of George Whitefield's dreams never materialized at Bethesda, but both orphans and boarding students were educated there. There were numerous private schools in Savannah at which one could take a variety of subjects including military drill and fencing, fancy work for girls, languages, mathematics, and scientific subjects. Classes were given day and night and private instruction could be arranged. Schools also existed in Georgia's other towns and on plantations, but with not so varied a curriculum as in Savannah. Education was available for those who wanted it and could afford to pay for it; few Georgians thought more was necessary.

Other social affairs in Georgia may be glimpsed briefly from mention in the *Georgia Gazette,* the colony's only newspaper, published weekly in Savannah, by James Johnston. Johnston was a born newspaperman in that he was anxious for news and would print any side of any controversy and seems to have injected a minimum of his personal feelings into the news which he published.

The social, political, and economic center of the colony was, of course, Savannah. Here most of the wealthy and important people lived at least a part of the time. Officials, the few professional men (doctors and lawyers), merchants, and wealthy planters made up the society of the town. Most of them were planters regardless of what other economic interests they had, and the entire group was small enough to work and play together with a minimum of friction. A few of this group lived most of their time upon their plantations, which might be as far away as the Altamaha, but such was the exception rather than the rule. For amusement there were occasional plays and musicales by visiting artists. Public balls and private dinner parties were frequently held. Holidays like the King's Birthday, Gunpowder Plot Day, St. George's Day, and St. Patrick's Day were generally celebrated by militia drills, speeches, or special sermons. Cricket matches and other athletic contests were occasionally mentioned, but by far the most popular sport was horse racing. There were several social clubs in Savannah, a Masonic lodge, and other civic and social organizations. The Union Society, Savannah's oldest philanthropic and civic organization, paid for the schooling of worthy poor, looked after orphans, and made presentations to worthy citizens who did something of special civic note. The Georgia Library Society maintained a circulating library for the benefit of its members.

Socially and economically Georgia in 1773 was a frontier community of about 35,000 people scattered along the coast, up the rivers a short distance, and up the Savannah River as far as Augusta. The back country was just beginning to fill out from Augusta. While there were enough of "the better sort of people" to give Savannah's society some of the "tone" so ardently desired by Governor Wright, there was no real aristocracy of wealth or blood such as existed in some of the older colonies. The rapid filling up of the back country in the 1770s was making Georgia primarily an area of yeomen farmers instead of aristocrats. Most Georgians naturally deferred to their "betters" in matters of government, but they were not dictated to by an aristocracy. The main concern of most people was to get more good farming land from the Indians. Cultural affairs would have to wait until the frontier had been conquered.

THE RISE
OF DISCONTENT
1764 - 1774

2

****

IN GEORGIA, as in all other royal and proprietary colonies, there had been arguments be-
tween the appointed governors and the elected assemblies as long
as the assemblies had existed; but such differences were not
necessarily a prelude to revolution. However, in the period after
1763 controversy became more frequent and more serious, consumed more legislative time, and was seldom satisfactorily com-
promised. Tensions were built up in all colonies, Georgia included. The biggest disputes came out of the new British colonial
policy and concerned the Sugar and Stamp Acts, the Townshend
Revenue Acts, and the Intolerable Acts. There was opposition to
all these acts in Georgia. Other differences between the governor
and the assembly might have been routine and have gone unno-
ticed except for the general controversy between the colonies and
the British government at the time. These disputes helped to build
up a climate of opinion against the British government that
eventually led Georgia to join the other colonies in revolt.

Besides the arguments between the assembly and the governor,
there were differences between the two houses of the assembly.
Two disputes that developed in many of the colonies concerned
the right of the upper house to introduce bills and its right to
amend or reject money bills. In Georgia most bills were introduced
in the Commons House, but the Upper House always introduced
bills if it desired, and argument over its right to do so never
developed. As in Parliament and most of the colonies, the Georgia
Commons House successfully maintained its right to introduce all

money bills and usually insisted that they could not be amended
by the Upper House. Controversy also developed between the two
houses concerning the nature of a money bill. The Upper House
maintained that the spending of money could be involved in a
bill without making it a money bill; it also maintained that it had
a right to share in matters of principle even though they involved
the spending of money.[1] Neither house won a clear-cut victory
in this argument, for sometimes one gave in and sometimes the
other. Besides money, the two houses often differed over the
support of the governor or the royal prerogative. In such case the
Upper House was the one which supported prerogative.

The first step in the "new" British policy of raising a revenue in
the American colonies to help defray the expense of imperial
defense of these colonies was a general act concerned with duties
on imports into the colonies. Usually referred to as the Sugar Act,
it became law in April, 1764. Massachusetts took the lead in
colonial opposition to this act, which, if strictly enforced, would
hurt New England rum distillation considerably. The Massachusetts House of Representatives sent a circular letter to all the
other colonial assemblies protesting the policy of laying of taxes
upon the colonials by Parliament, a policy which had been followed for many years without audible colonial opposition. Five
months after the Massachusetts circular was received by the Georgia Assembly, both houses voted to instruct Georgia's agent in
London to join with other colonial agents in protesting the new
requirements of the Sugar Act. Though the Massachusetts circular
had put stress upon the laying of taxes upon the colonies by
Parliament, the Georgia Assembly based its entire protest upon
an economic argument, that the new regulations would effectively
end the Georgia lumber trade with the West Indies. The new
regulations required certificates and bonds guaranteeing that the
lumber be landed in British territory. Because Georgia's lumber
was shipped in small transient vessels over which the shippers had
no control, the certificates stating where the lumber had been sold
might not be returned to the shipper. In this case he would lose his
bond, double the value of the goods sold.[2]

At the same time that the assembly directed its colonial agent
to protest against the Sugar Act of 1764, it also directed him to
protest against the proposed Stamp Act about which the ministry
had requested colonial comment. The committee of correspondence said that the proposed stamp duty was "as equal as any" that

might be imposed upon the colonies but objected to the manner of imposing the tax and to the added financial burden that it would impose upon Georgia, a burden which the assembly thought would be greater than Georgia could bear. There were also objections to the non-jury trials authorized by the proposed act and to the idea that all British subjects, even colonials, were virtually represented in the British House of Commons though they never voted for representatives in that body.[3] After the Stamp Act was passed, the committee of correspondence approved the fact that its agent had not questioned the authority of Parliament to levy such a tax. The committee directed the agent to join the other colonial agents in working for the repeal of the Stamp Act before some of the other colonies should go too far in denying the authority of Parliament to levy such a tax.[4] Georgians were meek and mild in their objections and preferred dutiful petitions to ringing declarations.

The Stamp Act, which became law on March 22, 1765, required that every newspaper, pamphlet, broadside, ship's clearance, college diploma, lease, license, insurance policy, bond, bill of sale, and every legal document be written or printed on stamped paper sold by public officials. All income from the sale of stamps was to be used for defending the colonies.

News of the passage of the Stamp Act, the rates of the act, and the objections to it in the Northern colonies all received adequate publicity in the *Georgia Gazette* without arousing public protest in Georgia. Georgians were informed that stamp collectors were unpopular people, were being hanged in effigy, were having their property destroyed, and were resigning in most places. The preliminaries of the intercolonial congress to object to the act were also carried in the *Gazette*.[5]

When the circular from the Massachusetts Assembly inviting the colonies to send delegates to the Stamp Act Congress arrived in Savannah, the assembly was not in session. Alexander Wylly, Speaker of the Commons House, requested the members of the House to meet and consult on the matter. Sixteen of the twenty-five members met in Savannah in September, but Governor Wright opposed sending delegates to the congress and refused to call the assembly into session to consider the matter. The assembled members wrote to the Massachusetts House of Representatives that no delegates would be sent to the congress because of Wright's objections but gave assurance that Georgia was concerned with the common welfare of all the colonies and would back whatever action the congress took.[6]

When the assembly met late in October, Alexander Wylly laid the documents about the Stamp Act Congress invitation before the Commons House and made a complete report. The House thanked Wylly for his actions and ordered the documents published in the *Gazette*.[7] The documents were published on October 31, the anniversary of the succession of George III to the throne and a day of public celebration in Savannah. That night a group of people in a celebrating mood carried the effigy of a stamp officer through the streets and then hanged and burned it "amidst the acclamations of a great concourse of people of all ranks."[8] The same day the *Gazette* reported that Simon Munro, George Baillie, and Thomas Moodie had received threatening letters signed "The Townsman" alleging that Munro had been appointed stamp master and that Baillie and Moodie had stamped papers in their possession. All three denied the truth of these accusations and offered a £50 reward for the name of the author of the false report. Later Governor Wright offered a reward for information as to who wrote threatening letters to James Habersham and Dennis Rolls accusing them of being stamp masters.[9]

The Stamp Act was scheduled to go into effect November 1, yet no stamp officer nor stamped paper had arrived in Georgia, not even a copy of the Stamp Act itself. The council advised Wright to stop warrants and grants for land until stamped paper was available but to allow vessels to clear the customs house with a certificate attached stating that no stamps were available.[10]

As Wright no doubt knew, his stamp troubles were just beginning. On November 5, Gunpowder Plot or Guy Fawkes Day, a day of public celebration, Savannah was treated to a most interesting entertainment. A group of sailors assembled together, placed one representing a stamp master on a scaffold, and carried him about the town. He had a rope fastened around his neck, a paper in his hand, and at certain intervals was obliged to call out "No stamps, no riot act, gentlemen, etc." After the stamp master had been shown to the entire town, he was hung up in front of Machenry's Tavern (the rope went under his arms as well as around his neck) and left hanging for awhile before he was cut down to the great amusement of the crowd of people which collected. The *Gazette* was careful to note that no property was damaged and that no outrages were committed during the demonstration.[11]

The next day the Sons of Liberty (the first time this name is mentioned in Georgia) met at Machenry's Tavern and unanimously agreed that upon the arrival of the stamp master in Savannah he be waited upon and informed that the people objected to the Stamp Act, that the execution of the act might be attended with very bad consequences, and that he must resign his office as stamp masters in other colonies had done.[12]

Wright was sure that there would be trouble upon the arrival of the stamp distributor and the stamps in Georgia and consulted with his council as to the proper steps to protect both. The council advised that both stamps and distributor be given the necessary protection and that a proclamation be issued forbidding riots and tumultuous assemblies and especially ordering all magistrates and peace officers to be vigilant in their duties.[13] Wright said that from this time there was a great increase in the "spirit of faction and sedition" and that the Sons of Liberty held numerous meetings and were reported to have signed an association to prevent the stamps from being sold or the act from taking effect. Wright worked publicly and privately to influence the more substantial people against such rebellious actions and to get their backing in the enforcement of the law once stamps and a distributor arrived. Wright said that he thought he would have been successful except for the constant stream of inflammatory papers, letters, and messages from the Liberty Boys in Charleston urging the Georgians to greater action.[14] While the South Carolinians did their utmost to instruct Georgians in their proper attitude and action in regard to the Stamp Act, it is doubtful that they should receive all the credit for what happened in Georgia.

The journal, petitions, and memorials of the Stamp Act Congress were delivered to the Commons House of Assembly by the speaker on November 25. After due consideration of these documents, the Commons House voted, December 14, that the petition to the King, the memorial to the Lords, and the petition to the Commons adopted by the Stamp Act Congress be signed by the speaker and dispatched to England on behalf of the Commons House.[15] Thus the Commons House made good the statement of its members that Georgia would back the action of the Stamp Act Congress.

Late in November Wright received a copy of the Stamp Act "in a private way" and took the oaths required by the act.[16] The stamps arrived on December 5, and Wright was immediately called upon by a deputation of Savannah citizens who assured him that the townspeople had no intentions of attempting to destroy the stamps. On December 16 Wright informed the council that the Stamp Act was now fully in force in Georgia, a month and a half late, but no stamp distributor had yet arrived. The same day the governor and council denied a petition of the merchants and ship captains that the loaded vessels in the harbor be allowed to depart without stamps because of the absence of a stamp distributor, an action which had been allowed in other colonies. The appointment of a temporary stamp distributor was considered, but no action was taken.[17]

After a militia muster on January 2, 1766, a number of people marched to the governor's gate to find out if he intended to appoint a temporary stamp distributor as he had been petitioned to do by a number of merchants. Wright replied that he would do what he thought best, lectured the people on the proper way to question their governor, and informed them that he was really more of a friend of liberty than they were and that his actions would uphold liberty while theirs would destroy it. Hearing that several hundred Liberty Boys were gathering in town to break open the royal storehouse and destroy the stamps, Wright collected from forty to fifty people (rangers, ship captains and sailors, and some local merchants and their clerks) and at their head removed the stamps from the royal storehouse to the rangers' guardhouse. A guard was kept for two weeks, and Wright said he did not have his clothes off for four days. He was sure that this prompt action was all that saved the stamps from destruction by the Liberty Boys.[18]

Mr. George Angus, the stamp distributor, arrived on January 3, 1766. He was met below Savannah by a party of rangers in a scout boat and brought to the governor's house. Several days later stamps were distributed and the port opened. About sixty vessels in the harbor were cleared with stamp papers. After that the people generally agreed not to buy any more stamps until the King's pleasure was known as to the repeal of the Stamp Act. Stamp Distributor Angus soon went into the country "to avoid the resentment of the people," where he remained for about two months.[19] No further stamps were sold in Georgia.

After this there were several weeks of relative peace in which Wright worked hard to quiet malcontents and objectors to the use of stamps. Toward the end of January a concerted effort was made by the Liberty Boys to end any possibility of future stamp sales in Georgia. Several hundred people were reported collecting near Savannah to destroy the stamps. Wright again moved the stamps, this time to Fort George on Cockspur Island where protection would be easier away from the town mob. The South Carolinians became very vehement in their protests against the vile Georgians who were so weak in the support of American liberties. A Charleston group voted to stop all trade with Georgia and to punish anyone selling provisions to Georgia with instant death and the burning of any vessel so trading.[20] In South Carolina the stamp distributors had resigned before the act went into effect. After the port of Charleston remained closed for three months because of the absence of stamps, Lieutenant Governor Bull opened it and allowed vessels to be cleared with a certificate that no stamps were available. The *South Carolina Gazette* began re-publication December 17, 1765, carrying above its masthead the legend "NO STAMPED PAPER to be had."[21]

By this time Wright had decided that it would take more than the small military force at his command to make Georgians buy and use stamps or even allow stamps to remain in the colony. Hence when HMS *Speedwell* (the vessel that had brought the stamps to Georgia) returned to Savannah on February 2, he was glad to put the stamps on board and send them away. A group of several hundred people came to Savannah to demand that the stamps be given to them to be destroyed instead of being sent away. But Wright with his force of rangers, sailors, and the usual "well disposed gentlemen" got the stamps safely on board the *Speedwell* and out of Georgia for good.[22] When Stamp Distributor Angus came back to Savannah from the country on March 26 he was immediately beset by Sons of Liberty to know if he intended to sell any more stamps. He said yes, if anyone applied for them. By the time enough Sons had collected to decide what should be done, Angus could not be found. Hence the Sons went to bed, and recorded Stamp Act violence ended in Georgia.[23]

Throughout February and March Wright continued to try to convince Georgians that they had acted foolishly during the Stamp Act troubles. He sent for leading citizens from the various parts of the colony and pointed out to them the folly of the actions and asked them to go home and convince their neighbors of it. He said he received assurance from most parts of the province that there would be no armed rebellion against established authority again.

Yet he knew there was still "a knot of rebellious turbulent Spirits" in Savannah kept hot by continual intercourse with Charleston who refused to admit the error of their actions.[24] Despite Wright's frequent mention of the "well disposed gentlemen" who backed him in upholding the royal authority and of the Sons of Liberty (Wright called them "Sons of Licentiousness") who opposed him, he never identified a single one of either group by name. Neither did articles in the *Georgia Gazette* or the *South Carolina Gazette* or any other source. They must remain anonymous.

During these Stamp Act troubles the assembly was in session, except for its Christmas recess from December 20 through January 13. The arrival of the stamps and the stamp distributor and the actual sale of stamps came during the recess, but at no time was there any official communication between the assembly and Wright about the troubles. The Commons House of this assembly voted the memorial and petitions of the Stamp Act Congress just as the Stamp Act was going into effect in Georgia,[25] and it authorized its committee of correspondence to call the members of the House together if there should be any further action necessary relative to these memorials and petitions.[26]

The *Georgia Gazette* ceased publication when the Stamp Act went into effect in Georgia. When it began re-publication on May 21, 1766, it carried notice that a bill to repeal the Stamp Act was being considered in Parliament. The next issues carried full information about the repeal until the act of repeal was printed in full on June 18. The publication of the Declaratory Act one week later evoked no recorded criticism in Georgia. When Wright called the assembly into session on July 16 to inform it officially of the repeal, he and the Commons House congratulated each other that there had been no violence or destruction of property in Georgia and that the assembly had not questioned the supremacy of Parliament or the Crown in America.[27] The Commons House proposed, and the Upper House agreed to, an address thanking the King for the repeal of the Stamp Act and for his consideration for the happiness of his American subjects. In transmitting this address to England Wright said that most Georgians were now grateful for the grace and favor received and were disposed to comply dutifully with the laws. Some still persisted in a "strange idea of Liberty" and insisted that internal taxes could be levied only by their representatives. Wright was doubtful that he could dissuade these deluded people, though he would do his best.[28] Wright's entire action in the Stamp Act troubles was approved fully by the government in England.[29]

In a sermon "The Stamp Act Repealed," the Reverend John J. Zubly said that nothing which had happened in British America was more deserving of public thanksgiving to God, to King, and to Parliament. For the people's privileges had been preserved, and America would not become a land of slaves. While stoutly upholding the rights of Americans and praising their remonstrance which helped secure the repeal of the Stamp Act, Zubly favored obedience to the laws of Parliament and respect for the Crown. He was careful to point out the differences between liberty and licentiousness, saying that Christianity taught rulers to consider the good of their subjects, and that subjects must be good citizens as well.[30]

The Stamp Act controversy was the first major disagreement between the people and the British government in which Georgia joined the other colonies. Georgia always acted later than other colonies and was influenced by happenings in them. It is impossible to know what Georgians would have done if left to themselves. There was certainly economic objection to the cost of the stamps. The number of the Sons of Liberty always available to oppose Wright's actions makes it obvious that there was some good organization in Georgia and contact with other colonies, but it is impossible to know who the leaders were. It seems that the opposition came mainly from Savannah and probably from the artisan and small merchant class. The importers and ship captains (who were not Georgians) were the people most willing to obey the law and to purchase the stamps.

A controversy between the two houses of the assembly over the colony's agent in London came out of the Stamp Act troubles. Georgia, like the other American colonies, kept an agent in London to oversee colonial matters that came before the British government.[31] This agent was elected by the assembly for a one-year term, and at the time of the Stamp Act, William Knox, the Provost Marshal of Georgia as well as property owner and former resident in the colony, was agent. Knox was lukewarm in presenting Georgia's objections to the Stamp Act,[32] and wrote a pamphlet defending the right of Parliament to levy internal taxes in the colonies, "The Claim of the Colonies to an Exemption from Internal Taxes Imposed by Authority of Parliament Examined." A portion of this pamphlet was published in the *Georgia Gazette,* August 8, 1765, and immediately roused objections on the part of many Georgians, especially members of the Commons House of Assembly.[33]

Angered by this action of Knox, the Commons House on November 15 adopted a resolution informing him that his services as agent were no longer needed. A copy of this resolution was sent to the Upper House, but its concurrence was not asked nor did it take any action.[34] The Commons House members of the joint committee to correspond with the agent informed Knox of this resolution when the Upper House members refused to join them.[35] The Upper House voted its thanks to Knox for his faithful services, which it said had been entirely satisfactory.[36] When it voted the memorial and petitions adopted by the Stamp Act Congress, the Commons House requested Charles Garth, provincial agent for South Carolina, to present these to the King and to Parliament.[37] Garth, a member of Parliament, had voted for the Stamp Act, but this fact may not have been known in Georgia.

When the assembly met in the fall of 1766 the Commons House voted an ordinance appointing Garth as Georgia's provincial agent. The Upper House refused to agree to this ordinance, maintaining that Garth could not properly represent both Georgia and South Carolina in London where frequent arguments between the two had to receive official adjudication.[38] When the tax bill was drawn by the Commons House, it included a year's salary for Garth as agent plus expenses for the services which he had already rendered.

The Commons House refused a conference with the Upper House because of its contention that the Upper House could not amend a money bill, and the Upper House passed the bill under protest rather than hold up all appropriations.[39] At the request of the Upper House, Wright wrote to the secretary of state setting forth the argument at length and requesting that no agent appointed by the Commons House alone be accepted by the government in London.[40] When the account of Garth was presented for payment under this appropriations bill, the council refused to pass it.[41]

When the assembly met in 1768, the Commons House again passed an ordinance appointing Garth as provincial agent, and the Upper House again refused to agree to it. In a conference between the two houses, it was agreed that Benjamin Franklin should be elected Georgia's agent, and the colony now had a fully accredited agent for the first time since 1765.[42] Franklin was

re-elected every year until 1774 when the Upper House refused
to agree to his election insisting that he had done nothing during
the years of his agency but accept the appointment and his yearly
salary. A quarrel developed between the two houses about their
cooperation with and trust of each other, in which the facts of
the case were entirely forgotten. The Commons House resolved,
seventeen to two, that the appointment of the agent should be
exclusively lodged in the representatives of the people, that
Franklin should be the agent, that he should follow the instructions of the Commons House, and that a salary of £150 a year
should be provided in the next tax bill. The Upper House resolved
that this was an attack upon its constitutional rights and upon the
prerogatives of the Crown. Wright again took the matter up with
the secretary of state, but no action had been taken in London
when the revolutionary troubles erupted.[43]

After the dying down of the Stamp Act agitation and the relative
quiet of 1766, 1767 was full of objections from the assembly to
action of Parliament. The first of these protests began in January
when Wright received a request from the commanding officer
of the British troops in Georgia for the barracks necessities (light
and heat, beds and bedding, barracks furniture and cooking
utensils, and rum or beer) required to be furnished by Parliamentary Mutiny Act of 1765.[44] This request met with prompt
refusal from the Commons House on the grounds that it would
violate the trust reposed in the assemblymen by their constituents
and would set a dangerous precedent. Wright reported this refusal
to the British government and to General Gage, Commander-in-
Chief of British forces in North America.[45] Despite its refusal to
furnish barracks necessities to the troops, the Commons House
two months later requested Wright to ask Gage to send more
soldiers to Georgia to replace the two troops of rangers recently
disbanded.[46] The same day that the Commons House formulated
this request, it resolved to provide sufficient funds to pay one
shilling per day to every officer and two pence per day to every
enlisted man stationed in the province, in lieu of barracks necessities. The Commons House refused to send this resolution to the
Upper House for concurrence as Wright suggested; so no funds
were paid out by the treasurer.[47]

Gage informed Wright that no troops would be sent unless
barracks necessities were provided.[48] The secretary of state wrote
that Parliament would not allow its rights to legislate for the

colonies to be questioned and that the King required that the Georgia Commons House comply fully with the Mutiny Act.[49] Wright called the assembly into session in October, 1767, and laid this letter before it. The Commons House voted, apparently without strong objections, that not over £200 should be included in the next tax bill to provide barracks necessities beginning November 1, 1767, or a payment of three pence per man in lieu thereof. The House also adopted a resolution declaring that it had made adequate provision for barracks necessities by its resolution at the last session.[50] The tax bill passed in April, 1768, provided for three pence per man per day in lieu of barracks necessities for troops stationed in Georgia.[51]

After more than a year of almost continual trouble, the barracks necessities argument was settled. Four months later the one officer and twenty-seven enlisted men over which the argument had raged were withdrawn from Georgia[52] and stationed in St. Augustine as a part of the new British policy of stationing troops in larger garrisons where they would be quickly available for any necessary duty instead of leaving them scattered in small detachments to guard the frontier. Wright and the assembly objected strenuously to this withdrawal and continued, until the Revolution broke out, to ask for troops to be stationed in Georgia.

There was trouble over the compliance of the colonial legislatures with the Mutiny Act in almost every mainland colony with a legislature. This trouble became serious in Massachusetts, New York, and New Jersey. The New York Assembly was suspended by action of Parliament in 1767 until it complied with the terms of the Mutiny Act. South Carolina's objections to furnishing barracks necessities came before Georgia's and were settled in the same way.[53]

The second argument of the Commons House against Parliamentary requirements concerned a statute of Queen Anne's reign that required postmen to be provided free passage on ferries. In the spring of 1767 the Commons House provided for the establishment of two ferries without specifying free passage for postmen. Wright called this matter to the attention of the Upper House, which amended the bills to comply with the statute. The Commons House failed to agree to the amendments on the grounds that it could not submit to the enforcement of the Parliamentary statutes alluded to, and the ferry bills were lost.[54] The next year the ferry laws were passed with free passage for postmen provided and with no objection from the Commons House, which had apparently decided that the Upper House would allow no ferries without free passage for postmen.[55]

The final, and by far most important, conflict which arose in 1767 came as a result of the passage of the Townshend Acts by Parliament in that year. Since so many Americans had objected to the "internal" taxes of the Stamp Act, Chancellor of the Exchequer Charles Townshend assumed that the Americans would not object to "external" taxes, or import duties laid by the act on glass, painters' colors, red and white lead, paper, and tea. Little did he know the American mind so far as taxes were concerned! The acts also created an American customs service to administer the laws of trade and legalized writs of assistance in America. The income derived from these duties was to be used to pay the salaries of royal governors and judges in the colonies. The first mention of the acts in the *Georgia Gazette* was the publication of the duties imposed by the acts on October 14, 1767. Throughout the winter the objections to the acts in the New England colonies and the non-consumption and non-importation agreements were published. From January 27 through April 27, 1768, John Dickinson's *Letters of a Pennsylvania Farmer,* in opposition to the acts, was published, together with considerable favorable comment on the *Letters.* The assembly instructed Georgia Agent Benjamin Franklin to work for the repeal of these acts.[56]

The Massachusetts House of Representatives again sent out a circular letter objecting to taxation of the colonies by Parliament. This letter was received in Georgia before a newly elected Commons House met. Alexander Wylly, the speaker of the last Commons House, wrote the Massachusetts speaker that the old Commons House before its dissolution had instructed the Georgia agent to join other agents in working for the repeal of the Townshend Acts and that no further action could be taken until the assembly met in November.[57] As a result of this letter of Wylly's, Governor Wright was instructed from London to disapprove Wylly should he be elected speaker of the next Commons House.[58]

Wright had expressed fear that the new Commons House elected in the spring of 1768 had a majority of Sons of Liberty and would give trouble when it met. He had no intention of calling it into session until the troubles caused by the farmer's *Letters* were somewhat forgotten.[59] When the assembly did meet in November, Wright told the body that the King did not approve the Massachusetts circular and had instructed him to dissolve the assembly if the circular should be considered. The Commons House assured Wright that it would concern itself with the necessary business of the colony, that it had not received the Massachusetts circular, and that it entertained the strictest loyalty and attachment to the King.[60] After more than a month of routine business, the Commons House on December 24 began a consideration of the Townshend Acts. It adopted a "dutiful and loyal address" to the King in which it avowed a readiness to acknowledge its constitutional subordination to Parliament but objected that Parliamentary taxation was a violation of the "indubitable right" of the colonists to grant away their own property.[61]

Wylly then presented the circulars objecting to the Townshend Acts which he had received from the Massachusetts and Virginia lower houses. The House resolved that these letters were not dangerous or factious, as the governor had maintained, but were a very proper exercise of the right to petition the throne, a right that belonged to British subjects in America or in England. The authors of both circulars were ordered informed that the Commons House approved their actions and sentiments. The circulars and the proceedings thereon were ordered published in the *Georgia Gazette*. Governor Wright immediately sent for the Commons House to attend him, approved the acts passed, and dissolved the assembly as he had been instructed to do. In his dissolution speech Wright put all the blame upon the Commons House because it had been warned that consideration of the Massachusetts circular would bring dissolution. Wright argued that to say Parliament was the supreme legislature of the empire but could not tax the colonies was a contradiction in the plainest terms. The authority of Parliament must be full and complete or of no value at all.[62]

Throughout the first half of 1769 the protests and resolutions of the various colonies were published in the *Georgia Gazette,* but they caused no trouble in Georgia. Wright said in August that things were "quiet and happy."[63] In July the recently adopted South Carolina non-importation agreement, in which the South Carolinians agreed to purchase nothing from Britain except certain necessities that could not be procured otherwise, was published in the *Gazette*. Enforcement was to be voluntary, and American manufactures were to be encouraged.[64]

The *Georgia Gazette* of September 6 carried a three-column

letter urging in strongest terms that Georgians join their fellow colonists in denouncing and defeating the evil designs of the Townshend Acts and uphold their rights as Englishmen. Rights specifically mentioned included no taxation without the consent of the taxed, trial by jury, and trials in the locality where a crime was committed—rights violated by the Townshend Acts. Georgia might be one of the youngest colonies but she was too old for such leading strings. Besides Georgians had "sucked the love of liberty at the same breast" with other Englishmen and Americans. Because petition had been ignored there was but one recourse, refusal to buy the "unconstitutionally" taxed items. "If we are no longer to be allowed the rights of Britons, WE MUST be Americans." Non-importation and home manufacture would secure the repeal of the new taxes. The same *Gazette* carried an announcement that at a meeting of the Amicable Society at "Liberty-Hall" on Saturday it was resolved to invite planters, merchants, tradesmen, and all other Georgians to a Savannah meeting on September 12 to consider ways of obtaining relief from the burdens imposed on Americans by the Townshend Acts. At this meeting a committee was chosen to prepare resolutions to be presented to a second mass meeting.[65]

On September 16 a group of Savannah merchants met at the house of Alexander Creighton, protested the Townshend Acts, agreed that they were unconstitutional and entirely inconsistent with the abilities of the people to pay, and said that in Georgia there was insufficient specie to pay the duties. The merchants resolved that as soon as they could stop their orders they would not purchase any items taxed by these laws and that people who violated this agreement ought to be treated with contempt and deemed enemies of their country.[66] However, no enforcement machinery was created by the merchants.

On September 19 the mass meeting, adjourned from September 12, resumed, and the committee presented its resolutions. The Townshend Acts were objected to as taking away property arbitrarily and unjustly, contrary to the spirit of the constitution. The following resolutions were presented and adopted: (1) American and Georgia manufacturing was to be encouraged. (2) The raising of sheep was to be encouraged, and lambs were not to be butchered. (3) The raising and manufacture of cotton and flax were to be encouraged. (4) Non-importation of British and European goods except what had already been ordered was agreed to with the exception of a considerable list of cheap textiles and clothing, cheap shoes and hose, hats, hardware and plantation tools, paper, firearms and munitions, mill and grindstones, cotton and wool cards and card wire, and items necessary to the Indian trade. All other orders to Britain were to be cancelled at once, and goods on hand were to be sold at former prices. Any goods shipped contrary to this agreement were to be returned or stored. (5) The giving of articles of mourning at funerals was to be discontinued. (6) No American Negroes were to be bought after January 1, nor African Negroes after June 1. (7) No wines were to be bought after March 1. (8) Nothing was to be purchased from Georgians or transients who did not sign the agreement within five weeks. Non-subscribers and those who signed but did not abide by the agreement were to be considered enemies of their country.[67]

This non-importation agreement generally followed the outline of the South Carolina agreement. It excepted more specific manu- factured goods than did the South Carolina agreement or the agreements of most of the other colonies. Jonathan Bryan, a mem- ber of the governor's council, presided at the meeting and was suspended for doing so.[68] Wright said that the meetings had been entirely orderly and had expressed ideas which would continue to be held until there was some real solution to the problem of the constitutional relationship between the colonies and the mother country. Mere repeal of the duties would be only a temporary solution.[69]

A brave beginning had been made by what was apparently a small Savannah group, but little else happened. One more meeting of the Amicable Club at Liberty Hall was announced. "A Mer- chant" objected in the *Gazette* to the "resolves of the Merchants of Savannah" as published and estimated that half the merchants did not approve them.[70] Neither of the agreements contained any enforcement machinery, nor were individual signatures of com- pliance secured. Wright worked privately to prevent signatures to the agreement or its enforcement. The majority of the mer- chants seemed to have opposed non-importation, and many planters were lukewarm. There is no evidence of excitement any- where in the colony outside of Savannah. The opposition was certainly not so obvious, so widespread, so well organized, or so violent as that against the Stamp Act. This type of import duties had long existed in the colonies, whereas stamp duties were entirely new to the colonials. The opposition aroused in other colonies because the income from the new duties was to be used to pay officials did not exist in Georgia. Such officials in Georgia had always been paid from England. From the very beginning the agreements seem to have had little effect on Georgia imports. One disappointed Liberty Boy consoled himself with the pleasing prospect that Savannah would become the chief exporter of Carolina produce just as soon as the port of Charleston closed.[71]

Wright was afraid that when the assembly met early in November the Commons House, as a result of the late trouble, might enter into resolutions against the Townshend Acts and in favor of constitutional rights of the colonies regarding taxation or trial by jury. The Virginia resolutions of May 16 were received and entered upon the journal at the opening of the session, but they were not taken up throughout the session that lasted until May 10, 1770.[72]

By May, 1770, Negroes and other goods which were not allowed to be landed in South Carolina were being reshipped to Georgia and apparently sold there. The next month a Charleston mass meeting voted to cut off all trade with Georgia and Rhode Island because they had traded with Britain while the other colonies were abiding by non-importation. Throughout the summer London merchants reported that they were receiving orders from both Georgia and South Carolina; non-importation was weakening in South Carolina, although it was not officially ended in that colony until December.[73] By the time the Georgia Assembly met in October, 1770, the Townsend Acts had been repealed except for the duty on tea, and were ignored by both the assembly and the governor.

The troubles over the Townsend Acts began in the assembly and resulted in a dissolution when the Commons House took up the Massachusetts circular letter in December, 1768; the entire non-importation movement developed outside the assembly. But at the same time the Commons House found two other things over which it differed with the governor and which were to bring on three more dissolutions in 1771 and 1772. It now seemed almost impossible for the governor and the Commons House to agree upon anything connected with the rights of the Commons House, the governor, or the British government. To see the development of these executive-legislative troubles, it will be necessary to go back a few years in the colony's history.

After the area between the Altahama and the St. Marys was

annexed to Georgia in 1763, it was divided into four new parishes —St. David, St. Patrick, St. Thomas, and St. Mary.[74] When settlers began to move into this area, Governor Wright in 1768 informed the British government that it would be expedient to allow representatives in the Commons House from these parishes.[75] On November 15, 1769, the Commons House asked Wright to issue writs of election for these parishes, stating that it was the "most valuable and inestimable Privelege [sic]" of British subjects to be represented in their law making body. Wright replied that he too thought the parishes should be represented but that his royal instructions did not allow him to increase the number of representatives in the Commons House. He would request royal permission for representation for the new parishes.[76] The Commons House insisted that the proclamation of 1763 specified that all the new areas affected by it should be represented and therefore counteracted Wright's royal instructions. The address ended with a statement that the Commons House dare not impose a general tax unless the four parishes were represented.[77]

The Commons House was taking the "no taxation without representation" argument quite literally, ignoring the fact that it had regularly taxed these four parishes previously without showing any concern about their lack of representation. The interpretation of Wright and his council that the statement of the proclamation of 1763 applied to new colonies and not to new sections in old colonies seems to be the correct interpretation, but the two houses of the assembly entered into a protracted argument over this matter.[78] However, in the end the tax bill was passed with the four southern parishes exempted, "they not being represented according to the true Intent and meaning thereof."[79]

When this assembly reassembled in October, 1770, the Commons House again requested that writs of election be issued for the four southern parishes, and Wright again explained that he could not issue the writs without positive orders from England, which he was expecting.[80] This time the Commons House refused to enact a tax bill because the four southern parishes were not represented.[81]

Two days before the Commons House refused to enact a tax bill, Thomas Moodie, deputy secretary of the colony, refused to take an oath when giving testimony before a house committee. Moodie said that oaths had not been required of witnesses previously and that he would not begin such a precedent. The House voted this a breach of its privilege and contempt of the committee and had Moodie arrested by its messenger and imprisoned in the common jail during its pleasure. Wright insisted that the Commons House had no right to require oaths without statutory sanction and pointed out that the House of Commons in London did not ordinarily require oaths at its committee hearings.[82]

Wright considered the refusal to pass a tax bill and the imprisonment of Moodie going beyond the rights of the Commons House. The King alone could grant representation, and certainly the Commons House could not take unto itself whatever powers it chose. Wright told the speaker that unless the two objectionable decisions of the Commons House were removed, the assembly would be dissolved. At the same time Wright told the speaker that permission had just been received from England to allow representation for the four southern parishes. No reconsideration came up during the next business day; so Wright dissolved the assembly with the approval of the council.[83]

In future assemblies the southern parishes were represented, in future tax bills they were taxed, and the matter was closed. To prevent trouble in the future, when Wright wrote to England about the political division of the lands acquired from the Indians in 1773, he advised that representation be allowed in the parishes which were to be created there as soon as there were 100 families or voters in each. This recommendation was promptly approved, and Wright was told to issue writs of election for any new parish as soon as it had sufficient inhabitants.[84] However, no representatives were elected from this area before the revolutionary troubles broke out.

Writs of election were issued immediately after the February, 1771, dissolution of the assembly, and the newly elected assembly met on April 23. The Commons House unanimously re-elected its late speaker, Noble Wimberly Jones. Governor Wright, exercising a power given him by royal instructions but never before used in Georgia, disapproved this choice. He did not give his reasons for disapproval, but it was probably because Jones was one of the leaders in the opposition to British measures. The Commons House immediately elected Archibald Bulloch as speaker and proceeded to business.[85] The next day after some debate the House thanked Jones for the way in which he had shown himself a loyal subject and true lover of his country by supporting the honor and dignity of the House and the rights and privileges of the people. A second resolution was adopted, stating that the rejection of the speaker was a high breach of the privilege of the House and tended to subvert the rights and liberties of the people. The House however would proceed to business because it was unwilling to delay the public business, which had already been too much delayed by the recent dissolution of the last assembly. The disapproval of the speaker was not to be admitted as a precedent.[86]

Naturally a resolution such as the second one acted as a red flag so far as Governor Wright was concerned. He immediately called into session his council, which agreed with him that the resolution was a "most indecent and Insolent denial of His Majesty's Authority" and that the assembly should be dissolved if it would not reconsider this resolution. After some councilmen tried unsuccessfully to convince the speaker that the resolution should be repealed, the assembly was dissolved on the fourth day of its session before it had transacted any business. In reporting this matter to England Wright insisted again that the powers of the assembly must be settled or its members would soon become "Petty Tyrants."[87] Apparently it never occurred to Wright that many of the assemblymen and colonists might consider him a "Petty Tyrant." Wright's actions were approved in England, and instructions were issued to inform the next assembly of the King's displeasure and of his intention to uphold the royal prerogative. The speaker of the next assembly was to be disapproved; and if there were objections again, the assembly was to be dissolved.[88]

In July Wright went to England on leave, and James Habersham, the secretary of the colony and president of the council, became acting governor. Habersham did not issue writs of election until the next spring, trying to wait until the excitement over the negative of the speaker died down and until he learned the opinion of the British government on Wright's actions. Throughout the fall and winter Habersham reported things quiet but was sure that "too much of the old Leaven of rancour" remained and would cause trouble again.[89] The new assembly, elected in the spring of 1772, included all the former representatives from Savannah who had led the opposition to the government in recent assemblies. Habersham said he did not think that friends of government could have been elected no matter what was done, and so he had done nothing.[90]

When the assembly met on April 21, 1772, the Commons

House unanimously elected Noble Wimberly Jones speaker. Habersham informed the House of his instructions to disapprove the speaker. The House elected Jones again. Habersham said that he had no personal objections to Jones, but disapproved him again in obedience to royal instructions. The next day Jones was elected again, but this time he thanked the House for the honor but declined to serve. The House then elected Archibald Bulloch, Habersham approved him, and the assembly went about its usual opening routine.[91] Habersham informed the Commons House of the royal disapproval of its actions in imprisoning Deputy Secretary Moodie and of its denial of the right of the governor to disapprove a speaker, a right clearly set forth in royal instructions. The House ignored these rebukes and indicated a determination to get on with its business.[92] Five days after the session began, Habersham informed the Commons House that he was extremely sorry to learn from its journal that it had elected Jones speaker again after his second disapproval and had elected Bulloch only after Jones' refusal to serve. Habersham requested the House to remove the minute at once or be dissolved. The House replied that the last election of Jones was not intended to be disrespectful to the King or to Habersham nor was it meant as an infringement of the prerogative. Neither could the House see that the election was contrary to strict parliamentary procedure or to anything that Habersham had told it. The House would leave the minute in its journal and proceed immediately to business. Without consulting his council, Habersham dissolved the assembly.[93]

This dissolution left the colony for two years without a tax bill and other needed laws, especially a militia law (which had expired). The secretary of state wrote Habersham that it did not appear that the Commons House had specifically questioned the King's right to disapprove a speaker and therefore had made the dissolution necessary. He hoped that the time allowed for reflection had improved the situation in Georgia and that the next assembly, which he thought should be called as soon as Habersham thought convenient, would go off smoothly.[94] The hope that reflection would improve the situation was vain as Habersham well knew. Throughout the summer, he said, the opposition attacked him upon almost any possible item that came up.[95] In the summer the Rev. John J. Zubly published a pamphlet in which he seriously questioned the right of the Crown to disapprove a speaker and argued that the choice of a speaker by the representatives must be as free as the choice of the representatives by the people. While his historical argument that the Crown could not negative a speaker was inaccurate, the pamphlet sounded good to Georgians who wanted additional support for their argument against prerogative.[96] Habersham blamed the troubles upon the bad example of South Carolina, insisted that the inflammatory matter published in the *Gazette* had kept the spirit of opposition alive, and said he thought the assembly was ashamed of its action.[97] This last statement seems doubtful for a majority of the members of the Commons House.

When the newly elected assembly met in December, 1772, Jones was again elected speaker. He thanked the House for the election but declined to serve, and William Young was elected. Habersham said that he told a few of Jones' friends that he would not do business with Jones as speaker and that Jones very prudently declined to serve.[98]

In February, 1773, Wright, now Sir James Wright, returned to Georgia and resumed his duties as governor. Habersham had not been very sure of himself as acting governor[99] and in his protracted arguments with the Commons House over the negative of the speaker had not shown very good political finesse. Though the troubles had begun when Wright was in Georgia, Habersham's handling of the assembly at the time of its April, 1772, dissolution seemed inept and somewhat more of an insistence upon the dignity of his office than Wright had usually exercised. The election of Jones, which he used as his excuse for dissolution, was no different from the other two which he had disapproved. There had been no resolution or questioning of the right of disapproval, merely another election of Jones. Habersham's trouble was probably that he was trying too hard to do a good job in a position where he was not quite sure of himself.

Relations between the Commons House and the governor improved after Wright's return; there was not another dissolution in colonial Georgia.

At the same time that the legislative-executive fight was going on there was also trouble between the British-appointed-and-paid chief justice and the American assistant justices. In 1772 the attorney general applied to the general court for general writs of assistance for use in fighting smuggling. Chief Justice Stokes, the only trained lawyer on the court, was of the opinion that the issue of such writs was mandatory upon application. The three assistant

justices professed themselves willing to give all necessary help
against custom frauds but did not think writs of assistance were
needed.[100] Upon a second application for writs of assistance in
1773 the chief justice favored issuance, one assistant justice
opposed, and the other assistant justices gave no opinion. No writs
of assistance were issued either time.[101]

The legislative-executive fight had made the opposition party
in the Commons House more insistent upon its rights and tended
to draw it closer to opposition parties in the other colonies. That
it was powerful in the Commons House was illustrated in the
spring of 1773 by the response of the House to the invitation of
the Virginia and Rhode Island assemblies that other colonial
assemblies appoint a committee of correspondence so that the
colonies might keep in touch with each other about matters
concerning all of them. The Georgia Commons House resolved
that the speaker and any five members of the regular committee
to correspond with the colonial agent be the new committee.[102]
A special committee of correspondence was appointed by the
House in January, 1774, and directed to correspond with other
such committees in all matters about the interest of Americans.[103]

No irreparable break between the King and his Georgia subjects
had yet been made, but many things that had happened since the
passage of the Stamp Act in 1765 had helped to pave the way for
such a break. A change in the attitude and policy of the British
government would be necessary for a return to the satisfactory
relationship of an earlier period. No real constitutional settlement
of the rights of the British and colonial governments, for which
Wright repeatedly called, was to come. Georgians were aware of
the fact that they were Americans. Most of them still wanted to
be British subjects. Action in the next two years would convince
many that it was impossible to be both.

THE REVOLUTION
DRAWS NEARER
1774 - 1775

3

****

THE TOWNSHEND ACTS had caused considerably more trouble in most of the other colonies than in Georgia and besides arousing the colonials to assert their rights, had decreased colonial imports from Britain. Hence all duties except that on tea were repealed in April, 1770, and the quartering act was allowed to expire. The Declaratory Act and the tea tax stood on the books, and happenings in the colonies kept the excitement of the "American Party" or Whigs at a pitch and intercolonial committees of correspondence busy. However, in Georgia there was relative quiet and no new major quarrel between the Commons House and the governor and no new protests by the Whigs against British policies. The effort of Parliament to force taxed tea upon Americans, which many had resolved not to drink, and to relieve the financial difficulties of the East India Company led to the Boston Tea Party in December, 1773, in which Bostonians dumped a shipload of tea into the harbor rather than allow it to be landed and the tax paid.

To punish Boston the ministry pushed through Parliament in the spring of 1774 four acts quickly named "Intolerable Acts" by the Americans. The port of Boston was closed until the tea should be paid for. Changes were made in the Massachusetts government that took certain powers away from the assembly and gave them to the governor. British officials could be tried in England for accusations made in the colonies. The quartering of troops upon the people was legalized. An act setting up a government for the new province of Quebec passed at the same time was often linked to these four acts by Americans.

39

These new threats to American liberty and the presence of troops in Boston stimulated quick and united colonial action against British coercion. Virginia sent out invitations for an inter-colonial congress to consider the situation, and other colonies reacted quickly. South Carolina held a general meeting in Charleston July 6-8, 1774, to formulate her policy and to elect delegates to the congress. Governor Wright reported that this South Carolina action set off troubles in Georgia again after several years of comparative quiet.[1] On July 14 an invitation in the *Georgia Gazette* signed by Noble W. Jones, Archibald Bulloch, John Houstoun, and George Walton and a broadside invited Georgians to a meeting at the "liberty pole" at Tondee's Tavern in Savannah on July 27 to consider the critical situation in America caused by the Intolerable Acts and the Parliamentary acts for raising a revenue in the colonies.[2] Wright reported that the sponsors of this meeting were using hand bills, letters, public invitations, newspaper publicity, and other means to get a large attendance.[3] There was also opposition by the same means. Some Georgians thought that the Bostonians should pay for the tea that they had destroyed and that the Creek Indian troubles on the Georgia frontier were too critical to risk arousing antipathy on the part of the British government.[4]

At the July 27 meeting held at the exchange in Savannah, letters and resolutions from committees of correspondence in Boston, Philadelphia, Annapolis, Williamsburg, North Carolina, and Charleston were read. A committee of thirty was appointed to draw up similar resolutions of objections to the Intolerable Acts. When it was objected that the meeting should not enter into reso-lutions at once because some of the more distant parishes had not had sufficient time to send delegates, the meeting adjourned until August 10, on which date all parishes were requested to send the same number of delegates that they had in the Commons House of Assembly to meet with the committee of thirty. Before adjourn-ing the meeting appointed a second committee of nine to receive subscriptions for the suffering poor of Boston.[5]

There is no record of how many people attended this meeting or which parishes were represented. A Charleston newspaper account said that upwards of one hundred people from one parish [proba-bly St. John] came resolved on an agreement not to import or use British manufactures until Americans were restored to their constitutional rights. The opponents of the meeting said most of the people who attended were from Christ Church and St. John's parishes,[6] an entirely logical situation. There was a group of artisans, small businessmen, and young men from the better Savannah families who early formed a group that consistently opposed the actions of Wright and the friends of government. Because of the physical isolation, religious dissent, and independence in thought and action, the St. John's Parish New England Congregationalists never became a part of the "court party" at Savannah but retained what Wright called "Oliverian principles."

John Glen, chairman of the committee of thirty, immediately issued invitations to the August 10 meeting.[7] Wright issued a proclamation saying that such meetings were unconstitutional and punishable by law,[8] yet every parish sent representatives to join the committee of thirty. The main work of this meeting was the adoption of eight resolutions which were the first real statement of revolutionary sentiment in Georgia. The first two resolutions covered old ground when they said that Americans were entitled to all the rights, privileges, and immunities of Britons and that Americans had a "clear and indisputable right" to petition the throne. The Boston Port Bill was objected to as being "contrary to our idea of the British constitution" because it deprived people of their property without the judgment of their peers, because it was an *ex post facto* law, and because it punished both the guilty and the innocent indiscriminately. Neither could it be justified by necessity. The abolition of the Massachusetts charter tended to subvert American rights. Parliament had no power to tax Americans; the constitution admitted no taxation without representation; requisition to their colonial assemblies was the proper method of getting funds from the colonies. It was contrary to natural justice and law to transport people away from the locality where the alleged crime had been committed and try them and thus deprive them of trial by their peers and the full benefit of witnesses. The meeting declared its concurrence with other colonies in all constitutional measures to obtain redress of grievances. The membership of the meeting was declared a general committee to take any future necessary action. Any eleven of its members were empowered to act as a committee to correspond with the other colonies, and copies of its proceedings were ordered transmitted to the other colonies.[9]

These resolutions were far from the radical revolutionary utterances their enemies declared them to be. They were similar to statements, common since the Stamp Act troubles, concerning the constitutional relationship between the colonies and the mother country. The whole appeal was to the constitution against unconstitutional action by the British government. The resolutions were a statement of grievances by loyal subjects—a procedure that had a long and hallowed tradition in English constitutional history.

This meeting also debated the selection of delegates to the general congress of all the colonies soon to be held in Philadelphia, but in the end decided not to send delegates. No reason for this decision has been found. In an unidentified letter from St. John's Parish, it was said that the defeat of the motion to send delegates to Philadelphia was carried by a number of people from Savannah who were not really a part of the meeting and who had no right to vote.[10] If this account is true, it is probable that these people gained admittance at this meeting for the express purpose of defeating the sending of delegates to Philadelphia. Members from St. John's led a second attempt to appoint delegates to Philadelphia but were defeated again. The First Continental Congress met and adjourned without any Georgia delegates being present.

Governor Wright did not think it advisable to oppose this meeting or its resolutions publicly, but he complained bitterly to London about such action and the lack of support given him in his efforts to uphold the government. As usual, he put the blame upon the South Carolinians.[11] After the adjournment of the meeting, petitions raising numerous objections to it were circulated throughout the province by friends of government (Tories), who were backed by Wright. It was alleged that the province was not fully represented, that the selection of delegates was irregular, that some who sought to attend were denied admission, that the purpose of the meeting was misrepresented, that protests from St. Paul's Parish tendered at the meeting were not received,[12] that such action as the meeting might stop the British government from sending the desired troops to protect the frontier against the feared Indian attack, and that the meeting should have made a dutiful petition rather than question the authority of the British government.

These objections were included in petitions circulated throughout the province for signature to prove that the August 10 meeting really did not show the feeling of the province. Seven petitions, which were circulated in four parishes and which contain 633 signatures, have been located.[13] In Savannah a number of colonial officials and wealthier merchants signed, as would be expected. The petitions from Savannah and the upper part of St. Paul's Parish include a number of signatures of people who later became leaders in the revolutionary movement. Edward Langworthy, James Habersham, Jr., Alexander Wylly, William Few, and Elijah Clarke are examples.

These petitions were followed in turn by objections to the objections. Defenders of the August 10 meeting argued that the Savannah petition contained only 103 signatures, one-third of them officials', while there were between five and six hundred men in the parish eligible to sign. Similar objections were raised in other parishes. In some areas more people than lived there were said to have signed, dead people's signatures were reported, and people were reported to have signed more than once. The contents of the petition were said to have been misrepresented and no public meetings held to get real public opinion. Because the August 10 meeting was made up of elected delegates, people without correct credentials were excluded. None of these objections to the petitions were signed.[14]

After the deputies from St. John's Parish at the August 10 meeting were defeated the second time in their attempt to get delegates appointed to the Continental Congress, they resolved that they would send delegates to the congress and abide by its decisions if a majority of the other parishes would join them. Two additional meetings were held at Midway in an effort to get agreement by other parishes. Four parishes—St. John, St. George, St. David, and St. Andrew—were represented or later approved the actions of the second meeting; resolutions were adopted; and Dr. Lyman Hall was elected as a delegate to Philadelphia. Although Hall had been a leader in the attempt to send delegates to the Continental Congress, he did not attend. Either his election was contingent upon approval of other parishes which did not come, or he did not think he had sufficient backing to speak for the colony. St. John's had to content itself with these attempts and with the collection and forwarding of some 200 barrels of rice and £50 in cash for the suffering poor of Boston.[15]

The Savannah meetings, the August 10 resolutions, the objecting petitions, the objections to the objections, and the Midway meetings prove beyond a doubt that sentiment in Georgia was badly divided about what Americans should do to secure their rights within the British Empire. There was a party for strong action and definite declaration of American rights, undoubtedly influenced by what was happening in South Carolina and the other colonies. This party took the lead and was able at the August 10 meeting to put Georgia on record as being in substantial agreement with the other colonies. There was a party, led by the governor and his friends, that still favored humble petitions and appeals to the King. This party was able to prevent the sending of delegates to the Continental Congress and to collect the signatures on the objecting petitions. Probably at this time a majority of Georgians were not in the first party; they certainly did not belong to the second party, but they tended in that direction. Many people who later decided that American rights could not be secured by constitutional means within the British Empire had not yet made up their minds. Taxation without representation and other unconstitutional actions of the British government were objected to. Nobody breathed a word about independence or a general resettlement of the constitutional relationship between London and the colonies. Revolution had not yet come to Georgia.

The First Continental Congress met in Philadelphia on September 5 with delegates from twelve colonies; they could only "lament Georgia with resentment" because she was absent.[16] Georgians could not blame Governor Wright for the absence as they had done at the Stamp Act Congress. Representatives of the province had made the decision themselves on August 10. Georgia, St. John's (Newfoundland), Nova Scotia, and the Floridas were sent information about the actions of the Congress, but there is no evidence that this report ever received any official consideration in Georgia.[17]

Late in 1774 Wright reported that things were tolerably quiet; but now that South Carolina deputies had returned from the Continental Congress, he knew there would be trouble again and was afraid that a large party in Georgia would try to carry out the dictates of the congress.[18] The assembly stood adjourned until November 15, and Wright prorogued it until January 17, by which time he hoped the furor created by the congress would have subsided.[19]

Wright showed that he knew Georgia when he said he expected more trouble. December was an exciting month. Many letters published in the *Gazette* urged Georgia to adopt the association (non-importation and non-exportation to Britain and the West

Indies) agreed to by the Continental Congress, while others urged that it be ignored. The committee of the August 10 meeting called a citizens' meeting in Savannah on December 3 which suggested that all parishes elect delegates to a provincial congress which should meet in Savannah at the same time the assembly met in January. The Savannah election for this congress was conducted as a regular poll at which everybody who paid toward the general tax was allowed to vote.[20] The *Gazette* carried accounts of elections in the rest of Christ Church and in St. Paul's and St. Matthew's parishes.[21] There seemed general agreement in commercial circles in Savannah that the Continental association would be adopted by the congress when it met. One observer reported that most of the Savannah objectors to the August 10 resolutions had voted for delegates and that two of the back parishes, St. Paul and St. George, that made the most noise in opposition to the August 10 resolutions had now "come over to us."[22]

As would be expected, St. John's Parish was in the vanguard of the movement for the adoption of the Continental association. At a parish meeting at Midway on December 6, it recommended that the other parishes elect delegates to the proposed congress at once and individually adopt the Continental association instead of waiting for the action of the provincial congress. Lists of non-signers could then be offered to the congress when it met. St. John's adopted the association fully, agreed to trade only with those who had agreed to it, and began getting individual signatures of those who agreed to the association.[23]

Meetings in early January at Darien, St. Andrew's Parish, under the leadership of Lachlan McIntosh and other Scots, adopted the Continental association without reservation. Stopping land grants, raising quit rents, and appointing absentee officials who remained in England were declared to be attempts of the British government to enslave America. Long-standing Scottish animosity toward England is seen in the statement, "such oppressions neither we nor our fathers were able to bear, and it drove us to the wilderness." Objections were raised to government by ministerial instructions and disallowance of colonial laws, payment of salaries of colonial officials from England was said to render these officials insolent, to allow the raising of exorbitant and illegal fees without the wholesome effect of legislative curbs, and to make the officials a corrupting influence more dangerous than a standing army. Slavery was declared an "unnatural practice . . . founded in

injustice and cruelty, and highly dangerous to our liberty (as well
as our lives) debasing part of our fellow creatures below men, and
corrupting the virtue and morals of the rest, and is laying the basis
of that liberty we contend for . . . upon a very wrong foundation."
A pledge was made to work for the manumission of the slaves in
the colony. These resolutions, adopted January 12, 1775, are one
of the better early statements of Georgians in the revolutionary
crisis and put the argument upon a considerably higher plane than
heretofore.[24]

Wright reported these activities, along with the promise of the
South Carolina delegates to the Continental Congress to be responsible personally for Georgia's agreeing to the association and
also told of the ensuing attempts by the delegates to carry out this
promise. He said that he intended to make one more effort to
oppose the liberty folk and to keep Georgia out of the rebellion.
With 200 troops and a sloop of war the effort would be much
easier. Wright was sure that things would be decided one way or
another soon and said that he would welcome a decision.[25]

The assembly met in Savannah on January 17, 1775, and the
provincial congress one day later.[26] Five parishes—Christ Church,
St. Paul, St. Matthew, St. Andrew, and St. George—sent delegates
to the congress. The St. John's delegates refused to join the
congress until it had agreed to the Continental association, saying
that their acceptance of the association prevented their joining
with non-associates.[27] Probably St. John's would have come nearer
to getting Georgia to adopt the association by joining the congress
and working within it as did St. Andrew's, which also had adopted
the association.

Six of the forty-five identified members of the provincial congress were members of the assembly, and others had been members
of earlier assemblies. The congress elected Archibald Bulloch,
Noble W. Jones, and John Houstoun, all members of the congress
from Christ Church Parish, as delegates to the Second Continental
Congress to meet in May. The Continental association was
adopted with some modifications. It was to become effective
March 15 and all other beginning dates were delayed the same
three and a half months. The non-consumption agreement of the
Continental association was ignored entirely, and Georgia did not
cut off trade with colonies which still traded with Britain. Goods
necessary to the Indian trade were to continue to be imported
subject to the decision of the Continental Congress when it met.

Other than as indicated above, the importation of all goods from Britain, Ireland, and the British West Indies, and of slaves from Africa was to stop on March 15. Exports to these areas were to stop on December 1. Sheep raising, manufacturing, and industry of all sorts were to be encouraged. Merchants agreed to sell their goods at the same prices as formerly. Horse racing and other amusements, giving and wearing of mourning clothing at funerals, and other unnecessary expenditures would be stopped. A committee, to be elected by all who paid taxes in every parish, town, or district, was to see that the association was carried out and to give publicity to any violators, who were to be boycotted by people living up to the association. Ship captains were not to be allowed to take on cargoes of forbidden goods. A committee was to inspect the customs house records frequently and to give violators publicity in Georgia and other provinces.[28]

The provincial congress felt itself severely restricted because it represented but five parishes and some of its delegates were under restrictions as to the type association they could adopt. The Continental delegates elected by the congress said that it got little encouragement in Savannah because the importers there were mostly against any interruption of trade and that the consumers were divided. Yet, with the absence of St. John's Parish, the leadership in the congress came from the artisan-small businessman group in Savannah, and several merchants who were members of the congress signed the association when it was adopted. The province was hopelessly divided on the adoption of the association. The congress felt that it had done what it could and that anything else must be done by the assembly which represented all the province. Hence the congress adjourned on January 25 leaving final approval of its actions to the assembly.[29] Wright took credit for preventing publication of the journal of the congress by threatening a proclamation against anything it might publish.[30]

Wright and his council decided to let the assembly meet at the same time as the provincial congress in an attempt to furnish some backing for conservatives instead of letting the radicals take the entire spotlight in the congress.[31] Wright delivered a well thought out and moderate opening address to the assembly, calculated to soothe the Commons House, rather than antagonize it. The address was a sincere attempt to get on with the ordinary business and discourage revolutionary activities; it showed the real concern of a man who believed in the complete powers of the British government and who had a real love for America. "You may be advocates of liberty, so am I, but in a constitutional and legal way. You, gentlemen, are Legislators, and let me entreat you to take care how you give sanction to trample on Law and Government; and be assured . . . that where there is no law there can be no liberty. It is the due course of law and support of Government which only can insure to you the enjoyment of your lives, your liberty, and your estates; and do not catch at the shadow and lose the substance." Wright, who said that he was speaking as a friend of Georgia, was grieved to behold the province that he had seen nurtured from infancy at the expense of the Crown plunged into distress and ruin by the rashness of some inconsiderate people.[32]

The Commons House replied that it too was worried about relations between Britain and America and felt that the numerous grievances of the colonies should be redressed in order to give the colonists their constitutional rights. The House would avoid anything not consistent with its duty to the King or with the welfare of its constituents.[33] The Upper House, which usually agreed with Wright and said nothing about American rights, may have startled him when it said that the King's American subjects should enjoy all the rights and privileges of British subjects and that it was necessary that American rights be clearly defined and firmly established to unite Britain and the colonies.[34]

The day the assembly met, the Upper House asked the Commons House for a conference to consider the best means for securing to Americans all the rights to which they were entitled as British subjects. The conference took place, but the two houses were unable to reach any agreement for united action.[35] Petitions signed by eighty inhabitants of Christ Church and by 180 inhabitants of St. George's Parish were presented to the Commons House objecting to the violent actions of some of the other colonies which they said tended to widen the breach with Great Britain rather than heal it. A temperate address to the King limited to the subject of no internal taxation without representation would, the signers felt, accomplish more.[36] The Commons House took no official notice of these petitions but considered the papers from the Continental Congress and the other colonies which had been before the provincial congress. It agreed with the declarations and resolves of the Continental Congress, thanked it for its wise and able action in the cause of American liberty, and resolved to elect delegates to the next Continental Congress.[37] To prevent the Commons

House from adopting the association and resolutions of the provincial congress, Wright prorogued it on February 10.[38] Thus ended the last session of the royal assembly in Georgia before the outbreak of fighting. The assembly had been plagued by the same division that paralyzed the provincial congress and showed the fundamental division in Georgia.

Noble W. Jones, Archibald Bulloch, and John Houstoun, the delegates to the Continental Congress selected by the provincial congress, declined to serve because they could not speak for a majority of the province. Their advice to Georgians to choose delegates again with some show of unanimity was of no avail. They wrote a long letter to the Continental Congress explaining what had happened in Georgia since the calling of the provincial congress and giving their reasons for declining to attend the Continental Congress. They closed with a ray of hope: "notwithstanding all that has passed, there are still men in Georgia, who, when an occasion shall require, will be ready to evince a steady, religious and manly attachment to the liberties of America." Jones said a month later that he thought nine out of ten Georgians were with the other colonies, though they had not shown it yet.[39]

The status of Georgia's trade remained confused. Georgians were free to abide by the association or not except in St. John's and St. Andrew's parishes, which had adopted the Continental association independently. St. John's Parish cut off trade with the rest of the province. South Carolina and several other provinces did likewise.[40] When the Second Continental Congress met in May it stopped trade with Georgia.[41] Joseph Clay, a Savannah merchant, said in April that anything could be imported into Georgia where the association was not operating.[42] Ardent Whigs blamed the trouble upon the selfish desire of the merchants to continue trade and profits and on the timidness of the people to take action. Andrew Elton Wells summed up this attitude well when he wrote his brother-in-law, Samuel Adams: "I truly blush for the want of Spirit of the Greatest part of this province. Who after their mock resolutions lukewarm Associations & faint conventions have Thrown off the Mark, & remain a Self Interest penurious Set not worthy the freedom of Americans or the Notice of its meanest Subjects."[43]

St. John's Parish was highly indignant because the rest of Georgia would not adopt the association and refused to acknowledge that the actions of the provincial congress had any authority.

St. John's tried to divorce itself from Georgia and to become a detached parish of South Carolina, and so be allowed to trade with Charleston. The Charleston committee offered sympathy but said it could not possibly grant the request of the parish, which must remain a part of Georgia.[44] After this rebuff from South Carolina, St. John's decided that it would have to carry on trade for necessities with Savannah because the parish could not possibly supply itself. All such trade would be carried on under the oversight of a committee which would decide what was necessary.[45] Despite its brave stand, St. John's found it impossible to carry out the association as a single parish and had to join the "unworthy" people of Georgia.

However, St. John's was determined to be represented in the Continental Congress that was to meet in May. It elected Dr. Lyman Hall as representative and sent him northward with 160 to 200 barrels of rice and £50 cash for the relief of the poor in Boston. When Hall presented himself to the Continental Congress on May 13, he was unanimously admitted but he declined to vote because each colony had but one vote and he represented but one parish.[46]

Despite the troubles of the St. John's Parish and of Savannah in getting the province to back the Continental Congress, the royal officials, during the first half of 1775, were having even more trouble enforcing their authority. On February 15 the collector at Savannah seized eight hogsheads of molasses and six hogsheads of French sugar for non-payment of duty at the warehouse of Andrew Elton Wells, a brother-in-law of Samuel Adams. At midnight a mob of about twenty people, with blackened faces and dressed as sailors, came to the wharf and took the tide waiter, stationed there as a guard, to the town common and tarred and feathered him with supplies taken from the yard of Wells. The tide waiter could not identify the people but believed they were Savannahians of the better sort. Two sailors, also acting as guards, were thrown into the river and one was believed drowned. The sugar and molasses disappeared during the confusion. To Wright's offer of a reward of £50 for information leading to conviction of the people responsible there was no response.[47]

Early in 1775 the London government informed Wright that one small cruiser and 100 soldiers had been ordered to Georgia in answer to the almost continual entreaties from Wright and the assembly.[48] These troops had originally been requested for frontier duty, but more recently Wright had requested them to uphold the dignity and authority of his government. When authorization came from General Gage to transfer 100 troops from St. Augustine to Savannah,[49] Wright and his council decided that this number was insufficient to take care of the changed conditions in Georgia. Troops in Savannah would probably arouse further resentment of the Whigs and might cause more trouble than Wright or the soldiers could prevent. At least 500 troops and two vessels were now considered necessary to maintain order, and these were requested. Wright stopped the transfer of the 100 authorized, and by the time the new request could be considered, armed rebellion had broken out to the north.[50]

When Wright realized that the American troubles were not temporary, he expressed fear that his mail would be tampered with in Charleston by the Whigs. Because there was no other way to send or receive mail in Georgia, it continued to go through Charleston. On June 27, 1775, Wright wrote to General Gage and Admiral Graves describing the dangerous situation in Georgia and South Carolina. He asked Graves for a larger vessel than the one authorized for Savannah, and requested Gage to send more troops and money to build a fort. The Whig secret committee in Charleston secured these letters from the post office and substituted letters saying that things were going well in Georgia, that no troops or vessels were needed, and not to believe Lord William Campbell, the newly arrived governor of South Carolina, if he showed worry about the situation.[51] By July 1 the Charleston committee was openly seizing public mail in Charleston, extracting pertinent items for transmission to the Georgia and South Carolina provincial congresses and the Continental Congress, and forwarding the mail with an endorsement that it had been opened. Wright said that the Georgia Provincial Congress ordered the postmaster in Savannah not to forward his mail to him but later rescinded this order.[52] Any hope of communication between Wright and London was now impossible unless there was a special conveyance, a means not often available.

Several days before the scheduled May meeting of the assembly, Wright informed his council of rumors that the Commons House would not meet. On the advice of the council a special proclamation was issued requiring the meeting of the assembly as scheduled, but the members of the Commons House did not meet, and the assembly was prorogued until November 7.[53]

The news of the battles of Lexington and Concord reached Savannah on May 10, and caused considerable excitement. The next night the public powder magazine was broken open and most of the powder stored there was removed. Wright offered the usual £50 reward for information leading to the conviction of the guilty parties but did not really expect to secure any information.[54] The powder was used by Georgia and South Carolina Whigs, and there is a strong tradition that part of it was used by the Americans at the Battle of Bunker Hill.

On the night of June 2 the twenty-one cannon on the battery in Savannah were spiked and thrown down the bluff to prevent their use in the coming celebration of the King's birthday and perhaps with the idea that they should be taken out of the hands of authorities. Some of these cannon were recovered, drilled out, and fired on the King's birthday, June 4. The usual drinking of the King's health under the flagpole was done by the governor, the council, and the gentlemen of the town. The next day (the birthday came on Sunday) the governor gave his usual entertainment for the public officials, and the town was illuminated at night. Not to be outdone by Tories, the Whigs also held a celebration on June 5. They erected a liberty pole and then retired to Tondee's long room for an elegant dinner and spent the day in the "utmost harmony," concluding with toasts to the accompaniment of the discharge of cannon placed under the liberty pole. Toasts were drunk to the King, American liberty, no taxation without representation, speedy reconciliation between Britain and America upon constitutional principles, American leaders, and the members of Parliament who had stood up for American rights.[55]

In late June and early July the public storehouse at Savannah was entered and guns, shot, and other military stores taken away. George Baillie, the commissary general, was present at the second raid and, on orders from Wright, forbade the raiders to take the stores. They ignored Baillie but did leave their names and a list of items which they took. Wright was powerless to prevent such action and could only report it to London.[56]

While there was more action against officials in Savannah than elsewhere in the colony, reports came from other areas also. On June 26 the schooner *Lively* arrived in St. Catherine's Sound with illegal goods on board. The collector at Sunbury, James Kitching, went down and seized the vessel, ordered it up to Sunbury, and sent the comptroller and searcher, Isaac Antrobus, aboard to decommission it. A group immediately collected under the liberty pole in Sunbury and told Antrobus to leave Sunbury within half an hour and not to return until the next morning. When he refused to obey, he was forcibly taken off the ship, sent out of town, and again instructed not to return until the next day. The ropes of the vessel were then cut, and it sailed away. Collector Kitching applied to a magistrate, the son of the chairman of the group who had signed the note ordering Antrobus to leave, but got no help. The deputy provost marshal at Sunbury was threatened with punishment if he tried to serve any writs in connection with the affair.[57] The records do not tell what happened to the *Lively*, but she probably unloaded her cargo somewhere along the coast.

Georgia and South Carolina Whigs laid plans to capture the regular shipment of gunpowder for the Indian trade, expected in Savannah in June. The South Carolinians sent several boats to guard the mouth of the river and to intercept the powder vessel upon its arrival. When the vessel arrived on July 10, it was stopped and the powder removed before it was allowed to proceed to Savannah. The powder, estimated at six tons, was divided between the Georgians and South Carolinians.[58]Tradition says that some of this powder was sent to the Continental Congress and used by Washington to drive the British out of Boston.

Throughout June and July people in and out of Georgia said that the colony was assuming the Whig viewpoint more than ever before. On June 1 Noble W. Jones reported that sixty-three barrels of rice and £122 in specie were on their way to the distressed in Boston, and that more was hoped for later from outside Savannah.[59] Even Charlestonians were willing to concede that Georgians were about to come out fully in support of the American cause and make up for their dilatory actions of the past.[60]

By July Wright and his neighboring governors were sure that Georgia was lost to the British cause. Wright said the friends of government were falling off daily because they got no support. Whigs had already warned some to leave the province. Wright thought the situation so intolerable that he requested leave to return to England the next spring. He said that he could not bear the daily insults that were a part of his lot and that the King did not need a governor any longer because that governor was powerless to stop the illegal and revolutionary activities taking place.[61] A man of Wright's ideas of law, order, and good government certainly found his situation intolerable, yet he was forced to endure it for six months longer. Royal government in Georgia had come on bad times, but worse times were to follow before the province decided which side it would back in the coming struggle.

TRANSITION FROM
COLONY TO STATE
1775 - 1776

4   **

B Y JUNE, 1775, Georgia's leading Whigs were certain they would uphold American rights, yet they still hoped to do this within the old government framework. A meeting of thirty-four prominent Savannah Whigs at Mrs. Cuyler's on June 13 made it clear that public peace should be preserved and that so far as this group was concerned, no person or his property should be molested so long as he conducted himself properly and expressed his opinions decently. The meeting suggested that a petition objecting to the Parliamentary acts for raising a revenue in America should be addressed to the King by a provincial congress inasmuch as the assembly was not sitting. Georgia should join with the other colonies in all just and legal measures to secure a restoration of American liberties, heal the division between Britain and the colonies, and restore the union so essential to peace and prosperity.[1] When such men as Noble W. Jones, Joseph Clay, John J. Zubly, John Glen, and George Houstoun could sign such resolutions, the colony was not irreparably lost to Britain. Both in personnel and resolutions this meeting was the last attempt of the two parties in Georgia to effect some sort of compromise before either side went so far there was no turning back. But the suggested program of petitioning the King had been tried frequently with no results. For the conservatives, a petition was one more attempt to keep peace; for the radicals, it was a measure so innocently worded that it could do their cause no harm.

At another meeting held at Tondee's Tavern in June,[2] the inhabitants of Savannah and some of the other parishes agreed to abide by the resolves of the Continental and provincial congresses, to secure the rights of Americans against Parliamentary oppression, and to secure reconciliation between Britain and America. A committee was appointed to put this agreement into effect and to recommend it to the rest of the province. Finally the meeting recommended that a provincial congress be held in July and that Savannah hold a meeting on June 22 to elect its delegates and to elect a committee to enforce the agreement just adopted.[3]

Throughout the rest of June there were frequent meetings of various groups in Savannah. There seem to have been two main groups: one, the more radical American rights (Whig) party that was mainly concerned with preparations for the coming provincial congress; the other, composed of both radicals and conservatives who were still trying to effect some sort of a compromise.[4] The first group elected the Savannah delegates to the provincial congress on June 22 and selected the committee to enforce the recently adopted Savannah agreement. This committee apparently was variously referred to as the general committee or council for safety. By the time a definite council of safety can be identified it consisted of William Ewen, president; William LeConte, Joseph Clay, Basil Cowper, Samuel Elbert, William Young, Elisha Butler, Edward Telfair, John Glen, George Houstoun, George Walton, Joseph Habersham, Francis H. Harris, John Smith, and John Morel, members; and Seth John Cuthbert, secretary.[5]

On July 4, 1775, Georgia's second provincial congress assembled in Savannah at Tondee's long room, with 102 delegates. Every parish was represented except St. Patrick and St. James, two small parishes south of the Altamaha. The representation was as follows:

Parish of Christ Church		39
Town and District of Savannah	25	
District of Vernonburg	2	
District of Acton	3	
Sea Island District	7	
District of Little Ogeechee	2	
Parish of Saint Matthew		12
Parish of Saint Philip		8
Parish of Saint George		8
Parish of Saint Andrew		13
Parish of Saint David		2

Parish of Saint Mary _____ 1
Parish of Saint Thomas _____ 1
Parish of Saint Paul _____ 7
Parish of Saint John _____ 11

The parishes most forward in upholding American rights, Christ Church and St. John, lacked but two votes of a majority and could easily lead the congress. There were a few delegates who later refused to go along with American liberty, but few who were conservatives in July, 1775, sat in the congress. Many of the delegates were well-known Whigs and others would become well known soon. Archibald Bulloch, of Savannah, was elected president, and George Walton, a delegate from St. Matthew though he may have lived in Savannah, secretary.[6]

After its organization, the congress adjourned to the meeting house where the Reverend John J. Zubly, one of its members, preached a sermon on the alarming state of American affairs, "The Law of Liberty," taking his text from James 2:12: "So speak ye, and so do, as they that shall be judged by the law of liberty." Zubly expounded at great length upon the oppressive measures of Rehoboam in Israel (I Kings 12) and the grievous burdens and taxes he laid upon the people. The likeness to George III and America was obvious. Laws are necessary, said Zubly, but the only perfect law is the law of God. The Gospel of Jesus is the law of liberty, for liberty must be regulated by law to be of any value. All will be judged in the end by this law of liberty and punished if they have not measured up to its standards. Christianity commands respect for superiors but does not give them license to do as they please. Christianity requires obedience only when magistrates act for the common good. The sermon thus far might be called an application of the ideas of Locke to religion.

Next came the immediate situation in America and its remedy. Because Zubly was a believer in monarchy as the best form of government, he fell back on the old explanation that the King had bad advisers and would do no wrong when he knew the true situation. Americans were urged never to lose sight of their glorious connection with Britain and never to think of separation. They should act in moderation in all things; their opposition should be to oppression, not to law.[7] From the position enunciated in this sermon, that the colonists should insist upon their constitutional rights under law within the empire, Zubly never departed.

The first business of the congress was to request Governor Wright to appoint a day of fasting and prayer for a happy reconciliation of the disputes between Britain and the colonies. Wright's council advised that he could not consider the congress a constitutional assembly, yet the request was put in such dutiful and loyal terms that it should be complied with. Thinking that the congress would have appointed the day itself had he not agreed to do so, Wright proclaimed July 19 as a day of fasting and prayer, but did not mention that the congress had requested such a day.[8] After arrangements had been made, word arrived that the Continental Congress had proclaimed July 20 as a fast day for the same purpose. The provincial congress decided that both days should be observed in Georgia. When the Reverend Haddon Smith, Rector of Christ Church, refused to observe July 20 because he had not been so directed by the governor although the congress twice requested him to observe both days, he was declared unfriendly to America and forbidden to preach longer in Savannah.[9]

July 6 was taken up by congress in the consideration of a motion to put the colony on the same footing as the other colonies. Sixteen resolutions were adopted declaring that Georgia would carry out all the recommendations of the late Continental Congress, that its American Declaration or Bill of Rights was adopted, and that the association as originally adopted by the Continental Congress was to go into effect immediately.[10] There was no doubt now that Georgia was fully bound by the association; the only problem henceforth would be enforcement. Georgians did not think this would be difficult.

On July 7 the congress elected five delegates (John Houstoun, Archibald Bulloch, the Reverend John J. Zubly, Noble W. Jones, and Lyman Hall) to the Second Continental Congress, then meeting in Philadelphia.[11] The first four were members of the provincial congress and had been prominent in its activities to date. Hall was in Philadelphia as the St. John's Parish delegate to the Continental Congress. A secret committee was created to discover and report to the congress or council of safety all matters that these bodies should consider.[12]

The congress approved a petition to the King drawn up by Dr. Zubly in much bolder language than had been used previously in Georgia. George III was reminded that he was the sovereign of the greatest empire on earth, recently enlarged by the acquisitions of 1763. Here the Catholic religion and arbitrary French law were approved in place of the just and mild British constitution and the protestant religion. The acts to raise a revenue in America would enslave the Americans and any attempt to enforce them would increase the expenses of the British taxpayer rather than lessen them. Even the Crown officers in America disapproved of these acts which were driving America to the brink of despair and endangering the empire. The King should listen to the Americans instead of his ministers, recall the armies and fleets, and see that justice and the constitution replace the arbitrary and unconstitutional actions of the ministry. Then he would find that he could easily command the last shilling of American property and the last drop of American blood.[13]

On July 10 the congress expressed its ideas about the unhappy state of American affairs in a set of nineteen resolutions. They began with the usual statement of American rights, and declared that in the British Empire the constitution was superior to every man. The colonies were declared to be subject to the Crown only and not to Parliament. Depriving a man of his property without his or his representative's consent was contrary to the law of nature and the British constitution. Civil war had begun in the North, yet the Georgia Assembly was not allowed to sit and the congress had to meet to preserve American rights and union with Britain. The first hint made in any public meeting that Georgians even considered separation from Britain was contained in the statement that nothing but being deprived of the privileges and natural rights as Britons could ever make the thought of separation possible. The congress admitted that the British government had a right to raise a revenue in the colonies when it said that if royal requisitions were made they should be granted according to the ability of the colonies. People who disobeyed the provincial and Continental congresses should have their names sent to the Continental Congress to be published in every gazette in America, and Georgians should have as little to do with them as possible. Debtors willing to pay their debts should have a stay in the payment of these debts when the confused situation made payment more difficult. The exception of Georgia from the list of American colonies with whom trade had been prohibited by a late act of Parliament was declared an insult meant to break the American union.[14]

These resolutions were a general compromise into which the conflicting ideas of the members of the congress were lumped. The only thing that they definitely advocated was American rights within the British Empire; here was the one point of agreement among all the members in the controversy at that date. There was no new suggestion as to how these rights should be secured. The hint of possible separation from the empire must have been slipped in by some radical while the moderates were not looking.

The congress sent Wright an address saying that it had met because action by the people was necessary and the assembly had not been allowed to deliberate unhampered. Most Georgians, the address continued, had always considered Parliamentary taxation illegal but had done little about it previously. Now they had joined with the other colonists by adopting the association and sending delegates to the Continental Congress. Letters of Wright recently published in England were objected to as favoring the ministry instead of giving the true situation in Georgia. However, the people were still ready to acknowledge whatever Wright might do for the good of the colony in the future.[15]

After considering Georgia's finances, the congress decided that £10,000 should be provided as there was no likelihood that the assembly would meet again soon. Certificates, to be sunk within three years after reconciliation between Britain and the colonies, were to be issued. All property holders were declared bound to contribute to a general tax to sink the certificates, but no actual procedure for collection was provided. Anyone who refused to accept these certificates was declared to be an enemy of the province.[16]

The congress had now done its major work, but there were certain other things to be done before adjournment. In providing for its own successors, it voted that future congresses should have a fixed representation of ninety-six delegates apportioned so as to lessen the predominance of Savannah, increase that of St. John's Parish, and give representation to the Indian cession of 1773 for the first time. Electors were all who paid toward the general tax.[17]

A general committee, consisting of the Savannah delegates plus all other delegates who happened to be in town, was to have power to superintend, direct, and advise parochial and district committees and to hear appeals from them. Appeals lay from the general committee to the congress.[18] A council of safety was created and given full power, during the recess of the congress, to give information, propose measures, and advise the Continental delegates.[19] A publicity committee was appointed to keep Georgians informed of the dispute between Britain and the colonies and of the doings of the congresses.[20]

The delegates to the Continental Congress were instructed to apply to it for full incorporation with the other provinces and to pledge Georgia's faith to contribute an adequate part of the expenses to defend American rights.[21] In his report to the Continental Congress, President Bulloch emphasized the fact that Georgia was now united. Every parish except two small and almost uninhabited ones had been represented in the provincial congress. Several parishes, previously backward in the American cause, had shown laudable zeal. Georgia promised full cooperation in whatever the Continental Congress might undertake.[22]

On July 17 the second provincial congress adjourned until August 19, the day before it would end officially.[23] There was no doubt now that Georgia had gone all the way with the other colonies in opposition to British action. The congress had made one more try at reconciliation, but it had adopted measures that were to be followed regardless of reconciliation. It had considered several matters that could be acted upon only by a legislative body (reform of the militia and the raising of money), and it stated that it met in place of the assembly which had not been allowed to hold uninterrupted sessions. The second provincial congress was Georgia's first revolutionary government.

After the adoption of the association by the congress on July 6, 1775, an all-out attempt was made to get the measure signed and enforced throughout the colony. High-pressure methods were used to secure signatures wherever they were not forthcoming voluntarily. Economic pressure and unfavorable publicity were the usual methods, but at times stronger methods were used. Governor Wright reported that a great part of the province signed.[24] Trouble immediately arose over the question of whether vessels that had sailed before the association was adopted should be allowed to land. The provincial congress agreed that vessels arriving within one month of the adoption of the association should be allowed to land their goods, which would be stored until the Continental Congress decided upon a proper disposition. After a heated debate in Philadelphia, it was decided that the cargoes could be sold and any profit used for Georgia's defense.[25] Even during this month some parochial committees would not allow cargo to be landed while another parochial committee might allow even the same vessel to land its cargo. Several slave ships which were not allowed to land their cargoes had difficulty in securing sufficient food to proceed elsewhere.[26]

Once the association was adopted, the Continental Congress and South Carolina removed their trade bans on Georgia.[27] Yet the association was not strictly enforced, especially in the export of Georgia produce. Exportation of indigo was not stopped until September 10. Georgians applied to the Continental Congress for permission to export their 1775 crop and to import for the Indian trade. No record of a decision by Congress has been found on this matter, but it would be safe to say that many Georgians exported, whether it was legal to do so or not. Some merchants favored exportation to pay their debts in England.[28]

Governor Wright reported that enforcement of the association took up much of the time of the provincial congress, the council of safety, and the parochial committees. Usually, adverse decisions of these bodies were sufficient to keep vessels from landing and selling forbidden cargoes.[29] Vessels were reported as loading and unloading illegal cargoes in the streams south of the Altamaha, where the population was sparse and chance of detection not very great.[30]

Besides enforcing the association, Georgia Whigs in the summer of 1775 continued the process begun by the second provincial congress of taking political power away from the royal government and giving it to Whig governmental agencies. The most important agencies of the new government were the provincial congress and the council of safety. These bodies were not bound by royal instructions, constitutions, or in any other way. They assumed what powers they considered necessary and could be checked only by the voters. The provincial congress, the only body elected by the voters, took ultimate authority; and the council of safety acted as an executive when the congress was not in session. But the council carried on legislative and judicial duties if it thought them necessary, and there was no clear-cut division between its work and powers and those of the congress. Three congresses were elected and served during 1775, and a fourth in January, 1776.

The council of safety, which met regularly once a week or oftener if necessary,[31] was elected by the general provincial committee or the provincial congress. It elected its own officers and sometimes filled vacancies in its own ranks and called elections or sessions of the provincial congress as needed.[32] It directed military activities completely—commissioned militia officers elected by their units, ordered militia organizations to duty, and took steps to secure arms and ammunition.[33] It undertook Indian negotiations to counteract the influence of the British Indian Department. It borrowed or issued monies and provided for expenditures.[34] It appointed a committee to oversee the *Gazette* and to take care that nothing unfavorable to the Whig cause was printed.[35]

The Savannah Parochial Committee took unto itself more and more of the functions of local government. It enforced the association, embargoed provisions needed locally,[36] appointed a layman to officiate in Christ Church after the rector had been silenced by the provincial congress,[37] and did whatever it thought needed doing for Savannah. The identified members of this committee in September, 1775, were Mordecai Sheftall, chairman, a Jewish merchant; _____ Lyons, a blacksmith; and Peter Tondee, an innkeeper. Wright lamented the lack of people of ability and substance on the commitee ("it is really terrible my Lord that such people should be suffered to overturn the Civil Government . . ."), but he was glad that the council of safety included planters, merchants, and men of substance.[38]

The second provincial congress considered new militia regulations but adjourned without taking any action. On August 8 the council of safety informed Wright that many of the militia officers were unacceptable (probably because they would not sign the association) to the men they commanded to a degree that would impair battle efficiency and requested that officers elected by the militiamen be commissioned. Some militia organizations had already elected officers who probably served without formal commissions when Wright refused to commission them. The first records of the council of safety, for November, 1775, show that it was commissioning militia officers by that date.[39] In October a party of back-country people forced the surrender of the garrison of rangers stationed at a small frontier fort for defense against Indians. The council of safety ordered the fort returned to the rangers, who would now come under the authority of the council of safety and not the governor.[40]

In taking over the courts, Georgians moved slower than they did with the other branches of government and were careful to preserve the legal practices and safeguards of the English legal system. In early March a group of people in St. George's Parish agreed to let no writs or processes be served against them and actually prevented the service of writs in the parish. Governor Wright sent a strong letter to the justices of the parish, and the leaders of the movement were arrested. The people who had entered into the agreement then said they did not realize the unlawfulness of their actions and were sorry for what they had done. At their request, all legal action against them was stopped.[41] After the summer of 1775 none of the assistant judges met with the chief justice to hold court. Noble Jones, the judge most likely to uphold royal government, was too ill. The other two judges were Whigs, one of them having been a member of the second provincial congress.[42] At the October term of the general court, the majority of the jurors refused to be sworn. Activity of the general court was thus severely curtailed, and the issuance of legal papers was about all the business that could be carried on henceforth.[43]

On December 1, 1775, the provincial congress ordered all actions for recovery of debt to stop unless approved by the parochial committee of the defendant. The attorney general, James Hume, ignored the regulations of the provincial congress; so in December it ordered him to leave the province. Chief Justice Stokes issued a rule of court striking from the roll of attorneys any who delayed cases on account of the regulations of the provincial congress, but he did not have it published for fear it would cause royal officials additional trouble and would not accomplish its desired end. In December armed men took possession of the courthouse in Savannah and Stokes gave up trying to enforce laws though he remained in Georgia until April, 1776.[44]

Such actions made it obvious that royal government had little power. The royal council continued to meet and consider rebel activities, but it could do nothing to prevent them. By the middle of September, 1775, Wright was sure that the power of royal government was gone entirely. Sometimes royal officials were not permitted to carry out their duties under threats of bodily harm, and those who tried to carry on as previously found themselves ignored by the people. Wright reported that he was governor in name only while the real power was exercised by the provincial congress, council of safety, general committee, and parochial committees. The British government recognized these facts and included Georgia in the colonies that might be abandoned by the royal officials whenever they thought it necessary to their safety.[45]

While the Georgia Whigs were taking over the colony's government, they insisted that everyone believe as they did about British tyranny and often used strong persuasion to see that their viewpoint prevailed. Certain instances show the strong feelings of 1775 and furnish background for the bloody partisan fighting of 1779-1781. As early as June, 1775, ship captains and merchants trading at Savannah were ordered by a committee of Whigs to leave the province because they were too forward in support of the King's cause.[46] Since all the people concerned were transients who soon left Georgia, the matter had no lasting effect. The first Savannah resident to get special "Liberty" treatment was a mariner and pilot, John Hopkins, who behaved disrespectfully toward the Sons of Liberty and was said to have drunk "Damnation to America" despite warnings that his conduct was not approved. On the night of July 24 he was taken from his home, tarred and feathered, and paraded through the streets of Savannah. At the liberty tree he was told that he would be hanged unless he drank "Damnation to all Tories and Success to American Liberty." He drank as directed and did not press charges against the mob leaders,[47] who were prominent Whigs, for fear of personal harm if he did so. Hopkins reported that he heard that the Reverend Mr. Smith, Rector of Christ Church, who had refused to observe the Continental Congress day of fasting and prayer, would be next and that all Tories would receive the same treatment. Smith said that a number of people entered his home the same night that Hopkins was visited but that he was out of town. Learning about this the next day, Smith went down to Tybee for a week and then took passage to England. Wright said he did not believe such conduct was approved by all the people but only the violent among the mob.[48]

The most famous tarring and feathering took place in Augusta on August 2. A body of Sons of Liberty went from Augusta to New Richmond, South Carolina, to bring to account William Thompson and Thomas Brown, lately come from England, who had expressed strong opposition to the measures adopted to support American liberty and had tried to persuade the people of the area to join them. Brown was reported to be a son of Lord North, who had been sent to poison the minds of Americans. Thompson was absent when the Sons arrived, and Brown refused to return to Augusta with them. He was taken to Augusta, tarred and feathered, and ridden about the town in a cart. The next day, "consenting voluntarily," he swore that he repented of his past actions and would do his utmost to protect American liberties in the future and try to persuade a party of men operating under Colonel Fletchall in Ninety Six District of South Carolina to do likewise. Brown reported that he lost the use of two toes and could not walk for six months as a result of the bad treatment he got in Augusta. As soon as he was released, Brown publicly retracted his "voluntary" oath to protect American liberties. It was reported that Brown and Thompson collected 150 sympathizers to demand satisfaction of the Augusta Sons of Liberty and that Colonel Fletchall with 700 men was ready to join them in securing the leaders of the group that had harmed Brown. The Augusta parochial committee applied to James Grierson, commander of the Augusta militia, for help in protecting themselves and the town, but Grierson refused any help unless Governor Wright ordered it. Some militia came to Augusta on the order of the council of safety in Savannah, but no battle developed. Brown retired into South Carolina before moving to St. Augustine.[49]

Such over-zealous action by Whigs drove some neutrals into the Tory camp and stored up resentment on the part of the Tories, which was repaid later with interest, especially in Brown's case.

In light of what was happening in Georgia and what Wright was saying about it, his proclamation of November 2, inviting loyalists from other colonies to settle in Georgia, sounds out of character. People who had been disturbed in person and property were told that in Georgia they could follow their occupations and enjoy their property peacefully with confidence that the laws of Britain would protect them.[50]

One opponent of independence who got better treatment than those mentioned above was the Reverend John J. Zubly, who had left Philadelphia when he discovered that he could not stem the trend toward independence in the Continental Congress. He had been accused of carrying on a treasonable correspondence with Wright by informing him of the actions of the Continental Congress. He was allowed to go at large and to argue with Whigs, though he had now lost his earlier popularity with them. Zubly still insisted on American rights in the British Empire, the position that he had originally taken.[51] By being consistent in his beliefs, Zubly came to be thought of as a reactionary Tory instead of the radical Whig he had been considered just a year earlier.

More important to most Georgians than what happened to a few Tories was the attitude of the neighboring Indians. In June, 1775, the South Carolina Provincial Congress accused Indian Superintendent John Stuart of trying to arouse the Indians against the frontier and sent emissaries to Savannah, where Stuart had gone hastily from Charleston, to get Whig help in returning Stuart to Charleston. Stuart met with Whig leaders and read them his correspondence with London and his deputies to convince them that

he was not trying to bring down Indians on the frontiers nor had
any orders to do such a thing. From Savannah Stuart went to St.
Augustine where he had no fear of capture by Whigs.[52]

The South Carolinians were mainly worried about the Cherokees, but the Creeks caused Georgians most concern. Relations
with the Creeks in the spring had been precarious because of a
shortage of trading supplies. When the gunpowder for the Indian
trade arrived at Savannah in July, it was captured by the Georgia
and South Carolina Whigs, and only a small amount of it ever got
to the Creeks. Stuart and Wright tried to get Indian supplies in
Savannah, Augusta, and St. Augustine to keep the Creeks quiet.
Stuart got some powder in St. Augustine, but part of it was
captured by Whigs on its way to the Creeks.[53] Both sides were
worried about what the Creeks might do and Stuart and Wright
worked hard to prevent any Indian trouble, which they knew the
Whigs would blame on them if it did come.

Georgia, South Carolina, and the Continental Congress sent
agents (usually Indian traders) to win Indian friendship and oppose the influence of Stuart and his deputies. Both Whigs and Tories wanted to keep the Indians neutral and to prevent their joining the other side. Stuart's correspondence throughout the fall of
1775 makes it plain that he was sincerely trying to keep the Indians
quiet and at the same time to counteract Whig actions and keep
the Indians friendly to the British.[54]

In the midst of this contest between the Whigs and the British
Indian Superintendent, a second vessel of powder for the Indian
trade was captured by the Whigs at Savannah on September 17.
Part of this powder was sent to the Indians as a gift, but the rest
was retained by the Georgians for their own use. Wright was so
concerned about what the Creeks might do after this second capture that he privately urged Georgia Whig leaders to send the
powder to the Creeks to maintain peace. All he could get was a
vague promise from the Whigs to do what they could to get supplies to the Creeks.[55]

To counteract the gifts and supplies which the Whigs were getting to the Creeks, Stuart got supplies from Britain sent to St.
Augustine where they would be safe from Whig interference.[56]
The threats heard in South Carolina and Georgia against Stuart
are proof of the high opinion the Whigs held of his abilities with
the Indians.[57] Stuart still wanted peace in the Indian country, and
even after he received definite orders to use the Indians against the

Whigs he hoped to use them with whites so they could be controlled. Indiscriminate Indian warfare was too horrible for Stuart to contemplate, and it would be harmful to the numerous Tory frontiersmen as well as to Whigs.[58]

Early in January, 1776, the council of safety received word from Charleston that British war vessels were unable to secure needed supplies there and probably would come to Savannah for them. The council of safety ordered militia to Savannah, sought additional military supplies, set up a defense system, and warned all coastal areas to be especially vigilant. As a protective measure, the houses of overseers and Negroes on both sides of the Savannah River for twenty-five miles above Savannah were ordered searched for arms and ammunition.[59]

By January 18 four men-of-war and several auxiliary vessels had arrived at the mouth of the Savannah River. Governor Wright sent for Noble W. Jones and Joseph Clay, leading Whigs, and told them that one of the vessels was to be stationed at the mouth of the Savannah, while the others desired only to purchase provisions. If the vessels were allowed to make their purchases peaceably, Wright offered to persuade the commander not to harm Savannah; otherwise Wright was sure the vessels would take what they needed and probably damage the town in the process.[60]

The council of safety differed with Wright's program and began the execution of its own plan by arresting Wright, his council, and other royal officials imediately. After two days under guard, the arrested officials were allowed to give their paroles not to go out of town or try to communicate with the British vessels. All non-associates were required to give a like parole. More militia were ordered to duty at Savannah, and the return of the powder "loaned" to South Carolina after its capture at Savannah was requested.[61]

In February additional vessels with some 200 troops on board arrived from Boston to purchase provisions for the British army there. Wright and several members of his council broke their parole on the night of February 11 and fled to Cockspur Island where they boarded HMS *Scarborough* at three the next morning.[62] Wright informed his council in Savannah that he was compelled to leave Savannah to communicate with the officers on the British vessels since the council of safety would not allow him to do so from Savannah. No harm would be done to Savannah if the vessels were allowed to procure the needed provisions. But the naval commander, Captain Barclay, announced his readiness to help any properly cleared vessels to proceed on their voyage regardless of actions of the council of safety or of the provincial congress. Wright announced that he was going to England to take advantage of leave that had been granted him.[63] This letter was Wright's last attempt to turn Georgians from their "mistaken" ways. He knew it would accomplish nothing, but he could not abandon Georgia and its government without this last try.

The British were anxious to secure the rice on several vessels in the river above Savannah. These vessels could legally sail after March 1, when the Continental non-exportation agreement expired. The South Carolina Provincial Congress urged a two-month extension of non-exportation until news of any possible extension by the Continental Congress could be secured, and the Georgia Council of Safety decreed an extension on March 1.[64] Since it was now impossible for these vessels to sail peacefully and for the British to secure provisions otherwise, it was assumed that the British would try to aid the rice vessels in getting past Savannah and to the mouth of the river.

The council of safety anticipated such action and took measures to oppose it. There were from two to five hundred militia in Savannah, perhaps a hundred South Carolinians who had come to help, two batteries of cannon on the bluff commanding the channel, and a vessel sunk in the channel to prevent the men-of-war from coming up to the town. Savannah houses and ships in the port belonging to people who had signed the association were ordered appraised so that damages might be paid if they were destroyed in the anticipated trouble. The shipping was ordered destroyed rather than let it fall into the hands of the British, and all Whigs were admonished to take part in the defense of the town rather than desert it for their own safety as some were doing.[65] South Carolina, appealed to for help, ordered Colonel Stephen Bull to take troops to Savannah and cooperate with the Georgia and Continental commanders there. Bull and his forces did not arrive until after the armed clashes of March 2-3, but his arrival gave Georgians a stronger sense of security.[66]

On the night of March 2 British troops landed on Hutchinson's Island, in the river opposite Savannah, and got on board the rice vessels anchored against the island above the town. The next day a party of men sent by the council of safety to take the riggings off these vessels, was surprised and detained by the British troops on the vessels. Other Americans sent to treat with the British were also detained. The council of safety retaliated by confining all royal officers in Savannah and several prominent Tories. The Whigs on shore fired upon the rice vessels, but they were out of range of the cannon. After prolonged negotiations, the Whigs sent down a fire vessel to set the rice ships aflame. Three or four were burned, but the rest got away by sailing down a channel back of Hutchinson's Island, which the American artillery could not reach and which was not guarded because it was assumed to be too shallow for the vessels to use.[67] Fourteen or fifteen vessels with 1,600 barrels of rice fell into the hands of the British. The prisoners taken on both sides were released, and the officials and Tories who had been imprisoned were allowed to leave Georgia, if they desired. Having secured what provisions they could, the British transports and their escort left.[68]

After Wright escaped to the *Scarborough* but before the March 2-3 troubles, he requested 500 to 1,000 troops and several vessels from Sir Henry Clinton to support royal government in Georgia and allow many back-country people to return to their correct loyalty from which they had been frightened by Whig actions and lack of support by Tories. Captain Barkley agreed that royal government could not be continued without armed support, but his troops were under orders to return to Boston. Clinton was engaged in military operations in North Carolina, and could send no help. Wright and most of the royal officials sailed away with the British vessels.[69] Royal government ended in Georgia, and the Whigs now had complete control.

At this point it may be well to pause and consider in summary the reasons why Georgia joined the other colonies in revolution. What forces contributed to revolution and what worked against it? There were many reasons why Georgia, the youngest of the rebellious colonies, should have remained loyal to the mother country. She had been settled only forty years and had received more financial help from England than any of the other colonies that rebelled. While the public and private help that had been lavished upon the colony at the time of her founding hardly influenced Georgians by 1770, the Parliamentary payment of the civil list lessened taxes and allowed her colonial officials to be more independent than those paid by the legislatures in other colonies.

Georgia, like many of the other colonies, had a diverse population background. The backbone of her population was English, either by direct immigration or from the other colonies, but this fact had little effect in determining if an individual became Whig or Tory. Other British elements in the population were Scotch and Scotch-Irish. The Scots of St. Andrew's Parish were mainly Whig from the beginning of the troubles. The Scotch-Irish, though somewhat slower in making a decision than the people on the coast, were independent-minded frontiersmen and generally became Whigs. The Scots who were most likely to be Tories were the Indian traders. They were often recent immigrants, and their business depended upon the British Indian Department and their standing with it. The next biggest national group in Georgia were the Germans. They lacked any background of representative government and individual rights. In Georgia they had found the religious freedom they sought, they had prospered economically and many feared that they would lose their land if they opposed the royal government. They lived apart from the main stream of Georgia life because of the language barrier. At first the Germans tended to be loyal to the King, but in the end they split, with the majority probably becoming Whigs. The small number of Jews in Georgia had received some insults and unequal treatment from representatives of established church and government, and so were Whigs from the beginning.

Georgia was also divided religiously, and different religions had a greater influence upon life than national backgrounds except for the Germans. Certainly the Church of England clergymen in the colony tended to be Tories because they had not been in America long enough to lose their English viewpoint. However, the Church of England was at best a slim support to the British cause in Georgia. Its churches, clergy, and communicants were too few, though the communicants were often leaders in the colony. There were no outstanding or popular Anglican clergymen among the five in the colony.[70] Anglicans became both Whigs and Tories, but the church had no noticeable influence upon their decision. The strong religious bodies in Georgia were the Congregationalists in St. John's Parish, the Lutherans at Ebenezer, and Zubly's Presbyterian Meeting House in Savannah. There was never any doubt about the Congregationalists; they were leading Whigs from the very first. Zubly's congregation tended to be Whigs and at first the Lutherans tended to be Tory; but in the end both split. The great majority of frontiersmen were without religious organization. It is doubtful if religion *per se* was of any consequence in the division between Whig and Tory in the early revolutionary struggle in Georgia. If it was a determining factor, it probably made more Whigs than Tories.[71]

The varied elements in Georgia's population and the physical isolation of different groups made it difficult for Georgians to cooperate fully and to agree upon a common policy in opposition to the royal government. These differences were taken advantage of by the Tories in the early days in their attempts to discount or counteract the opposition to the acts of the British government. If the diverse background of her population was not an item in favor of loyalism in Georgia, the small population and the sparse settlement, in comparison with the number and proximity of Indian neighbors, were reasons to cling to the protection that the royal government could give the frontier.

Georgia's fighting population had always been outnumbered by that of her Indian neighbors, most of whom were fairly well controlled by the British Indian Department in the 1770s. The fear of Indian trouble seems to have acted as a real deterrent to opposition to the royal government by frontiersmen at first, but the British government's constant refusal to send military help against the threatened Indian war in 1774 certainly worked to the favor of the Whigs.[72] The proximity of the British garrison at St. Augustine to the lower parishes and the long, exposed coastline with no protection against naval depredations made some people delay open repudiation of the British.

The number and caliber of royal officials in Georgia was a definite reason for Georgia's early backwardness in revolutionary activity. Because the leading officials were often sent from England and paid by Parliament, they kept the British viewpoint. Georgia's council, being appointed mainly from these officials, was an effective check on the popularly elected Commons House of Assembly.[73] By far the most able and influential official in Georgia was Governor Wright, whose opposition to revolutionary activity has already been pointed out. Wright knew the colonial mind thoroughly, but he never lost his sense of duty to the British government and never let the colonial opposition take the initiative out of his hands until mid-1775. Wright put law and order above everything else and always insisted that there could be no liberty without law. His ability and interest in Georgia made him respected by both Georgians and British officials.[74] More colonial officials of his type would have given the British imperial machinery a much better name than it enjoyed in 1770.

Wright could never understand the Whig constitutional arguments. If people were willing to admit that Parliament was the supreme legislative body of the empire, then it must, Wright argued, have absolute power to tax the colonies or do anything else. While he could not see the justice of the colonial arguments, he understood the colonists well enough to know that these arguments must be settled if peace was to return to America.[75] Wright was the virtually undisputed leader of Georgia's government until the Stamp Act troubles. After 1765 he did not always think the acts of the British government wise, but he tried to enforce them all regardless of the difficulties he knew his attempts would create. He thought that once a decision had been made it should be adhered to and that the repeal of the acts, regardless of how unpopular they were in America, was a mistake and could only create more American demands.[76] His solution was to enforce the laws, with troops if necessary, and he often thought British enforcement halfhearted. Such inflexibility lost Wright his earlier universal political leadership and respect and made him instead the leader of one faction. Perhaps a governor who thought compromise possible would have been better at this stage, but it is doubtful that any official in America could have prevented revolution in Georgia. Governors who did not try to enforce the unpopular acts in other colonies did not prevent revolution there. Personal respect for Wright certainly delayed open opposition to the royal government on the part of many Georgians in the early phases of the struggle.

Other than the officials sent from England, the people most influential in keeping Georgia out of the Whig ranks were leading citizens who had come to Georgia in their youth, attained wealth and position in the colony, and had been given a seat on the governor's council and/or an office. James Habersham and Noble Jones were the best examples of this type. They had been born and reared in England and had ties there which they did not want to give up. They had lived so long in the colonies that they were thorough colonials. They were of both parties and did not want to take sides with either. They upheld the right of the British government to govern the colonies but argued strongly against the expedience of the Stamp Act, Townshend Acts, and other acts unpopular in America. Habersham said, "It is easy for People in England to speculate and refine, but here we must act as *Necessity requires,* which is an infallible Rule."[77] Both Habersham and Jones, who had been towers of strength to Georgia and Wright, died in 1775 before Georgia made the final break with England.

Georgia's leaders were a relatively small and homogeneous group with no notable divisions or factions. They sat in the assembly and council and occupied the important executive offices. They were the economic and social leaders of the colony. Most of them lived in or near Savannah and knew each other well personally. Governor Wright was the natural and conscious leader of this group.

These men, being the natural leaders of the colony, were able to delay revolutionary action until many Georgians were thoroughly aroused and new leaders had developed. The younger Habershams and Jones, Joseph Clay, and other consistent Whig leaders came from this influential group, and they must have found it difficult to break with their old associates and ways of doing things.

So far as the press is concerned, it does not seem to have been any clear-cut influence on the Whig-Tory division. James Johnston, the editor of Georgia's one newspaper, the *Georgia Gazette,* was a loyalist so far as personal sentiments went; but his newspaper shows no evidence cᶠ having been conducted in the interest of the royal cause. He printed much on all sides of any argument, and he certainly kept Georgians informed of growing opposition in other colonies. Johnston was first a journalist and second a partisan.[78]

Few Georgians owned vessels to violate the navigation laws. After the Townshend Acts troubles there was little objection to the Parliamentary acts on economic grounds. The argument against Britain paralleled that in the other colonies. "No taxation without representation" was first heard at the time of the Stamp Act and continued until 1775. Georgians, as did most colonials, placed great faith in petitions to the King and insisted that George III was really their friend once he knew the true facts. Most Georgians were reluctant to take sides until relatively late. They kept hoping that some sort of compromise could be worked out and that it would not be necessary to take sides. As late as the second provincial congress, in the summer of 1775, there was attempt at compromise; but this congress also took the first major stand for revolution in Georgia. By the end of the summer of 1775 it was necessary for people to take sides. The loyalist position was a negative one that would maintain the *status quo,* a fairly confused *status quo* after the Stamp Act. The Whigs advanced a positive and progressive argument for the safeguarding of American rights, an argument that developed into the eventual demand for independence. The positive and progressive argument always has an advantage over the negative and static one in winning advocates in such a confused situation as existed from 1765 to 1775.

The original split in Georgia was between the conservative and wealthier merchant-planter class and a group of younger and less wealthy Savannahians, some of whom were the sons of the first group and some of whom were small tradesmen and artisans. The more radical Savannahians were joined by the St. John's Parish group (that often wanted to go further and faster than the Savannah group), and by the Scots from St. Andrew's Parish, to create the original Whig group. The Tories consisted of the officeholders and clergymen from England, the wealthier Savannah citizens, most of the Indian traders, recent immigrants from Britain, a good number of Germans of Ebenezer, and the Quakers from Wrightsborough. The last two groups were by no means homogeneous and were to furnish recruits for both sides as the argument continued. The frontiersmen were slow to break with the established government, but later they made up for lost time.

From the time of the Stamp Act, it was obvious that there was a party in Georgia in essential agreement with the more radical parties in the other colonies.[79] This party showed itself in every dispute between the colonies and the mother country. It is impossible to identify individual members of the opposition until 1774-1775, but it seems that there was a continuity of personnel for the entire decade. Certainly Georgia radicals and those in other colonies took similar action. Georgians were conscious of the fact that they were Americans and must do what other Americans did. The fifteen years of rapid physical and economic expansion, and of growth in population and political independence had given Georgians a sense of belonging. With the help of the other colonies, they now felt strong enough to stand alone. Georgia was still too young and weak to begin troubles with the mother country, but she could participate in them. Her inspiration came from the other colonies —especially South Carolina,[80] Massachusetts, and Virginia. Her actions often did not go so far as those in other colonies, and they always came later. There would certainly have been no revolution had it been left to Georgians to begin!

WHIG

POLITICAL AFFAIRS

1776 - 1778

5

****

THE departure of Governor Wright and the complete collapse of royal government emphasized the fact that the temporary Whig government needed to be regularized and legalized. The contract theory of government was entirely acceptable to most Georgians, but the contract needed concrete expression. The old contract of colonial government had been broken, and a new contract of state government must be drawn up. Out of such a situation in all the revolting colonies came the writing of state constitutions.

Georgians lost no time once the royal governor was gone. While the British men-of-war were still off Cockspur, the provincial congress must have been considering the changed conditions of government; for on April 15, 1776, it issued Georgia's first temporary state constitution, known as the Rules and Regulations of 1776.[1] The preamble stated that when Wright left, carrying with him the great seal of the province, many of the magistrates doubted that their authority still existed and most of them had refused to act further. Judicial powers, which had been totally suspended, were vitally needed. While no general system of government could be concluded until application was made to the Continental Congress for advice, some temporary government was necessary for the protection of people and property. This temporary government the Rules and Regulations set up.

A government of the usual three departments was created with all real authority residing in the legislature. The chief executive was a president and commander-in-chief, who was appointed by the legislature for a six months' term. He was bound to consult and follow the advice of the council of safety in all matters and was legally no more than the chairman of that council. The council of safety, also appointed by the legislature, consisted of thirteen members plus the delegates to the Continental Congress; seven were a quorum.

All legislative power was vested in a one-house provincial congress which was limited by no higher authority or executive veto and could do anything not specifically delegated to some other department. In actual practice it controlled the executive, though this particular power was not formally provided for in the Rules and Regulations. All laws in force in Georgia were continued if they did not interfere with the actions of the Continental or provincial congresses. All resolves of both congresses were to have full force and validity unless otherwise directed.

The court of sessions, which replaced the old general court, was to consist of a chief justice, two assistant judges, an attorney general, a provost marshal, and a clerk—all appointed by the congress to serve during its pleasure. Courts were to be held twice a year and were to observe all former rules and methods of procedure as nearly as the changed situation allowed. Local magistrates were appointed by the president and the council of safety and were directed to conform as nearly as possible to the old methods of procedure.

The Rules and Regulations, a simple document of thirteen brief paragraphs, contained only the broadest outline for the government, leaving the rest to be filled in by the congress and the council of safety. It continued the governmental machinery which had already developed and all colonial practices that did not conflict with the new situation. Its court system was the first one created by the revolutionary government, and it is quite possible that the need for courts was the reason the document was drawn up, as the preface stated. The document voiced good Whig doctrines when it said that governmental power originated with the people and that governments existed for their benefit. Certainly Georgia now had a full-fledged revolutionary government resting upon a constitutional basis. The separation from England was completed with the provincial congress's statement on June 12 that henceforth justice should run in the name of the province instead of the King,[2] and with the adoption of the Declaration of Independence by the Continental Congress on July 4, 1776.

Archibald Bulloch, an early and consistent leader of the revolutionary movement in Georgia and the president of the provincial congress, was elected president and commander-in-chief under the new government which went into effect on May 1.[3] At the first session of the provincial congress after Bulloch's election as president, he showed that he had a good grasp of Georgia's problems and made sensible recommendations for their solution. He recommended further regulation of the courts, of the continental battalion, and of the militia. The Indian situation should be considered seriously to prevent troubles on the frontier and to improve defense. Provisions should be made for foreign trade, for the promotion of domestic manufactures, and for keeping down inflation. Non-associates and other enemies of American liberty should be watched closely.[4]

The structure of government was considerably augmented and altered by the provincial congress and the council of safety as the need arose. The property, especially slaves, of absent loyalists was used to construct and repair civil and military installations. The council of safety did not hesitate to change appropriations made by the provincial congress,[5] to overrule the courts and order the re-arrest of people of doubtful loyalty freed by the chief justice,[6] or to appoint executors while the courts were not functioning.[7] The council carried on all normal executive functions, including the pardoning of criminals.[8] It oversaw the parochial committees in the enforcement of the association[9] and otherwise saw that the Whig cause was forwarded and that its enemies did not get out of line.[10] It began the raising of a fighting force and issued letters of marque to privateers to prey upon British shipping.[11]

The Rules and Regulations continued as Georgia's fundamental law for a year and made a satisfactory temporary government to effect the transition from province to state, a period during which there were no grave political problems. President Bulloch, a capable executive, died mysteriously late in February, 1777. He was succeeded by Button Gwinnett, who remained in office until a new constitution went into effect in May.[12]

The Rules and Regulations made it obvious that Georgia was ready for independence when it was declared by the Continental Congress in July, 1776. Georgia had no conspicuous part in the adoption of the Declaration of Independence, but she did not delay it as did some other states. In April, 1776, Georgia's provincial congress reminded her delegates to the Continental Congress that the American cause was continental, not provincial, and instructed them to do what they thought best for the common good.[13] In the discussions of independence that took place in the Continental Congress in the first half of 1776, it was generally assumed that Georgia would go along with independence. Her delegates favored independence, and their April instructions gave them a free hand.[14] Georgia had three delegates—Button Gwinnett, George Walton, and Lyman Hall—who voted for and signed the Declaration, but there is no record of their actions in the debates that preceded its adoption.

Independence was announced in Georgia when President Bulloch read a letter announcing the adoption of the Declaration, from John Hancock, President of the Continental Congress, to the council of safety on August 8. Two days later Bulloch, accompanied by the council of safety, other officials, and military forces, read the Declaration publicly at the assembly, the liberty pole, and the battery. The reading was followed by a public dinner at which toasts were drunk to the "United, Free, and Independent States of America." The day was concluded with a funeral procession and the interment of "George the Third" before the courthouse.[15] Georgia did not specifically affirm the Declaration, but all acts of the Continental Congress were law in Georgia. There can be no doubt that the dominant Whig element approved the Declaration wholeheartedly.

Prior to the adoption of the Declaration of Independence, the Continental Congress advised the states, in May, 1776, to set up adequate governments if they did not already exist.[16] This action removed the temporary aspect of Georgia's new government and appears to have been the beginning of a move to write a new and permanent state constitution. Late in the summer President Bulloch called for the election of what he called a convention, but there was nothing in the election call to indicate that the convention was any different from the provincial congresses that had been meeting for the last year.[17] This convention, or congress, met in several sessions and carried on ordinary legislative business. Nothing is known as to when the move for a new constitution first was considered by the convention or who were its prime movers, but a movement was well along by December. There is extant a partial journal beginning January 24, 1777, which is concerned with the final revision and adoption of the new constitution; but the journal records only the personnel of a committee of form and the fact that the constitution was debated in its final form January 29 through February 5, on which day it was unanimously adopted.[18]

Though it is impossible to know who were the leaders in the writing of the new constitution, one thing is certain. They were Whigs of the more radical type, and there was probably general agreement among the Whig leaders concerning the new constitution. Whig doctrine is obvious in the preamble statement that separation from Britain came because of the insistence of Parliament on legislating for the colonies without their consent. The convention, as representatives of the people ("from whom all power originates, and for whose benefit all government is intended"), adopted the constitution without submitting it to the voters.[19]

The legislative, executive, and judicial departments of government were declared separate and distinct, but far more power was given to the legislative than to the other two departments. "The legislature of this state shall be composed of the people," declared Paragraph II. Representatives were to be elected and to meet yearly in assembly. They must be residents of the counties they represented, of the Protestant religion, twenty-one years of age, and owners of 250 acres of land or property worth £250.[20] Representation was to be apportioned by the number of electors in each county. Camden and Glynn counties, largely unsettled, were initially given one representative each. Every other county received ten representatives except Liberty, which was given fourteen. In addition, Savannah was allowed four representatives and Sunbury two "to represent their trade."

A one-house legislature, the House of Assembly, was given all power to make (or repeal) laws and regulations provided they were not repugnant to the true intent of the constitution itself—the first statement in Georgia that the constitution was superior law. There was no executive veto or check of any kind upon the legislature. The assembly was given power to elect its speaker and other officers, draw up its own rules, direct the issuance of writs of election to fill vacancies, and to adjourn itself. No person holding a civil or military office in any state (except officers of the militia) and no clergyman could be a member. The Continental delegates, though elected by the assembly, were also full members of it.

Although it was not an upper house of assembly as in colonial times, the executive council did have certain legislative functions. During assembly sessions, the entire council was required to attend and to examine all proposed laws and ordinances after their second reading in the assembly. The council could propose amendments and make other suggestions but had no legislative authority. In practice, the council seldom tried to influence pending legislation. When the council performed its legislative functions the governor did not attend, but the president of the council presided, and a journal was kept, separate from one for executive actions.

All male whites twenty-one years of age and six months Georgia residents, who were owners of property worth £10 subject to state tax or who followed a mechanic trade, were qualified to vote. Elections were to be by ballot, free and open, and no officer or soldier could appear at elections in a military character. No person was entitled to more than one vote,[21] and no person claiming a title of nobility could vote. Every person qualified to vote who did not do so was subject to a fine of not over five pounds unless he could give a good excuse for not voting, but this portion of the constitution apparently was never enforced.

The governor, styled Honorable, was to be elected by the assembly on the first day it met. The executive council, which was to advise the governor on all matters, was elected the same day by the assembly from among its members. Two members came from each county entitled to send ten representatives to the assembly, and one member from each county was to attend the governor in a system of rotation. The council appointed its own officers and drew up its own rules of procedure. The executive, the term used to denote governor and council acting together, was vested with executive powers except the granting of pardons or the remitting of fines, which powers were reserved to the assembly. The executive could call the assembly in emergencies but could not adjourn it. The executive commissioned all state officials and filled vacancies when the assembly was not in session. The governor was commander-in-chief of the militia and all other military and naval forces of the state. No governor could hold office for more than one year out of three. The president of the council exercised the governor's powers in his absence.

The creation of Georgia's first counties necessitated a change in court structure. A superior court, the ordinary trial court, was created for each county. There was to be one chief justice to preside over all superior courts in rotation, and he was assisted by three or more assistant justices who resided in each county. There was no higher court in Georgia, but any party to a civil suit who was dissatisfied with the verdict could file an appeal for a new trial within three days of the decision. Such appeals were retried in the superior court by a special jury, and its decision was final. There was no provision for appeals in criminal cases. Courts of conscience, or justice courts, were to continue as previously for small offenses and civil matters involving no more than ten pounds. Courts merchant were indirectly mentioned in the constitution, but no provision was made for their creation. Captures, by land or by sea, were to be tried by what amounted to a specially appointed superior court, and appeals would be made to the Continental Congress. If any county had insufficient population to form a jury, its cases should be tried in an adjoining county. Court costs in the superior courts were not to exceed three pounds, and no case was to be held over for more than two terms (one year). The fact that juries were made the judge of both fact and law was an indication of the control of government by the people. In case of doubtful legal points, the jury might apply to the bench for advice, and such requests were to be answered by the justices in rotation. In reality juries interpreted the constitution as it applied to their cases. The only organizational link among the courts that might work for uniformity of decisions was the fact that the chief justice presided over all courts and the same attorney general was public prosecutor in all courts.

Besides the governor and council and the court officials, no other state officials were specifically provided for in the constitution. The assembly annually elected a chief justice, an attorney general, a treasurer, a secretary, and any others thought necessary. The provost marshal was replaced by county sheriffs.

The militia was established on a basis of county battalions; however, depending upon its population, a county might have more or less than one battalion. Although the constitution did not so specify, company officers continued to be elected by the men of the company and field officers by their company officers. Officers were commissioned by the executive after elections.

Because of the physical growth of Georgia and the revolutionary belief in control of government by the people concerned, the colonial parishes were replaced by counties which were real units of government and not simply administrative subdivisions. All the counties were named for English politicians who had taken the side of the colonies in the American struggle except for the county containing St. John's Parish, which was given the distinctive name of Liberty. The former parishes, the new counties, and their principal towns follow:[22]

Indian cession of 1773, north of the Ogeechee—Wilkes County
St. Paul's Parish—Richmond County—Augusta
St. George's Parish—Burke County
St. Matthew's Parish and the upper part of St. Philip, above the
    Canouchee River—Effingham County—Ebenezer
Christ Church Parish, and the lower part of St. Philip—Chat-
    ham County—Savannah
St. John's, St. Andrew's, and St. James' Parishes—Liberty Coun-
    ty—Midway, Sunbury, and Darien
St. David's and St. Patrick's Parishes—Glynn County
St. Thomas' and St. Mary's Parishes—Camden County.

Civil officials of the counties were to be elected by county voters
on the day of the general election. Justices of the peace, registers of
probate, tax collectors, road commissioners, and other officers who
performed state functions on a local level were to be elected by the
assembly. Schools were to be erected in each county and supported
by the state. Courthouses and jails were directed to be built in each
county.

Scattered throughout the constitution were several paragraphs
which together made up a bill of rights, guaranteeing certain economic and social gains. Entail of estates was forbidden; property
of people dying intestate was to be divided equally among the
widow and children, or the widow could have her dower. Free
exercise of religion, provided it was not repugnant to the peace and
safety of the state, was guaranteed to all, and no one was to be compelled to support any teacher of a religious denomination except
his own. These provisions effected the disestablishment of the
Church of England without any specific statement to that effect.
Excessive amounts for fines or bail were forbidden. Freedom of the
press and trial by jury were to remain inviolate. The principles of
the habeas corpus act were declared a part of the constitution.

The constitution prescribed the design for a new seal of state.
On one side was a scroll containing the words "The Constitution
of the state of Georgia," and the Latin motto *"Pro Bono Publico."*
(For the Public Good). On the other side was to be an elegant
house with other buildings, fields of corn and meadows with sheep
and cattle, a river running through the meadow with a ship under
full sail, and the Latin motto, *"Deus nobis haec otis fecit,"* (God
created these opportunities, or blessings, for us).[23]

A clumsy amending system provided that amendments were to

originate in petitions from a majority of the counties and signed
by a majority of the voters in each county. When these petitions
were presented to the assembly, it was to call an amending convention, and specify the alterations to be framed from the petitions.

The constitution was marked by simplicity of style and brevity;
it restricted itself to the barest of fundamentals—a characteristic
that Georgia's later constitutions would have done well to emulate.
It was divided into sixty-two numbered paragraphs, most of which
were short and could be easily understood by a layman.

The political philosophy behind the constitution was that of the
eighteenth-century Whig—natural rights, separation of powers,
government deriving its power from the consent of the governed,
guarantees of citizens against arbitrary government—philosophy
that had been ably expounded by Locke, Montesquieu, and others.
From a purely practical viewpoint, many of the provisions of the
constitution came from colonial and early revolutionary experience. The belief in government as close to the people as possible
and the dislike of a strong executive in the colonial period were
responsible for the creation of a strong legislature and a weak executive. Hence there was created a one-house legislature,[24] elected
directly by the people and with no veto or other executive check
upon it. It was colonial tradition coupled with the fear of strong
executives that was responsible for the creation of a plural executive, a governor and council. Since the governor was elected by
the assembly and could serve but one year, he was effectively limited and was hardly able to carry through any extensive program
of his own. Making juries the judge of both fact and law, the absence of any appeal court, and the use of local assistant judges kept
all judicial power in the hands of the local citizens.

Because Georgia's conservatives were so effectively silenced,
church disestablishment and the killing of entail were easily effected without the long and bitter battle that was necessary to end
them in Virginia, where conservative Whigs were more powerful.
All outside checks, even of the Continental Congress, were eliminated; and the voters, practically the entire white male population, were in ultimate control. Politically the radicals had over-
thrown the old order with its aristocratic checks and had established a new one without any checks. They had achieved their
revolutionary victory and were ready to enjoy it.[25]

Conservative Whigs did not approve the extreme democratic
tendencies of the new constitution. One, who had been a member

of the convention and who protested privately about the shortcomings of the constitution after it was written, was Joseph Clay, Savannah merchant and deputy paymaster for Continental troops in Georgia. Clay complained that Joseph Wood, just elected as a Continental delegate, had several times been convicted by the courts of dishonest dealings. Election of such a man, said Clay, arose from a defect in the constitution, "which is so very Democratical & has thrown power into such Hands as must ruin the Country if not timely prevented by some alteration in it. . . ." Too many of the old leaders in Georgia were now Tories, and government had got "into the Hands of those whose ability or situation in Life does not intitle them to it. . . ." Later Clay complained that many people now in power "from their levelling Principles & Conduct" were as great enemies to Georgia as the King. As an illustration Clay described the passage of a bill through the assembly in which a clause that had been defeated was included in the engrossed bill signed by the speaker. But, said Clay, this was not to be wondered at with the type of assemblies Georgia then had, for their main concern was to fleece the state and then go home and enjoy the spoils. The Chatham County Grand Jury presented as grievances the lack of any check upon the assembly and the unequal representation in the assembly—two items that undoubtedly showed Savannah's discontent at the loss of her dominant role in Georgia's government.[26]

Having treated the constitutional history, it will be well to consider political conditions from the summer of 1776 through 1778, the period in which the radical Whigs were in complete control. During the summer of 1776 the majority of politically active Georgians were willing to back independence by force of arms if necessary. While rough treatment of Tories had abated, people deemed dangerous to American liberty were banished or arrested.[27] Many loyalists removed to East Florida where they formed themselves into the Florida Scouts to harass south Georgia. By fall, there were reports that there was much dissatisfaction in Georgia, that the Continental battalion was generally considered insufficient to protect the state, that British sympathizers were impatiently awaiting the arrival of British soldiers to help them, that there were numerous squabbles between Whig factions, and that many Whigs contemplated leaving Georgia and removing to South Carolina.[28]

Certainly squabbles among Whig factions had much to do with discontent and almost paralyzed concerted action against Georgia's internal and external enemies—Tories, Florida Scouts, and Indians. A year later Joseph Clay described Georgia in rather unhopeful terms: her money had depreciated drastically; unwise and poorly led military expeditions had brought the state low and promised to bring it still lower; Georgia could not possibly defend herself, yet her boasting manner discouraged outside help; about the only hope was her importance to the United States.[29]

The new constitution went into effect in May, 1777, but it made no great difference in governmental organization or action. The pattern of a weak plural executive and a strong legislature continued. Button Gwinnett was defeated in his desire to be the governor under the new constitution, probably because of his recent and disastrous expedition against East Florida.[30] Instead that honor went to John Adam Treutlen, a merchant and planter and leading citizen of Ebenezer who had come from humble beginnings but was a substantial citizen with colonial and early revolutionary legislative experience; he served until January, 1778. The executive continued to refer all important decisions to the assembly;[31] the assembly, in continuing to give directions to the executive and the judges, showed that it considered itself superior to them.[32] The executive council proved a frail check upon the governor, for twice in times of military danger the council requested him to take upon himself the whole executive power and to act without consulting it until the danger was passed.[33] Such a course of action was both efficient and unconstitutional.

The action of the assembly between May, 1777, and December, 1778, as well as can be determined,[34] was mainly concerned with normal governmental functions, with military organization and protection of the state, and with the changes necessitated by political and economic dislocations stemming from separation from Britain. Many ordinary governmental functions continued the same as previously: pilots were regulated, roads were ordered built or repaired, the state's paper circulating medium was kept up, militia regulations were amended, taxes were levied with the change that religious objectors to military duty and absentees were taxed doubly.[35] All laws not in conflict with Georgia's new status were continued.[36]

Legislation growing out of the new political status was concerned with several topics. Counties and superior courts needed further regulation. In June, 1777, the granting of land was resumed on the old colonial headright system. Merchants from non-

British areas were encouraged to trade with Georgia, and a state insurance office was set up to insure vessels owned by Georgians and to further encourage trade.[37] The assembly and executive issued numerous regulations for the control or expulsion of enemies of the state, but these were allowed to lapse as soon as any immediate fear was over.[38]

Georgia was one of the last states to enact legislation against her citizens who remained loyal to Britain. Loyalists were expelled in the fall of 1777, but no details of the law have been discovered.[39] The estates of some Tories were used for defense purposes early in 1777, but it was March, 1778, before an act was passed to attaint 177 Tories for high treason and to confiscate their estates.[40] Refusal of allegiance to the state after April 19, 1775, was taken as sufficient reason for inclusion in this list. People listed in the act who returned to the state or who were taken fighting against the United States were to be tried for high treason and upon conviction were to suffer death. Commissioners were appointed to manage and sell confiscated property in the interest of the state. Money realized from this property was to be used to redeem the paper money of the state and to pay the state's requisitions from the Continental Congress. A supplementary act of November, 1778, provided that the property of people over twenty-one years of age who resided in British territory and who did not return to Georgia within twelve months and take oaths to support the state should be sold under the terms of the original act.[41] Little is known of how much property was sold under these acts or the amount of income the state derived from it, but the asumption is that not very much was done.

Not only did Georgia Whigs fight Tories, but they often considered it necessary to fight other Whigs as well. In 1776 and 1777 there were two main Whig groups which may be called the radical or popular or country party on one side, and the conservative or city or merchant party on the other. When the officers of the Georgia Continental battalion were elected by the provincial congress in January, 1776, the Whig factions had not become as pronounced as they did later, and Lachlan McIntosh (who later became identified with the conservative Whigs) was elected colonel. Button Gwinnett, a leading radical Whig, had hoped for this command. As the Whig ranks diverged further throughout 1776, Gwinnett and McIntosh became estranged, and the radicals secured complete control of state politics. The election of McIntosh as brigadier general by the Continental Congress, in September, 1776, did not help the feeling between him and Gwinnett.

While Gwinnett was president and McIntosh was Continental commander, the 1777 expedition against St. Augustine was undertaken.[42] There was insufficient cooperation between McIntosh and Gwinnett,[43] because of the existing ill feeling and the desire of Gwinnett to command in the field and prove that he had real military ability. This rivalry went so far that the council of safety requested both Gwinnett and McIntosh to return to Savannah and to allow Colonel Samuel Elbert the field command.

About the middle of March, just before the Florida expedition, Lachlan McIntosh's brother George was arrested on order from President Gwinnett and put in irons in the common jail. This arrest resulted from a recommendation of the Continental Congress after it considered an intercepted letter of Governor Tonyn, of East Florida, which intimated that George McIntosh, a member of the Georgia Council of Safety, was friendly to the British cause. Gwinnett refused bail because the charge was treason, and George McIntosh said that he was not even informed of the charges against him. When the council met in the absence of Gwinnett, it released McIntosh on £20,000 bail and gave him copies of the papers received from the Continental Congress so that he could prepare a defense of himself. Gwinnett said that three relatives of McIntosh on the council allowed his release on bail.[44]

When George McIntosh was released from jail, it was specified that he could go to Congress to present his case but must give security to the executive before his departure. After the executive had refused McIntosh a trial in Georgia, he set out for Congress without notifying the executive. As the assembly had specified that McIntosh be sent to Congress under guard, Governor Treutlen sent a guard after him which overtook him in North Carolina and delivered him to Congress.[45] The case was considered in Congress on October 2-10, 1777, and the decision was that there was insufficient evidence to detain McIntosh for trial. He was accordingly released.[46]

As best as can be determined from the mass of conflicting evidence, George McIntosh had joined several other St. Andrew's Parish planters in loading a vessel of rice intended for Dutch Guiana in May, 1776. William Panton, a notorious Tory, had become associated with the vessel just before it sailed. He sailed with it, took it to St. Augustine and got new papers for it, sailed to the

British West Indies, sold the cargo, bought a new cargo, and returned to St. Augustine. There is no evidence that McIntosh knew of Panton's plans, but he certainly can be censured for association with a known Tory while he was a member of the council of safety. The St. Andrew's committee seems to have been rather lax in enforcement of the association, and East Florida had secured considerable rice from the parish.[47]

When the assembly under the constitution of 1777 met, it considered the recent Florida expedition. The arrest and bad treatment of George McIntosh was fresh in Lachlan's mind, and the case had not yet been determined. After hearing Gwinnett and Lachlan McIntosh, the assembly approved the conduct of Gwinnett and his council. When this approval was announced, Lachlan McIntosh is said to have called Gwinnett "A Scoundrell & lying Rascal" to his face before the assembly. This brought the McIntosh-Gwinnett feud to a head. Gwinnett challenged McIntosh to a duel, which was fought in Governor Wright's meadow outside Savannah on May 16, 1777. Both men fell wounded, and Gwinnett died three days later.[48]

No notice of the duel was taken by the civil authorities until the next session of the assembly. McIntosh was then arrested, tried, and acquitted. Lyman Hall and Joseph Wood led the movement against McIntosh in the assembly and throughout the state. Petitions asking the removal of McIntosh from his command were circulated and secured 574 signatures in Richmond, Liberty, Chatham, Wilkes, and Effingham counties. These, together with a petition from the assembly, were forwarded to Congress.[49] However, before the assembly could formulate its petition, McIntosh's friends in Congress (George Walton of Georgia and Henry Laurens of South Carolina) had requested his transfer, and he was ordered to report to Washington for reassignment on August 6, a month before the Georgia Assembly petition was voted.[50]

Arguments among Georgia Whig factions were not the only excitement that 1777 brought to Georgia politics. The suggested union of Georgia and South Carolina caused considerable furor. Late in 1776 the South Carolina Assembly proposed the union and sent William Henry Drayton and John Smith to Georgia to promote it. Drayton arrived in Savannah in January, 1777, and reported that he found all officeholders opposed to the union but that there was some sentiment in favor of it among the people. Appearing before the Georgia convention on January 23, he pre-

sented a very elaborate argument as to why Georgia should join
South Carolina but gave no consideration to the objections which
might be raised by Georgians. By soil, climate, economy, and general interests the two states should be one. The Savannah River
could be more effectively improved and used by one state than
split between two. The jealousies that had always existed between
the two states could cease, and the people of both could work for
the common good. Agriculture, trade, and industry would all improve markedly. Carolina planters would extend their improve-
ments into Georgia, where land prices would rise as a result. South
Carolina merchants would improve Georgia trade, which already
depended upon them. Savannah would become the natural metropolis of the entire Savannah River valley and grow in economic
importance, though it would lose its political importance. If there
were no union, South Carolina would probably build a rival city
across the river to retain all its trade within its own borders, and
Savannah would decay rapidly. Government and public defense
would improve, yet the cost would be less. Georgia currency, which
was of less value than South Carolina's, would rise in value. Georgians would not have to pay any of the South Carolina debt, but
South Carolina would probably help pay the Georgia public debt.
South Carolinians would not take up great tracts of land in Georgia as some feared; rather they would be willing, on this and other
items, to grant whatever reasonable terms Georgians might require
in a treaty of union.

The convention excluded Drayton from any participation in
the debate on his propositions, but he attended privately. Button
Gwinnett led the opposition to union. Drayton said that several
members of the Georgia convention agreed with him that Gwinnett's arguments were not so good as Drayton's, but this made
no difference since the convention already opposed union. The
convention rejected Drayton's proposals on the grounds that they
were contrary to the Articles of Confederation to which Georgia
had agreed but which had not gone into effect.[51]

Although Drayton was not allowed to answer the convention, he
kept up his efforts by sending letters into Georgia, circulating petitions for the union, and doing everything else he could to stir up
agitation in favor of union and against those who opposed it. In
July the executive council requested Governor Treutlen to issue
a proclamation offering £100 reward to anyone who would apprehend Drayton or anyone working with him in the interest of the

union.[52] Drayton replied with a stinging and sarcastic letter to Treutlen in which he delivered a long tirade against rulers who opposed petitions, with apt references to the Stuart kings and their well-known tyranny. He accused the governor and council of being concealed Tories and said he did not doubt but that the people of Georgia would prefer British rule to anything they could get from their present rulers. He threatened to show the illegality of the proclamation and any action under it by paying for the defense of anyone arrested under it. He offered to continue the argument as long as Treutlen and his council desired. But he was careful to remain in South Carolina out of the reach of Georgia authorities.[53] So far as the records show, here ended the proposed union; and the two states soon fell to quarreling over their boundary, just as Drayton had predicted they would.

Of more importance than her relations with South Carolina were Georgia's relations with the Continental Congress. These began on July 7, 1775, when the second provincial congress elected Archibald Bulloch, John Houstoun, the Reverend John J. Zubly, Noble Wimberly Jones, and Lyman Hall delegates to the Continental Congress, any three of them to be a quorum. The delegates were instructed to work for the preservation and defense of American rights and liberties and for the restoration of harmony with Britain upon constitutional principles. The provincial congress promised to do whatever the delegates agreed to in the Continental Congress.[54] Bulloch, Houstoun, and Zubly left at once for Philadelphia. By the time they arrived in Philadelphia, Dr. Lyman Hall, who had been representing St. John's Parish in the Continental Congress since May 13, had left for Georgia. When Congress reconvened on September 13, the three delegates were seated. Two of them being clothed in homespun aroused favorable comment. John Adams was especially impressed with the learning and zealous spirit of Zubly.[55]

Georgia's first request to the Congress was for a decision on what should be done with the goods landed in Georgia during the month after the association went into effect. After a heated debate, Congress recommended that the goods be sent back or sold at auction for the benefit of the public.[56] Georgia wanted to allow importations for the Indian trade and the exportation of her 1775 crop as usual but made no definite application on these points. Zubly led a debate in which he maintained that only through trade could the colonies secure much that was necessary, but he was strenuously opposed by Samuel Chase. No decision was reached nor was any modification of the association approved.[57]

Zubly had championed American rights from the very beginning of the argument with Britain. From the Stamp Act until he went to Philadelphia, he had emphasized his belief that American rights must be upheld and that a constitutional union with Britain must be maintained. He was opposed to republics, considering them inherently evil, and he said so publicly several times.[58] He refused to go along with the steadily increasing sentiment for independence and left Congress somewhat under a cloud about the middle of November and returned to Georgia.[59] The other delegates left about the end of November.

Georgia was unrepresented from November, 1775, until the arrival of Button Gwinnett and Lyman Hall on May 20, 1776. They brought with them very broad instructions from the provincial congress stressing Georgia's weakness and exposed situation and hence the need of union for protection, declaring that America's cause was Continental and not provincial, and complaining that Georgia was too far away to know the current thinking in Congress. The delegates were told to use their best judgment in promoting the cause of Georgia and America. Georgia had delegates in Congress throughout the rest of 1776 and during most of 1777 and 1778.[60]

The Continental business with which Georgia was most concerned throughout these years was the raising and equipping of troops for the defense of the state. While the Georgia delegates devoted themselves to these matters, the efforts of Henry Laurens of South Carolina probably produced more results. Laurens had a better over-all picture of Southern conditions than any other delegate and had considerable influence in Congress. He tried to impress upon Congress the importance of Georgia and South Carolina in the general defense picture, an importance which he said the Northern states did not realize properly.[61]

Congress voted some funds for the support of Georgia's Continental troops from the time they were authorized in 1775; but the majority of their support through 1777 came from the state itself, which soon issued more bills of credit for their support than the state's credit could sustain. Georgia's currency depreciated in value considerably below Continental curency or that of its neighboring states. By the summer of 1777, the treasury was so empty that the commissary general in Georgia was forced to appeal to the public for funds or supplies to keep the troops going, and Governor Treutlen laid the situation before Congress. Congress voted $400,000 to redeem the Georgia bills of credit issued to support the troops and $300,000 for future expenses.[62]

Upon the urging of General Robert Howe, Continental commander in the South in the fall of 1777,[63] Congress appointed Joseph Clay, a Savannah merchant and friend of Henry Laurens, as Continental paymaster for Georgia. By May, 1778, Clay and Howe still complained that little money had come to Georgia except to redeem bills of credit; but in June Clay said he hoped to be able soon to pay all back pay due.[64] After continual complaints from state and army officials, Congress in September voted another $1,000,000 for Georgia military expenses.[65] Laurens continued in Congress to press for consideration of Georgia's condition, but other matters pushed it into the background. Few people in Congress could see the necessity for action when most of the British army was much farther north, and Georgia did not have enough weight in Congress to demand attention.[66]

In the debates on the writing and adoption of the Articles of Confederation, Georgia took little part. Button Gwinnett was Georgia's member on the committee of thirteen appointed in the summer of 1776 to write the articles, but not even his enthusiastic biographer could find any influence that he exerted in the original draft of the articles.[67] In the debate which followed, both Gwinnett and George Walton (another Georgia delegate) argued that Congress should have complete control of Indian affairs and trade as the articles specified.[68] When methods of representation were debated, in October, 1777, the Georgia delegates Walton and Nathan Brownson favored equal representation for all the states.[69]

The Articles were sent to the states in November with a request that they be ready to ratify by March 10, 1778. When Congress called for a report on ratification from all states on June 25, Edward Langworthy, the only Georgian present, said he had no recent instructions but was sure that Georgia would ratify.[70] Edward Telfair arrived from Georgia on July 13 and said that he was authorized to sign for Georgia. Not until the arrival of John Walton on July 23 was Georgia's authorization for ratification laid before Congress. Walton and Telfair signed the next day; and Edward Langworthy, who was not present then, signed after he returned to Congress in August.[71]

The Georgia Assembly had actually approved the Articles on

February 26, 1778, but sent no notification to Congress until Telfair arrived. The assembly proposed four minor amendments to the Articles. The first two concerned the first sentence in article four. This sentence is given with Georgia amendments inserted in brackets. "The better to secure and perpetuate mutual friendship and intercourse among the people of the different states in this union, the free [white] inhabitants of each of these states, paupers, vagabonds [all persons who refuse to bear Arms in defense of the State to which they belong, and all persons who have been or shall be attainted and Judged guilty of high treason in any of the United States], and fugitives from justice excepted, shall be entitled to all privileges and immunities of free citizens in the several states; . . ." The fifth paragraph of the ninth article should be so amended that when Congress reported to the states on monies borrowed or bills of credit emitted, an account of how the money had been spent should be given. Article eleven should be amended so as to admit East and West Florida as well as Canada into the Confederation should they so desire. South Carolina had made several attempts to get "free white" substituted for "free." The second amendment to article four was in line with Georgia policy. In case Congress would not agree to Georgia's proposed amendments, the delegates were to ratify the Articles as they were; and this they did.[72]

MILITARY
ACTIVITIES
1776 - 1778

6

****

BEFORE fighting can be done, armies must be raised and supplied. In the American Revolution this was done by the Continental Congress and the individual states. The first consideration of the defense of South Carolina and Georgia by the Continental Congress culminated in an authorization on November 4, 1775, to raise three battalions of Continental troops for South Carolina and one for Georgia. The officers were to be designated by the South Carolina and Georgia Whig governments, and enlistments might be made in Virginia and North Carolina if there were insufficient men in South Carolina and Georgia.[1] On January 29 and 30, 1776, the Georgia Provincial Congress elected Lachlan McIntosh, colonel; Samuel Elbert, lieutenant colonel; and Joseph Habersham, major, of the Georgia battalion.[2] Recruiting was held up by lack of currency which could be used outside Georgia, the promised money from Congress not having arrived. McIntosh said that he expected few enlistments in Georgia and even fewer in South Carolina, which latter state paid larger bounties than Georgia. On April 28, McIntosh reported 286 men enlisted for the Georgia battalion, and a week later 400 were reported. The state was also raising two troops of horsemen to guard the southern frontier against cattle raids from East Florida and the western frontier against Indians. About 600 militia were reported on duty.[3]

On February 27, 1776, the Continental Congress created a Southern Military Department of Virginia, the Carolinas, and Georgia, commanded by Major General Charles Lee. Georgia and

95

South Carolina were commanded by Brigadier General John Armstrong.[4] In March and May Congressional committees recommended that additional troops be raised for South Carolina and Georgia, and General Lee added his plea for 2,000 men before he arrived in Charleston.[5] State and Continental authorities in the spring and summer of 1776 agreed that more men were needed.

In considering Georgia's defense it is necessary to picture a settled area from thirty to sixty miles wide from above Augusta down the Savannah River to the sea and down the coast to the Altamaha. From the Altamaha to the St. Marys, settlement was thin and near the coast. Highest estimates gave 4,000 white men capable of military duty, all members of the militia. No more than half of these could be used for military duty at once if the area was to continue to exist economically. The back country must have sufficient men present at all times to protect itself from the Indians. The coast with its islands, inlets, and river mouths had a number of good harbors and necessitated a considerable naval force to patrol it. There were from 500 to 1,000 British regulars at St. Augustine plus Indians and Tories from Georgia and South Carolina. All needed to be fed, and south Georgia was the most obvious source of food.

The Creek Indians, Georgia's nearest red neighbors, outnumbered the Georgians in fighting men and were on fairly good terms with the British Indian Department. Georgia, being a frontier province, must bear the brunt of any attack from St. Augustine or from the Creeks, and her defense would also protect South Carolina and the colonies to the north. To secure and maintain the land and the naval forces necessary to protect Georgia made too formidable a task for the youngest and weakest colony, and it was only fair that she should receive help because of her frontier position.[6]

When General Lee arrived in Charleston in the summer of 1776, he called a conference of South Carolina and Georgia representatives to consider the military needs of the area. The Georgia delegates, headed by Colonel McIntosh, pointed out Georgia's weakness, her importance to the union, and her fear of attacks from British troops. They said that Georgia needed men, fortifications, and an understanding with the Indians. Six battalions of Continental troops, which Georgia could not raise, were requested. The four troops of horsemen already raised could be turned over to Continental command, and another regiment of horsemen should be raised. Horsemen should be used to protect the Georgia and South Carolina frontier and to cut off the Indian contacts with the British in the Floridas. Congress was also asked to furnish funds to build forts on the frontier and to man war galleys on the coast. Finally, Congress was asked to furnish sufficient Indian presents to satisfy the Creeks and to pay for the cattle which Georgia could furnish the Indians.[7]

While Lee was not convinced on all these points, he was impressed with the importance of Georgia to the American cause and the impossibility of her defending herself. Lee and South Carolina urged Georgia to augment her frontier patrols and to send presents to the Indians at once, and assured her that Congress would pay for what she could not.[8]

In the last half of August, Lee came to Savannah for a personal inspection and for conferences. He reported that the state's defense depended upon McIntosh's battalion and some 2,500 militia. McIntosh and his battalion Lee praised very highly but said the Georgia troops should be exchanged for South Carolina troops because too many of the Georgians had Tory friends and relatives in East Florida who were continually raiding southern Georgia. The militia was unreliable for the same reason. Lee recommended a large number of row galleys to guard the inland passage and coast, and the building of forts south of the Altamaha to serve as places of refuge and refreshment to the horsemen patrolling that area. Lee personally favored abandoning all Georgia south of the Altamaha; but because he did not think it possible to persuade Georgians to do so, he was ready to defend this area. Lee's report showed a good understanding of the Georgia situation and a well-formulated plan of action.[9] Lee saw the difficulties in carrying out his plans, and he graphically described them to General John Armstrong, his South Carolina and Georgia deputy.

The people here are if possible more harum skarum than their sister colony [South Carolina]. They will propose anything, and after they have propos'd it, discover that they are incapable of performing the least. They have propos'd securing their Frontiers by constant patrols of horse Rangers, when the scheme is approv'd of they scratch their heads for some days, and at length inform you that there is a small difficulty in the way; that of the impossibility to procure a single horse—their next project is to keep their inland Navigation clear of Tenders by a numerous fleet of Guarda Costa arm'd boats, when this is agreed to, they recollect that they have not a single boat—Upon the whole I shou'd not be surpris'd if they were to propose mounting a body of Mermaids on Alligators. . . .[10]

Lee offended the council of safety by informing it that he was the best judge of what should be done and would merely requisition what he needed without explanation as to its intended use.[11] The question as to the degree of authority Georgia had over Continental troops had already come up and was going to continue to cause trouble throughout the war.[12] Lee recommended that tighter security measures be adopted, especially against leaks of military plans to East Florida, where Georgia plans were known almost as soon as they were known in Savannah.[13]

While Lee was making enemies in Savannah, Congress decided to augment the Continental establishment of Georgia by two additional battalions of foot troops, one to serve as riflemen, and a regiment of rangers to act as horsemen or foot soldiers. Virginia and North Carolina were asked to allow recruiting within their borders and to give the recruiting officers all possible help. Two companies of artillery to garrison forts at Savannah and Sunbury were also authorized. Four row galleys were to be built at Continental expense for coastal defense. In the fall another Georgia battalion was authorized.[14] Congress appointed Colonel McIntosh as Brigadier General to head the Georgia brigade,[15] and recruiting officers immediately began work in Virginia and North Carolina, where they secured considerable help from the state governments. Bounties of $70 and 100 acres of land were offered for recruits who would enlist for the duration of the war.[16] By the end of 1776 McIntosh reported 538 men in the First Georgia Battalion, dispersed throughout the state on guard duty, and about forty men between the two companies of artillery. The regiment of light horse, doing patrol duty on the frontiers, had some 300 men; but its discipline was poor and would remain so as long as it was a separate unit. No recruits from Virginia and North Carolina had yet arrived for the second and third battalions. Georgia had little ordnance and almost no military stores.[17]

To help fill the Georgia and South Carolina units, General Lee gave authority in September to enlist troops from Virginia and North Carolina then serving in Georgia and South Carolina. This order so incensed North Carolina that she recalled all her Continental troops, but she sent them south again by the end of the year.[18] North Carolina refused to allow the Fourth Georgia Battalion to recruit in North Carolina in the spring of 1777, but she did furnish supplies to troops who were recruited in Pennsylvania and were marching to Georgia.[19] At the same time that Continen-

tal troops were being recruited outside the state, Georgia was trying to recruit state troops in other states as well.[20]

Early in 1776 the council of safety took steps to secure military
supplies and arms. All available arms in Georgia were ordered collected and put into usable condition. Samuel Elbert, Edward Telfair, and Joseph Habersham were appointed to arrange for the importation of munitions and the exportation of Georgia produce to
pay for them, a modification of the association allowed by the Continental Congress. Originally 400 stands of arms with bayonets,
20,000 pounds of gunpowder, 60,000 pounds of lead, and bullets
and shot were authorized;[21] but this was only a beginning. Munitions were secured from various West Indian islands—apparently
the Bahamas and perhaps a few other British islands supplied
some, and Captains Oliver Bowen and Job Pray carried on trade
for munitions and tried to recruit seamen at Cape Francais and St.
Thomas.[22] Such trade was dangerous because of the possibility of
capture by British vessels. There are records of at least one trader
who worked for Georgia and East Florida at the same time.
Thomas Young was appointed by Georgia to secure clothing for
the Georgia Battalion and by Governor Tonyn of East Florida to
supply the West Indies with provisions from Georgia. Young was
later discovered by both sides to be dealing with the other. As a
result he lost the clothing that he had imported to Georgia and his
name was placed on the 1778 Georgia act of confiscation and banishment.[23] There were probably others who professed loyalty to
both sides for personal profit.

In November, 1776, the Continental Congress recommended to
the states that they lay up magazines of munitions and provisions
for the use of troops and militia. General Lee reported the establishing of food magazines on the Altamaha and the Ogeechee, at
Augusta, and between Savannah and Augusta.[24] Rice and salt meat
could be collected easily in Georgia, but there were almost never
enough munitions. General Lee recommended, and the council of
safety approved, the removal of cattle from the sea islands in August, 1776, to augment the food supply and to prevent their falling
into the hands of the British. Some cattle were removed and used
to feed the army, but there were still cattle on the islands for the
British to capture in 1777 and 1778.[25]

Before any troops were raised or supplied, there was much talk
of marching against St. Augustine to capture it and wipe out the
small British garrison (about 150 in the fall of 1775) and the head-

quarters of Georgia and South Carolina loyalists and of Indian Superintendent John Stuart. Refugees in St. Augustine were reported so afraid of such an expedition that they were fleeing to the West Indies.[26]

Under British rule East Florida between the St. Marys and St. Johns rivers had developed a plantation economy like that of the other Southern colonies, but it had not progressed far enough to feed the colony and garrison at St. Augustine. Ordinarily food was imported from Georgia. Many of the Southern loyalists who moved to East Florida in 1775 and 1776 began planting activities in this area and kept up contacts with friends and relatives who remained in Georgia and Carolina. With the augmented civil and military population in East Florida by spring of 1776, additional food was needed just when Georgia tried to stop all exportation to British areas. Many of the newly-arrived loyalists formed themselves into troops of horsemen known as the Florida Rangers, whose main duty seems to have been stealing cattle and otherwise harrying southern Georgia, which was so sparsely inhabited that it could do little to protect itself. Thomas Brown, tarred and feathered as a loyalist at Augusta, was the commander of this provincial troop and never forgot his desire for revenge on Georgia Whigs. The Florida Rangers and the Georgians who wanted to continue to sell their produce in East Florida made it impossible to stop the flow of provisions from Georgia to East Florida.

On January 1, 1776, the Continental Congress recommended to North Carolina, South Carolina, and Georgia that they undertake a joint expedition at Continental expense to capture St. Augustine.[27] News of this recommendation reached St. Augustine almost as soon as it did Savannah and set off talk of an immediate expedition against Georgia. Governor Patrick Tonyn of East Florida suggested that he be made a brigadier to lead the 580 troops at St. Augustine against Georgia at the time of Sir Henry Clinton's proposed attack against Charleston. Tonyn was sure that he could draw troops which would otherwise oppose Clinton and probably be able to overrun Georgia and return it to British allegiance.[28]

Border incidents in the vicinity of the St. Marys River did not await the opening of a formal expedition. South Georgia militia operated against Florida Rangers, and in May the Georgia Council of Safety ordered Captain William McIntosh and his troop of horsemen to destroy the forts and magazines near the St. Marys River and destroy or drive south all Florida troops found in the area. It was also suggested that forts be built for the Georgia troops and that vessels on the river be captured. Four days later Tonyn presented these Georgia plans to his council in St. Augustine.[29] Throughout July preparations on both sides were intensified. There were reports of increasing cattle stealing. Florida expected reinforcements from the Carolina and Georgia back country. Tonyn protested the impossibility of protecting a 300-mile frontier and the plantations between the St. Marys and the St. Johns with a garrison consisting mainly of raw recruits.[30] In July there was a false report of a British fleet on the Georgia coast and fear of an imminent attack. South Carolina refused any help despite Lee's request and insistence that the best defense of South Carolina was on the Georgia-Florida frontier.[31] Regardless of false rumors and future plans, the almost daily raids in the St. Marys area continued; cattle were driven off, and Georgia and East Florida troops of horsemen and militia met in small engagements.

By August Lee was planning an expedition to break up the settlements and plantations between the St. Marys and St. Johns rivers, though he doubted that he had sufficient troops and supplies to capture St. Augustine. The expedition should be able to stop the raids into south Georgia, help to wean the Creeks from their allegiance to Britain, and give the Georgians a sense of victory. Of the estimated 1,000 troops needed, Lee and Georgia could raise about 600 and must apply to South Carolina again for the rest. Just at this time Lee was notified that several South Carolina units had been put on the Continental establishment; so he could take them without fear of a South Carolina veto as in July.[32] Lee collected the Virginia, North Carolina, and South Carolina troops in Charleston and set out for Georgia.[33] As usual Tonyn in St. Augustine knew the American plans almost as soon as they were formulated and long before they could be put into operation.[34]

In early August Colonel McIntosh raided northern East Florida, broke up every settlement north of the St. Johns, and caused the withdrawal of the forces on the St. Marys which had been so troublesome to Georgians.[35] On August 19 Lee asked the Georgia Council of Safety if the proposed expedition was needed since the area north of the St. Johns had been broken up and since it was impossible to collect or transport supplies for a reduction of St. Augustine. The council of safety thought that if the area north of the St. Johns was invaded in force all of its inhabitants would withdraw to St. Augustine where they could not be fed or housed and that the fort might surrender to the Americans upon their arrival. The old arguments about breaking up the country between the St. Marys and the St. Johns, stopping raids into south Georgia, and impressing the Indians were repeated. After such a raid in force, the council said one troop of horsemen should be sufficient to protect the Georgia border.[36]

The council of safety did not anticipate the transportation troubles that worried Lee but began the collection of boats and supplies.[37] The Florida authorities were genuinely worried, especially for fear that Floridians would prove disloyal when an American army appeared.[38] The expedition took place in September, and some American troops got as far as the St. Johns and laid waste the country. Certainly the majority of the troops did not get that far. Tonyn said they got no further than Sunbury, and none of them saw St. Augustine. Various reasons were given for this failure: sickness of the troops, hot weather, insufficient transportation, the size of the St. Augustine garrison (which had recently been reinforced), hostilities of the Cherokees against back settlements, the general inability of the Americans to get things done, and the lack of cooperation between Lee and civilian authorities.[39]

Cattle stealing from East Florida began again, and by October Georgians were calling for help against the Florida Rangers. The area south of the Altamaha was overrun, and it was impossible to raise militia just north of that river as the people were moving their families to places of safety. By November the raiders had penetrated north of the Altamaha.[40] Sir William Howe recommended that Georgia and South Carolina should be the target of British winter expeditions,[41] but nothing was done. Trouble from Florida loyalists continued throughout the winter.

During most of 1776 there were British naval vessels stationed off Savannah and St. Augustine. The vessels at the mouth of the Savannah River hurt trade and prevented any military reinforcements and supplies that might have come by water. However, the inland passage from South Carolina to the Altamaha was generally open.[42] The British vessels were reported to have left the mouth of the Savannah early in October but there were constant rumors that they would return.[43]

Failure of the 1776 St. Augustine expedition did not restore peace to the Georgia-East Florida frontier. Raids into Georgia and talk of another expedition against St. Augustine continued. In January, 1777, St. Augustine was reported in a good state of defense with Indians coming in to help the garrison.[44] On February 18 Captain Richard Winn surrendered Fort McIntosh, a small stockade fort on the Satilla River (between the Altamaha and the St. Marys), and its garrison of fifty men to British Regulars and Florida Scouts from St. Augustine.[45] The fear that this attack might be prelude to a more extended operation against Georgia resulted in the sending south of the Continental troops in Savannah and the calling out of militia in several parishes. On February 22, just before the death of President Bulloch, the council of safety gave him the entire executive power for a period of one month because of the possibility that a council could not be assembled quickly enough to take action during the expected emergency.[46]

General Robert Howe, the new Continental commander in the South, came to Savannah early in March and conferred with the president and council. The Georgia regiment of light horse refused to do duty, and many disaffected people in the back country were not to be trusted. This left only the First Georgia Battalion of some 400 troops available for duty. Gwinnett and his council were sure that with proper help they could stop all supplies going from Georgia to St. Augustine, get many of the East Florida people to join them, capture St. Augustine, and end all the East Florida trouble. The militia was called out. Georgia's navy of seven armed galleys was put in readiness. Georgia was ready, with Howe's help, to blot St. Augustine off the map. Howe refused to send any troops from South Carolina to Florida, although he did order one battalion to Sunbury; he took the rest of his troops back to Charleston with him. "He came, he saw, and left us in low Estate," said Gwinnett. Gwinnett did not think that Howe liked the idea of working with a civilian even though he was the head of the military forces of the state. It never occurred to Gwinnett that Howe might think him dictatorial and incompetent. Howe later explained that he lacked troops and supplies necessary to capture the fort at St. Augustine, that it was the wrong time of the year to undertake military operations in the South, and that the state officials wanted to dictate the expedition and had no conception of what was necessary to win.[47]

Gwinnett proceeded with his plans for the expedition but asked for no help from General McIntosh, who said that he was ready to cooperate but had not been informed of the plans for the expedition. The militia was slow in coming in. The arrest of George McIntosh came during March and interfered with any cooperation that might have been possible between McIntosh and Gwinnett. Not until March 27 did Gwinnett and the council of safety request aid from McIntosh; McIntosh said that this request came then only because so few (not over 200) militia could be raised.[48]

As usual, the plans of the expedition were known in St. Augustine in time to oppose them. Governor Tonyn asked Superintendent Stuart to call out Creeks and Cherokees to ravage the Georgia frontiers, and he redoubled his efforts to get disaffected people from the Georgia and Carolina back country to join his forces in St. Augustine.[49]

Militia and Continental troops set out in early April and reached Sunbury by the middle of the month. Here the old enmity between McIntosh and Gwinnett flared again, and cooperation was impossible. Each insisted that he should command the expedition, and neither would allow the other to do so. Upon the advice of the council of safety, both returned to Savannah and left command to Colonel Samuel Elbert, the ranking Continental officer.[50] On May 1 Elbert embarked his troops and proceeded down the inland passage. A group of mounted militia, commanded by Colonel John Baker, went overland. Progress by water was slower than anticipated, and the militia reached the St. Johns before the Continentals did. Here the militia was attacked by British Regulars and Florida Rangers, and most of them fled at once. The progress of Elbert's flotilla south was kept up with by the Florida authorities, but they made no attack against it. Provisions ran short, and the troops, hot and confined on the transports, became sick and disgusted. It was impossible to get the boats through Amelia Narrows just below the St. Marys, and Elbert was worried about the condition of his troops and the leakage of his plans to Florida. So on May 26 he decided to abandon the expedition and return to Savannah where he and his troops arrived on June 15. The only concrete result of the expedition was the collection of some 1,000 head of cattle by the Georgia troops.[51]

The ending of the expedition was the signal for the Florida Rangers to begin their raids into Georgia again. Tonyn reported that they got to within five miles of Savannah and went through Augusta. They seemed able to penetrate to the Ogeechee without any trouble and drove off much stock. These raiding parties were generally not over 150, and there was much complaint that the Georgia Continentals and militia were seldom able to give them any real opposition. Many Georgians feared a real attack from Florida in the fall.[52]

Not only must Georgia fight the British and Tories from East Florida, but she also had serious military recruiting, finance, and supply problems in 1777. Recruiting continued in North Carolina and Virginia for the Second and Third Georgia Battalions and extended into Pennsylvania for the Fourth Battalion. Returns of the first three Continental battalions, the regiment of horse, and the artillery companies in August, 1777, showed a total of 1,526 troops. However, in October only 600 were reported available for duty. Not over 2,000 militia could possibly be collected.[53] Being unable to secure qualified engineer and artillery officers locally, the assembly, in May, 1777, sent blank Continental commissions to an agent in France to be issued to qualified personnel. The Continental Congress disapproved of this action when it heard of it, but the presence of artillery officers with French names in Georgia leads to the conclusion that some of the commissions must have been issued.[54]

Georgia's military situation was considered at length by the Continental Congress in the summer of 1777. When Henry Laurens arrived in Congress he found an expedition against West Florida agreed upon but no men or money yet voted. He set to work to kill this expedition and to substitute for it defense of Georgia. A committee headed by Laurens recommended, and Congress approved, $600,000 for Georgia troops' expenses and the appointment of Joseph Clay, a Savannah merchant and friend of Laurens, as deputy paymaster for Georgia.[55] By the summer of 1778 the back pay due Georgia troops was largely paid, and Congress was induced to vote $1,000,000 additional for support of the Georgia troops.[56] More Continental housekeeping officers were appointed for Georgia; and supply, on paper at least, was taken over entirely by the Continental authorities. In the spring of 1778 it was reported that no state funds were available to Continental troops and there was the old difficulty in getting sufficient funds to feed and supply the troops.[57]

General McIntosh left Georgia to assume his new command in the North on October 10, 1777, and was replaced by Colonel Samuel Elbert as commander of the Georgia brigade.[58] When the Continental troops got back to Savannah in June, 1777, from the Florida expedition, they were sent into healthier locations as frontier guards. Garrison and guard duty proved disagreeable, or perhaps the troops tired of army life in Georgia. At any rate, desertions and poor discipline were much in evidence throughout the rest of the year, though Colonel Elbert made a determined effort to improve conditions.[59]

Early in 1778, Georgians began to plan their annual expedition against St. Augustine. On January 29 the assembly recommended to General Howe that he carry out an expedition against East Florida and promised all possible assistance. Howe and the Continental field officers considered the matter and decided that it would be unsafe to send troops to attack St. Augustine at that time. The 1,500 considered necessary to capture St. Augustine were not available and there were no other troops to protect Georgia during the expedition. It was recommended instead that strong bodies of troops be stationed along the Georgia-Florida frontier to make it secure. Howe said that if the assembly determined upon a Florida expedition anyway, he would be glad to be of whatever help he could. He questioned the use of militia at the season when militiamen were needed to look after farming operations.[60]

The assembly resolved that Howe's letter was highly disrespectful to the governor. It was sure that there were sufficient supplies in Georgia for the proposed expedition and asked for specific recommendations of what further supplies were needed so that they could be acquired. Governor Houstoun was asked to call a council of war to consider the expedition, the council to be attended by the general and field officers of Continental and state troops, the governor, and a committee of the assembly. When the old trouble of civilian-military prestige came up, Howe refused to attend this council in his official capacity but offered to attend as a private citizen and give any advice he could. The assembly requested the governor to send a report of Howe's insubordinate conduct to Congress.[61]

Cattle raids and other troubles from the Florida Rangers continued. On March 9 the executive council authorized any person who would raise fifteen or more volunteers to plunder at will in East Florida under a commission from Georgia. All Georgians who would settle for three months on lands between the St. Marys and the St. Johns (in East Florida) could have a grant of 500 acres in this area.[62] Such offers may have gotten a few adventurous people to operate against East Florida, but to settle in that disputed area for three months was impossible. A state that had to fight its battles with volunteers who supplied themselves and were to be rewarded by being given what they personally captured, and which still insisted to the Continental authorities that it had ample men and supplies for an extended operation in that same area, was not being realistic.

Governor Tonyn, the Florida Rangers, and the British army in St. Augustine were not idle. In February, Tonyn sent German emissaries to try to influence Germans in the Georgia units to desert and come to East Florida. Tonyn was sure that the forces then in Florida were sufficient to capture Georgia but objected that Colonel Prevost, the British commander, would not move without orders from his commander. Prevost, like Howe, wanted more troops and cooler weather before he undertook any extended expedition.[63]

By mid-April Georgians were sure an attack was being planned from East Florida. A large band of disaffected people, estimated at from 400 to 700, from the South Carolina back country went to St. Augustine. These people were called Scoffellites or Scopholites after their leader, a Colonel Scophol, and had been roused through the efforts of Thomas Brown and his connections in the Carolina and Georgia back country. Continental troops and militia were sent to oppose their passage through Georgia but apparently did not make contact with them.[64]

A proclamation was issued by Governor Houstoun calling upon all friends of freedom to repair to a state camp established in Burke County. Houstoun was to command, provisions and ammunition were to be furnished by Georgia, but all plunder was to be retained by its captors.[65] When Houstoun took the field, the executive council gave him full powers in regard to the campaign, saying that quick action was necessary in battle and that the constitution did not make consent of the council necessary in military matters. Houstoun said he had no desire to exercise power alone but he realized the difficulties of getting quick action otherwise and so would take the power. The assembly was to meet in ten days and could cancel this grant of power if it wished.[66]

By the end of April there were about 2,000 troops consisting of Georgia and Carolina Continentals under Howe, Georgia militia under Houstoun, South Carolina militia under Colonel Andrew Williamson, and naval units under Commodore Oliver Bowen.[67] The old argument of command immediately appeared. Howe and Houtoun had already differed. Howe, the senior officer and the Continental commander of the Southern Department, claimed command by right. Houstoun, about thirty years old and with no military experience, refused to take orders from Howe. Colonel

Williamson said his militia would not take orders from Howe but caused little trouble in the confused command picture. Bowen refused to take orders from either Houstoun or Howe as there was some dispute as to whether the galleys were Continental or state vessels. Howe, Houstoun, and Bowen held a council in the general's tent on the Florida border but could not agree on a plan of action.

As the expedition approached the St. Marys on June 29, the Florida Rangers hastily destroyed their own supplies and their rendezvous, Fort Tonyn, on the Florida side of the river, and withdrew. Because of the confused command picture and the destruction of Fort Tonyn, Howe asked and received approval of the Continental officers to end the expedition. He and the Continentals started north in mid-July and were back in Savannah by the end of the month. Houstoun still wanted to proceed against St. Augustine, but he and Williamson decided an expedition was impossible without more troops, and returned to Savannah.

Thus ended the third and last attempt of Georgians to capture St. Augustine. It had gone no further than the Florida-Georgia border and had met no serious opposition. Some 1,200 Regulars, Florida Scouts, and Indians were reported to have marched out of St. Augustine; but Prevost, the British commander, had no intention of any serious opposition until the force reached the St. Johns, a river it did not see. The Whigs had about twice as many men as the British and certainly had a better chance of taking St. Augustine than on either of the earlier expeditions. The season was bad, but the inability to agree on a common commander or plan of action was the major cause of the failure of the expedition.[68]

As soon as the Georgians returned to Savannah, the cattle stealing raids from East Florida began again. Late in August the assembly ordered that families of many Florida Scouts, who had been left on the Ogeechee and who carried Georgia plans to Florida, be moved onto forfeited estates where they could be more easily watched and prevented from communicating with Florida.[69]

Both General Howe and Henry Laurens proposed another expedition against St. Augustine by fall. Congress authorized an expedition with specially enlisted troops, if necessary, for the winter of 1778-1779.[70] But by the time this expedition could be got ready, Georgia Whigs had British troops closer than St. Augustine to worry them.

The three expeditions against East Florida were the major military effort of Georgia in the first phase of military activity and should be analyzed before the next phase of the fighting is considered. Throughout this fighting neither the Continental nor British military commanders thought they had sufficient troops to destroy or decisively defeat the other and never wanted to undertake the expeditions. It was the civilian authorities who were so anxious to defeat the enemy and who were sure that this could be done easily. The two greatest weaknesses of the Americans were the lack of strong executives, Continental or state, to carry out any unified program over any period of time and the divided command that a stronger executive and a state government less jealous of its prerogative might have eliminated. Because the major effort was left to the civilian authorities, it is possible to say that Governor Tonyn won with his Florida Rangers. This was a relatively small group of loyalists from Georgia and Carolina who were organized and supported by Tonyn and commanded by Thomas Brown, a man who knew what he wanted and how to get it. The military commanders at St. Augustine opposed the Rangers and would have little to do with them. But it was the Rangers who kept up continual raids into Georgia and never gave the state any peace. Brown and his loyalists all hated Whigs and were anxious to get even because of the loss of their property and the rough treatment they had received earlier. They knew well the area in which they operated. Georgians often said they needed such a force, but they never created one. Neither Continental nor state troops nor militia could equal the Florida Rangers, though they often outnumbered the Rangers. It is possible to say that Florida got the better of this three years of fighting because of superior administrative organization, wherein the early revolutionary governments in America were notably weak. Perhaps the administrator himself, Tonyn, should also be given much of the credit for this success.

Troop life in the Georgia Continental Line varied little during 1776-1778, and in many respects a description of it sounds strikingly modern. Garrison life was monotonous with a routine of guard, parades, drill, policing the barracks and surrounding area, orders to stay out of houses of ill repute, and admonitions to respect civilians. Colonel Elbert's Order Book indicates that the concern of the army with the soldiers was almost entirely negative. Little or no effort was made by the army or civilians, except by the ones who could profit personally, to improve soldier morale. Discipline was bad among both officers and men. Death sentences for desertion were fairly common. Ten convictions for desertion on one day brought seven sentences of shooting, one of hanging, and two of 100 lashes. The most common punishment for desertion, 100 lashes, was also meted out for abusive language. One sentence of 400 lashes for desertion to the enemy is recorded.[71]

Army supply left much to be desired. On the 1778 Florida expedition a list of men without shoes was ordered made so that cowhide could be procured to make moccasins. At another time men who had never had blankets were ordered to apply for them.[72] Near the end of the summer in 1778, barracks for the Savannah garrison were finished outside the town. These must have provided improvement over the previous arrangement of quartering the men in crowded billets. Often only a part of the Continental troops were kept in Savannah, and the rest were scattered over the frontier for guard duty.[73]

One of the greatest complaints of Continental troops in 1776 and 1777 was that they were paid in Georgia currency, which had considerably less value than Continental currency and was of no value outside the state. Many of the men did not live in Georgia and needed money that they could send to their families in other states. Both General Howe and Deputy Paymaster Joseph Clay made repeated attempts to get Continental funds to pay the troops. Howe said that there would be a mutiny unless such payments were made; and a majority of the desertions were blamed on the small value of the money paid to the troops, the lack of any pay at all, or the high cost of necessities that the troops had to buy.[74] After funds were voted by the Continental Congress in the summer of 1777, it was still a year before the situation was corrected.[75]

Besides Continental troops, militia was often mobilized for independent action or cooperation with Continentals on operations like the Florida expeditions. When Continental troops were needed elsewhere, guard duty on the western frontier was usually assumed by the state. Militia was supposed to do this duty, but it was considered bad policy to give militiamen continuous duty during the summer months when they were needed for farm work. Often little or no militia could be assembled if there was no immediate danger obvious to the militiamen. To get more reliable troops and to relieve the militia during the planting season, the state resorted to various types of special troops. Invariably these units did not measure up to expectations and were abolished or they faded away and some other type of state troops was ordered raised. But the "other type" were never any better than the units they were supposed to replace. State troops either could not be raised in the desired number, or they began to desert before recruiting was finished, or there was insufficient equipment for them, or the discipline was so poor as to render them useless, or they could not be found when needed, or something else happened to render them useless. Often these troops were raised for a short period for some specific duty, but several attempts were made to raise frontier minute battalions to do duty for the duration of the war. In 1777 a company of frontier scouts to be composed of Indians was authorized, but it probably never materialized. In 1778 there were minute battalions, two troops of horsemen, five independent companies, special magazine and jail guards, a combination artillery and fire company for Savannah, and six companies given no special name. When the five independent companies were ordered disbanded, only six men were known to be on duty; and the clerk of the executive council was ordered to inform what officers he could locate that the companies were disbanded.[76] State troops were more a hope than a reality. Georgia authorities throughout the war attempted to recruit both state and Continental troops outside the state. Because better bounties were usually given by other states and service in Georgia did not have a very good name, out-of-state recruitment was usually a false hope. But the state clung to it, perhaps because there were not enough men in Georgia to do the necessary military duty.

Besides the army action that has been described, there was naval activity along the Georgia coast. All early Whig defense plans emphasized the necessity of naval protection of the coast, and a navy grew up as an adjunct to the army and was never clearly separated from it. Oliver Bowen, its commander, was originally commissioned a captain in the Continental Battalion formed in February, 1776. In January, 1777, Bowen was elected by the assembly as "Commodore or Commander" of Georgia's navy to rank as a colonel in the army.[77] Ship carpenters were brought from Philadelphia to build vessels, and by spring of 1777 there were at least five galleys, eight row galleys, and two sloops belonging to the state.[78] There was a naval board appointed by the executive council, presumably to handle supply matters. In April, 1778, the executive council noted that the galleys had originally been commissioned by the state to guard its coast. The fact that the ships had been taken over by the Continental establishment did not change the purpose

or direction of their activities, all of which was still in the hands of
state authorities. The state promised to supplement naval funds
if the Continental Congress did not supply enough.[79] Since Bowen
refused to take orders from the governor on the Florida expedition
of 1778, the executive instructed the captains of the vessels to take
orders direct from the council and not from Bowen, and Bowen
was suspended from his command because of contempt of the
executive.[80]

The earliest Whig naval action, capture of powder vessels at
Savannah, has already been described. There was a certain amount
of naval action connected with the East Florida troubles, stemming
mainly from the fact that most of the rice taken from south Georgia
to East Florida went by small vessels that could go up the rivers
and ply the inland passage. Sometimes Whig naval activity was directed by naval commanders and sometimes by army commanders.
Though Bowen refused to cooperate during the 1778 Florida expedition, Colonel Elbert and other army officers were responsible
for the capture of several British naval vessels along the Georgia-
Florida coast.[81] British men-of-war stationed on the Georgia coast
never had any opposition from the Georgia navy because it had no
vessels large enough to fight major British vessels.

The Continental Marine Committee appointed John Wereat
its agent in 1776 and instructed him to supply all Continental vessels with provisions, stores, money, and other necessities. Wereat
was to seize, libel, and sell all captured vessels brought into Georgia as prizes by Continental cruisers. He was to supply cargoes,
public or private, for the *Georgia Packet,* a Continental vessel,
which regularly sailed between Philadelphia and Savannah as a
mail and supply boat.[82]

One thing that had always affected the military situation in
Georgia was relations with Indians, especially the Creeks. As the
struggle between the colonials and Britain intensified, the struggle
for control and friendship of the Southern Indians also intensified.
The British Indian Department got along well with the Indians
and had an initial advantage in this struggle. In 1776 Superintendent Stuart had Indian gifts and trade items sent through the Floridas, and prevailed upon some Indian traders to remove from
Augusta to Pensacola, where he intended to create a new center
of the Southern Indian trade.[83]

The Georgia Council of Safety, in January, 1776, instructed
local committees to be sure that nothing was done to antagonize

the Indians and saw that some ammunition was distributed to the Creeks. An unsuccessful attempt was made to get the Creeks to apprehend and deliver to the Whigs David Taitt, Stuart's deputy to the Creeks.[84] Like Stuart, the Whig Indian commissioners wanted to prevent a general Indian attack on the frontier but wanted to get Indian cooperation when there was military activity.

In the late spring of 1776 the Continental Indian Commissioners held a conference of Creeks and Cherokees at Augusta, at which the British Indian Department was unable to prevent Indian attendance. Apparently the aim of this conference was to distribute presents and try to win the Indians away from British friendship.[85] No definite results have been ascertained, but the meeting did illustrate the split Indian loyalties that worried both sides throughout the war. There were always Indians who would meet with representatives of either side, take their presents, and make promises of friendship. There were always other Indians of the same tribes or groups who would repudiate the first group and any promises it had made to the whites. The whites always tried to deprecate the number and importance of the Indians who attended the meetings of their enemies.

In the summer of 1776 the Cherokees began troubles, known as the Cherokee War, on the Carolina frontier. The British tried to get the Creeks to help the Cherokees; the Americans tried to prevent this, and few Creeks helped the Cherokees. Actual hostilities began between the Cherokees and South Carolina. The Continental Congress requested Virginia, North Carolina, and Georgia to help South Carolina. Georgia militia around Augusta was already mobilized and some of it or state troops participated in the war, but most of the fighting was done by the other states. Georgia participated in the treaty of De Witt's Corner, which ended the war, on May 20, 1777. The defeated Cherokees gave little additional trouble throughout the Revolution.[86]

The Continental Congress and the state government in Savannah always differed with frontiersmen on the subject of the Creeks and the Creek trade. While the council of safety was assuring the Creeks in the summer of 1776 that Georgians intended to begin the manufacture of goods to supply the Indians, the inhabitants of the frontier parishes were requesting that the Indian trade be stopped. George Galphin, the Continental Indian Commissioner, had his hands full preventing the people on the 1773 Indian cession from starting a war with the Creeks. Stuart likewise tried to prevent hostilities between the Creeks and the Whigs.[87] The timely arrival of suitable Indian presents from the French West Indies and the defeat of the Cherokees assured Creek friendship in the summer of 1777. After a conference which Galphin held in June, Stuart said he had no hopes of Indian cooperation against the Whigs until fall.[88] In September when Stuart had well-laid plans for white and Creek cooperation against the Whigs, Galphin held another conference in Charleston and was able to prevent the Creeks from carrying out Stuart's plans.[89]

While Galphin and his colleagues were working so hard to maintain Creek peace, the people in upcountry Georgia were trying to begin a Creek war and in late summer almost succeeded in persuading the assembly to declare a war that the state could not possibly have won without outside help. At the request of General Howe, the Continental Congress urged the Georgia Assembly to try to cultivate Indian peace and to punish the people who sought a war with the Creeks.[90] Throughout the fall and winter there were frontier incidents but no major trouble. In the summer of 1778 the Creeks were reported willing to settle their differences, but in August twenty whites were killed in Wilkes County. Georgia and South Carolina militia were called out for the expected war, but an uneasy peace was restored for the winter.[91]

This account of 1776-1778 Creek affairs makes it clear that the Creeks had returned to the situation which had existed before 1763 when two nations of whites competed for Creek friendship, and the Creeks could often play one against the other to their own benefit. South Carolina often took the initiative in diplomacy or military preparations, because Georgia was too poor and weak to buy the needed presents or to fight the Creeks on her frontier alone.

Because there were no major British military operations in the South during this period, British-Indian affairs were pretty much left to Stuart and the governors of East and West Florida. Stuart and his deputies usually deprecated the efforts of George Galphin, the leading Continental commissioner, but their concern about his actions showed that they knew he had more influence than they would admit. The Creeks tended to be mainly pro-British, but there was always a Galphin party in the nation. The Creeks were not willing to fight a full-scale war against Georgia because there were insufficient British troops available to cooperate. The Indians never took to Stuart's idea of military cooperation with whites but preferred their old system of warfare which they understood. It is exceedingly doubtful that they seriously contemplated prolonged war against Georgia such as the British wanted. Regardless of how much Indian help could be got by either side, both sides continued to work hard for Indian friendship.

BRITISH RETURN
TO GEORGIA, 1779

7

****

N O SOONER had the British officials been
forced by the Whigs to leave Georgia and
South Carolina than they began presenting plans to the government in London for the recapture of these provinces. The early
ideas of Governor Wright were not favorably received by the secretary of state, who wrote, "Sir James Wright can be of little use at
present, his ideas of military operations are most extraordinary. He
gave me a plan for keeping a few oxen in an island, which would
employ a fleet. I have another plan for subduing Georgia and S.
Carolina, where he desires the alliance and assistance of all the
Indians, and only 11,000 regular troops."[1] The governors and lieutenant governors of South Carolina and Georgia presented a
formal memorial in August, 1777, in which they said that the loyalists in both provinces had been subdued by the rebels but were
only awaiting help and protection to resume their loyalty to the
King. Help should be sent before the areas were overrun entirely
by rebels, for 1,500 from Virginia were reported to have moved to
Georgia. The memorial continued that the Southern colonies were
essential to the rebel economy because they produced the exports
which paid for rebel military supplies. The colonial products that
made up these exports could be used by the British. Occupation
of Charleston and Savannah would make it easy to control the entire provinces.[2] A year later Georgia's governor and lieutenant
governor presented another memorial in which they urged that
Georgia be subdued even if it were not possible to subdue South
Carolina at the same time. Georgia lands could be given to loyalists

116

in other rebel colonies, her ports would help naval operations in the South, food and lumber would be supplied to the army and the West Indian colonies, and the cost of the entire operation could be paid for by the confiscation and sale of property of Georgia rebels.[3]

The first evidence that the British government had decided to begin operations in South Carolina and Georgia was a "Most Secret" letter of March 8, 1778, informing Sir Henry Clinton that he had been appointed commander-in-chief in America and outlining plans for operations in the South as they had been developed in London. The basis of this plan was information from officials and loyalists who had left the two colonies. Once the subdued loyalists were allowed to reassert their loyalty to the King and once those who had left returned, civil government could be re-established. Other rebellious colonies would see the blessings of restored British rule and would be willing to return to it—or so it was reasoned in London.

It was estimated that it would take 2,000 troops to capture Savannah and 5,000 to capture Charleston. If enough for both were not available at once, Clinton was urged to capture Savannah as the easier of the two. Then it would be possible to make contact with the loyalists in the back country of both provinces and isolate the rebels on the Carolina coast until more troops were available to capture Charleston and all of South Carolina. James Simpson, a former South Carolina attorney general and representative of the back country in the assembly, was sent to the Carolina back country to see how the people felt about the return of royal government and to pave the way for such a return.

Clinton was directed to begin the operation just as soon as the troops could be spared from operations in the North, probably in October. He was instructed to attack Maryland and Virginia at the same time if there were enough troops available.[4] General Augustine Prevost, British commander in St. Augustine, and Moses Kirkland, a deputy Indian Superintendent for the Southern Department who was in New York, advised that the expedition be undertaken in the winter because the climate made operations easier in the South then and troops could not be used in the North. Clinton's orders for the expedition were based upon a plan submitted by Kirkland on October 13, 1778, which suggested that General Prevost march against southern Georgia at the time the troops from New York arrived and that Augusta be taken as soon as possible to open communications with the loyalists in the back country and to cut off rebel communications with the Indians. Indian Superintendent Stuart should be instructed to raise all Indians possible to cooperate with the British. It might be well to influence the Indians to attack the Virginia back country to prevent Virginia sending any help to Georgia and South Carolina.[5]

The British Commissioners for Restoring Peace in America, of whom Clinton was a member, formulated a plan to use the recapture of the Southern provinces as a part of their peace offensive. They instructed the commander of the expedition to use the military only to furnish sufficient support to loyalists in the provinces and to allow them to resume their ordinary civil government. Any legal action against rebels or their property should be taken by the civil government, not the military. Should this plan work well in Georgia, then the commissioners planned to use it in other areas which they hoped would be captured by the British.[6]

Preparations of an expedition of this size could not escape notice, and various rumors as to its destination were soon current in both British and American areas. A South Carolina loyalist who had been in New York informed Henry Laurens, then President of the Continental Congress, of the proposed expedition; but Laurens was doubtful of the truth of the information, because of the circumstances of its delivery.[7] However, Virginia was requested to send 1,000 troops and North Carolina 3,000 to help South Carolina and Georgia. North Carolina quickly collected her troops and started them south under General Ashe. Two thousand additional troops requested later were also sent.[8] The dispatches from Laurens containing his information about the proposed expedition were laid before the Georgia Executive Council on November 19, 1778, and a few precautionary measures were taken.[9]

At this time Congress was considering another expedition against East Florida and authorized the enlistment of special troops for it. Laurens opposed this expedition and presented additional information about the British expedition which was preparing in New York, but Congress did not cancel its East Florida expedition.[10] In December Laurens gave Congress a full report of conditions in South Carolina and Georgia, their value to Congress and the British, and the improbability that the Americans could recapture them soon if the British occupied them.[11]

In New York Clinton assembled an expedition of British, German, and loyalist troops under the command of Lieutenant Colonel Archibald Campbell, 71st Scottish Regiment. There were at least two battalions of the 71st Regiment, two regiments of Hessians, three or four battalions of New York loyalists, and a detachment of royal artillery. Contemporary estimates of total strength vary from 2,500 to 3,500. A naval detachment commanded by Commodore Hyde Parker was to accompany the transports to Georgia.[12]

Clinton ordered that General Prevost march his troops from St. Augustine to the St. Marys to cooperate with Campbell when he arrived in Georgia.[13] Prevost sent two expeditions against lower Georgia, one by land and one by sea, in the latter part of November, 1778. Georgians were warned that their state was being invaded by four British armies but were told that if they remained peacefully in their homes and surrendered their arms upon demand they would have nothing to fear. Otherwise their property might be destroyed. When British troops arrived at Sunbury, their commander, Lieutenant Colonel L. V. Fuser, demanded that Lieutenant Colonel John McIntosh surrender Fort Morris to him. McIntosh replied that he and his troops were fighting the battles of America and would prefer to perish in defense of the fort. "As to surrendering the fort, receive this laconic reply, 'COME AND TAKE IT.'" When Fuser discovered that the other expedition from St. Augustine had not arrived to cooperate with him, he returned to Florida without making any attempt to take the fort. The other British expedition under Lieutenant Colonel Mark Prevost met American troops under Colonel John White and contented itself with burning the meeting house and other buildings at Midway before retiring to Florida.[14]

Just as the invasion from Florida began, General Robert Howe was relieved as Continental Commander of the Southern Department and was replaced by Major General Benjamin Lincoln. Howe delayed his departure long enough to go to Georgia to do what he could to drive out the British. Georgia troops were busy against Indians on the frontier, and Howe reported that Georgia was totally unprepared to defend itself against further attack.[15] This invasion was not generally connected by Georgians or Continental officers with the rumored British invasion from New York. General Lincoln reporting from his headquarters in Charleston did not connect the two, though he enclosed a deposition from a deserter of a British ship just arrived at Tybee which said that his vessel was one of the expedition prepared in New York. Lincoln did urge North Carolina to rush the troops authorized for service in Georgia.[16] The Georgia Executive Council, after sending agents to Charleston to urge that defense measures be taken, busied itself with putting military matters in the best possible condition.[17]

The Georgia expedition in New York weighed anchor on November 12, but a heavy gale drove it back to Staten Island and damaged several of the vessels. It sailed a second time on November 27 and had a rough passage south. It was off Charleston on December 17 and arrived at Tybee Island December 23, totally ignorant of the military situation in Georgia. From two local residents the British learned that the Carolina troops which had come to Georgia during the recent Florida troubles had returned to South Carolina and that there were only a few hundred troops and militia in Savannah. Campbell's troops, two or three times as many as Howe had under his command, landed unopposed below Savannah on the morning of December 29.[18]

From start to finish the defense of Savannah was handled poorly. The British landed unopposed at one of the obvious landing places which Howe had visited the day before. General Howe, Governor John Houstoun, and Colonel George Walton, commander of the Georgia militia, did not get along with each other, probably because of the troubles Howe and Houstoun had on the 1778 Florida expedition; and there was insufficient liaison between them and no real central command. It was the old story of divided command and no real cooperation between the commanders. Howe defended the main road from the landing place to the city and said that he guarded all the approaches to the city as best he could with the 600 to 1,000 troops in Savannah. Walton later said that he pointed out to Howe additional unguarded passes through the swamps after the battle had already begun; in fact the British got around the American army and into Savannah with the help of a Negro who showed them a little-used path through the swamps. Once it was known that the British were in Savannah, panic seized the Whigs. Some officers and soldiers deserted their duty to look after families and personal property. Individual officers tried to rally troops, but there was no general effort or central control. It was practically every man for himself.

With the warnings that the Americans had received, Savannah should have been better defended. Howe had made recommendations to the state government earlier, but little had been done. Howe apparently was taken by surprise and did not use his troops to best advantage. There is no evidence that he made a determined effort to prevent the British landings or to intercept the troops before they could organize for battle. He had fewer troops than the British, but the town was surrounded by swamps and was fairly easy to defend. Everything was confused and no single person seemed able to take hold and direct the American forces. A few days' delay would have given time for Lincoln and his Carolina troops to arrive and perhaps prevent the capture of Savannah.

Many Americans were captured before they could escape from Savannah; the height of the water in the surrounding creeks prevented many from making their escape. Some who attempted it were drowned, and some of those who did escape lost their arms and equipment. Campbell reported that he captured some 450 Americans and that about 100 were killed or lost their lives through drowning. He reported British losses as seven killed and nineteen wounded. The battle was over so quickly that the city itself was damaged little.

In his account of the defeat written on December 30, Howe showed his complete confusion as to what happened. He did not know how many men he commanded during the battle nor how many were lost. He still hoped that many of the missing would appear and report to his headquarters, as some were doing. He praised all officers that he mentioned but offered no explanation or satisfactory account of what had happened. He recommended that the British be attacked or at least confined to Savannah if sufficient American troops were available for that task.[19]

No sooner had the British captured Savannah than they took steps to reclaim Georgia loyalty. On January 4, 1779, Commodore Parker and Colonel Campbell issued a proclamation stating that they had come to Georgia to protect loyal subjects of the King in all Southern provinces and inviting all such to join them. Protection was to be based upon future loyalty rather than past disloyalties, and all who would swear loyalty to the King and renounce the Continental Congress were to enjoy their property unmolested. People of every description were given three months to take the oath and receive full pardon for past offenses. Those who opposed the royal authority were warned that they would be severely dealt with, and loyal inhabitants were urged to report "ringleaders of sedition" who refused to accept royal clemency to army headquarters for punishment.[20]

General Prevost again led his forces into Georgia from St. Augustine and captured Sunbury with its garrison on January 10,

1779.[21] With the arrival of Prevost in Savannah, Campbell presented his plan for an immediate advance to Augusta to complete the control of the province by the British and, as Campbell put it, make him the first officer "to take a stripe and star from the rebel flag of Congress."[22] The reaction of people outside Savannah to the British was mixed. Pastor Triebner at Ebenezer rushed to take the oath of allegiance to the British, but he could not carry his entire congregation with him. Campbell reported that many respectable inhabitants joined his army, while American observers reported that many Georgians were fleeing the state in advance of the British.[23]

Campbell set out for Augusta on January 24 with about 1,000 troops and arrived, after some organized opposition from Whig militia, on January 31 without the loss of a man. He scoured the country around Augusta for sixty miles to get supplies and to make his presence known to the inhabitants. About 1,400 men submitted, swore allegiance to the King, and allowed themselves to be formed into twenty militia companies for the protection of Georgia against South Carolina Whigs.[24]

After the loss of Savannah, Howe retreated up the Savannah River with the part of his army that had escaped and crossed over into South Carolina where he turned over his troops to General Lincoln and left the South. Lincoln had come to Purrysburg when Savannah fell and had collected an army of North Carolina, South Carolina, Virginia, and Georgia troops with which he hoped to attack the British and drive them out of Georgia or confine them to Savannah where they could not draw supplies from the back country or contact the Indians or back-country loyalists.[25]

As soon as the shock of invasion had passed, Georgia Whigs began to try to regain as much of their state as possible. By the middle of January several hundred militia were reported collected at Burke Jail under the leadership of Lieutenant Colonel James Ingram who was cooperating with Lincoln and South Carolina militia. Ingram was unable to attack Campbell upon his march to Augusta but continued to attack small parties of British and loyalists.[26] In the back-country Wilkes County, Whigs collected under militia Colonels Elijah Clarke, John Twiggs, and John Dooly. By the middle of February it was obvious that the British were not going to overrun all of Georgia at once, and many people in the back country began to doubt the wisdom of their oath to the King which they had taken when the British first arrived. Many renounced the oath and entered the Whig forces.[27]

The British had anticipated considerable help from the Indians once there were sufficient troops for them to rally round. Stuart had given repeated assurances that the Creeks and Cherokees would cooperate with the British once British troops arrived. However he was not informed of the planned invasion in time to collect Indians for military cooperation. When Campbell arrived at Augusta he saw but few Indians and they were interested only in presents. Neither did the numerous back-country loyalists who were supposedly waiting to be freed from their Whig oppressors rise *en masse* to join Campbell at Augusta. The more ardent British sympathizers probably had left and joined the Florida Rangers, while others had lost some of their love for the British cause since the disappearance of royal government in 1776.

When Campbell realized that he was not going to get his anticipated reinforcements and that the Whig opposition was gaining strength daily, he became doubtful of the wisdom of his rapid advance to Augusta. With the arrival of General John Ashe and some 1,200 North Carolina troops opposite Augusta, Campbell discovered that his newly organized loyalist militia was of extremely doubtful value. Since he was outnumbered and saw no hopes for reinforcements, he marched out of Augusta on February 14 and took station at Hudson's Ferry, some twenty-four miles above Ebenezer.[28]

The same day that Campbell withdrew from Augusta, Whig militia under Colonels Andrew Pickens, John Dooly, and Elijah Clarke surprised a group of about 700 Tories under Colonel Boyd at Kettle Creek, in Wilkes County near where the town of Washington is now located. After a brisk encounter, the Tories were defeated and many were captured or killed. Boyd, who had expected to join some 500 more Tories and ravage upper Georgia, was killed; and his planned expedition did not take place.[29]

Although all Tory operations in Wilkes County were not ended, the defeat of Boyd and the withdrawal of Campbell from Augusta insured Whig predominance in the upcountry. Kettle Creek was an illustration of how well militia could fight when well led, and the encounter was a forerunner of the savage Tory-Whig fighting that was to take place in the upcountry during the next three years.

Throughout February Lincoln pushed the collection of troops in South Carolina.[30] After Campbell evacuated Augusta, General Ashe crossed the Savannah River and took post on Briar Creek to cover the area above the British outposts at Hudson's Ferry. On

March 3, Ashe was surprised at his camp, near where the creek empties into the Savannah, by a body of British and Tories under Lieutenant Colonel Mark Prevost. The Americans had about fifteen minutes' warning of the British approach and were drawing ammunition and taking position when the attack came. Despite personal bravery of many officers and men, there was no chance against a well-disciplined army. Ashe could not rally his troops, who escaped through the swamps, swam the creek, or got away as best they could. The main loss to the Americans was the effect the battle had upon morale and the disruption of Lincoln's offensive plans against the British, which were entirely abandoned for the time being. Ashe was absolved of any personal cowardice by a court martial but he was blamed for a poorly selected camp site and insufficient security.[31]

Having no immediate military problems, Campbell was free to carry out his instructions to reinstate civil government at the earliest practicable moment. The initial proclamation inviting Georgians to return to their old loyalty had informed them that Parliament had given up any attempts to tax the colonies. On March 4, 1779, civilian government was restored with Lieutenant Colonel James Mark Prevost, brother of General Prevost, as lieutenant governor. A council and complete slate of provincial officials were appointed and all laws of 1775 were declared in force.[32] Georgia now had both a British colonial government and a Whig state government (at a rather low ebb just now), each acting in the area controlled by its military forces.

Governor Prevost invited loyalists from other Southern areas to come to Georgia and urged all Georgia loyalists to cooperate with his government and the army, especially in furnishing needed supplies. Finding the provincial treasury non-existent, he drew on the British Treasury for necessary expenses and for support of loyalist refugees. He took steps to provide for frontier defense and to regain Indian friendship.[33]

But Prevost's term as governor was only temporary. Some of Georgia's old provincial officials had been ordered back to the province even before Campbell's success was known in London.[34] The instructions to Governor Wright indicate the thinking of the British government about the restoration of provincial government. Wright was authorized to restore Georgia to the "Peace of the King" if he thought it advisable upon his arrival in Savannah, and he was advised to call an assembly soon thereafter to convince the inhabitants that civil government was a reality. Nothing should be recommended to this assembly that it would not approve, and any punishment of rebels should appear to come from the assembly and not from the governor. It would be well if the assembly would vote something toward imperial expenses to set a good example now that Parliamentary taxation of the colonies had been abandoned. Loyalists coming from other colonies should be granted lands if they wished to settle. A royal council was to be created by Wright out of the best people available.[35]

Governor Wright, Lieutenant Governor John Graham, and Chief Justice Anthony Stokes arrived in Savannah and took up their duties in July, 1779. Wright answered the congratulatory address of welcome from the inhabitants with assurances that Parliament had granted the points for which Americans said they were fighting.[36] Wright did not find Georgia in as good shape as he had hoped and did not think that there were sufficient troops to protect it from rebels who persisted in rejecting the blessings of restored colonial government. He said that the people thought the restoration of civil government restored the King's peace; therefore he issued a proclamation restoring it, but he was doubtful if Georgia was really ready yet.[37] Before he left England, Wright had expressed doubts if many who took the oath of allegiance to the King could be trusted. He believed that such doubtful people could control any assembly elected if they were allowed to vote— hardly an encouraging picture for a restored province.[38] Wright held to this opinion after his return to Georgia and did not call an assembly election for almost a year.

Soon after Savannah's capture, the army advertised for needed supplies.[39] By February, 1779, a vessel arrived from the Bahama Islands to secure food to relieve the shortage in those islands and to bring several families of loyalists who had fled to the islands and were now returning to Georgia to live. Other loyalists in St. Augustine and the West Indies were reported to be preparing to return to Georgia.[40] One of the arguments for the recapture of Georgia was that it could furnish food to the army and to the West Indies. Yet within a few months both the army and navy were ordering provisions from elsewhere with the explanation that only rice was available in Georgia and that the troops and sailors did not like it. Immediately after the capture, the navy set Georgians and refugee Negroes to work getting needed timbers and naval stores from the forests.[41]

After the British success at Briar Creek, Campbell was sure that 3,000 to 4,000 more troops could subjugate Georgia and South Carolina, and he urged Clinton to send them. However, he did not wait to complete the conquest but, together with Commodore Parker, left Savannah for England on March 12, 1779.[42] Throughout the spring and summer Georgia was uneasy. The British controlled Savannah and the area for twenty-five to forty miles around it. The Whigs controlled the back country and part of the lower coast. Provincial and state militia composed of neighbors sometimes operated in the same area. Whigs often raided to within a few miles of Savannah, and the British raided the Whig areas. The border area between Whig and Tory Georgia, sort of a no man's land, was badly devastated. Whig planters and backwoodsmen went into South Carolina in considerable numbers if the British pressed hard, but they came back into Georgia when the pressure was removed. Many Whigs from the area occupied by the British moved to South Carolina. There was considerable trouble on the frontier between state militia and the Creeks, probably urged on by the British.[43]

In the spring General Lincoln decided that the 5,000 men under his command were enough to attack the British, confine them to the Savannah area, and cut off their contacts with the back country.[44] By the end of April Lincoln and most of his army had crossed into Georgia at Augusta and had begun an advance on Savannah. General Prevost, soon discovering the weakened condition of the American army left at Purrysburg under General Moultrie, crossed into South Carolina, and marched toward Charleston. When Lincoln saw that Moultrie could not stop Prevost, he abandoned operations in Georgia and rushed back to Charleston in mid-May to save it from the British. After a slow progress through the Carolina low country, the British army returned to Savannah, and both armies gave up any plans for immediate offensive actions.[45] Military activity settled down to raids into the territory held by the enemy with no important results or change in territory controlled.

Wright and the Tories continued to complain that the 1,000 British troops in Georgia were not enough to protect the loyal subjects or to conquer the rest of the province, but no more troops arrived.[46] Neither Whigs nor British were sure of their power, and both thought the other side stronger than it actually was. There were rumors of British reinforcements which did not materialize. In August General Lachlan McIntosh wrote General Lincoln from

Augusta that he had heard rumors of an imminent British attack in that area and was afraid it would be successful. He painted a dark picture of American chances in Richmond County and the back country. The state government sent urgent appeals to General Lincoln and South Carolina for help. Georgia's treasury was empty, and South Carolina granted her a $100,000 loan to support back-country militia on duty.[47] At the same time Wright wrote that Augusta was occupied by McIntosh and that the country above Briar Creek was ravaged by the rebels. He thought 4,000 to 5,000 troops and "a few Ships" could control all of Georgia.[48]

From the time of Campbell's arrival in Augusta in February, it was obvious that the Indians were not going to flock to the British standard. Hence the British began to court Indian friendship and tried to get Indians to cooperate in their warfare against the Whigs. The British insisted that the Indians join them in organized combat; the Indians objected to British attempts to prevent looting and indiscriminate frontier warfare.[49] Few Indians joined the British army, and the ones who did remained only a short time.[50] There were continual complaints that Superintendent Stuart was not doing his job as well as formerly. Stuart died after a long illness on March 21, 1779, and the Southern Indian Department was divided into two sections. Alexander Cameron, a deputy, was given the Choctaws, Chickasaws, and other Indians along the Mississippi. Thomas Brown, the notorious Georgia Tory and leader of the Florida Rangers, was given the Creeks, Cherokees, Catawbas, and other Indians toward the Atlantic.[51]

Soon after Savannah's capture by the British Congress and General Washington considered the loss. They realized the importance of its reconquest, but Washington said he could spare no troops, and the only hope for reconquest was with French or Spanish aid.[52] Henry Laurens kept this subject before Congress, which, in January and February, 1779, requested Virginia and North Carolina to send what troops they could to Lincoln in South Carolina and ordered Count Pulaski and his legion to the Southern Department.[53] At the same time, Congress debated requesting Count d'Estaing, commander of the French fleet and troops in American waters, to help recover Georgia. The French minister objected that d'Estaing was busy in the West Indies; so Congress sent no request to him. But Governor John Rutledge of South Carolina asked d'Estaing's aid to reconquer Savannah.[54]

This invitation of Rutledge's set in motion the most interesting and most spectacular military action that took place in Georgia after the capture of Savannah. Since there was really little hope for French help, the Americans and British were greatly surprised when d'Estaing arrived off the Georgia coast on September 1, 1779, with twenty-two vessels of the line and about 4,000 troops. D'Estaing had come to add the conquest of Savannah to his accomplishments before his return to France, and he intended to make short work of it. Governor Rutledge told him that the British would probably surrender at once if their escape was cut off.[55] General Lincoln began collecting the Continental troops and militia in Georgia and South Carolina.[56] General Prevost rushed to get the defenses of Savannah in shape and dispatched a call to Lieutenant Colonel Maitland to hold his 800 troops at Beaufort in readiness to come to Savannah. Governor Wright and his council ordered in four to five hundred Negroes to work on the fortifications under the able direction of the engineer, Captain Moncrief. The British forces from outlying areas were concentrated in Savannah, and guns from naval vessels were landed and manned by sailors.[57]

Lincoln spent September 11-13 getting his troops across the Savannah at Zubly's Ferry, making a juncture with General McIntosh and his troops from Augusta, and establishing a camp near Ebenezer. On the 16th Lincoln and d'Estaing made contact and began what might be called a joint operation.[58] Before they saw each other, d'Estaing had demanded that Prevost surrender to the French, but it was now agreed that all future negotiations would be conducted jointly. Surrender negotiations went on for two days while the British strengthened their fortifications and got Maitland's 800 troops from Beaufort into Savannah. Then the demand to surrender was refused.[59]

On September 23 the French began entrenching operations for regular siege approaches to the city. Heavy artillery was brought from the ships and a bombardment of the city begun on the night of October 4 or 5—contemporary accounts often differ a day on the dating of happenings in the siege. This bombardment continued through October 8 and caused considerable damage inside the city. D'Estaing had already overstayed his proposed time and was afraid of hurricanes and the possibility of a British naval attack; besides, there were shortages of provisions and supplies and much sickness because the fleet had been so long at sea. The siege seemed to make no real progress against the determined British inside Savannah. Therefore the attackers determined to try to take the city by storm.

The French and Americans, led by d'Estaing in person, stormed the British lines on October 9. Despite the gallant heroism and wounds of d'Estaing and many more and considerable loss of life, all was in vain. The main bodies of French and American troops left the lines on October 18. The French spent the next two days embarking and then sailed away. The Americans went up the river to Zubly's Ferry and crossed into South Carolina.

Thus ended a "joint" operation that might have been highly successful had it really been joint. There was never sufficient cooperation between the French and the Americans. D'Estaing was so sure of his superiority in military matters that he tended to ignore the Americans. He was so sure that his superior numbers would make the outcome certain that he delayed or gave in to Prevost on all points. In short, he allowed himself to be outsmarted by the British. Had he stormed Savannah upon landing, even before the Americans arrived, there seems little doubt that he could have captured the town. If there was any reason for his delay, d'Estaing did not report it. Instead of attacking immediately he waited until the defenses had been strengthened and Maitland's and other troops had been brought into Savannah. Any real understanding between d'Estaing and the Americans would have prevented Maitland's entry into Savannah. Some warning to the Americans of d'Estaing's anticipated arrival would have allowed them time to collect troops and otherwise prepare for him, but it might have done the same for the British in Savannah. Real French-American cooperation and quick action should have gained Savannah and might have changed the entire course of the war in the South.[60]

While Congress was laboring under the misapprehension that the French and Americans had been successful at Savannah, it debated a recommendation to set aside a day for thanksgiving to God for the victory.[61] Governor Wright and his council, who were better informed of happenings at Savannah, set aside October 29 as a day of thanksgiving and prayer for God's deliverance of the city from the French and Americans.[62] The commanding officer at St. Augustine, Colonel Fuser, gave a ball in honor of the deliverance of Savannah.[63]

FIGHTING AFTER THE
SIEGE OF SAVANNAH
1779 - 1782

8 **

ALTHOUGH the failure of the Americans and French to take Savannah in 1779 dealt a severe blow to American military plans, the idea of Savannah's reconquest was not abandoned. Lincoln's headquarters began to plan for the recapture whenever enough Continental troops could be sent south. A Congressional committee recommended that Virginia and the Carolinas be urged to fill their troop quotas and that Washington be directed to send 1,000 troops to Lincoln, but Congress took no action. Washington sent a few troops but not enough to make any real difference.[1]

Before the arrival of d'Estaing at Savannah, Clinton had assembled an expedition with which he hoped to capture Charleston. Its sailing was delayed until the outcome of the action at Savannah was known, for Clinton said he had little hopes of capturing South Carolina or regaining Georgia if Savannah was lost.[2] When the British victory at Savannah was known in New York, the Charleston expedition moved forward again. It sailed late in December, 1779, and arrived at the mouth of the Savannah River at the end of January, 1780. Clinton set up his base and depots on Tybee Island.[3]

Despite local objections, Clinton stripped Georgia and East Florida of most of their British troops and left Georgia outside Savannah pretty much at the mercy of Whig partisans and militia.[4] Governor Wright complained bitterly that from the British viewpoint things were so bad that a Whig assembly could meet at Augusta and elect a full state government, and that Whigs often raided to within a few miles of Savannah. Wright estimated Georgia's troop needs until South Carolina could be completely subdued at 500 at Savannah, 500 at Augusta, 1,500 to 2,000 operating from Augusta in Georgia and South Carolina back country, 200 at Ebenezer or Hudson's Ferry, 150 at Zubly's Ferry, 70 horsemen for patrols in the Savannah area, and several armed galleys to cruise off the coast.[5] Wright's estimates of troops needed in Georgia were always considered high by the military authorities, and were never filled.

During the Charleston campaign, General Lincoln removed Continental troops from Georgia, despite the protests of Georgia Whigs.[6] The state government asked South Carolina for military help to guard its western frontiers. General Andrew Williamson brought his brigade of South Carolina militia to Augusta in early March and remained until May 29 when his duties were taken over by Georgia militia.[7] Charleston surrendered to Clinton's superior numbers on May 12, and Lincoln and his entire army became prisoners of war.

Clinton and part of his army returned to New York, but Lord Cornwallis and the rest of the British troops were left to complete the conquest and occupation of the Carolinas and Georgia. Throughout 1780-1781 the main fighting in the South was between British troops under Cornwallis and Americans under Gates and Greene in the Carolinas. So far as the military commanders on both sides were concerned, Georgia was out of the main picture and was largely ignored. In spite of the objections by state and colonial civil governments to what they termed insufficient consideration by the military, Georgia secured no more consideration or troops. The British troops taken out of Georgia before the capture of Charleston were never returned; and after Cornwallis moved into North Carolina in the fall of 1780, the Whigs in the back country felt safer than they had since the siege of Savannah the year before.

After the evacuation of Augusta by General Williamson in May, 1780, Tory troops under Colonels Thomas Brown and James Grierson soon moved in and took possession. Brown still remembered the suit of tar and feathers he had received there in August, 1775, and he became the bane of all back-country Whigs in his dual capacity of military commander and Indian superintendent. Throughout June and July both Brown and Governor Wright were of the opinion that resistance in Georgia might really end. Many people took the oath of allegiance to the King, apparently because they believed that the Whig cause was dead in Georgia and the Carolinas, not because they had any love for the British. People around Augusta, in the Ogeechee country, and along the coast south of Savannah, submitted. Brown reported that several Whig militia officers, including Colonel John Dooly, had offered to surrender their units as prisoners of war.[8] Dooly evidently changed his mind, if he ever intended to surrender, because he was murdered in his home by a band of Tories in the summer.

Out of the murder of Dooly comes the best known and most interesting legend of the Revolution in Georgia, the story of Nancy Hart. Five of the murderers, says the legend, called soon after their gory deed at the cabin of Nancy Hart in frontier Wilkes County and demanded food. While the food was being prepared, they stacked their muskets in the corner and made merry by emptying a well-filled jug. Nancy sent her daughter to the spring for water and to warn the Whig men in the neighborhood that Tories were in the cabin. When the meal began more water was needed, and the daughter was dispatched with instructions to signal the Whigs to come to the cabin. Then Nancy began to slip the muskets through a crack between the logs. The Tories discovered this, but before they could do anything Nancy, musket in hand, warned them that she would shoot the first one who moved. A Tory moved, Nancy fired, and the Tory fell to the floor dead. A second musket was instantly in Nancy's hands and the daughter returned with word that Whig men would arrive soon. Nancy's reputation with firearms was well known, but her being cross-eyed made it difficult for her prisoners to know just which one she was watching. If they were to escape, they must do so before the Whig men arrived. Another Tory moved and joined his companion on the floor. The other three accepted Nancy's demand that they "surrender their ugly Tory carcasses to a Whig woman" and were hanged without further ado when the Whig men arrived.[9] According to legend, Nancy and her fellow Whigs did other notable services in Wilkes County that matched the deeds of Colonel Brown and other fiendish Tories.

Brown joined Wright in distrust of many who had taken the oath to the King, and he reported that some of the turncoats caused trouble to real loyalists despite his threat to hang anyone caught molesting peaceable inhabitants. By July, 1780, it was reported that most of the upcountry had submitted to British authority except some 800 to 900 frontiersmen in Wilkes County who did not seem disposed to submit.[10] Cornwallis was so sure that Georgia was safe that he sent troops from the colony to St. Augustine in the early summer.[11]

The only part of Georgia left under Whig control was Wilkes County and the upper part of Richmond County. The state civil government, located in Wilkes County, could do little. Wright alternated between the fear that the rebels would show up in force —there were a few British troops in Savannah and Augusta—and the hope that the inhabitants of the ceded lands (Wilkes County, to the Whigs) would submit. He now reduced his troop requests to from 600 to 800 foot and 150 horsemen, and was sure that with these the back country would submit completely. Some people, he said, had not submitted because of the reports that British troops would soon leave Augusta.[12] There were troops only at Savannah and Augusta, hardly enough to control all of the province.

Many Whigs left Georgia for the Carolinas or states farther north. Others on the frontier built stockade forts for protection against bands of roving Tories and Indians. There were bands of Whig and Tory militia and partisans operating throughout the back country. Some of them were more interested in loot and personal gain than in which side eventually won in the bigger struggle. Militia activities resulted from the personal inclination of the militiamen and their leaders—Elijah Clarke, John Twiggs, Benjamin and William Few, James Jackson, and John Dooly for the Whigs and James and Daniel McGirth, Thomas Brown, and James Grierson for the Tories. The Tories got some help from the British commander in Savannah, but it was 1781 before the Whigs got much help from the Continental military commander in the South. This Whig militia must have had a remarkable intelligence system, for its leaders always seemed to know when a band of Tories was nearby and how large it was. The militiamen assembled if there was any chance of success, attacked the Tories, and then dispersed to their homes to become ordinary frontiersmen until there was another chance to strike at the Tories. Sometimes they returned from an expedition to find their homes burned, their families murdered, or their crops destroyed; yet they always seemed ready for the next action. South Carolina and Georgia Whigs fought together on both sides of the Savannah River. There were reports of Georgia militia in many of the battles fought in both the Carolinas during 1780 and 1781.

Georgia militia activity can be illustrated well by Elijah Clarke and his men in the summer and fall of 1780. In mid-August Clarke and a small band of Georgians joined North Carolinians in a small action at Musgrove's Mill in North Carolina. Clarke's party then returned through Tory-occupied South Carolina to Wilkes County, Georgia. The men were dismissed to go to their homes, see their families, and put their business in order. After about ten days 300 men reassembled and marched with Clarke toward Augusta, which they attacked in mid-September. Before Thomas Brown and his Tories were forced to surrender to the Whigs, reinforcements under Colonel Cruger arrived from Ninety Six, and Clarke's men had to beat a hasty retreat.

It was after this action that tradition says one of Brown's most famous cruelties took place. Brown's troops and his Indian allies had been hard pressed and had taken refuge in an Indian trading post, the White House, outside Augusta. Brown was injured and confined to his bed by the time he was relieved by Cruger. According to the story, Brown picked twelve of the wounded Whigs left by Clarke in his hasty retreat and had them hanged from the staircase of the house so that he could watch their dying agonies from his bed. A contemporary account by Wright reported the hanging of thirteen rebels who had broken their paroles and fought with the Whigs. These are evidently Tory and Whig versions of the same action.[13]

Clarke and his men, after their failure at Augusta, went upcountry to Little River where they dispersed. When they met again in late September, they found 400 women and children who were trying to escape Tory ravaging of upcountry Georgia. Clarke and his men escorted these refugees to the only place of safety Clarke knew, the Watauga Valley in a section of North Carolina (now Tennessee) unvexed by Tories. Clarke's men returning from this trip helped to bring on the Battle of King's Mountain when the British tried to intercept them.[14]

Despite the efforts of Brown, Wright, and others, Wilkes County did not submit to the royal government. After Clarke's failure to take Augusta, Brown sent raiding parties through the area that had not submitted, and Wright reported that about 100 plantations or settlements of people who had attacked Augusta were laid waste and burnt. Lieutenant Governor Graham went through the country and forced many to give security for good behavior and disarmed all that he did not trust. A list made by Graham in November of some 723 males from the ceded lands (Wilkes County) area showed 255 loyal men formed into a militia regiment; 159 left in the area, from whom twenty-one hostages were carried to Savannah; forty-two prisoners sent to Charleston; fifty-seven of unknown character in the area; forty-nine notorious rebels hiding from the British; and 140 who had left with Clarke.[15] Wright still begged for a troop of horsemen, if only fifty in number, to guard the frontier. He was sure that if Cornwallis took his army into North Carolina, rebels would rise up to plague Georgia and South Carolina.[16]

By April, 1781, it was evident that Nathanael Greene, now Continental commander in the Southern Department, was preparing to take the offensive in Georgia and the Carolinas. When about 250 men under Colonel Shelby came from Tennessee into Wilkes County in April and killed some forty loyalists, Grierson and Brown did not have sufficient troops at Augusta to go against the Whigs. Wright was sure that there were not enough British troops to oppose the Whigs if they moved in force against Georgia.[17] Both Ninety Six and Augusta were invested by forces under Greene in May.[18]

Georgia and South Carolina Whig militia began the siege of Augusta in April, 1781, under the command of Micajah Williamson and Elijah Clarke. About May 20 General Andrew Pickens and Lieutenant Colonel Henry Lee, with some Continental troops, arrived at Augusta and joined Clarke. First the Whigs captured a British supply depot and got some badly needed supplies. The two forts guarding Augusta were captured on May 25 and June 5. At the fall of this second fort, Colonel Grierson, who had been a scourge of many upcountry Whigs, was killed by enraged Whigs after he had surrendered.[19]

Throughout May many upcountry posts in South Carolina and Georgia were surrendered to the Americans or evacuated by the British. By June 15 Greene reported that the British had evacuated every post they held in the upcountry except Ninety Six, and it was abandoned by the British on July 3, though Greene had raised the siege. But there were still large numbers of Tories to trouble the back country, and Greene strongly urged Georgia to put her militia on a better footing to control these Tories.[20]

With all the back country in Whig hands, the whole military picture changed. Many loyalists fled to the area controlled by the British, where their economic support created additional problems. Wright formed new militia units out of the back-country loyalists in the Savannah area but did not think they could oppose the Whigs successfully without regulars.[21] By December General Leslie, the British commander in Charleston, and Wright had painted so dark a picture to Clinton that he authorized Leslie to abandon Georgia if he thought best.[22]

But Whigs also were worried about conditions in Georgia. There were rumors that more British troops would be sent to Georgia and that the British were going to retake Augusta. Requests from Greene for help from the state government met with as little success as did those from Wright to Clinton. The Whigs continued to gain ground slowly, and by December were back in Ebenezer.[23]

Before recounting the military activity that culminated in the evacuation of Savannah by the British, general military conditions for the period 1779 through 1782 will be considered. In December, 1778, Campbell brought between 2,000 and 2,500 British troops to Georgia, and Prevost brought 1,000 from Florida. During the siege of Savannah in September, 1779, there were 2,350 troops of all sorts in Savannah. After Georgia was stripped of British troops to help in the reduction of Charleston, there were about 600 left fit for duty. Throughout 1780 and 1781 this number remained fairly constant but rose to 970 fit for duty by the end of 1781. About two-thirds of these troops were loyalists, about two-ninths were Hessians, and less than one-ninth were British Regulars. There was no appreciable change by May 1, 1782, the date of the last return.[24]

Sickness accounted for the largest number of absentees among the troops, usually running as high as thirty per cent and sometimes reaching almost fifty per cent. If the complaints of the British and Hessian officers can be believed, most of this sickness was due to the climate. The most constant complainer about Savannah climate was Lieutenant Colonel Friedrich von Porbeck, commander of the Hessians in Georgia throughout the British occupation. He complained of the heat in December and January, said that troops could not be drilled after March 15, and said that troops who remained in Savannah long were permanently weakened and were not fit for full duty. He described various strange diseases, which he blamed on the climate and on Savannah's lack of a sewage disposal system and pure drinking water. Some years, according to Porbeck, 500 to 600 whites died of fever, and a constant supply of convicts from Britain and the Northern colonies was necessary to keep up the population. No white who could afford to leave ever spent a summer in Georgia. The fact that one-third of his recruits were sick enough to be hospitalized upon arrival in Savannah in no wise affected his opinions of Savannah climate. In every letter he asked for a transfer to the North and said that promotions were the only thing that would improve morale. Since he got neither a transfer nor a promotion, his morale must have been very low the entire time he was in Savannah.[25]

Governor Wright had numerous dealings with and many complaints about the military commanders in Savannah. General Prevost, in command when Wright arrived in 1779, remained until May, 1780. It was during his tenure that the largest British garrison was in Georgia, that the colony was almost entirely recaptured, and that British military operations were most successful. Prevost seems to have been a competent commander, and Wright got along with him much better than with either of his successors. Prevost was replaced by Lieutenant Colonel Alured Clarke as commander of East Florida and Georgia.[26] Clarke took part of his troops and went to St. Augustine in April, 1781, when there was fear of a Spanish attack there. Von Porbeck was left as senior officer in Georgia. Wright objected to a commander who did not understand English government and law and who he understood claimed to be totally exempt from civil authority.[27] Von Porbeck had complained earlier that there was a civil government in Georgia; and though he made no direct reference to Wright, there is no reason to think that they got along well. Clarke returned to Savannah by June 7, 1781, and remained until the evacuation. During Clarke's command there were fewer troops in Georgia, the British were on the defensive much of the time, and Wright was generally harder to get along with than when Prevost commanded.

The main trouble between Wright and military commanders (in Savannah, Charleston, or New York) was that they could not see the defense of Georgia as he did and consequently, so he said, did not have the welfare of the province at heart. Wright always put Georgia first, and he was convinced that there were enough British troops available to spare the 500 to 1,000 that he thought necessary to subdue all of the province. If military commanders did not agree, they were shortsighted, and Wright reserved his choicest tirades for them. Wright summed up his opinion of the generals after he had lost hope of getting any more troops:

The Generals &c. have always Set their faces against this Province, as I have frequently Wrote you, and I can't tell why, unless it is because the King has thought Proper to Re-establish his Civil Government here—which the Military Cannot bear—and I have long Seen they will do Nothing for us, without a Positive order from Home & which may now be too late.[28]

The military officers and political officials in London, realizing it was impossible to convince Wright, quit trying, and merely told him that no more troops were available. All military commanders who dealt with Wright must have agreed with Lieutenant Colonel Balfour who said of Wright and his council that they "are the most Absurd of all people."[29]

Relations between Georgia loyalists and British and Hessian troops were those that usually exist between a "friendly" population and an army during combat. The army took what it wanted, and the civilians complained. In Savannah the barracks built by the Whigs were used by the British until they were destroyed in the siege of 1779. After that soldiers were billeted in private houses in the town. The army said that there was plenty of room for troops and civilians, but the civilians disagreed. Both said the other took the best houses. Outside Savannah and away from the watchful eye of Wright, civilians fared worse. Ebenezer suffered especially from army occupation. It was either a halfway station to Augusta or an outpost, and troops were usually stationed there and were often passing through. The inhabitants complained that the troops took their Negroes, horses, cattle, and wagons and destroyed their farms and homes. The church, schoolhouses, and mills were damaged or destroyed.[30] Similar conditions existed wherever troops were stationed, and there is little evidence that the army tried to prevent such damage.

Not only did Wright complain that there were insufficient troops in Georgia, but he also complained because there were no mounted troops to protect loyal inhabitants against rebel raids. Infantry were quite ineffective in opposing these raids, which were hit-and-run affairs often carried out by mounted men. The British army was never convinced and refused to send horsemen to Georgia. After the siege of Savannah, Wright got his council to approve mounted militia patrols. General Prevost agreed to pay these patrols but refused to ration them.[31] During the Charleston campaign, Clinton approved pay and rations for militia patrols. Later Wright paid similar patrols out of his own pocket and had trouble collecting from the army.[32] The British commanders usually opposed such special provincial troops that were not directly under their command and claimed that they did as much looting as they prevented.[33]

After the fall of Charleston, Clinton ordered all young unmarried men to be formed into active militia units subject to service half of the time and to be paid and rationed by the army while on duty. Besides this, the regular militia was to continue for local areas. Wright objected that these regulations could not apply to Georgia, where a civil government existed, and again he demanded his troop of horsemen, which had been approved by Clinton but never raised. Cornwallis opposed the horsemen but could never convince Wright that they were no longer needed.[34]

After the unsuccessful siege of Augusta by the Whigs in 1780, Wright called a special assembly session to consider defense. Upon his recommendation a bill was passed that allowed the drafting of slaves to work on defenses and the arming of Negroes in time of extreme danger. The entire militia system was tightened. Wright immediately ordered out some 400 Negroes to work on the defenses of Savannah.[35]

Early in 1781 Wright and the council authorized three patrols of twenty mounted militiamen each, and two months later raised a troop of horsemen to protect the back country. The British government approved this use of horsemen and ordered the army to pay for it. Two troops of horsemen were actually raised and put into the field, and British officers tried to recruit dragoons for service in Georgia.[36]

To turn from British to Whig troop activity is in many ways to repeat a similar story, especially as regards a troop shortage. The Whigs probably had more trouble keeping their units filled than did the British; certainly they had fewer regular troops. The Continental Congress approved a total of four battalions of infantry and one regiment of light dragoons for Georgia. Only the first battalion of infantry and the dragoons were raised in Georgia. The other battalions were raised in the Carolinas, Virginia, and Pennsylvania. Troops enlisted from out of the state complained about low pay, the small value of Georgia currency, distance from home, and hot climate. Probably these battalions were never up to strength. Few replacements could be secured for men who deserted or went home when their enlistments expired. In 1779 Congress ordered a reduction to one battalion of infantry and one regiment of horse. Early in 1780 there was a recommendation of two battalions with one to consist of Negroes, but the original reduction held. No Negro troops were ever raised, and in 1782 the Continental troops were further reduced to one battalion.[37]

From the time of the capture of Savannah by the British until mid-1781, the state government was too weak and irregular to be of any real assistance in military matters. After the upcountry was freed of British troops, a revived state government began to do what it could to raise militia and state troops to cooperate with the Continentals. The best known state unit, the Georgia State Legion or Jackson's Legion, commanded by Lieutenant Colonel James Jackson, was raised at the suggestion of General Greene in the summer of 1781.[38] It, like other state units, was to be composed of people who wanted to transfer their allegiance from Britain to the United States now that the war seemed to be going against the British. Other state troops were ordered raised, usually for a short time to help the Continentals or to do frontier guard duty. Often such troops were to furnish their own arms and mounts, since none could be procured by the state. State troops proved no more satisfactory than they had before 1779 and continued to be more a hope than a reality. The greatest trouble about state troops was that the state government had no funds with which to pay them. It resorted to such expedients as land, mounts, Negroes, clothing, provisions, salt, and anything else that it could get its hands on (usually from confiscated Tory estates). But for the need of many to prove their loyalty to the United States, it is doubtful if there would have been any state troops worth mentioning.[39]

Militia continued to be a main source of military manpower, especially on the frontier and in the partisan fighting in the back country. At the time of the capture of Augusta there were militia reported present who had been in the field for a year but who had received little pay or subsistence.[40] Such long term militiamen in many ways were more like partisans than militia. They remained in the field because of their hatred of the British, because of their regard for their leaders, because they considered military duty safer than civilian life with the unsettled conditions in the back country, or because they might possibly get a better living from the state (if it had any provisions and supplies) than they could hope to produce upon their own ravaged farms. The state authorities usually opposed long terms for militia because of the interruption of farming, but the Continental commanders often called for militia because it was the only source of additional manpower available. The old troubles of militia undependability remained. On April 22, 1782, a return of Burke and Richmond county militia serving with the Continental troops showed eight officers and twenty enlisted men present, and twenty-three deserters.[41]

The matter of Indian cooperation continued to be one of importance to both sides in the struggle. Despite the failure of anticipated Indian help upon the initial conquest of Georgia, the British continued to cultivate Indian allies. The Indian Department tried to keep several hundred Indian allies ready to cooperate with British troops when they were needed. Thomas Brown, in his dual capacity as Indian superintendent and commander at Augusta, especially used Indians to supplement his military actions. While the British sought active Indian allies, the Whigs usually tried to frighten the Indians away from friendship with the British into neutrality. By 1779 the Whigs had little to offer the Indians to get any active assistance from them. Whenever the British had special need of Creek help, the Whigs would send out a threatening expedition toward the Creek country to frighten the Indians into remaining at home for self-protection. Despite Whig accusations about British cruelty in using Indian allies and encouraging scalping parties, it is probable that the British policy of encouraging Indian cooperation with white soldiers actually lessened Indian cruelties. It was usually possible for the British to get Indian allies for a short campaign or single action if they had plenty of gifts, but it was very difficult to keep Indians in camp if there was no action.

After the foregoing treatment of general military conditions the specific happenings of 1782 will be recounted. After the defeat of Cornwallis at Yorktown in October, 1781, the Continental army in the Southern Department got more consideration than previously. General Greene wanted to keep the British shut up in Charleston and Savannah but saw little chance of capturing either without reinforcements. In early January, 1782, Brigadier General Anthony Wayne, who had come south after Yorktown, was sent to Georgia as Continental commander to reinstate the authority of the United States. A regiment of dragoons and a detachment of artillery were sent with Wayne, and Georgia and South Carolina troops and militia were to be under his command.[42] At the same time General Leslie in Charleston ordered 200 British troops to Savannah and promised 300 more if needed. This brought British strength to 1,000,[43] while Wayne had about 500. Despite Wayne's shortage in troops,

he immediately took the offensive, forced the British to withdraw from several points a few miles from Savannah, and began
intercepting Indians coming to aid the British.[44]

When Greene sent Wayne to Georgia, he requested the cooperation of Georgia's new governor, John Martin, and suggested that
the state take steps to win wavering people from British to American allegiance. Martin ordered out half the militia, which he estimated at about 300 men, to act with Wayne and took steps to
procure food for men and horses in the areas recently abandoned
by the British.[45] Wayne showed more determination than any
Whig had exhibited for many months in Georgia, and Martin cooperated fully. The Whigs now seemed ready psychologically to
drive out the British even if they did not have the military resources. The British strengthened the defenses of Savannah and
brought in Indians.[46] Wright's letters took on the note of pessi-
mism of a man who knew that he was doomed.[47]

It soon looked as though Wayne's presence in Georgia might
come to naught. The South Carolina state troops that came with
him had but thirteen days of their enlistment left and went home
promptly at the end of this period. As late as February 6, no Georgia militia had joined Wayne because of a campaign of Elijah
Clarke against the Cherokees. Only 130 state troops and militia
reported during February. General Leslie was sure that Wayne
could do nothing but annoy the loyalists outside Savannah.[48]
Wayne himself said,

> The duty we have done in Georgia is more difficult than that imposed
> upon the children of Israel. They had only to make bricks without
> straw, but we have had provision, forage, and almost every other
> apparatus of war to procure without money: boats, bridges, &c. to
> build without materials except those taken from the stump: and, what
> was more difficult than all, to make *Whigs* out of *Tories.* But this we
> have effected, and have wrested the country out of the hands of the
> enemy, with the exception only of the town of Savannah. How to keep
> it without some additional force is a matter worthy of consideration.[49]

Wayne exerted himself in every possible way to get men to fill
his depleted ranks. He urged the state government to do everything possible to fill its Continental quota: increase the bounty
offered for enlistments, raise a Negro corps, encourage desertions
from the British, and restore any Tory or absent citizen to good
standing if he would enlist.[50] On February 20 Governor Martin

issued a proclamation aimed at securing desertions from the Hessians, who were especially dissatisfied because of the prolonged service in Georgia. The proclamation, circulated in German, increased Hessian desertions.[51] The Germans at Ebenezer helped persuade the Hessians to desert. Von Porbeck said, "The women are the best recruiting agents for the rebels." It was reported that any Hessians stationed outside Savannah immediately deserted. Patrols of Indians and Negroes roamed the woods beyond the British lines at night and brought in Hessian deserters for which they were paid two guineas each, dead or alive.[52] Hessian deserters from Georgia are said to have migrated as far as North Carolina where they settled permanently.[53] Loyalists and militia also deserted in large numbers, probably with the idea of saving their property from the Whigs. Some months desertions reached a total of fifty. Sir Patrick Houstoun, noted for being loyal to whichever side was in power in Savannah, surrendered at Wayne's headquarters on February 21 with a group of Hessian and loyalist deserters. On March 10 a group of thirty-eight mounted loyalist militia reported to Wayne's headquarters and joined the Georgia volunteers for duty until the British left Georgia.[54]

Throughout the spring there was little change in the military situation. Wayne was usually able to intercept the Indians trying to get into Savannah to help the troops there. The state tried hard to raise troops and militia to help but secured few men. Wayne, continuing to strike the enemy whenever he had a chance, had some successes, and kept the British effectively penned up in Savannah.[55]

On May 21, General Leslie, having received official notice of the progress of peace negotiations, proposed to Greene a cessation of hostilities; but Greene refused any such move without instructions from Congress. On May 29 General Clarke and Governor Wright in Savannah suggested to Wayne a cessation of hostilities, but Wayne referred the matter to Greene. Nothing came of these requests.[56]

In April, Clinton called on Leslie for 2,000 of the 6,000 troops in South Carolina, Georgia, and East Florida. Rather than weaken the British position in South Carolina and East Florida, Leslie suggested that Georgia be evacuated.[57] Just at this juncture, Clinton was replaced as British commander in North America by Sir Guy Carleton, who was instructed to withdraw the British troops from New York, Charleston, and Savannah.[58] Carleton informed Leslie that Savannah was to be evacuated immediately and Charleston soon. Wright and the royal assembly expressed amazement at this evacuation of Georgia and insisted that it was unnecessary and that only a few troops could protect the province. They first suggested that the St. Augustine garrison be brought to Savannah; finally they asked that East Florida remain in British hands until loyalists could make arrangements as to where they would go to begin life anew.[59] Wright protested the evacuation strenuously, but his strongest objections came after his return to England. In "A Concise View of the Situation of the Province of Georgia for 3 Years Past" he set forth in detail Georgia's progress after its recapture in 1778, the lack of military protection to loyalists, the lack of necessity for abandoning the province, and the hardships undergone by the loyalists as a result of the evacuation.[60]

No destruction, even of fortifications, was allowed in the evacuation of Savannah; and new fortifications, thrown up on Tybee Island just before the evacuation, were apparently temporary protection for refugees awaiting transports.[61] On July 10 and 11 the last of the British troops left Savannah, and Whigs took possession. Lieutenant Colonel James Jackson of the Georgia troops received the keys to the city and was the first Whig officer to command the city since December, 1778. British troops remained at Tybee for ten to twelve days, and Thomas Brown's loyalists were near the town as late as July 31 before they went to St. Augustine overland.[62]

Wayne allowed the merchants in Savannah six months to dispose of their inventories, adjust their affairs, and leave the state. They were ordered to turn in an inventory of their stocks to Wayne so that the Whigs could get needed supplies. This agreement was approved by Governor Martin, the state assembly, and the Continental Congress.[63] Loyalists who had aided the British and who wished to remain in Georgia could clear their past conduct by enlisting in the Georgia Continental battalion for two years or for the duration of the war. Two hundred had joined by July 12.[64]

The British troops evacuated from Savannah were sent to New York and Charleston. Greene, afraid that Leslie would undertake an offensive action in South Carolina with these reinforcements, ordered Wayne and all his Continentals, except the newly-enlisted Georgia battalion, to report to his headquarters outside Charleston at once. Although the presence of Brown's loyalists and sickness of Wayne's troops delayed this departure, pleas from the Georgia government and from Wayne that the troops be left were of no avail. The Georgia battalion under Major John Habersham and Jackson's legion were all the troops left to defend the state.[65]

Loyalists who wished to leave Georgia were promised transportation to other points in the empire, but insufficient transports were sent to Savannah and many loyalists were forced to go to St. Augustine overland or via the inland passage in what small vessels they could procure locally. About two-thirds of the transports sent to Savannah were used to transport troops and military stores to New York and Charleston. The remaining 3,500 tons of transport space was divided about equally between loyalists going to St. Augustine and to Jamaica.[66] There are no exact figures of how many loyalists left Savannah. Just before the evacuation, Wayne said that there were 6,000 people, black and white, encamped at Savannah, awaiting transportation out of Georgia.[67] Governor Tonyn said that refugees began to arrive in East Florida early in the spring of 1782 and were still coming in November, probably from South Carolina that late. A return of Georgia loyalists in East Florida in December, 1782, lists 911 whites and 1,786 Negroes. An undated return received from General Leslie in July, 1782, lists 1,042 whites and 1,956 Negroes, a total of 2,998. It lists heads of families by name and the number of people in each family. Tonyn said that the great majority of refugees were very poor back-country people, but there were a few people of quality.[68] Governor Wright requested transportation to Jamaica for 2,000 Negroes, and General Carleton said that ten families with 1,568 Negroes went from Savannah to Jamaica. An unidentified return dated Charleston, December 13, 1786, says fifty white men and 1,600 Negroes went from Georgia to Jamaica. The slaves of William Knox, Governor Wright, and other large slave owners were reported in Jamaica.[69] Taking the highest estimate given above makes about 3,100 whites and something over 3,500 Negroes who left Savannah at the evacuation. Almost 5,000 of these went to East Florida, and some returned to Georgia when the British evacuated East Florida in 1783-85.

James Jackson said that no less than 5,000 to 6,000 Negroes were taken away at the evacuation, and others said that between three-fourths and seven-eighths of the slaves of the state were taken away.[70] Both the total number and percentages seem excessive. Though the slave population had decreased during the war, it had been 15,000 in 1773 and could hardly have declined by one-half. Both Leslie and Clarke seem to have tried to prevent the taking away of slaves not the *bona fide* property of loyalists.[71] Negroes who had served in the British army were not considered American property but loyalists entitled to evacuation. Carleton said that any who had been promised their freedom for army service must be freed, and he left the status of all doubtful Negroes to be determined by Leslie.[72] There were some Negroes in Savannah whose army services entitled them to their freedom, but probably not very many. Three free Negro families were on the East Florida refugee list.[73] The biggest Negro problem came out of the confusion about ownership that resulted from confiscation laws, conflicting governments and their court decisions, abandoned property, escapes, and the general confusion of the period. The state assembly directed that negotiations be entered into for the purchase by the state of the Negroes about to be carried away, but it refused to let individuals make purchases. It also requested Governor Martin to allow Whigs who had property within the British lines to go into Savannah and claim this property before the evacuation.[74] No agreement was reached about the purchase of the slaves by the state, and it is extremely doubtful that individuals were able to reclaim property that was also claimed by evacuees. Thus, a badly needed labor supply was carried out of the state and would make itself felt for several years to come.

CIVIL GOVERNMENT
1779 - 1782

9

****

PROVINCIAL government was restored in Georgia in March, 1779, and Governor Wright and other officials returned from England in the summer to assume their old jobs. During the siege of Savannah in 1779 Wright and his council secured slaves to work on the defenses and encouraged civilians to cooperate with the military. After the siege, the civil government checked the conduct of all residents of Savannah who had taken the oath of loyalty to the King but had not helped with the defense of the city. Any whose loyalty was suspect were required to post a £100 bond for good behavior for the next year and to take the oath of loyalty again.[1]

At the first session of the general court after the siege, probably the first session since the return of the British to Georgia, the civil government tried to show its real strength. Chief Justice Stokes charged the grand jury to investigate, for the purpose of indicting for treason any questionable conduct during the siege, and at least seven people were indicted. Three of these were found guilty of treasonable misdemeanors. Two were fined £300 and £200 each, but no punishment for the third is recorded. Two confessed their indictments and were fined £100 and £20 each. One was tried for high treason and acquitted. The last was held over for trial by the next court, and no further record of the case has been discovered. Wright hoped that this action would convince others that treason would not go unpunished by the provincial government.[2]

The British government suggested that Wright call an assembly soon after his return to Georgia, but he had delayed because the entire province had not been regained and because he feared that an assembly might be controlled by those who had taken the oath of loyalty to the King for reasons of expediency and not because of real loyalty. Early in 1780 Wright and his council planned to hold an assembly election when the British troops moved out of Georgia to help Clinton at Charleston. The plan was to send the troops up to Augusta before they crossed into South Carolina, and thus impress the back country with the strength of the royal government, in the hope that this show of power would secure a more loyal assembly than might be elected otherwise. But the troops crossed the Savannah River at Savannah, and the election was not held.[3] On March 3, Clinton issued from his headquarters before Charleston a proclamation offering pardon for past treasonable offenses to all who speedily returned to their allegiance to the King.[4] Wright objected to this proclamation as being too broad and including many former inhabitants of Georgia who had been active in the rebellion. To prevent such people from getting control of the provincial government, writs for an assembly election were issued at once.[5] The election was held in April in every parish except St. Paul (Augusta), where the deputy provost marshal said an attempt to hold an election would be dangerous.[6]

When the assembly met, four parishes (St. Paul, St. David, St. Matthew, and St. Mary) were not represented, and only fifteen of the twenty-six elected members qualified. Eighteen had been the quorum of the Commons House in former assemblies. However, Wright and his council decided to treat the Commons House as a legal one, and it lowered its quorum to eleven early in the session.[7] In his opening address, Wright said that Britain had given up levying taxes on its colonies except the duties for the regulation of commerce, the net proceeds of which were to go to the colonies. All arrears of quit rents were remitted, and future collections of quit rents and fines and forfeitures were to accrue to the colony. The replies of both houses expressed appreciation for the return of British government to Georgia and for Britain's giving up colonial taxation, which the Commons House thought "ought to remove every discontent and doubt of the most bigotted Zealots for American Independence." Both houses voted a joint address thanking the King for re-establishing civil government, for returning Wright to Georgia, and for doing other good things for the colony.[8]

The assembly remained in session from May 9 through July 10, with a two-week adjournment in mid-June. It worked hard to restore Georgia to its pre-revolutionary status by renewing expired laws and passing needed ones. Of the nine acts passed, only three can be traced directly to the rebellion. One of these set up a method of proving property ownership when records had been carried out of Georgia by the Whigs. Another took all political rights away from 151 prominent rebels and anyone else who had occupied any official position under the rebel state government. The third declared all actions of the Whig governments illegal and void.[9]

Wright seemed well pleased with this assembly session. He said that there were several other matters he would have liked done, but since the weather was hot and the assemblyman seemed tired he judged it best to let them go home.[10] By the time the assembly was prorogued, Charleston was in British hands and there was hope that peace would return to the Southern colonies with all of Georgia and South Carolina under British control. Augusta and the great majority of Georgia except the Indian cession of 1773 (Wilkes County to the Whigs) were in British hands.

Throughout the summer of 1780 the provincial government gained strength and control of more Georgia territory. But despite a better position than it had enjoyed since its return early in 1779, there was still opposition—active on the frontiers, passive nearer Savannah where the British army was in control. The June grand jury complained that many notorious rebels were allowed to pass freely through the province and recommended that all old paper currency be called in and that the colony's currency be given a general overhaul.[11] In Savannah at least, it was government as usual, rebellion or not.

A full contingent of provincial officials had been appointed with the return of Wright to Georgia. Throughout the summer of 1780 justices of the peace, commissioners of roads and ferries, commissioners of the loan office, and commissioners of pilotage at Savannah were appointed. In August the appointment of officials for St. Paul's Parish and the 1773 Indian cession was evidence that effective control of these areas was hoped for in the near future if not already achieved. Militia officers were appointed for the entire province in September.[12]

During the attack on Augusta in 1780, Wright called the assembly into session to consider defense. After a two-week session, in which little business was transacted by the Commons House, the assembly requested adjournment because of the meeting of the general court. The bill for reorganization of the militia had not been passed, but Wright adjourned the assembly as requested.[13]

By this time, the pattern of assembly action for the rest of the colonial period was evident. It was hard to get assemblymen to remain in session long enough to do the necessary business, and they showed little desire to carry out Wright's suggestions. The attitude was one of passive resistance rather than active objection to Wright's program. By the end of 1780 Wright was doubtful of the cooperation he could expect from the assembly. He reported that assemblymen did not attend sessions, that some resigned, and that many elected since the original election were hard to get along with.[14] As long as the British remained in Georgia there were frequent short sessions. Three acts were approved in the fall of 1780, nineteen during the first six months of 1781, and four on August 2, 1781. No record of acts approved after August 2 has been found, but it seems that acts were passed and approved later than this.[15]

The provincial assembly tried to ignore, for legal purposes, the years during which there had been no provincial government. It removed legal disabilities created by the lapse of time or lack of positive action on the part of the Whig governments and cancelled all Whig political action. All abandoned property was ordered taken over and managed for the benefit of the province. Several laws had to do with the defense of the province. There were two acts concerned with rebel treason and its punishment. The rest of the legislation of the assembly consisted of ordinary peace-time measures, a type that might have been passed had there been no rebellion. Wright reported that thirty-three acts were passed between July, 1780, and August, 1781.[16]

Of the ordinary legislative business, the most noteworthy item was the attempt to take care of the physical growth of Georgia. The lands of the Indian cession of 1773 had not been organized into parishes when royal government ended in Georgia in 1776 but had been made into Wilkes County by the state constitution of 1777. In the spring of 1781 these lands and the western part of St. Paul's Parish were divided into two new parishes, St. Peter and St. Mark. The same act also created a western circuit court for the parishes of St. Paul, St. Peter, and St. Mark. This court, equal in power to that at Savannah and conducted by the same judges and officials, was to meet twice a year at Wrightsborough. The governor and council were given power to establish other circuit courts if they were needed.[17] This act was passed about a month before the beginning of Whig operations that resulted in the capture of Augusta, and it is doubtful if the new parishes ever attempted to operate. Certainly the western circuit court did not.

Throughout the period when there was no provincial government in Georgia, 1776-1778, Parliament continued the yearly appropriations to pay Georgia officials who were in England. The temporary officials appointed by the military in 1779 were paid half the salary plus emoluments of office, the amount usually paid to temporary officials in the absence of the appointee.[18] Because of the destruction in Georgia, the necessity for giving relief to many loyalists, and the inability of loyal Georgians to pay taxes, the British government furnished an extra £5,000 contingent fund for Georgia for 1780 and 1781.[19]

Georgia's restored colonial government was willing to live off the bounty of the British government, and no record of the introduction or discussion of a tax bill in the assembly has been found. Provincial taxes before 1776 had brought in about £3,000 a year, and the extra £5,000 for 1780 and 1781 made taxes unnecessary. By the time of the 1782 assembly sessions, too little of Georgia was under British control for the assembly to make a tax bill of any value. Besides the funds granted in England for the support of Georgia, the provincial government used the funds collected from British customs duties in Georgia.[20] The only records of taxes actually levied and collected in provincial Georgia between 1779 and 1782 are the parish levies for Christ Church Parish.[21] There were probably similar levies in other parishes.

Although not interested in provincial tax bills, the British government did urge Wright to get the assembly to vote a permanent sum as Georgia's share of imperial expenses to replace the colonial taxation given up by Parliament.[22] In 1781 the assembly complied by granting a 2½% duty on all exports produced in the colony.[23] Chief Justice Anthony Stokes said that he drafted the original bill but that it was so changed in the Commons House that he was not responsible for its final form.[24] The Board of Trade did not approve certain parts of the bill; but, instead of recommending disapproval on technicalities, it recommended approval. It complimented Wright and Georgia for setting an example for other American colonies and for suggesting that certain points of the bill be changed by future legislation.[25] This bill was approved by Wright on March 6 and by the Privy Council on June 24, something of a record for speed in approving bills in England. No record has been found of what amounts, if any, were collected under this act.

A problem that worried loyalist Georgians more than the support of their government was the treatment of rebels. Soon after the return of the British to Savannah, Colonel Campbell appointed a police board to have charge of deserted and rebel plantations. In March a permanent board of five commissioners of claims was created to manage, in the interest of the province, all such property, including wandering Negroes.[26] In the summer of 1779 Georgia and South Carolina loyalists in England were ordered to Georgia with the suggestion that those qualified be used as managers of vacant estates until their own property was freed from rebel control. Income from vacant estates was to be used to support needy loyalists.[27] Considerable income was expected, and an elaborate organization for estate management was created. However, by the end of 1780 Wright reported that little had been received and nothing more could be expected. The fact that many Negroes were carried into South Carolina by the rebels rendered the plantations useless. After the destruction of the barracks at Savannah during the siege of 1779, rebel houses in the town were occupied by the British troops stationed there. Vacant estates were plundered by partisans of both sides, and much that was movable was carried off. Many loyalists returned and took over their own estates. Nothing of any value was left.[28]

Besides temporary management of vacant estates, there was the question of permanent disposition of both rebels and their estates. At the first session of the restored royal assembly, bills were passed by both houses to attaint 112 prominent rebels for high treason and to confiscate all their property. But since the two houses were unable to agree to a single bill no law on the subject was enacted.[29] The assembly did pass an act that disqualified politically 151 prominent rebels listed in the act and all others who had held official position under the state government. Most of the people named in the proposed act of attainder were in this disqualification act. The governor and council could remove the disqualifications imposed when the people concerned showed the proper loyalty to the King. Any who had given up their loyalty after November 1, 1779, must take an oath of allegiance to the King, renounce any allegiance to the state government, and give bond for twelve months' good behavior. Any person in the province who refused to fulfill these conditions must join the British army or be impressed into the navy.

This act was Wright's answer to Clinton's proclamation of amnesty issued upon the reduction of Charleston. But by 1781 Wright thought the act did not go far enough and should be strengthened because there were still rebels going at large in Georgia, even in Savannah.[30]

In April, 1781, the assembly attainted for high treason twenty-four individuals and all others who had held civil or military office under the state government except those who had conformed under the disqualifying act. All their property was forfeited, subject to debts due to loyal subjects and a one-third reserve for any wives or children who were loyalists. The people attainted could stand trial for treason before October 9 if they preferred, in which case the provisions of the act would not apply to them. This act was not to go into effect until it received royal approval, and there is no indication that such approval was ever received or that the act was put into effect.[31] The rebel property advertised for sale in the *Royal Georgia Gazette* was usually on attachment for debt or was to settle suits that had gone by default because the defendants did not appear in court.

The provincial government had difficulties with the British military authorities in enforcing its disqualifying act. A number of Georgia Whigs, captured when Charleston fell to the British in 1780, returned to Savannah as military prisoners on parole with the permission of the British commander in Charleston. When arrested by the civil authorities under the disqualifying act, such people always claimed that these arrests were illegal and got the backing of the military and the British commissioners for restoring peace. The only two such cases that can be traced to a conclusion are those of John Glen, the first state chief justice, and Dr. James Houstoun, a surgeon in the Continental Army. Glen took the oath of allegiance to the King and Houstoun submitted to trial for treason, the outcome of which has not been discovered.[32] The British government allowed the Georgia civil government, rather than the military, to decide the status of the people arrested. Wright and his council were consistent in disregarding paroles, maintaining that a parole given by the Whigs was illegal and did not excuse British subjects in Georgia from doing militia duty.[33] Most of the people arrested under the disqualifying act apparently took the oath of allegiance to the King and were released.

Ten days after the disqualifying act was passed in July, 1780, Sir Patrick Houstoun and Andrew McLean, both named in it, attended council to explain their conduct during the rebellion and to have their disqualifications removed. McLean had his disqualifications removed on July 24, but it was November 13 before Sir Patrick's case was completed.[34] Records of five other removals have been found,[35] and it is supposed that there were more of which no record has been discovered. Six other people[36] on the provincial disqualifying act were included in the state act of confiscation and banishment of 1782, apparently because they had their disqualifications removed and resumed their loyalty to the King. Records are too fragmentary to give complete information about the operation of the disqualifying act.

To understand the operation of the provincial government from 1779 through 1782, the influence and actions of Governor Wright must be considered. When Wright returned to Georgia in 1779 he hoped to restore the province to its old place in the British Empire. His first disappointment was in finding only part of Georgia under British control. But with the work of re-establishing royal government and the siege of Savannah and its aftermath, Wright had sufficient activity to keep him busy. Things became worse when the province was stripped of troops to help capture Charleston, but the situation improved after Charleston was taken and the British occupied much of South Carolina and most of Georgia in late 1780 and early 1781.

Wright never thought that there were enough troops in Georgia to control all of it and to protect all loyalists against the rebels who refused to accept the blessings of restored colonial status. If Georgia were to be an example in showing the other revolted colonies the errors of their ways, then the loyalists must be protected from rebels who continued to cause so much damage. Wright expressed himself clearly on this matter to the military and to the authorities in London. The military operated in a bigger field and never agreed with Wright on the importance of controlling all of Georgia. The British government agreed with the military. Wright developed a feud with the military that must have caused both to disregard the viewpoint of the other, regardless of the merits of individual cases.[37] By the end of 1780 Wright's letters lost their old force and reason and became increasingly the futile objections of a man in an impossible position who knew he could do little about it but wanted to get his position on the record. The caliber of Wright's work and leadership did not measure up to his earlier competency. Several times he requested leave to return to London, saying that he was of little use in Georgia.[38]

Despite Wright's disgust during the last part of his stay in Georgia, he continued to be the real leader of the provincial government. He generally got the complete backing of his council, more and more made up of officeholders, and he had no fights with the assembly. The British government backed him in all but military matters. He was given especially high praise after the passage of the duty act granting a permanent income to the British government.[39] But this praise was small consolation in Wright's argument with the military and for his constantly shrinking province. When the order to evacuate Georgia came in the summer of 1782 he objected strenuously, and insisted that a few more troops would return the province to its old loyalty.[40] He must have left the scene of his greatest successes and failures with a deep feeling of frustration and disappointment and "gone home" to England a tired and embittered old man. He spent the last three years of his life fighting for some measure of financial compensation from the British government for the services and losses of himself and of other loyalists who had been forced to leave their positions, homes, and property to the victorious Americans.

Besides the provincial government, there was also a state government in the Whig part of Georgia after the return of the British. After the minutes of the state executive council for December 26, 1778, is the following notation, "The Town of Savannah being taken by the British Troops, on the twenty eighth of December put a final end to public business of a civil nature."[41] This statement came very near being literally true. A new assembly had been elected on the first Tuesday in December, 1778, but the capture of Savannah came before it met. An attempt was made to convene this assembly in Augusta on the first Tuesday in January, 1779, but representatives appeared from only Wilkes, Richmond, and Burke counties—approximately half the state. The area overrun by the British was not represented. When it became apparent that only three counties would be represented, the meeting adopted the name convention instead of assembly; it did not try to act as an ordinary assembly but merely sought to keep a state government in existence.[42] There are no minutes of this convention and little is known of its actions. It did not elect a governor but by January 8 chose a committee, which organized itself as the executive council of the state on January 21 and elected William Glascock as its president.[43] Governor John Houstoun, who had been present at the capture of Savannah, apparently considered this council the new state executive, for he made no attempt to act as governor in 1779.

What happened to the executive council and any other state government that existed when the British occupied Augusta for the first part of February is not recorded. With the British raiding the back country, it could have done little. The state government returned to Augusta when the British withdrew to Hudson's Ferry. One interesting item of business of the council in July was to order an election to be held at Spirit Creek on July 2, apparently by the voters, to choose a delegate to the Continental Congress. No hint is given as to why the council did not itself elect the delegate, and apparently no delegate was elected by the people on July 2.[44]

In April and May Georgia refugees in South Carolina took steps to reconstitute a Georgia government, but it is impossible to determine just what they accomplished.[45] On July 24 a body calling itself "the Representatives of the Counties of Wilkes, Richmond, Burke, Effingham, Chatham, Liberty, Glynn and Camden and other free men of the State," but never using the term assembly, met in Augusta, to consider "the present disturbed situation of this State; and applying as far as in our power some remedy thereto." Considering itself inadequate to act as an assembly and never claiming any legal authority for itself, this body appointed a supreme executive council of nine men (John Wereat, Joseph Clay, Joseph Habersham, Humphry Wells, William Few, John Dooly, Seth John Cuthbert, William Gibbons, Sr., and Myrick Davies) to serve until the first Tuesday in January, the day when the assembly should meet under the constitution, "unless sooner revoked by a majority of the freemen of this State." This body gave the supreme executive council full governmental powers, subject to the approval of the citizens of the state, and directed the council to follow the constitution as closely as possible.[46] Some 500 citizens of the three northern counties signed statements approving the creation and powers of the supreme executive council.[47] The council announced that it claimed only executive powers and intended to uphold the constitution as best it could.[48] The supreme executive council did not claim a better legal base than the executive council it replaced, although apparently it was selected by representatives of a larger number of counties.

On July 24, the day of its election, the supreme executive council organized, with Seth John Cuthbert as president *pro tempore;* it selected John Wereat as permanent president on August 6.

Courts were ordered opened in Wilkes and Richmond counties and were actually operated. Sentences of civil and military courts were approved, and pardons were issued—even for notorious Tories—by the council. Commissioners for these two counties were appointed to receive plunder, to return that belonging to Whigs, and to keep that belonging to Tories. The state treasurers were ordered to return to Georgia with their money and accounts, and North Carolina was requested to give Georgia militia officers help in returning the treasurers if they refused to return of their own accord.[49] The supreme executive council was willing and able to act as Georgia's executive over the part of the state subject to its authority, but it was weak and at times had to content itself with requests rather than with orders.

One of the major problems of the supreme executive council was to secure sufficient money to operate the government, to pay and feed militia on duty, and to feed the people who had fled from their homes or who were unable to cultivate crops because of the devastated condition of the state. The council was given all financial power and urged to get finances and currency in better shape, but it could do little. No tax bill had been passed since 1778, and few taxes could have been collected even had there been a tax bill on the books. The state's credit was so low that no one would lend it money. General Lincoln and Joseph Clay, Continental Paymaster General for the Southern Department, refused to turn over money voted by the Continental Congress for Georgia to the supreme executive council because it was not a constitutional executive, but they did entertain applications from it for specific expenditures.[50]

After additional unsuccessful attempts to convene an assembly, on November 4 the supreme executive council ordered the election of an assembly on the first Tuesday in December, the day specified by the constitution. The Whig inhabitants of the counties overrun by the British were asked to repair to some convenient place in the area under Whig control and vote, so that as full an assembly as possible might be elected.[51]

Late in November a group of people calling themselves an assembly, but in number apparently considerably short of a constitutional quorum, met in Augusta. How the members of this body were selected is not known, but it is possible that some of them were elected by their counties. The Richmond County Grand Jury in its March, 1780, presentments said that this body "assumed and exercised the legislative and executive powers of government, contrary to the express letter and spirit of the constitution," and apparently met to further the "private purposes of some artful and designing individuals."[52] This "assembly" elected William Glascock speaker, George Walton governor, and an executive council with delegates from five counties (Liberty, Effingham, Burke, Richmond, and Wilkes).

Walton issued a proclamation declaring the laws of the state in full force and requiring all officers to enforce the same. He recommended to his "assembly" that it send representatives to Congress, restore the credit of the state's paper money, raise a corps of horsemen to check British and Indian raids, and find some method of effectively dealing with the Tories who lived in Whig Georgia. Walton and his group called the supreme executive council the "Tory Council" although Walton's group had no better claim to being a legal government. Evidently both Walton and his council and the supreme executive council claimed to be the legitimate Georgia executive until the new assembly met in January, 1780. Walton applied to the Continental Congress and its agents, General Lincoln and Joseph Clay, for the $500,000 voted for the use of Georgia, but the money was not paid to him.[53]

During the meeting of the Walton "assembly" there were objections to Lachlan McIntosh's presence in the state as a Continental officer. He had returned earlier in 1779. After the session ended, letters of Walton and Glascock were sent to Congress saying that there was a general aversion to McIntosh in Georgia and that it would be better for the war effort if he were used elsewhere. Congress removed McIntosh from his Southern command on February 14, 1780, without giving him a hearing.[54] When McIntosh asked Glascock about his letter, Glascock denied having written such a letter or having harbored such beliefs.[55]

Glascock's statement set off a Congressional investigation in the fall of 1780. Walton, who was then a member of Congress, said that during the session of his "assembly" a committee informed him that it had been appointed to draw a letter to Congress protesting McIntosh's return to Georgia. The "assembly" adjourned suddenly before the letter was written, and Glascock, a member of the committee, authorized it to sign his name to the letter. When the letter was finished it was signed for Glascock and sent to Congress by Walton. Richard Howley and George Seegar, both members of the 1779 "assembly," appeared before the Congressional committee and testified that the Glascock letter represented the general opinion of the 1779 "assembly." The Congressional committee decided that this letter plus the one from "Governor" Walton were sufficient grounds for removing McIntosh from his command, and Congress agreed.[56] In 1781 Congress, at the instigation of James Mitchell Varnum, repealed its February 15, 1780, resolution against McIntosh. Walton and Howley, both in Congress, tried to insert an amendment to keep McIntosh from getting another command in Georgia, but their attempt failed.[57]

The Georgia assembly considered the matter in 1783 and came to the conclusion that the executive objections to McIntosh were "unjust, illiberal, and a misrepresentation of the facts." Glascock's letter was declared a forgery "in Violation of law and truth and highly injurious to the interest of the State." The attorney general was directed to investigate the matter and enter such prosecutions as appeared necessary.[58]

Here the case ends so far as the record goes. Nobody ever questioned Walton's story. The real answer to what happened is lost in the confused situation at the time. There was a political split between the radical or country group, led by Walton and Howley, and the more conservative group, led by Wereat and the supreme executive council. McIntosh apparently adhered to the conservative group, though he said he tried not to take sides. Walton had defended McIntosh in Congress at the time of his first removal from Georgia but had since broken with him.[59]

The assembly elected at the call of the supreme executive council assembled in Augusta in January, 1780, and was controlled by the Walton faction. It elected Richard Howley, president of Walton's executive council, as governor and Walton as one of the delegates to the Continental Congress. It elected a full slate of state officials and declared the acts of the supreme executive council illegal.[60] The fact that the state government was now back in the hands of one group and existed according to the constitution should have compensated for some of what conservative Whigs considered the shortcomings of the actual government. General Lincoln and Joseph Clay turned over to the new government $597,000 in Congressional funds voted for Georgia.[61]

Although the British seemed firmly entrenched in coastal Georgia, the 1780 state assembly formulated plans for the development of the upcountry. This, the first government body not dominated by the coast, struck out to fulfill Georgia's destiny in the rich lands of the Piedmont. One of the two acts known to have been passed by this assembly stressed upcountry development. Augusta was made the seat of the government and public offices were to be opened there, but in times of danger the executive might move elsewhere. One-acre lots were to be laid out from the vacant lands at Augusta and sold at public auction for one-half cash and one-half to be paid within twelve months. Purchasers must build houses at least 20' x 16' or forfeit their lots. The streets were to be regularized and straightened; the jail and the courthouse were to be moved from Brownsborough to the public lot on Broad Street. Public lots were to be reserved for houses of worship, for schools, and for a burying ground.

An attempt to get more settlers for Georgia was embodied in the provision that anyone who would settle in the state and take an oath to support it would be granted 200 acres of land plus 50 acres for each additional member of his family. Settlers in Wilkes County would be exempt from militia duty for two years except for local defense. A town of 100 lots, named Washington, was to be laid out adjacent to the Wilkes County courthouse and its lots disposed of on the same terms as those in Augusta. The governor was requested to issue a proclamation inviting settlers to take up Georgia's rich lands, and a land office was ordered opened at once.[62]

When the state was stripped of troops to help fight Clinton at Charleston, the executive council resolved that it and the governor leave Augusta and, if necessary, carry on executive business outside the state. On February 5, 1780, the council resolved to adjourn to Heard's Fort, some eight miles from Washington in Wilkes County, but it is not clear if it actually left Augusta.[63] Governor Howley called upon all Georgians to stand firm against the British and to exert themselves in the defense of the United States. The winter and spring of 1780 were so confused that at times the executive council felt it necessary to call on the militia to carry out ordinary civil orders.[64]

Governor Howley had ignored the February 5 urging of his council to go to Congress for his personal safety; but on May 25 when he was again urged to do so, he decided to take advantage of the option allowed him by the assembly and go to Philadelphia. Stephen Heard, president of the council, now assumed the governor's duties; and the government moved out of Augusta (if that was the location), probably to Heard's Fort.[65] The British moved into the Georgia and Carolina upcountry and occupied Augusta.

From the end of May, 1780, until July, 1781, the whereabouts or existence of the Georgia state government is unknown. Augusta was in the hands of the British until June, 1781. Tradition has it that the government moved about in Wilkes County to keep out of British hands and possibly crossed into South Carolina. It seems certain that council president Stephen Heard went into South Carolina and was succeeded by Myrick Davies in August, 1780. No assembly was elected or met during this period. Militia that operated in Wilkes County and South Carolina did so because of the leadership of its commanders and not because there was any central direction from a state government. Truly, state government was in default and it was every man for himself in Whig Georgia. Wilkes County and perhaps part of Richmond were the only areas not subject to British control for most of this period, and they were subject to Tory and Indian raids. In June and July, 1781, General Greene tried to re-establish a state government where apparently there was none. He sent Joseph Clay to Augusta after its capture by the Whigs early in June, to form a temporary council to govern Georgia until constitutional government could be re-established. Clay said that he did this.[66] In August, Dr. Nathan Brownson, Continental Army hospital head in the South, went to Georgia to try to unite the various militia commanders under one head. General Greene said that the late governor of Georgia (otherwise unidentified) proposed to appoint Brownson brigadier general of Georgia, but Brownson's status and just what he did in Georgia are not known.[67]

After the capture of Augusta from the British in June and their withdrawal from Ninety Six early in July, the Georgia state government could operate again. An assembly was elected and met in Augusta on August 17 with representatives from every county except Camden. The assembly first elected Nathan Brownson its speaker but immediately thereafter elected him governor. An executive council, a full slate of state officers, county officers for every county except Glynn and Camden, and Congressional delegates were elected. All state laws, expiring or near expiring and not repealed or repugnant to the constitution, were extended.[68]

Militia field officers for six counties were elected, and enlistment bounties and pay for a state legion of 200 men then enlisting at the recommendation of General Greene were authorized. Attempts were also made to procure needed supplies for militia and state troops. The militia act subjected people who refused to do militia duty to a fine of £15 sterling in specie for the first offense, confiscation of half their property for the second offense, and service as Continental soldiers for the duration of the war for the third offense.[69]

Reclaiming Georgians who had taken the oath of loyalty to the King was begun by an act which allowed such people to remain in the area under state control if they had committed no crimes against Whigs and had joined the American army. Others who desired to reclaim their state citizenship could do so if they joined the army, gave security to stand trial for any crimes committed, and took an oath to the state and renounced their loyalty to the King. The loyalty of any suspected citizens was to be investigated, and the families of loyalists within the British lines were ordered to move within the British lines themselves. Commissioners were appointed to search out and take into their possession Tory property so that it could be rented or sold for the benefit of the state.[70]

At the request of the assembly, the governor issued a proclamation requiring citizens who had fled northward from the state to return and help fight the British. People in South Carolina were to have thirty days to return, those in North Carolina sixty days, those in Virginia ninety days, and those farther north four months. Any who did not return were to have treble taxes assessed against all real estate they owned in Georgia.[71]

This session of the assembly lasted only five days and was concerned almost entirely with the restoration of constitutional government. It took up no involved or controversial legislation and did not even suggest a tax bill. It passed only four laws, copies of only two of which have been located.[72]

Although constitutional government had been restored, it was very weak during the four and a half months that Brownson was governor.[73] There were almost continual drafts of militia and less frequent requests to General Greene for troops to protect Georgia against Tories and Indians. In September a group of Tories tried unsuccessfully to capture Governor Brownson and his council. Myrick Davies, president of the executive council, was captured and murdered in December. Another unsuccessful attempt was made to capture Governor Martin in March, 1782.[74] The financial condition of the state was desperate. Military supplies and food for troops were bought on four-months credit if anyone could be found who would sell on such terms; supplies were taken off loyalists' estates, were begged from anyone who had anything needed, were impressed, and probably were taken without any formalities by hungry troops. Cattle from the lower part of the state were collected to feed troops and civilians and to be traded for other needed supplies. Purchase of horses for state troops at the exorbitant price of £45 sterling each was authorized. Much of the time of the governor and council was taken up in ordering rations and salt issued to families of militiamen and to others who were in need.[75] Dr. Brownson must have been glad when his term as governor ended in January and he could return to the relative quiet of his position as head of the military hospitals under General Greene.

When the 1781 elections were announced, people from the counties still in alarm were urged to meet in Augusta and vote for representatives from their counties, so that the new assembly would have a full representation. Every county was represented in the assembly which met on January 1, 1782, in Augusta.[76] By then the majority of the state was in Whig hands; and after the arrival of General Wayne in Georgia early in January, the British were confined to the Savannah area.

After electing William Gibbons speaker and John Martin governor "by a large majority,"[77] the assembly went on to consider the state's financial condition. All state salaries were reduced, and the assemblymen voted to serve gratis.[78] Many salaries were past due; some militiamen had not been paid since 1778. In the first real attempt to audit state accounts since the British invasion, an auditor general was appointed and all who had received state funds since 1778 were ordered to make an accounting of them at once.[79] Certificates to the amount of £22,100 specie, were ordered issued to pay current expenses, and military officials were empowered to issue similar certificates to purchase needed supplies. All certificates issued were to be redeemed by November from funds derived from the sale of confiscated estates. Prices for purchases were to be the same as those paid in 1774-1775 except that corn was to be bought at 2s6d per bushel.[80] Other payments by the state were made in kind, especially in Negroes from confiscated estates. To get a jail built in Augusta subscriptions for Negro labor were to be requested; and if there should not be sufficient voluntary labor, Negroes were to be impressed "from such Persons as Can best spare them."[81] The assembly considered no tax bill but instructed its delegates to inform Congress of its deplorable situation and to endeavor to secure funds for military use at least.[82]

Although several matters of importance that deserved consideration had been received from Congress, the assembly ordered a
letter to Congress saying that the deplorable conditions in Georgia
made their consideration impossible at present. Two superintendents of Indian affairs, James Rae and Daniel McMurphy, were appointed and recommended to Congress as suitable Continental Indian Commissioners.[83] On January 12, after a twelve-day session,
the assembly adjourned.[84]

Throughout the first six months of 1782, there was no material
change in the status of the state government. The British were
confined closely to Savannah except for occasional raids to the
south and along the Ogeechee. Food was scarce, and many people,
including the governor and council, were fed from public stores.
When grain ran short in the spring, the executive secured rice
from South Carolina but had difficulty arranging transportation
into Georgia and finally had to agree to give one-third of the rice
to get the rest transported to Augusta.[85] The low salaries and prices
set by the assembly made it impossible to procure many needed
items or for the governor to hire a clerk to do his executive work.
The executive spent much time trying to keep militia or state
troops in the field to cooperate with the few Continentals in Georgia. Both Wayne and Greene urged the state government not to be
too severe with people who had taken the oath to the King but to
reclaim them as state citizens if possible. Things were still so confused that in January the council members voted themselves half
a dozen cartridges apiece for personal protection.[86]

Despite the meager results from the previous two sessions, the
executive called an assembly session in April. This session sat from
April 20 until May 4 and spent much of its time in hearing individual petitions about the ownership of property, especially Negroes, and in arriving at decisions on them. Individuals were ordered to turn in their accounts and to pay any funds due to the
state. Many people presented their accounts against the state and
asked for payment. The main work of this session was the passing
of a new confiscation and banishment act against Tories.[87]

Joseph Clay and Ex-Governor Richard Howley were the leaders
of this session and served on every important committee. If committee membership is an indication, Clay and Howley must have
done two-thirds of the work at this session. The day before adjournment, the assembly recommended that the executive remove to
Ebenezer or some part of the state that it thought most convenient.

It seems that the executive did move to Ebenezer, where Wayne had long had his headquarters, but definite confirmation is lacking.

On July 3, the assembly was called to meet at Ebenezer to consider the British evacuation of Savannah, but no quorum assembled. The members who met elected Joseph Clay chairman and passed resolutions attempting to prevent the carrying away of the Negroes within the British lines and allowing Tory merchants to remain in Savannah and dispose of their goods after the evacuation.[88] The assembly met in Savannah on July 13 and the executive council on July 14.[89] The government had returned to the capital, from which it had been driven December 28, 1778. The British were evacuating the state, and Georgians were free to begin recovering from the ravages of seven years of war. Well might they be thankful and look forward to better days!

Throughout the war years, Georgia's relations with the Continental Congress were rather limited and confined almost entirely to military matters. Having ratified the Articles of Confederation in 1778 and shown her belief in the place of Congress, Georgia continued her accustomed support of Congress until British occupation interfered. There were Georgia delegates in Congress most of the time except April, 1779, through May, 1780, when the assembly was unable to meet and elect any. The delegation usually consisted of two men, but there were long periods when only one delegate was present. From 1775 through 1782 seventeen Georgians were elected to Congress, some of them several times, but only fourteen actually attended.[90]

Available evidence indicates that Georgia delegates took little part in debates and that none of them could be considered Congressional leaders. Perhaps the most active Georgia delegate was George Walton, who was not noted for hiding his light under a bushel. Walton would join debate on almost any subject, but was not responsible for any major accomplishment.[91] Governor Richard Howley was also a delegate to make his presence known. He was well characterized by a fellow delegate:

Governor Howley of Georgia is a man of great reading and knowledge which he generally displays without system or design straying far from the object in question, so that he often leaves it in doubt what side of the question he is on. He is loud but not very eloquent, therefore rather excels in Declamation than argument, and of course is not closely attended to, but when he entertains the House with strokes of wit or sports of knowledge. He would shine more in a Democratic assembly.[92]

Howley is given credit by one of his colleagues for demolishing the attempt to vote Washington dictatorial powers in the fall of 1780.[93] South Carolina's Henry Laurens continued to be Georgia's best delegate in Congress. Laurens got much of his information about conditions in Georgia from his friend, Joseph Clay, and usually did what Clay recommended. Georgia was usually considered along with South Carolina and the Southern Military Department, and Laurens was almost inevitably an important member of committees considering these subjects.

Georgia's main need from Congress was military and financial help. From 1779 through 1782 Georgia could not support her delegates, and they had to get their actual living expenses from Congress. Congress voted $1,000,000 for the service of Georgia in August, 1777, $500,000 in the summer of 1779 and $1,000,000 on February 11, 1780.[94] Throughout this period Georgia requested more funds than she got from Congress and paid in nothing upon requisitions. Congress did not expect Georgia to make payments on her requisitions while she was occupied by the British, and she was not assigned a quota in 1780.[95] Georgia did furnish supplies for Continental troops early in the war, and she continued to do so whenever Continental troops operated in the state.

To replenish its chronically empty treasury, early in 1781 Congress proposed to the states that it be given authority to levy a five per cent duty upon all imports for the purpose of paying the principal and interest on the war debt. This recommendation had been approved by all the states except Georgia and Rhode Island by the fall of 1782. Rhode Island rejected this grant of power to Congress, but Georgia never considered it. The assembly that met in January, 1782, apologized to Congress for not taking up Continental matters and expressed the opinion that the next session would act. However, the matter never received consideration in any assembly.[96]

When Congress was trying to get Spain as an ally against Britain, Americans assumed that Spain would want the Floridas in return for any help. In this debate Congress passed a resolution defining the southern boundary of the United States as the thirty-first degree of latitude from the Mississippi to the Chattahoochee, down the Chattahoochee to the Flint, from this junction a straight line to the head of the St. Marys, and along the St. Marys to the Atlantic.[97] This was the boundary of Georgia as described in the proclamation of 1763 and included the area given to West Florida in 1764. After the capture of Mobile by the Spanish in March, 1780, Congress instructed John Jay in Madrid to see to it that the United States was allowed the use of rivers running out of Georgia through West Florida to the Gulf of Mexico if Spain captured West Florida. In return for this right, the United States was willing to guarantee the Floridas to Spain. Georgia's delegates in Congress, Walton and Howley, were willing to have the United States give up any claim to the navigation of the Mississippi and even to a small amount of territory north of the thirty-first parallel if Spain agreed to a treaty of alliance and made grants and loans to the United States during the war.[98]

There were rumors in Congress in the spring of 1780 that Britain would offer to make peace that acknowledged the independence of the United States, but she would retain Georgia and South Carolina for herself.[99] Early in January, 1781, Georgia's delegates (George Walton, Richard Howley, and William Few) published a pamphlet, "Observations Upon the Effects of Certain Late Political Suggestions," arguing that all the states had joined the war together and that none should be left under British control. However, the main argument emphasized Georgia's advantages to the United States. Her agricultural products, ship timbers and naval stores, excellent harbors, and commerce were valuable to the other states and should not be left in British hands. Britain in control of both ends of the Atlantic coast could certainly cause trouble in the future. Georgia's rapid physical and economic growth in the past twenty years was pointed out with a prediction of a bigger and better future.[100] Congress never seriously considered making peace without South Carolina and Georgia, and it is doubtful if she would have done so even without the objections of the Georgia delegates.

ECONOMIC AND
SOCIAL MATTERS
1775 - 1782

10

****

BESIDES military and political opposition, the revolting colonies used economic weapons against Britain. Non-importation, which had been used first at the time of the Stamp Act troubles, was an obvious weapon in the early days of colonial opposition. Georgia did not adopt the Continental Association until July, 1775, seven months after it was adopted by the Continental Congress, and many Georgians hoped that they would be allowed to export their 1775 crop.[1] The evidence indicates that after adoption the provincial congresses and council of safety tried to enforce the association, but because of insufficient policing or exceptions made by local committees, some rice and other items were exported. Some contemporary accounts for late 1775 and early 1776 say that all exports had ceased; others say that Georgia produce was being exported.[2]

Rice exportation was reported stopped in September, 1775; and on January 8, 1776, the council of safety, agreeable to Continental regulations, prohibited the exportation of rice until March 1. When South Carolina urged that Georgia continue non-exportation beyond March 1 until the feeling of Congress could be ascertained, the Georgia Council of Safety replied that there was great pressure among Savannah merchants to allow exportation to be resumed. However, because British war vessels at the mouth of the Savannah River were attempting to secure provisions, non-exportation was extended. Throughout the summer vessels leaving Savannah were required to abide by the resolves of the Continental and Georgia congresses.[3]

In the fall small vessels were transporting provisions from south Georgia plantation landings to St. Augustine. Georgia and South Carolina authorities tried to stop such traffic, but they did not have sufficient naval forces to do so. East Florida had been accustomed to getting food from south Georgia, and apparently some Georgians were quite willing to sell their produce to East Florida, regardless of attempts to prevent them. Such exportations continued, at intervals anyway, throughout 1778 despite the fact that Georgia agreed to continue the embargo on the export of provisions as recommended by the Continental Congress.[4]

The disruption of normal shipping and supply channels created shortages in imported items and surpluses in local produce in 1776. Abundant supplies of leather, rice, and indigo were reported in Savannah in November, with little trade going on. A packet boat instituted by the Continental Congress between Savannah and Philadelphia carried freight and helped the situation slightly.[5]

By the spring of 1777 Savannah was free of British vessels and was building up trade with the French and Dutch West Indies, which sometimes acted only as an exchange point for goods on the way to or from Europe. There was coastal trade with Charleston and the ports to the north. Throughout 1777 and 1778 the volume of this trade was small, but the profits were considerable for anyone with sufficient capital who cared to take the risk.[6] Georgia merchants were perfectly willing to re-export scarce imported goods if a profit could be made. Several proclamations were issued against this practice and against the exportation of provisions when the supply was short.[7]

The government, as well as the Savannah merchants, was aware that trade was necessary to the economic and military life of Georgia. To increase foreign trade, the state bought vessels and carried on trade itself, appointed John Wereat commissioner of public trade, and set up an insurance office to insure cargoes of Georgia traders. General Howe, while military commander of the Southern Department, urged the state to undertake more state trade to help its economic life.[8] Often the state either exported local produce itself or licensed individuals to do so as a means of securing funds to purchase needed military stores.

The rapidly growing Indian trade of Augusta was hurt by the war because Superintendent Stuart tried to divert all Southern Indian trade through Pensacola. Stuart succeeded in persuading at least one Augusta Indian trader to remove to Pensacola, although he was soon back in Augusta. In the early years of the war, the Whigs were divided as to the desirability of continuing the Indian trade and were able to get few trading goods anyway. During the British occupation of Augusta, 1780-1781, an attempt was made to revive the Indian trade, but little was accomplished. Augusta's great days as an Indian trading center ended during the Revolution.

Tied directly to the commerce of colonial Georgia was its agricultural production. Most of Georgia's large plantations that produced crops for export were located on the coast, and many of them were owned by loyalists who left by 1777. Although the state government tried to operate these plantations to secure an income, it accomplished little in the attempt. After the return of the British, there was never a planting season when large amounts of territory did not change hands, at least temporarily, between Whigs and Tories. Raids from the sea and from East Florida also accounted for considerable disruption of plantation routine. Partisan warfare in the back country brought considerable destruction there. Anything movable was carried off, and buildings and growing crops were often damaged or destroyed. Abandonment and neglect damaged or ruined many plantations, especially the irrigation systems so necessary in rice planting. Before the fighting began, Georgia had exported from 20,000 to 25,000 barrels of rice a year, and had consumed a good bit locally. In 1780 Governor Wright said that not over 2,000 barrels would be put on the market and that none of this would be available for export.[9]

One of the greatest damages the war brought to plantations was the disruption of the slave labor system. Slaves disappeared because of the absence of owners or overseers or because of military operations in the area. Regaining runaways was difficult under war conditions. Slaves became camp followers of both armies, joined or were carried off by the Indians, or escaped and set up Negro communities of their own. Both armies used slaves to work on fortifications and for supply, transport, and housekeeping functions. Ownership was confused by these conditions, by the attempts at confiscation of property by both state and provincial government, and by the general and legal confusion of the war years. Many Whigs took their slaves into South Carolina or other states. The state government's use of slaves as bounties or for payment of its obligations during the last two years of the war removed many from their accustomed locations. Importation was stopped during the war, and several thousand slaves were taken out of the state at the time of the British evacuation. Without slaves plantations could produce nothing.

Since Georgia's founding, the lack of good currency had been a problem that created confusion and hurt business. With the closing of the normal trade channels, this problem became worse. The state government issued paper bills of credit to care for the needs of the troops and to serve as a circulating medium. But Georgia currency was never accepted outside the state; it depreciated in value rapidly, and was a constant source of complaint from businessmen and soldiers paid in it. Continental currency and South Carolina paper currency were also used in Georgia and were worth considerably more than Georgia currency.[10]

A few illustrations of inflation will give point to these complaints. In 1781 a horse cost more than £30 in state certificates to be redeemed in four months. Office fees for signing land grants were $16, and the signing of a marriage license cost $80.[11] The paper currency bothered not only Georgia Whigs, but Tories and British also were worried with it after their return to Georgia.[12] By 1781 state paper of various sorts was of so little value that even the state government stopped trying to use it and turned instead to making payments in kind. Land bounties for army enlistments and service had been given since 1776. Now horses, cattle, clothing, and Negroes from confiscated estates were used as well. As the British were pushed out of the state, any movable property, especially Negroes, which they left behind was seized by the state to pay its obligations.

Army supply was another matter that worried both the state government and the troops operating in Georgia. Before 1779 the state furnished more of the supplies used than did Congress. By 1780 Continental troops, state troops, and militia got what supplies they could where they could, often without formal purchase. Congress supplied considerable munitions and clothing to state troops and militia. Most of the provisions used by all troops operating in Georgia were supplied by the state. With most of the state overrun by the British, Georgia could secure little locally and was begging for whatever she could get from Continental sources.[13] In 1782 she could not supply the small contingent of Continental troops under the command of General Wayne.[14] The state made attempts throughout the war to encourage the manufacture of guns, gunpowder, and other military supplies, but little was actually produced.[15]

One of the main arguments among the British for the recapture
of Georgia was the valuable trade she could supply to the rest of the
empire. Hence on January 15, 1779, two weeks after the capture of
Savannah, a proclamation was issued there allowing exports to
Britain, Ireland, the West Indies, and the loyal North American
colonies. Savannah merchants were allowed to trade with all in the
colony who took the oath of allegiance to the King. Two weeks
later Governor Tonyn opened trade between East Florida and
Georgia.[16] By summer trade was going full blast between Georgia,
New York, and the West Indies. Early in 1780 full trade was allowed between Georgia and Britain in compliance with a royal
proclamation of March 24, 1779, and Georgians were urged to send
needed items to the British West Indies.[17] In that year over 100 vessels cleared from Savannah, many loaded with lumber and naval
stores.[18]

In economic matters the British tried to return to the pre-war
conditions, even to the re-establishment of the public market at
Savannah under its old regulations. But the war made for changed
conditions, some good and some bad. The British army and navy
secured and paid for in gold and silver considerable supplies for
use in other parts of America. The provincial government imposed
embargoes frequently to safeguard provisions in short supply. At
least one incident of price fixing is recorded when cost of provisions
seemed to be getting out of hand.[19] Throughout the period that
Georgia was split between colony and state, there were commercial
and financial dealings between both parts of Georgia and South
Carolina with or without the approval of the provincial and state
governments.[20]

From all available evidence it seems there were fewer professional people and tradesmen in Savannah during the British occupation than had been there before 1779, and the assumption is that
there were similar decreases in the rest of Georgia. Not nearly so
many advertised in the *Gazette;* and apparently immigration from
Britain and other parts of Europe was slowed down or cut off by
the war. A few doctors, lawyers, and musicians advertised their
services to the public. About thirty-six mercantile concerns advertised in the *Gazette* for the years 1779-1781, fewer than had existed
before the outbreak of war. Savannah had her usual assortment of
tavern keepers, hatters, tailors, shoemakers, hairdressers, saddle
makers, gunsmiths, painters, and other tradesmen.[21] Some people
who had been in business in 1775 remained throughout the British

period and after the Americans returned, and others came and went depending upon which government controlled. Peter Tondee, the tavern keeper and early Revolutionary leader, died in 1775, but his wife continued to operate a tavern under American, British, and returned American governments.

To give any exact information about population changes during the fighting years is impossible. The upcountry, especially the Indian cession of 1773, continued to gain population except for the period 1780-1781 when most of Georgia was controlled by the British. The total white population seems to have increased in the back country, but there may have been a decrease along the coast.

From the time the revolutionary troubles became serious until the return of the British in 1778, many loyalists left and went to the Floridas and the West Indies. Some of them left their families in Georgia, and many returned in 1779 and 1780. Loyalists from other Southern colonies came into Georgia at the same time, some of them taking up lands and settling "permanently." Others came from West Florida after its capture by the Spanish in 1780-1781. Probably most of these recent arrivals left when the British evacuated the province in 1782.

Whig refugees began to leave Georgia with the British capture of Savannah in 1778, and they continued to do so as the British gained control of more and more of Georgia throughout 1779 and 1780. Probably most of them went to Whig areas in South Carolina, but others went into North Carolina, Virginia, and Maryland, where they were well treated. North Carolina excused them from tax payments or militia duty. Virginia allowed them to bring their slaves into the state, despite a law that forbade further importations, and did not tax such slaves the first year they were in Virginia.[22] In July, 1781, Congress recommended that subscriptions and loans be solicited in the states not overrun by the British for the relief of South Carolinians and Georgians driven from their homes by the war. Collections are known to have been taken in New Jersey and Massachusetts, and were no doubt taken elsewhere.[23] Perhaps some Bostonians remembered the relief sent from Georgia when the Boston Port Bill was in effect, and wanted to reciprocate. When the British were driven out of the Georgia upcountry the Georgia executive asked the states in which Georgia refugees were living to cooperate in helping them to return to Georgia.[24] Refugees began to return to the upcountry in 1781, and most were back in all parts of the state by the end of 1782.

For about a year after the capture of Augusta from the British in June, 1781, the state government was faced with a major relief problem to feed and care for refugees who returned to Georgia without resources and could do little to support themselves until the 1782 crops could be planted and harvested. The executive secured rations for such people and for the troops and militia operating in the state. Often civil officials, even the executive itself, and families of people absent with the army had to be fed. Sometimes food had to be bought outside the state to carry on these relief activities. By the spring of 1782 the food situation had become so desperate that corn was impressed when its possessors refused to sell it to the state.[25]

Salt supply was a persistent problem from the beginning of the war. Most salt had been imported in the colonial period, and there is no record that Georgians tried to produce this vital commodity in appreciable quantities during the fighting. Consequently salt was in constant short supply. As early as 1777 the executive forbade the exportation of salt, and took up much time throughout the war with the procurement and distribution of salt. At various times salt was ordered issued only on the personal order of the governor, was issued on the basis of one quart per family, and was used as a reward for satisfactory militia service.[26]

The provincial government, as well as the state government, had its relief problems. After its initial occupation of Georgia the British army appointed an inspector to take care of refugees, but discontinued such help by March, 1781, because most of the refugees were able to support themselves.[27] But when the British lost the upcountry, many refugees were driven into the Savannah area, and it was necessary for the government to feed them. Special church collections, lotteries, and dramatic performances were all used to secure funds for relief purposes.[28]

Besides its impact on the here and now, the war had a considerable effect upon the organization concerned with the hereafter—the church. The denomination most changed was the Church of England. When the fighting began, there were five Anglican priests in Georgia: Haddon Smith, Christ Church Parish; James Seymour, St. Paul; James Holmes, St. George; John Rennie, St. Philip; and William Piercy, superintendent of Bethesda Orphanage. Smith and Rennie were Tories and soon left.[29] Holmes evidently remained in Georgia and became a Whig, but no positive knowledge of his wartime activities has been found. Piercy joined the Whigs but was soon lost sight of, until 1784, when he appears in England.[30] He apparently never returned to Georgia.

Seymour had by far the most interesting and unusual story. He remained in Augusta after colonial government ended and said that he was allowed to continue his clerical duties without molestation, except from the more vulgar, for about two years. Then, because people who attended his services were called Tories by their neighbors, he discontinued public worship but remained in Augusta and carried on his other pastoral duties. He welcomed Lieutenant Colonel Campbell to Augusta with the British troops in February, 1779, and was arrested by the Whigs when Campbell retired. As a prisoner Seymour said he was well treated by express order of General Andrew Williamson, and he was soon released. Upon his release Seymour went to Savannah for a few weeks but returned to Augusta because of sickness in his family. Again he was well treated until the siege of Savannah in September. During the siege the church and glebe were used by American forces in Augusta; so Seymour and his family moved to his farm a few miles out of town. With the British occupation of Augusta in 1780, Seymour had the chance to conduct public worship again in his damaged church. The parsonage and glebe were returned to him, but he soon gave up the parsonage, for use as a military hospital. When the Whigs laid siege to Augusta, a fort was built in the churchyard; so services were held in a private house. After the Whig capture of Augusta, Seymour, considering himself unsafe on his farm, removed to Savannah but left his family in St. Paul. In Savannah he served in the provincial assembly for St. Paul's Parish, assisted the acting rector of Christ Church, and taught school. He remained in Savannah as a school teacher until the evacuation and then went to St. Augustine.[31]

After the return of the British in 1779, an attempt was made to revive the Anglican Church. In March, 1780, James Brown, who had been a Georgia schoolmaster before he left in 1777 because of his loyalist sympathies, returned to be missionary to St. George's Parish for the Society for the Propagation of the Gospel in Foreign Parts. Governor Wright did not think it safe for Brown to go to St. George's because of rebel activity there; hence, he remained in Savannah, where there was no Anglican clergyman, and carried out the rector's duties. The rector, Haddon Smith, drew the salary in England but the assembly allowed Brown a small salary, and he secured the rector's fees. In the fall of 1781 Smith sent a curate to

Savannah who took possession of the parsonage and forbade Brown to say services in Christ Church. Brown's payments from the assembly stopped, and seeing that his presence in Savannah only created clerical confusion, he soon went to Charleston.[32]

To turn from Anglicans to dissenters, the first clergyman who comes to mind is the Reverend John J. Zubly, of the Independent Presbyterian Church in Savannah. Zubly's early Whig leadership and opposition to separation from Britain have already been related.[33] After Zubly's return from the Continental Congress in late 1775, he continued his political sentiments and religious activities unmolested for some time. When he was called upon to take the oath of allegiance to the United States in the fall of 1777 he refused to do so, offering instead to take an oath to Georgia. Finding it impossible to remain in Georgia an unsworn neutral, Zubly retired to Black Swamp in South Carolina where he remained until 1781, when he returned to Savannah. Zubly, now worn out physically and mentally, died three months later, "still praying for his king and country."[34]

At Ebenezer, the Reverend Christopher F. Triebner, the Lutheran pastor, welcomed the British in 1779, took the oath of allegiance to the King, and actively supported the restored provincial government. Triebner could not carry all his congregation with him. His church and the town were considerably damaged by British army use and the ravages of war. Triebner left with the British army in 1782, apparently at odds with much of his congregation.[35]

The Congregational meeting house at Midway, in St. John's Parish, was burned by the British during the invasion of November, 1778. Little is known of the specific activities of the congregation or church during the war years, but an organization must have continued because it was active immediately after the fighting stopped. Moses Allen, the young minister of Midway, became the chaplain of the First Georgia Continental Battalion when it was raised. He was captured by the British at Savannah in 1778, imprisoned on a prison ship there, and drowned while attempting to swim ashore.[36]

The Baptists had begun to come into upcountry Georgia in the 1770s; and there were at least three churches, of which Kiokee in St. Paul's Parish was the most important, when the war broke out. Strickland identifies six Baptists (Daniel Marshall, Saunders Walker, Abraham Marshall, Edmund Botsford, Silas Mercer, and Alexander Scott) among the eleven Georgia chaplains in the American army. Botsford left during the fighting, but Marshall remained at Kiokee during the hard days of partisan fighting there.[37] The Baptists suffered less in church organization and ministerial recruitment from the war than most other denominations. The denomination seems to have taken no specific stand on the Revolution but left such matters to individual members, most of whom were probably Whigs. Relatively speaking, the Baptists were in better shape in 1782 than they had been in 1775.

Religious influence on the Whig-Tory split in Revolutionary Georgia has been best summed up by Strickland, who says,

It seems reasonably certain that a large number, but not a majority, of the Anglicans remained loyal to the Crown. Although many Highlanders and Scotch-Irish were loyalists, most of the Presbyterians were rebels. Probably all, or nearly all, Midway Congregationalists, Baptists and Jews were patriots. The Lutherans were split, but the majority appear to have favored independence. The Quakers were loyal or at least neutral. Except for the latter, it appears that all the dissenting sects tended to favor liberty and those which, in Europe or America, had suffered religious persecution were most ardent in their support of the American cause. Indeed, this seems to have been a much stronger controlling factor than economic interests in determining the side to which individuals gave their allegiance.[38]

There was less educational than religious activity in Georgia during the war years, as had been the case in the colonial period. Private schools continued in Savannah under whichever government controlled the city, but there seemed to have been fewer than formerly. Fees ranged from twenty shillings a quarter for reading and writing to ten pounds per year for Latin, Greek, French, or mathematics.[39] Not much is known about education outside Savannah, but it is extremely doubtful if there were many, if any, schools on plantations or in other towns after 1778. The parochial school at Ebenezer was abandoned when the British arrived, and there was no chance for any formal education in the upcountry.

Like religion and education, organized recreation declined during the war. Early in the troubles, the Whigs attempted to curtail recreation and to devote themselves to more serious things. Horse racing was frowned upon, and commercial recreation fell off. The few traveling entertainers who had come to Georgia in the colonial period were stopped by the war. Little record of Whig amusements has been found, but it is logical to assume that the colonial pattern was resumed as nearly as possible once the immediate urgency of 1775 and early 1776 had passed.

After the return of the British, little commercial recreation is evident until the middle of 1780. By 1781 there was an attempt in British Georgia to return to "life as usual" as it had been before 1775. Plays were presented in Savannah by "Gentlemen of the Garrison" for the benefit of public charity, though some had to be postponed when the actors went out of town on military duty. Dancing assemblies were held, with civilian and military managers. The St. Andrew's Society met on St. Andrew's Day and elected officers as formerly. The Ugly Club was revived, but nothing about the nature of its activities was divulged. The King's Birthday was celebrated, as was "The Glorious Ninth of October," the day on which the French and American attack on Savannah was repulsed.[40]

Little evidence of amusements outside Savannah has been found. There is no reason to believe that the pattern of frontier amusements, the creation of people living in the area and not dependent upon outsiders, changed, regardless of which government controlled an area. Military action in the upcountry did somewhat interfere with recreation. Undoubtedly sophisticated entertainment in Augusta declined during the war years.

All phases of ordinary life for most people—recreation and work, joys and sorrows, religion and education—went on about the same as formerly except when military activity at a distance took away men to fight, or when fighting in the immediate vicinity upset the economic and social pattern and made the old life impossible. Life was changed less for the poor frontier families; but all suffered, hoped for better days, and worked to support themselves and to compensate for the changes brought by the war.

INDEPENDENCE
A REALITY
1782 - 1785

11   **

THE STATE government was waiting at the
gates and moved into Savannah with the Amer-
ican army immediately after the British evacuation. The assembly
convened in Savannah on July 13, two days after the British left;
and the council had its first session in the old capital the next day.
With the appointment of county officials for Chatham County,
July 18, the governmental organization for the recently-evacuated
area was completed.[1] Physically, Savannah was hardly ready to receive the state government. The governor and council took steps to
secure goods from the merchants for use by the army, governmental
officials, and inhabitants; and the assembly appointed a committee
to secure food and lodging for its members.[2]

Six of the state's eight counties were represented when the assembly convened in Savannah, and Glynn County sent a representative two days later. This assembly first met in the church but
soon moved to the long room of Mrs. Tondee's tavern for the rest
of its session.[3] A committee which recommended matters for the
consideration of the assembly listed defense, finances, and Continental matters in that order of importance. General Greene should
be requested to supply sufficient Continental troops to protect the
state, which should furnish the necessary military supplies.
Amounts due the state should be ordered paid, and state accounts
for the war years were to be audited and prepared for settlement.
After these matters of pressing importance, Continental matters
should be considered.[4]

This session lasted three weeks (July 13-August 5) and was con-

cerned almost entirely with immediate relief and the organization
of government upon a regular and constitutional basis. Only three
bills are known to have been passed. One reopened the courts of
the state with the same jurisdiction they had possessed before the
British invasion. Delays of up to two years were allowed in settling
civil judgments in favor of the plaintiffs, and umpires were directed to determine the value of depreciated paper currency used in
settlement. The period July 1, 1775, through July 12, 1782, was
not to count in reckoning elapsed time under the statute of limita-
tions. The second act amerced certain people who had been amen-
able to British control in Georgia but who were not named in the
1782 confiscation and banishment act. The third act set up certain
categories of undesirable people who were not to be allowed to
settle in Georgia.[5]

Because General Greene had ordered General Wayne and his
Continental troops to report to Charleston as soon as possible, the
state had to take over its own defense, except for the small battalion of Continentals being raised from ex-British sympathizers
who wanted to reinstate their loyalty to Georgia and thus save their
property. The assembly ordered all British arms collected and additional arms purchased for the state troops. Greene was requested to
return the troops he had ordered to Charleston because Thomas
Brown and the Florida Rangers were still near Savannah, but no
Continentals were returned until after the Rangers left. The assembly suggested that two troops of horsemen be drawn from the
new Continental battalion, with Congress defraying the necessary
expenses for mounted troops and two galleys to guard the coast.[6]
There is no indication that any of the Continental troops were ever
mounted (something that Greene disapproved) or that the galleys
were ever built. Early in 1783 the assembly authorized the purchase of one galley to be paid for and controlled by the state.[7] Despite continual urgings from Greene, Georgia never provided the
necessary provisions for the Continental troops. Governor Hall
brought up the necessity of provisions in February, 1783, so that
the troops would not have to pilfer from honest citizens; but the
assembly directed the governor to draw supplies "in such manner
as may prove least burdensome to the inhabitants," until a better
mode of supply could be devised. Later there were complaints that
the courts would not allow the troops to impress provisions and
that the troops were in actual need.[8]

Peace negotiations between Britain and the United States, begun in the spring of 1782, resulted in a preliminary treaty in November, 1782. Congress, in April, 1783, decreed the suspension of hostilities, and the demobilization of the army. Greene, in June, 1783, ordered Wayne to march north at once the Continental troops which had just been sent to Georgia to oppose a feared attack from East Florida. Georgia's Continental battalion of ex-British sympathizers, its ranks depleted by desertions, was of little value to the defense of the state, and it was furloughed as no longer necessary and was discharged in December.[9] Georgia's defense was now entirely up to the state.

Trouble with British sympathizers had been feared after the British evacuation. The first such trouble came in August, 1782, from a group of people who had slipped out of Savannah just before its evacuation, congregated northwest of Augusta and preyed upon travelers, raided settlements along the Ogeechee in Burke County, and aroused the Creeks against Georgians. Militia sent against this group and its Indian allies apparently ended any immediate danger despite the fear of some that much of Burke County would be broken up.[10]

The large number of ex-Georgia loyalists in East Florida fanned the old animosities from that area. At the same time that the troubles above Augusta were being settled by the militia, attempts were being made to quiet fears of Georgians and East Floridians. Georgia commissioners were sent to St. Augustine to treat with Governor Tonyn, who insisted that he desired peace and had given positive orders that no raids would be made into Georgia unless Georgians raided East Florida. The commissioners assured Tonyn that Georgia intended to begin no trouble.[11] There were repeated complaints of raids from both sides of the Georgia-East Florida boundary, but the raiders seem to have been unlawful banditti rather than units backed by either government.[12]

Until the British evacuation of East Florida in 1785, there was considerable intercourse between loyalists there and relatives and acquaintances in Georgia. This contact was supposed to be carried on with official approval through flags of truce, but there were numerous flag violations and rumors of an invasion of Georgia in the spring of 1783. General Greene, authorized to take the necessary precautions, sent General Wayne and troops to Georgia from South Carolina.[13] However, nothing happened, and Georgia-East Florida relations remained harmonious. Georgians went to East Florida to try to recover stolen or runaway horses, slaves, and other

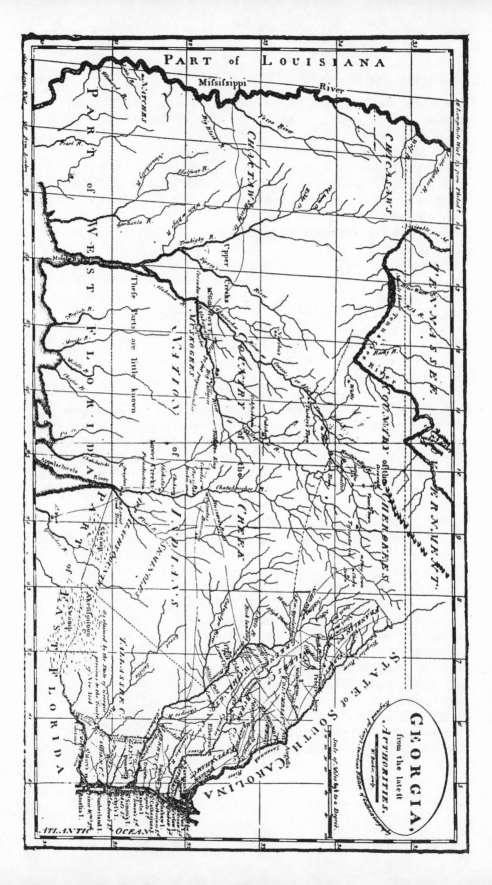

PART of LOUISIANA

Mifsifsippi   River

CHICKASAWS

TENNASSEE

PART of WEST

These Parts are little known

PART of FLORIDA

CHACTAWS

NATION

COUNTRY of the

CREEK

CHEROKEES

TERRITORY of the

Appalachicola   River

INDIANS

EAST FLORIDA

STATE OF SOUTH CAROLINA

ATLANTIC   OCEAN

GEORGIA,
from the latest
AUTHORITIES.

property. Some slaves taken out of Georgia at its evacuation were returned, by purchase or otherwise.[14]

The final peace treaty, signed at Paris on September 3, 1783, provided that East and West Florida be ceded by Britain to Spain. After news of the treaty was received, Governor Lyman Hall wrote to Governor Tonyn and suggested that, if East Florida was to be evacuated by the British, Georgia might be glad to receive many of its inhabitants. Hall intimated that Tories from Georgia and other states might be allowed to come to Georgia but said that this would have to be determined by the assembly. Hall asked that Georgia property in East Florida, especially slaves, not be evacuated; later he sent a commissioner to claim such property.[15] In the spring of 1784, requests from people in East Florida to settle in Georgia were approved by the executive; there also were reports of undesirables coming without official permission.[16] The evacuation began in 1783 and lasted through the summer of 1785. Georgians, who congratulated themselves upon the return of the Spanish to the Floridas, were soon to discover that it was as bad to have the Floridas in Spanish hands as in British hands, and probably worse.

Another of the loyalists' postwar problems that caused as much trouble as relations with Florida was enforcement of the confiscation and banishment acts. In January, 1782, the estates of all people within the British lines whose property had not been confiscated in 1778 or who had not returned to state citizenship under the act of 1781 was confiscated to furnish security for the certificates being issued to pay the current expenses of the state government.[17]

The May, 1782, assembly banished and confiscated the property of all people named in the original state act of 1778, plus any who had since adhered to the British cause or given aid to the British military in Georgia. The act, which named 279 people, applied to any others who might be convicted in state courts of having aided the British. Such people who returned to Georgia were to be arrested and sent to British territory. Any who returned again were to suffer death without benefit of clergy. Georgia property owned by people who were included in similar acts of other states was also confiscated. All Georgia property of British subjects was confiscated, regardless of the owner's connection with the fighting in America. Any property title transfers of the affected persons since April 19, 1775, were declared void, to prevent circumvention of confiscation. United States citizens or friends were allowed to present for payment any claims they might have against confiscated property. If the families of banished people remained in Georgia, they could get temporary support from the proceeds of the property confiscated from their family. County boards of commissioners were appointed to receive confiscated estates, and public sales were directed to begin within forty days.[18]

Almost as soon as the ink was dry on the confiscation and banishment act, the assembly began to mitigate its provisions. Before the passage of the act, General Wayne had urged that loyalists be treated leniently, so that many of them could be reclaimed as state citizens.[19] In July, 1782, the assembly considered restoring to Georgia citizenship those loyalists who were not named in the act, and appointed county commitees to draw up lists of such people. Those who had taken protection under the British were allowed no political rights until they had renounced their allegiance to the King and sworn allegiance to Georgia and the United States. Disaffected people from other states were prohibited from coming to Georgia and settling.[20]

Ninety-three people, forty-eight of whom had been listed in the confiscation and banishment act, were named in an amercement act in August. One group of these people were to pay twelve per cent of their property to the state; another group, eight per cent; and the rest were to serve as soldiers in the Georgia battalion of Continental troops or to find substitutes. All penalties of confiscation and banishment were to be removed upon payment of the amercement, and all political privileges were restored except the right to vote or hold office until three years after the war's end.[21]

It is impossible to say exactly how many people left Georgia because of the confiscation and banishment acts of 1778 and 1782. These acts named 342 individuals, and the blanket provisions applied to many other persons. When the British evacuated Savannah, most of the people who left went to East Florida or Jamaica. A few went direct to England. In 1782, the number of white Georgia refugees in East Florida was reported to be 1,042. Of these, 402 were heads of families, and 91 of them were on the Georgia confiscation and banishment act. Of the fifty white men reported in Jamaica, fifteen were named in the Georgia act.[22] Thus, it seems that not more than 1,250 to 1,500 white loyalists left Georgia. This number plus approximately 3,500 slaves make a total of 4,500 to 5,000 persons who left Georgia because of their British loyalty.

Upon the British evacuation of East Florida, many of its inhab-

itants came to Georgia. It is impossible to tell how many loyalists
returned to Georgia in 1783 and 1784, but it appears that many
small farmers not named in the confiscation and banishment act
must have done so. Others from East Florida went to the Bahamas,
where records of thirty-three people on the Georgia confiscation
and banishment act have been located.[23] A few went from East
Florida to other West Indian colonies, to Nova Scotia, or to England.

The banishment part of the act was never completely enforced.
As early as July 31, 1782, there were reports that people named in
the act were going at large in the state, and such people were
ordered jailed until they could be sent out of Georgia. Yet in August, Dr. Andrew Johnson, named in the act, was allowed the freedom of Savannah because of the need for doctors.[24] During the
next decade many other people named in the act were ordered
arrested, ordered to leave the state, or were allowed to remain.
Associations which were organized in Savannah and in several
counties in the fall of 1783 to prevent proscribed persons from returning to the state, became inactive after 1783.[25]

By assembly action throughout the 1780s, 1790s, and early 1800s,
twenty-one people were removed from the penalties of the act so
far as banishment was concerned; forty-seven were removed entirely, some being restored to full citizenship. The property of at
least nineteen deceased people named in the act was vested in their
heirs, with the same effect as removal of living people. Probably at
least thirty people named in the 1782 act were dead at its passage
but were included so that their property might be confiscated.
Wives and families of banished people often remained in Georgia.
A list prepared in the executive department of the state in 1813
showed 342 people originally subject to confiscation and banishment and some 263 still subject to the penalties of the acts.[26] These
figures agree approximately with the researches of the present
writer. Thus, it seems that at least 250 people named in the acts
were forced to leave the state and to lose all their property. Families leaving with these might bring the total number who left
permanently to 750 or 1,000, but no definite figures are available.

The Georgia state government was most interested in enforcing
the acts against loyalists who had considerable property or who
had been especially obnoxious to Whigs during the war. Many
Georgia loyalists had taken the oath of allegiance to the King only
because the British were in control of Georgia and were perfectly

willing to take an oath to the United States after the British left. Those in this category who returned from East Florida in 1784 and 1785 were allowed to settle and become citizens when the bitterness of the war years died down.

The sale of confiscated estates began in the summer of 1782 and continued at least through 1785.[27] Payment specified by law was one half in specie and the other half in state certificates or accounts against the state, with up to seven years to pay the full purchase price. Accounts of officers and soldiers of the Continental line were received as specie plus a discount of 12½ per cent for prompt payment, because such accounts entitled the state to a discount on its Continental quota.[28] When the personal bonds given in payment for confiscated estates became due, many of them were defaulted. By the summer of 1787 bonds valued at £281,716. 7.0 had been received in the treasury for payment of confiscated estates, and £93,783. 1.1½ worth of them had been paid. Bonds worth £22,607. 1.1 fell due in 1786, but only £1,818.19. 1¾ principal and interest was paid.[29] It is impossible to tell the proportion of the bonds defaulted, but there is no reason to suppose that 1786 was an unusual year. Besides defaulted bonds, the amount received from confiscated estates was further reduced by claims of Whigs against these estates, which were still being received in 1786.[30] While the state received some income from the sale of confiscated estates, the amount was far below the figure envisioned by early advocates of confiscation.

Besides punishment for loyalists, Georgia was concerned with rewarding Whigs for their war services. During the war, promises of land bounties had been used to recruit state and Continental troops and to bring new citizens to the state. After the fighting ended, the state fulfilled its bounty promises and made special grants to outstanding officers and soldiers for their combat services. Two hundred fifty acres of land exempt from taxes for ten years were allowed to all who had remained in the state and done militia duty during the British occupation. Those who had left the state but had done army duty elsewhere were allowed the same amount of land.[31] Members of the Georgia Continental units were entitled to both Continental and state bounties in Georgia. Often they could qualify for a headright grant as well. One application for Continental bounties from Connecticut troops was granted because it could be charged against what Georgia owed the United States.[32] Most state troops were given bounties of land, Negroes, or clothing. Land bounties continued to be authorized for militia and state troops who participated in the Indian troubles of the 1780s; and in 1788 the militia was voted 300 acres for every three-month tour of duty, more as pay than as a bounty.[33]

Most of the high ranking officers who served in Georgia were given special grants as a reward for their services. Five thousand guineas was voted to General Greene and 4,000 guineas to General Wayne, from which the state purchased two choice confiscated estates. For Greene was purchased Mulberry Grove, just outside Savannah—the former property of Lieutenant Governor John Graham and described as "by far the most pleasant seat on the Savannah with an Ellegant tasty house & Gardens & a large Quantity of highly cultivated rice land." A plantation formerly the property of Alexander Wright was bought for Wayne.[34] One hundred guineas with the thanks of the state was voted for every officer in the Georgia Continental Line. This payment was made in certificates which would be received as specie for the purchase of confiscated estates.[35] Colonel Elijah Clarke, Lieutenant Colonel James Jackson, and other officers of the militia and state troops were given confiscated estates as a reward for their war services. Count d'Estaing was granted 20,000 acres of land and made a free citizen of the state in reward for his services at the siege of Savannah.[36]

Besides gifts to living heroes, grants were made to the children of dead heroes in honor of the services of their fathers. Five hundred acres were granted to the son of the Reverend Moses Allen, the Midway parson and army chaplain who had drowned in attempting to swim ashore from a British prison ship at Savannah. Thomas and John Mitchell Dooly, sons of Colonel John Dooly, who was murdered in his Wilkes County home by Tories, were given 500 acres each. The two daughters of General James Screven, of the Georgia Continental Line, were granted 1,000 acres each. At the motion of George Walton, the Continental Congress requested Georgia to erect a monument to Screven at Sunbury at the expense of the United States, but it was the twentieth century before a monument was erected, at Midway. John and George Galphin, the sons of the Indian trader who had been so helpful to the early Revolutionary government, received 15,000 acres in a new Indian cession of 1784.[37]

Permanently maimed veterans were granted annual pensions, ranging from £5 for the loss of one eye to £30 to those who lost both hands or both eyes or were otherwise maimed so as to be incapable of self-support. Widows of soldiers killed in the war were granted £10 a year plus four shillings for each child under age fourteen. Provision was made for orphans of both Continental and state troops.[38] The state, upon the recommendation of the Continental Congress, granted half pay to totally disabled Continental officers living in Georgia. Disabled noncommissioned officers and soldiers were to receive five dollars a month, and those partially disabled were to receive amounts proportional to their disability.[39]

Three instances have been found of the emancipation of slaves for war services. David Monday was appraised at 100 guineas, which amount was ordered paid by the state to his owner. Austin, a mulatto, was praised for his actions against the British, "which would have honored a freeman," was freed, and declared "entitled to all the liberties, privileges and immunities of a free citizen . . . so far as free negroes and mulattoes are allowed." Austin had been disabled through his war services and was paid the same pension received by other disabled veterans.[40]

POLITICS
AND FINANCE
1782 - 1789

12 **

W ITH the evacuation of Savannah by the British in July, 1782, the state government controlled all of Georgia for the first time since December, 1778. The state government's first task was to bring some sort of order out of the chaos resulting from the war and the prolonged British occupation. First, physical destruction must be repaired. Citizens who had left must be induced to return, and the influx of new settlers that the war had slowed down must be encouraged anew, so that Georgia could gain much needed economic and military strength. Adjustments must be made for the loyalists who had left and the slaves that they had taken away. The legal confusion of property ownership, debts, confiscation, and other war disruption must be remedied, so that legal and economic life could flow in usual channels. Finally, Georgia must resume its relations with the United States, which had been virtually ignored since the British invasion.

Priority was given to the generally confused situation of the state, to the providing of food for needy people, and to the disposition of Tories who had not left with the British. The assembly that convened in Savannah in July, 1782, was concerned almost entirely with temporary relief measures and did little of a permanent reform nature.

Throughout the 1780s assemblymen were notoriously slow in convening. Often a week to ten days elapsed between the announced date of meeting and the time a quorum assembled. The initial meeting of each assembly began in early January and lasted about a month or six weeks. The assembly then adjourned until

July or August, when it might or might not be able to get a quorum for a second session. Several meetings called in times of Indian alarm or other emergencies were unable to secure a quorum. Twenty assembly sessions were scheduled between the evacuation of the British in 1782 and the adoption of a new state constitution in 1789, but only eleven secured a quorum and proceeded to business.[1]

Assembly sessions often began by appointing a committee to consider what business needed to be transacted during the session. The January, 1783, session may be taken as an example. On January 11, a committee reported sixteen items that needed consideration.[2] When the session adjourned on February 18, ten of these items had not been settled. Means of meeting state expenses and paying the Continental quota were ignored or postponed. No action was taken to renew laws that were expiring. Nothing was done to regulate customhouses, to build and repair roads and ferries, to establish schools and promote religion, to erect courthouses and jails, or to instruct the state delegates to Congress. Matters which received attention were settlement of accounts due the state, the holding of an Indian congress and arranging the disposition of any lands which might be acquired by the state from the Indians, and the appointment of agents to settle the boundary dispute with South Carolina. Before adjournment, the assembly resolved that two representatives from each county assemble ten days before its summer meeting to consider what new or unfinished business should come before this session.[3]

This assembly appointed a commitee to examine the actions of the government during the war years. The committee reported that from December 29, 1778, until January 7, 1783, since it was impracticable to convene a legislature agreeable to the constitution, various bodies had acted as assemblies and executives and had done what appeared best at the time. Such actions should be reviewed and passed upon by a constitutional government, and those beneficial to the state should be ratified.[4] The assembly took no action on this excellent suggestion.

When this assembly reconvened in July, Governor Lyman Hall laid before it a message that gave a complete picture of the state and suggested necessary actions—one of the few attempts at real executive leadership in Georgia during this period. After congratulating the assembly upon the conclusion of peace, Hall said he was sure that British subjects in Georgia and their reclamation by the state would receive just consideration and that he had written the governor of East Florida on the subject. Indian affairs were serious and needed attention. At a recent conference with the Creeks the anticipated cession of land had not been obtained. Instead, the Indians had left in bad humor because their horses and cattle had been stolen by whites. Whites continued to violate the Indian lands and to mark out lands for eventual settlement before they were even ceded by the Indians. Hall hoped that the assembly would take the drastic measures necessary to hold the whites in check and to prevent an Indian war—an excellent suggestion, but one that no Georgia assembly would take seriously. A sufficient tax to meet the obligations of the state should be imposed, to be paid in specie or produce out of the proceeds of the current crop. Hall had little hopes of realizing any income from confiscated estates, because of the large number of demands upon the estates to settle public accounts and because of the inability of the executive to secure all confiscated property. To improve the moral tenor and to prevent unlawful acts, schools supported by land grants should be established, and all possible encouragement should be given to organized religion. The land laws needed revision in order to guard against monopoly, to encourage settlement, and to secure the future resources of the state. The amount of interest to be paid on pre-Revolutionary debts needed consideration. Finally, attention needed to be given to the military defenses of the state.[5] In line with Hall's recommendations, the assembly revised the land law and imposed the first general tax a state government had enacted since 1778. Others of Hall's recommendations were enacted into law throughout the next few years, but many of his excellent recommendations were completely ignored.

Throughout the 1780s assemblies became more like legislative bodies and seemed less affected by the psychology of recovery. They deliberated more over ordinary legislative business and less over recovery from the war. Procedure became more businesslike in that more standing committees were appointed, less consideration was given to individual petitions on the floor, and more laws were passed as the decade progressed.

A brief review of legislation in the1780s will indicate the main items with which assemblies were concerned. In 1784 all provincial laws and all common or statute law of England in force in Georgia on May 14, 1776, and not contrary to the state constitution and statutes, were declared in force until repealed.[6] The 1785 assembly made a concerted effort to settle the unfinished business from the war years. Back salaries, payments due soldiers and officials, and accounts against the state for supplies used by troops during the war were ordered paid. Much was done to unsnarl land titles which had become confused because of loss of records, incomplete sales, delayed payments, confiscations, conflicting provincial and state action, and general confusion of the war years.[7]

Throughout the decade, petitions of all sorts (especially those praying payment for war services or supplies not adequately documented) took up much legislative time. At first, many received individual attention by the assembly; but later they were referred to standing committees and large numbers were disposed of quickly once these committees had reported. Most assemblies were concerned with the laying out or the improvement of roads, navigation improvement, and regulation of and inspection of imports and exports. Changes in methods of land granting took up considerable time and were closely watched by speculators and those interested in the development of the state. Regulations for sale of confiscated estates were changed often. The application of the acts of confiscation and banishment to individuals was often stayed. Making state income equal to obligations was an annual problem that became less serious throughout the decade.

The assemblies of 1786 and 1787 were especially well organized and run. They worked with dispatch, refused to take up great amounts of time with minor petitions, appointed more standing committees, and showed more trust in the executive than other assemblies. Most assemblies seemed to assume that the executive and former assemblies could not be trusted and that their acts must be scrutinized carefully.

Each assembly adopted a set of rules, usually from nine to fifteen in number, to govern its operation and the conduct of its members. Generally daily sessions began at eight or nine and lasted until two or three in the afternoon, six days a week. The insistence of the rules that members attend promptly or be fined is an indication that attendance was not always good. The rules of 1785 and 1786 may be taken as typical of those adopted throughout the decade. Members were to speak no more than twice in the same debate unless they received the leave of the assembly. All motions and amendments were to be written out by the mover and made a part of the record. Members called to order were to be fined until the third offense, which carried the penalty of expulsion. The fine for the use of indecent language in debate was one dollar for the first time and doubled each time thereafter. There were fines for leaving the floor during a sitting without permission of the chair. Nonmembers were not allowed on the floor during debate.[8]

After the assembly, the next most important part of the state government was the executive, the governor and council acting together. The governor alone could take little action. Ordinarily the council met several times a week, sometimes daily, under the presidency of the governor. The constitution specified that one councilman from each county should always be in attendance upon the governor, but the practice developed of considering a council with representatives from four counties competent to do executive business. The executive considered this matter in 1784 and voted to continue the existing practice, although it did not agree with the constitution.[9]

The biggest item of executive business was the granting of lands and the hearing of caveats about disputed grants. Other duties were the issuing of licenses and passports, qualifying and commissioning civil and militia officers, reviewing petitions when the assembly was not in session, appointing officials in the recess of the assembly or those whose appointment the assembly vested in the executive, offering rewards for the apprehension of criminals, issuing warrants for payment of state debts, and performing other executive duties as instructed by the assembly. Throughout the 1780s the tendency was for the executive to make few decisions that could be referred to the assembly, even though there was a wait of several months.

Besides the governor and council there were other administrative officials elected by the assembly—secretary, treasurer, surveyor general, attorney general, auditor, collectors and other port officials for Savannah and Sunbury, and Indian commissioners. Most state offices were open either from nine until two or from nine until noon and from two until five, as ordered by the executive. Fees ranging from two pence to fourteen shillings were set by the executive or the assembly for most of the services of executive officers.[10] These fees comprised a substantial part of the income of all officials, but no record has been discovered of the total income that any officials derived from fees.

Election campaigns, as that term is now understood, did not take place in post-Revolutionary Georgia. Ordinarily anyone desiring a public office left his name with the clerk of the assembly or a committee for transmission to assemblymen at the time of elections. Frequently assemblymen refused to serve after election, and some councilmen and local officials also refused to serve after election by the assembly. In 1788, James Jackson, a thirty-year-old hero of the Revolution, refused to serve as governor after his election by an assembly because he said that he was too young and inexperienced. William O'Bryan, elected as president of the executive council, also refused to serve and was replaced by George Handley. Handley then took over as acting governor until the assembly elected him governor.[11]

The third department of government, the courts, consisted of a superior court in each county and courts of conscience (justice courts) for local matters. The superior courts were composed of the state chief justice, elected annually by the assembly, and assistant justices designated for each county when its superior court was created.[12] Two sessions of the superior courts, held annually in March and April and in October and November, usually lasted not over a week in each county. The chief justice went from county to county and sat as presiding justice with the local assistant justices. Because of the lack of sufficient jails to hold criminals until the superior court sessions, the chief justice or assistant justices were authorized, upon the approval of the executive, to hold special criminal courts between superior court sessions, with the same jurisdiction as the superior courts. At these criminal sessions, people accused of a felony that was not bailable could be tried.[13]

High points in court week often were the charge of the chief justice to the grand jury and the presentments of the grand jury. Some chief justices, especially George Walton and Henry Osborne, brought up matters of state-wide and national interest in their charges and usually got a response in the grand jury presentments. If a majority of the grand juries presented the same grievance, the assembly would probably consider the matter at its next meeting. Charges and presentments were laid before the executive and assembly and printed in the newspapers. They are often good indications of popular feeling throughout the state.

George Walton was elected chief justice in 1783. Walton was a leader in upcountry political circles and of the opponents to General McIntosh who were responsible for the "forged" letter against McIntosh sent to Congress in 1779. The day after Walton's election as chief justice, the assembly investigated the "forged" letter and ordered the attorney general to bring charges against all those involved in the matter. At the March, 1783, session of the Chatham County Superior Court, the grand jury objected that Walton, the center of the McIntosh troubles and a man who should be prosecuted by the assembly's order, was chief justice. Walton refused to receive the presentments of the grand jury and adjourned the court instead. The grand jury requested Governor Hall to suspend Chief Justice Walton, and Hall did so for the rest of the session. This suspension was reported to the assembly in July, but the body took no action. Walton held the fall circuit of court and was generally thanked for his excellent charges, even in Chatham County.[14] The action of Walton, Hall, and the Chatham grand jury was another incident in the coastal-upcountry struggle for political power.

The absence of any supreme court or appeals machinery in Georgia made for a lack of judicial uniformity and might have created legal confusion. The chief justice could be a unifying force if he were strong enough. Usually he was a trained lawyer; but he could always be outvoted by the assistant justices, many of whom had no legal training. There were some complaints about this lack of judicial uniformity but little demand that a supreme court be created.[15]

Sentences of the courts always reflect the society of the day, and typical sentences of Georgia courts give a good economic and social picture of the times. Sentences varied widely because of the lack of legislative specification or judicial uniformity and also according to the mood of the court or past record of the criminal. Horse stealing might be punished with penalties varying from thirty-nine lashes to hanging. Negro stealing usually brought only whipping. The punishment for murder varied from branding in the hand to hanging, while counterfeiting South Carolina paper currency almost inevitably drew a death penalty.[16]

Admission to practice law in Georgia courts was secured by individual application to the assembly. A 1784 statute required the chief justice to investigate all applicants and to recommend to the speaker those he thought qualified by training and experience. Applicants coming from other states must be recommended by their governor or chief justice and reside in Georgia for six months before they applied to practice in her courts.[17]

Despite the statement of the constitution that the three departments of government were separate and distinct, the assembly and executive exercised considerable control over the courts. The executive suspended two chief justices and the assistant justices of Chatham County at different times. When John Houstoun was suspended as chief justice in 1786, he pointed out that he had refused to assume the duties of chief justice and hence could not be suspended. Had he assumed the office, he said, he would have ignored the suspension which was clearly illegal under the constitution. The executive appointed William Stith, a defeated candidate for the office when Houstoun was elected, as chief justice along with three assistant justices for Chatham County. The assembly considered this suspension and resolved that the executive could not suspend a member of the superior court. However, because Houstoun had declined to accept his appointment, Stith should exercise the office of chief justice until the next election. The suspended assistant justices for Chatham County ignored their suspension, met, and conducted judicial business on April 25, 1786, at which time the attorney general pleaded before them.[18]

The assembly, rather than the courts, was the final authority in constitutional interpretation. It passed at least three acts or resolutions in the 1780s to explain a portion of the constitution.[19] At one time the chief justice requested a constitutional construction from the executive on a recently-passed law. The fact that the matter involved the pardoning of criminals, an executive concern, may be the reason the chief justice requested the opinion of the executive.[20] Several people expressed the belief that in case of a conflict between the constitution and a law, the constitution must prevail;[21] but there is no record of a court declaring an act of the assembly unconstitutional.

Georgia's laws had never been digested, codified, or even collected. Most laws passed after 1763 were printed at the end of each assembly session, except that during the British occupation, 1779-1782, apparently no state laws were printed. There were frequent complaints that copies of the laws were not available to justices to aid them in law enforcement. To rectify this matter, the 1786 assembly appointed Nathaniel Pendleton, one of the leading lawyers of the state, to collect, digest, and arrange all laws and ordinances then in force.[22] Apparently the digest was never made; certainly it was never published.

Georgians had participated in their provincial assembly and courts ever since the creation of royal government in 1754; but there had been only one government in the colony, that at Savannah. The need for local governmental units was not felt until the physical expansion of the 1770s, and the first such units, counties, were created by the state constitution of 1777. Counties had little chance to function properly until the state was cleared of the British in 1782; hence it may be said that local self-government did not really begin until the postwar decade. The constitution did not attempt to divide governmental functions between the state and the counties, but left this to the assembly which gradually gave the counties more powers and duties.

For road construction and maintenance the colonial practice of appointing special commissioners for each road was continued after the war ended, but in 1785 commissioners were appointed by the assembly for each county. Yet the next year when a new road was ordered built between Sunbury and Augusta, the assembly returned to the old program of specially appointed commissioners. In the summer of 1786, the assembly ended its concern with roads by vesting regulation of ferries and roads in the superior courts of each county.[23] In 1789, the executive did order a road constructed by fatigue parties of state troops from the Big Shoals of the Ogeechee to Rock Landing on the Oconee. This road was entirely within Washington County, but it was in a new portion of the state and was ordered built for use in the anticipated Creek war.[24] Before the passage of the 1786 act, the assembly itself sometimes acted to establish ferries and sometimes referred the matter to local authorities.[25] After 1786, improvement of navigable streams continued under the old system of special commissioners.[26] Labor for both road and stream improvement was furnished by requiring a certain number of days of work from all males living along the route traversed.

The establishment of counties, the location of county seats and places for holding elections, the erection of courthouses and jails with the initial appropriation therefor, and the creation of superior courts were all matters determined by the assembly. Tax collectors, registers of probate, county surveyors, and justices were state officials and were elected by the assembly. County officers elected in every county were the sheriff, the clerk of the court, and the coroner. Generally assemblymen and county officials tended to remain in office for several years, especially in the older counties. Only one incident of "campaigning" for county office, that of clerk of the court of Chatham County, has been discovered.[27]

The first machinery of local government was that used in the older colonies, the county court or the justices acting collectively. First superior courts were given control over roads and ferries.

Funds derived from the tolling of strays (cattle) were to be used by the courts in the building and upkeep of bridges.[28] Superior courts had power to lay out districts for courts of conscience.[29] In Wilkes County the court was given the power to levy a tax to supplement the legislative appropriation to build the courthouse and jail.[30] County justices meeting together had authority to oversee the poor and to levy a small tax for this purpose.[31] These were the more important powers acquired by counties in the 1780s.

Town self-government also developed in the 1780s. In 1783 the assembly considered the incorporation of Savannah but took no action. In 1785 all laws relating to the city were collected into one act. Town commissioners were appointed and given control of public property in the city, were directed to oversee sanitary and police regulations, and were empowered to assess and to collect taxes for the necessary expenses of the city government. The commissioners organized at once and levied a tax of three shillings and six pence on every fire hearth, shop or store without a chimney, and unimproved lot.[32] The next year the incorporation of Savannah was again considered, but instead the commissioners were given additional powers.[33] Incorporation came in 1787 when the town was divided into wards, and proprietors of lots or houses within each ward were directed to elect a warden annually. The wardens were to elect a president from their membership, appoint a clerk and other needed officials, levy necessary taxes for the city government, control public property in the city, regulate the public docks, and make all laws and regulations necessary for the city. All other laws regulating Savannah were repealed, and the city had control of its local affairs for the first time since its founding.[34]

The act of 1785 also appointed commissioners for Sunbury and gave them the same powers as the Savannah commissioners.[35] The next year the trustees of Richmond Academy were given the same powers for the government of Augusta.[36] In 1788, the assembly appointed commissioners for Brunswick, in Glynn County.[37] Washington, in Wilkes County, was given no single government but continued to be governed by several sets of commissioners each responsible to the assembly for specific duties— the old pattern of town government in Georgia. The origin of any town-governing body, except in Savannah, was in the need to lay out the town or enlarge it, sell the lots, and use the income thus secured to erect public buildings, especially a building to serve as a church and public school. This combination of duties undoubtedly resulted from the fact that all these things needed to be done and that the income from the sale of lots was essential to the erection of public buildings.

Besides problems of governmental machinery and its operation, there were several political questions of importance that Georgia was concerned with during these times. One of these was the location of the state capital. After the British evacuation Savannah again became the capital. But coastal Georgia had lost its political pre-eminence and much of its economic importance during the war years, and the state had become attuned to the desires of the frontiersmen. Since 1779, Augusta, the center of the rapidly growing upcountry, had been the capital when it was free of the British. In the summer of 1783, the executive began residing in Augusta a part of the time to facilitate land granting, and between 1783 and 1785 moved ten times between Savannah and Augusta. During the same years the assembly held sessions in first one city and then the other. Some of the executive offices moved with the executive; but the permanent offices, except the surveyor general, tended to remain in Savannah.

In January, 1786, the assembly directed that a new town to be called Louisville and located within twenty miles of Galphin's Old Town be laid out as the capital and seat of the university. Until the new town was ready to receive the government, the assembly agreed to meet in Augusta, and directed the executive and executive offices to reside there. Despite this law, in 1789 the attorney general and auditor had not yet moved to Augusta.[38] Louisville did not become the capital until 1795.

Savannah did not like this loss of political importance but was powerless to prevent the moving of the capital. However, she did make her feelings obvious when the secretary's office prepared to move to Augusta. In the colonial period, the secretary's office was the sole office of record in the colony; but the constitution of 1777 directed counties to keep their own records. Before the records in the secretary's office were moved to Augusta, the newly elected chief justice, John Houstoun, and the Chatham County justices went through the records, extracted what they considered Chatham County records, and deposited them in the office of the clerk of the superior court in Savannah. The executive immediately suspended the chief justice and the county justices involved. A newspaper controversy ensued in which the justices set forth their viewpoint at great length. They maintained that they were upholding the constitution and that the moving of county records ordered by the executive was unconstitutional. The assembly considered the matter and decided that the executive had exceeded its powers in this suspension. In November, the disrupted records were reported to be in the secretary's office.[39] For two years Georgia had been reclaiming her public records, which had been scattered from Charleston to Maryland during the war years, and she did not intend to lose them to one of her own counties despite the constitutional opinion of the county justices.[40]

Because of Georgia's need for new settlers and her desire to exclude ex-Tories, another matter of concern was citizenship legislation. The first act on this subject was passed just after the British evacuation and provided that people from other states who desired to become citizens must produce certificates of their attachment to United States independence and of their personal honesty and industry, from a magistrate in the area of their last residence. Natives of Scotland, unless they had fought for United States independence, were forbidden entry into Georgia.[41]

The same act declared that all who neither cultivated sufficient land to support their families nor followed a trade should be termed vagrants and either be sent out of the state or required to serve two years in the Continental Army. Later, a vagrant was defined as anyone who did not cultivate three acres of land or follow a trade. People convicted as vagrants were to give bond for good behavior and for engaging in employment, or they might be bound out for a year's service. Vagrants who could not be bound out because no one would take them for the year's service might either be given thirty-nine lashes and released or enlist as state soldiers. Transported felons from other states or countries were not allowed to settle in Georgia.[42]

To carry out the 1782 law, all transients who came into the state were required to register with the attorney general or a justice of the peace.[43] A number of aliens who did not come under the provisions of the act made application to the assembly for citizenship, which was usually granted.[44] A general naturalization bill passed in 1785 provided that aliens who desired to become citizens must, after twelve months' residence in the state, obtain certificates of their honesty and friendship for Georgia from a grand jury. Citizenship was then conferred by their taking an oath of loyalty to Georgia, but voting and office-holding were not allowed for seven years. No one who had fought against the United States or who was named in any act of confiscation or banishment could be naturalized. Aliens who were citizens of friendly powers could own or rent land and could sue in state courts for debts that arose after July 20, 1782.[45] After this act, the assembly continued to admit some individuals to citizenship by special act without the prescribed waiting period. Frenchmen who were properly introduced were allowed to become full citizens after three years' residence, or after one year if they married a United States or a Georgia citizen.[46]

In many respects one of the most persistent problems before the state government in the 1780s was finances. During the occupation of the state by the British, no tax bill had been passed, and state government had lived as best it could by borrowing and by informal financial arrangements. At the British evacuation the only source of state income was from the sale of confiscated estates or payments by people named in the act of amercement. It was hoped that confiscated estates would meet the state's immediate financial needs; but, in the summer of 1783, Governor Hall reported that little more could be expected from that service and that a general tax was necessary. The 1783 assembly passed a tax bill, directed the collection of taxes and duties in arrears, and imposed a tax on items sold at public vendue.[47] The first postwar import duties were imposed early in 1784.[48] The state's income henceforth came from taxes, import duties, license fees, land sales, and a small amount from the sale of confiscated estates. Throughout the 1780s continuous attempts were made to force people who had received public funds during the war to settle their accounts.

In Georgia, as in other states, large amounts of bills of credit and other paper money were issued during the war to meet current expenses. Purchase or impressment of military and civilian supplies was made by numerous officials on the credit of the state. When the war ended, the state did not know how much it owed, because no accounts had been kept. People with accounts for or against the state were directed to have them audited. After the auditor had checked and approved accounts against the state, he issued certificates for the indebtedness, known as audits or audited certificates, which could be used in payment of half the purchase price of confiscated estates.[49]

The same law provided that certificates or audited accounts of state indebtedness not exchanged for confiscated property might be exchanged for new certificates—commonly known as funded certificates—bearing interest at seven per cent per annum in specie and redeemable in seven years. People entitled to funded certificates rushed to secure them; consequently, the state's interest payments increased greatly. Because many bonds given in payment for confiscated estates were defaulted, and because there was never enough specie in the treasury, funded certificates were issued and received at the treasury in lieu of specie. Taxes were poorly collected, and collectors were often several years behind in their accounts with the treasury. Import duties were evaded because of insufficient collection personnel. Confusion reigned supreme in the treasury, and the only sure thing was that the state owed more than it could pay and never had enough specie.

Early in 1783, a table of depreciation for paper money issued during the war was established by law, to be used in settling both public and private accounts. In January, 1777, paper money and specie were declared equal in value. By January, 1778, the ratio was specie 100, paper 287½; January, 1779, specie 100, paper 798 1/10; January, 1780, specie 100, paper 3,378 3/10; and June, 1780 (when the table ended), specie 100, paper 8,114 7/10. Continental currency was made to depreciate even faster, so that by June, 1780, its value was specie 100, paper 16,229 1/10.[50] Two years later, a law required that all Revolutionary bills of credit be exchanged with the auditor for specie certificates at the rate of £1 specie for £1,000 bills of credit if still in the hands of the original holders, or at the depreciated rate if in the hands of others.[51] By these two acts, most of the war indebtedness of the state was repudiated or greatly reduced in value.

It is impossible to make any exact accounting of the state's financial condition throughout the 1780s. Until 1786, no official was able to present a complete picture. Records had been fragmentary before 1782, and after 1782 they were often poorly kept and not promptly turned over to new officials. Every assembly appointed a finance committee, but the reports from year to year show little continuity. Most committees seemed concerned only with the affairs of the current year, and showed little concern for the total financial picture. It was often recommended that a complete accounting be made, but nothing was done until 1785-1786.

Treasurer Seth J. Cuthbert made a complete report of the state finances to the assembly that convened in January, 1786. He pointed out how the funding law of 1783 had increased the amount of interest payable until it consumed practically the entire specie income and that little interest was paid on the bonds due to the state. Because there was no specie in the treasury, the executive had authorized the acceptance of interest certificates on funded certificates for specie payment due to the state, and much of the taxes and import duties paid since the summer of 1785 had been paid thus. Cuthbert was afraid that specie payments would cease entirely because of the increase in the amount of funded certificates. He suggested that both interest and principal of funded certificates be accepted in payment for personal bonds, when they fell due, to take up funded certificates and stop payment of interest by the state for which no specie was available. This plan would cancel state debts upon which interest was due in specie with indebtedness to the state upon which no interest could be collected. Cuthbert also recommended that a system of allocating certain income for specific expenses be devised so that the state's rapidly deteriorating credit could be improved.[52]

The assembly took no action on these recommendations but did object to the executive allowing the treasurer to accept interest certificates in lieu of specie and also objected to a subordinate officer applying to the executive on a matter about which the law was very specific. The assembly was sure that sufficient funds had been appropriated in 1785 to support the government had specie been paid into the treasury as directed by law. No funds were available, yet nothing was done to pay pressing demands and past due salaries.

The assembly was not able to determine the status of suits by the state against defaulted bonds in the treasury, but it did not think that much income could be realized in this way. It had no hopes of collecting any specie as long as funded certificates and current expense warrants were outstanding. £21,780.13. 4 was appropriated for the current year; and the executive was ordered to anticipate the entire expected income from taxes by the issuance of £8,000 in treasury drafts to be received for all taxes and other specie payments due the state, except duties on tonnage and shipping.[53] Despite assembly objections to the executive's handling of finances and accepting certificates in lieu of specie, it had no better ideas itself and ordered the issuance of new certificates whose acceptance as specie would preclude any specie coming into the treasury. After much labor, not even a molehill was brought forth.

Governor Edward Telfair gave a complete report of state finances to the summer session of the 1786 assembly. A total of £220,633.10. 3¼ was due to the state, most of it in personal bonds received in payment for confiscated estates. The public debt was listed at £204,424. 0. 1½ — £119,368. 9.1½ in audited accounts, £72,523.15. 5 in funded certificates, and small amounts of other types of obligations. Telfair recommended that a system be devised to liquidate the state debt with the sums owed to the state, so that the state could operate on a specie basis. Especially, he recommended that the old debt be drawn into one debt to relieve the complicated bookkeeping in the treasury. If this were done, Telfair was sure that all funded demands upon the treasury would be reduced and the state's credit improved.[54]

Instead of action on the governor's request for a general overhaul of the state's finances, the assembly refused even to act upon the finance committee's recommendation that the next assembly study the matter. It did provide for the issuance of £50,000 in bills of credit to meet the pressing needs of the treasury and cancelled the £8,000 treasury drafts authorized in February.[55]

A report of January 1, 1787, showed a reduction in the state debt to £185,649. 6. 2½ — £155,382. 2. 2¾ in audited or funded certificates and the rest in current indebtedness. During 1786, £29,930.18. 3¼ in audited and funded certificates had been received in the treasury along with £24,729. 9.10¼ in other types of income. This was an indication that the state's financial condition was improving, a fact which Governor George Mathews confirmed early in 1787. However, Mathews lamented that the paper medium was in "low credit." Collection of personal bonds and interest due the state had not improved.[56]

In 1787, £45,410. 7. 3 in state emissions was taken into the treasury. Since many tax collectors had not reported their collections when this report was made, the state's income and reduction in indebtedness was really greater. In 1787, £47,358.11.10 was reported paid out of the treasury—£26,131. 9. 8½ for current expenses and the rest for audited and funded certificates and the bills of credit issued in 1786. In 1788 the assembly approved the treasurer's receiving any type current obligations of the state for sums due to the state.[57]

State income and expenses are hard to determine because often the only figures available are estimates at the beginning of the year; and all figures of actual income and expenditures are incomplete because of the slowness of many county officials in reporting. The largest regular items of expense were salaries and per diem for councilors, assemblymen, and members of Congress. Executive salaries amounted to between £2,000 and £3,000 a year. The governor received from £300 to £500, usually £400; the chief justice and auditor usually £300 each; and other officials from £20 to £200.[58] Total estimates of state governmental expenses ranged from £15,000 to £20,000 a year exclusive of Continental requisitions, Indian treaties, and military expenses. For 1789 regular state expenses were as follows:[59]

Salaries and office expenses of executive officers	£3,020
Payments to tax receivers	2,480
Contingent fund	2,000
Members of assembly at $2 per day	3,000
Members of executive council	3,000
Continental delegates, with arrears	1,500
Total	£15,000

Because the treasury was usually empty of specie or negotiable instruments, the state often had difficulty in securing funds for ordinary expenses. As long as any resources were left from confiscated estates, they were used; but this source was about exhausted by the end of 1783. The state frequently resorted to barter. To get £1,500 in goods needed for a 1783 Indian treaty, rice was exported to East Florida to pay for goods secured from British Indian traders. Disabled veterans were paid their pensions with drafts on the treasury which would be received in payment of custom duties from any merchant who let the original recipients have the goods he desired. The little specie was usually paid out to Continental delegates, who could not be paid in state paper. When Joseph Clay tried to collect 7,253 livres due for military stores purchased during the war from merchants in Cape Francais, the treasurer was directed to deliver to Clay bonds due to the state that would produce this sum when sold or collected. When Benjamin Franklin requested payment for his services as colonial agent, the assembly said that it could not order a specie draft but ordered 3,000 acres of land granted to Franklin, survey expenses to be paid by the state.[60] The regular method of paying salaries and state expenses was to issue warrants signed by the governor or speaker, directing that the funds be paid by the treasury. The recipients of these drafts used them to pay taxes and amounts owed to the state or sold them to someone who did have state obligations to pay. Favored creditors got drafts "for the first specie that comes into the Treasury," but usually there was no specie.

Upon the recommendation of Governor Lyman Hall, the assembly passed in the summer of 1783 the first general tax bill since 1778. Because of the distressed condition of the state, the tax was confined to a quarter of a dollar on every 100 acres of land, every slave, and every town lot; one dollar on every free Negro or Mulatto; and two dollars on every male twenty-one or older who did not follow a profession or trade or cultivate at least five acres of land. The executive remonstrated that the tax was too small to fulfill the needs of the state and that one-half of a dollar was the absolute minimum required, but the assembly was deaf to these entreaties.[61]

The summer session of the 1784 assembly never secured a quorum; so no tax bill was passed that year. The 1785 tax rates are quoted as typical of the postwar years.

£. s. d.

4. 0 per £400 value of lands granted or surveyed. Land was classified into fifty-two types and values according to its location.

4. 8 poll tax on all free white males 21 or over, entitled to vote

2. 4 on all slaves

4. 0 on every £100 value in town lots, wharves, buildings, etc.

9. 8 on every four-wheeled carriage except wagons, carts, and drays

4. 8 on every two-wheeled carriage except wagons, carts, and drays

1. 1. 9 on every free Negro, Mulatto, or Mestizo 21 to 60 years old

4. 0 on every £100 stock in trade

1. 1. 9 license fee on doctors, lawyers, factors, brokers, and vendue masters.

Double tax was levied on all vacant lands owned by adult males who did not live in the state and on vacant lands over 2,000 acres regardless of ownership. Half of the tax might be paid in audited or funded certificates.[62] Tax rates varied from year to year and were considerably higher in 1787 and 1788 than in 1785.[63]

Despite the need for revenues and stiff penalties for non-payment, tax collection was very poor. In every tax law, tax receivers and collectors were appointed for the counties and were paid on a commission basis for the amounts collected. Many of these refused to act or delayed making returns or payments to the treasury. Of the thirty-three tax returns due from collectors for 1785-1787, fourteen had not been made by March, 1788.[64] Repeated instructions from the executive to take action against delinquent tax collectors did not improve the matter. At the end of 1786 only £1,322. 0. 7½ tax money had been paid into the treasury, and most of it came from Chatham County. Later four counties made complete returns, and £8,377. 3. 4 for 1786 taxes had been paid into the treasury by 1788.[65]

In addition to the regular taxes, there was for 1788 a specific tax of six shillings and three pence on every £100 worth of property, levied to support state troops raised to fight the Creeks. This tax could be paid in foodstuffs, and at the end of the year £4,925.12. 8½ had been received while £3,515.15. 6 was yet due from county collectors. Because of the Indian troubles in Liberty, Glynn, Camden, Washington, Greene, and Franklin counties, the assembly allowed the collection of arrears in these counties to be suspended, and apparently no more was collected.[66]

Import and export duties on foreign trade had been standard in colonial Georgia. The only duty that was in effect when the British evacuated Savannah in 1782 was a duty on raw hides exported to any area except Great Britain, and this duty was probably not collected. A transient duty may have been in effect, but this is uncertain.[67] Certainly a transient duty was imposed on July 30, 1783, but it was soon reported as being studiously evaded by importers.[68] The first general duty levied after the war was 2½ per cent of the prime cost of all goods imported, imposed by an assembly resolution of February 11, 1784. The same assembly passed an act for regulating trade, laying duties on imports, and impost on tonnage and shipping; but no copy of this act has been located and nothing is known of its contents. The next year the assembly agreed that transient duties should not apply to citizens of other states because they did not apply to Georgians.[69]

The three tariff acts for the 1780s that have been located[70] are similar as to items taxed, amount of duty, and general provisions. Specific duties were laid on most items imported regardless of value. A few items and all imports not given specific duties were taxed according to value. Rates were set to discourage or prohibit the importation of slaves from other states or the West Indies, unless the importer intended to settle in Georgia, in which case there was no import duty. Imports from British possessions were taxed one-third to three times higher than the same items from non-British territory. Any import not the product of the United States was taxed even if it came from another state, but products of the other states entered duty free. Goods ordinarily entered through the ports of Savannah and Sunbury (Brunswick and St. Marys were added by the end of the 1780s) and overland from Charleston, mainly at Augusta.[71] Although a collector for Augusta was appointed after 1787, collection was difficult for overland imports. Imports in United States-owned vessels were entitled to a twenty-five per cent reduction in duties; if the vessel were built in the United States there was an additional ten per cent reduction. There were port fees and tonnage duties that were applied to the expense of port operation and the upkeep of the seamen's hospital in Savannah. The 1787 and 1789 duty acts specified that they were to remain in force only so long as they did not conflict with acts of the United States Congress.

A report of income from customs duties has been found only for the period February 1-December 31, 1788, and shows a total of £4,637. 5. 9½. £4,082. 1.11 was paid into the treasury and the rest used for harbor and office expenses. Treasurer Seth J. Cuthbert in his 1786 report to the assembly estimated that £500 had been evaded by importers in the past several months, and there were other reports of customs duty evasions at Augusta and the state ports.[72]

ECONOMIC AFFAIRS
1782 - 1789

13

****

WHEN fighting stopped in the summer of 1782, most Georgians hoped the economic expansion that had been interrupted by the war would begin anew and soon compensate for the losses of the war years. Joseph Clay, a Savannah merchant and conservative Whig leader, said that things looked better every day. Old inhabitants were returning and new ones were coming in rapidly. The richness of the back-country lands had impressed soldiers from other states who saw Georgia during the war; and the opening of the land office early in 1783 helped migrations, especially from Virginia and the Carolinas. In April, 1783, five hundred families were reported to have settled in the back country in the past six months.[1] A North Carolinian wrote, "Georgia must, *I think,* in a few years be one of the Richest States in the Union, and Where I've no doubt, you may live happy and secure a lasting and Valuable Estate for your self & family. . . ."[2]

As soon as the British left, Joseph Clay returned to Savannah and entered into business again. He endeavored to resume his old business relations with merchants in England, Philadelphia, and the West Indies and insisted that he intended to pay his pre-war debts. This would take time because plantations must be repaired of war ravages and be supplied with implements, work stock, and slaves. However, Clay said he was willing to deed land to his creditors at market prices if they desired it.[3]

Because of the great need for goods in Georgia, the state was anxious to trade and in 1783 opened its port to all who had

209

anything to sell.[4] The stocks that the British merchants had in Savannah at the evacuation were soon exhausted, and merchants were looking for permanent sources of supply. Joseph Clay thought that trade with the West Indies would be good, especially with the non-British islands, as long as the strong anti-British feeling lasted. He carried on extensive trade with Cuba and Jamaica before it was slowed by a state embargo on the export of provisions, imposed from November, 1782, through June, 1783. Naval stores, masts, spars, staves, shingles, and all sorts of lumber were reported available for export, but few provisions were offered before the embargo. Clay was sure that Georgia would need to import more than formerly because of the influx of new settlers, but he thought there would be little to export before the 1783 crop was ready for market and possibly not much before the 1784 crops could be marketed. Georgia needed plantation supplies and tools, Negroes, and cheap textiles and clothing in 1783. The demand for goods in Savannah made prices there considerably higher than in Charleston. Clay thought there would be insufficient trade between Savannah and Philadelphia in 1783 to fill a regular vessel, but that vessels between Philadelphia and the West Indies could profitably stop at Savannah.[5] In the spring of 1784, he reported that Georgia trade was thriving, that prices of imports were good, and that much trade was back in old channels with a good demand for farm supplies.[6]

The absence of customs house records and Joseph Clay's letter books for most of the 1780s makes precise information about Georgia's foreign trade difficult to secure. There are records of ship arrivals from June, 1783, through September, 1786, and for most of 1788, as well as customs house figures for part of 1788 and 1789. However, available information does indicate the general directions that trade took and the types of things that were imported and exported.

The efforts of Georgia merchants to establish trade between Georgia and Europe were helped by the appointment of consuls by several European governments and the desires of European merchants for American trade. A French consul general for the states from Maryland south was appointed in 1783, and there was a Georgia deputy by 1785. A Dutch consul for the three Southern states, Jan Bonner Graves, appointed in 1785, resided in Charleston. A British consul, George Miller, was appointed for the three Southern states in 1787; and he appointed a Savannah deputy, John Wallace, in March, 1788.[7]

In 1782, Casper Voght and Company, of Hamburg, in a letter to the governor and assembly of Georgia, pointed out the superiority and cheapness of German goods in comparison with British goods usually bought by Americans. Items available were listed with the offer to send a personal representative and samples if desired. Three years later Arnold Delius, of Bremen, was in South Carolina and Georgia to buy local produce and to sell German goods.[8] Available records of ship arrivals and departures show little direct trade between Europe and Savannah. London and Liverpool were the European ports most often mentioned. Amsterdam, Rotterdam, Hamburg, Lisbon, and Bordeaux are mentioned only a few times each.

Arrivals and departures of vessels in Savannah indicate that there continued to be more trade with Charleston than with any other port and that Charleston continued to act as port for much of Georgia's foreign trade. There was considerable intercourse with St. Augustine as long as it was British, but this stopped almost entirely after it became Spanish in 1785. After Charleston, West Indian ports are most frequently listed for ship destinations and sources. The British islands—Jamaica, Barbados, and New Providence—outranked the Danish, French, and Spanish possessions represented by St. Croix, Cape Francais, Hispaniola, and Cuba. So far as the United States was concerned, Philadelphia ranked first, Baltimore second, and New York third.[9] Georgia continued to do most of her trade with Britain and her possessions despite British restrictions against American trade, objections of Georgians to these restrictions,[10] and higher import duties on British goods. Britain was the one sure source of manufactured goods that Americans knew and wanted.

Savannah and Sunbury had been colonial ports of entry. In 1785 the executive appointed Henry Osborne the first collector for St. Marys and other areas south of the jurisdiction of the collector at Sunbury. In 1787 a separate collector was appointed for Brunswick.[11] The trade of Georgia ports other than Savannah was inconsequential and confined almost entirely to Savannah, Charleston, and the West Indies. Import and export figures for Georgia's ports have been found for only the months of March through October, 1788. Exports were valued at about £55,433 and imports at £50,000. Duty of £1,565 was collected on imports.[12]

Georgia's trade retained its colonial pattern so far as items of export and import were concerned. Exports were mainly rice, lumber, lumber products, naval stores, and some tobacco. Imports were West Indian sugar and rum, manufactured goods (from plantation tools to fine clothing—mainly from Europe), bar iron for a little local manufacture of hardware, flour and biscuit, and other food products not produced in sufficient quantity in Georgia (e.g., apples, potatoes, wine). To maintain the quality of its exports, Georgia continued the colonial practice of insisting that all items be inspected before export. A full complement of port authorities, including a "health officer and Surgeon" who headed the seamen's hospital, were kept at Savannah. Other ports got along with fewer officials because of the smaller amount of business carried on through them.

Local trade was carried on by merchants who might or might not have connections with foreign or Northern merchants. The main items sold were farm and plantation supplies, clothing, Negroes, some luxuries, and items used in the Indian trade. Some prewar merchants (Joseph Clay is the best example) continued in business after the war. Many old merchants did not survive, and new arrivals were added. Big merchants continued to import European goods and to export Georgia produce, and smaller merchants often bought imports from and sold Georgia produce to a larger merchant. The British merchants allowed to remain at the evacuation of Savannah got their time extended, and there were complaints that they were still present in 1784. Crookshanks and Spiers, one of the larger of the houses remaining, advertised in January, 1785, that they would close their business and leave Georgia as soon as possible. Evidently these British merchants stayed so long in an effort to collect old debts which they knew they would have little chance of collecting once they left Georgia, and to keep connections for British houses interested in the American trade.[13] From the advertisements in the *Gazette,* there seem to have been fewer mercantile houses in Savannah in the 1780s than in the colonial period, but they may have done as much or more business. There were more merchants in Augusta; they became increasingly general supply merchants and factors for the rapidly expanding upcountry of which Augusta was the economic and political capital. Savannah and Augusta merchants continued to do some Indian trade, but this became relatively less important, probably because of more farming in the back country and because the British firm of Leslie, Panton and Company remained in the Indian supply business at Pensacola after the Floridas became Spanish territory.

As before the war, a number of tradesmen and artisans advertised that they were just arrived from Europe and were thus conversant with the latest styles. There was an increase in the number who advertised themselves as coming from Paris or France and fewer from London. Some came from Philadelphia and other Northern cities. The fact that a number of such tradespeople located in Augusta is an indication that it was a growing town and that the people of the upcountry were demanding more of the better things of life. One watch and clock maker evidently found insufficient business in the frontier town of Washington, Wilkes County, for in the fall of 1787 he advertised his removal from Washington to Augusta.[14]

Manufacturing, encouraged by both private individuals and the state, made some progress. In 1785, Clay, Telfair and Company of Savannah contracted with Jeremiah Fox, tobacco and snuff maker of Philadelphia, to come to Augusta and set up a tobacco and snuff manufactory, teach the employees the necessary operations, and superintend the factory for the first eighteen months. Fifteen months later Fox endorsed the contract as completed with cash settlement by Clay, Telfair and Company; but no record of the success of the venture has been found.[15] In 1788 Thomas Glascock advertised that he had erected bolting cloths at his mill, in or near Augusta, and had a white attendant from Pennsylvania who completely understood flour manufacturing.[16] When James White and David Robertson asked help in erecting an ironworks, the assembly voted them 5,000 acres of pine land if the work should be finished in three years, a premium of £50 for the first ton of good bar iron produced, and exemption of all employees from militia duty and the payment of poll taxes for five years. Benjamin and Adoniram Allen were granted £500 upon giving satisfactory security to erect an iron bloomery in Wilkes County within two years.[17] No record has been found of the amount of iron produced, if any, by these two ventures.

An acute shortage of currency continued to plague business. Specie was especially short, and drafts on the Northern states or London were difficult to procure. To entice specie into Georgia, the assembly voted to give all foreigners, even if their nation was at war with the United States, the right to loan money at 7 per cent interest and to have equality with citizens in recovering current debts in the state courts.[18] This law was probably intended to bring British funds into Georgia by guaranteeing equal treatment to foreigners, though not recovery of prewar debts.

To relieve the currency shortage and to provide expenses for an anticipated Creek war, £50,000 in bills of credit was authorized for issue in 1786. These bills were to be redeemed in four years out of the proceeds of the sale of lands between the Altamaha and the St. Marys, were declared legal tender, and were to be taken for all specie payments due the state. The bills were to be issued in denominations from six pence to twenty shillings, to encourage their use in ordinary business. Four shillings and eight pence was declared equal to one dollar. Only £30,000 in bills was issued, presumably because the Creek war did not materialize.[19]

There was immediate objection to these bills, mainly from Savannah merchants and artisans, many of whom agreed not to take the money. The upcountry approved the issue of the bills just as strongly as Savannah objected. At a public meeting in Augusta on December 2, 1786, action was taken to encourage the use of the bills and to bring unfavorable public opinion upon any who refused to accept them.[20] Punishment prescribed for counterfeiting these bills was death, but reports were soon current that they were being counterfeited.[21] The lands pledged to the support of the bills could not be sold because of Indian troubles; and despite all efforts of the government and the upcountry, the bills depreciated rapidly. The assembly was willing to admit a depreciation of 33⅓ per cent by January, 1789, and directed that £5,000 of the bills be withdrawn from circulation and burned immediately and each year thereafter for the next four years, while the time for their complete redemption was extended until January 15, 1794.[22]

In agriculture, as in politics, one of the most notable changes after the Revolution was the development of the upcountry. The lands north and west of Augusta had been opened to white settlement by the Indian cession of 1773 and had filled up rapidly before the Revolution began. The partisan fighting in the back country had hurt settlement during the war, but land-hungry pioneers rushed in once the fighting had stopped. These lands were suited to the production of small grain, livestock, and tobacco. Large plantations or rice and indigo were not suitable to the upcountry as they were to the low country. Most new settlers were relatively poor and owned few, if any, slaves. A small-farmer subsistence type of agriculture developed with grain or flour, meat, furs, and lumber products the main money crops.[23]

The large number of slaves carried away by the British and the influx of new settlers created a shortage that made slaves hard to get and high in price in the 1780s. Just after the British evacuation, slaves were reported selling as high as 200 guineas, but six months later the price was 70 to 100 guineas. Prices from £50 to £100 or more for field hands continued to be quoted throughout the decade. Because of the insistence that slaves brought into the state come from Africa and not from West Indian plantations, it was harder to secure the desired number; but Joseph Clay and other merchants tried to make arrangements with London merchants for a supply direct from Africa. As late as 1787, Clay reported a good market for Negroes—more of a demand for them than there was money to pay for them.[24]

Georgia's 1783 crops were insufficient to meet her own needs, let alone to pay for the large amount of imported goods needed. Clay estimated that three times as much land would be planted in 1784 as in 1783.[25] Production and the amount of land cultivated increased rapidly throughout the decade; there was also an increase in land granted and in population.

Rice planting continued upon the coastal plantations, but it never regained its former position of predominance. Because irrigation systems on many plantations had been damaged during the war and the slaves carried off, recovery of large coastal plantations was delayed; and the coast was put at a disadvantage when compared to the new lands in the back country.

Perhaps the crop that increased greatest in importance was tobacco, which was raised in the fertile upcountry area. This crop could be used locally or exported; the state insisted that the quality of tobacco exported be kept up to standard by continuing the colonial practice of inspection. In 1783, the assembly appointed inspectors, who were to receive one dollar per hogshead inspected, set standards for exportation, and set up official warehouses where tobacco might be inspected and stored. Because no public warehouse existed in Augusta, the inspectors there were to build one at their own expense and were given the exclusive right of storing all tobacco brought to Augusta in the next twenty years. Under the inspection law of 1785 warehouses were to be maintained at Augusta, Savannah, on Broad River, and at the mouth of the Ogeechee River. A public warehouse large enough to accommodate 300 hogsheads of tobacco was erected at Washington in 1789 by the town commissioners.[26]

Indigo continued to be cultivated for several years after the Revolution, as contemporary newspapers and export figures for 1789 show. Evidently the disruption of the old trade with Britain, the loss of the British bounty, the British encouragement of indigo production in the East Indies, and the introduction of cotton were responsible for the decline of indigo production in the 1780s and 1790s.[27]

The first cotton had been grown and exported from Georgia in the colonial period. Sea-island and upland cotton were grown for domestic use and on an experimental basis in the 1780s. Roller gins were used for separating the seed from the lint of sea-island cotton, but no satisfactory gin was developed for upland cotton until Eli Whitney's gin of 1793.[28] In 1788 a Charleston newspaper reported that a large hogshead of cotton in seed had been rolled to Charleston from Wilkes County, Georgia, in the same manner that tobacco was rolled, and that the man who brought it reported that considerable cotton was grown in his area of Wilkes County.[29] During the 1780s better methods of growing upland cotton were discovered, and all was prepared for the great rush in cotton production that was to begin in the early 1800s.

Some effort was made to stimulate hemp production in Georgia and the other Southern states. A small amount of hemp continued to be grown, as in the colonial period, but not enough to be of much commercial value.[30] Cattle raising continued on the frontier and on uncultivated lands in the older part of the state. During the war there had been much confusion as to cattle ownership because of the great amount of cattle raiding done by both Whigs and Tories into areas each held and because branding and care of cattle were often neglected. The state declared in 1783 that all cattle with obliterated marks were state property and should be collected to feed the state troops and people in need.[31] Cattle-production methods continued much as before the Revolution, with the use of brands (which were recorded by the state to protect them), drovers, cowpens, and slaughtering and salting of meat for export. A few horses were exported during the 1780s.[32]

Prices of coastal lands held up for awhile immediately after the war despite the fact that much land could not be cultivated

because of the lack of slaves. Prices quoted in 1782 ranged from
£2 to £8 per acre. The next year Joseph Clay priced land to correspondents at £12 sterling per acre for unimproved swamp,
£22 sterling for improved tide swamps, and sixty shillings for rice
land at the head of swamps. By the end of the decade, prices of
coastal lands had declined considerably.[33] Most of the land sold
from confiscated estates brought between five and twenty shillings
an acre. One tract of 2,500 acres sold for £10 an acre, the highest
price discovered for confiscated land. No prices for upcountry
improved lands have been found.[34]

Not only agriculture, but almost everything in post-Revolutionary Georgia was tied to the land-granting system and the
number of new settlers who moved in. After the fighting stopped,
the hunger of frontiersmen for good virgin land set off a great
rush into Georgia's back country. Veterans of the Revolution
wanted the land bounties promised during the war, and the old
southward drift of frontiersmen in search of good land brought
others to take up the best virgin land then available in the South.
Land speculators helped advertise the movement. Georgians
realized that economic and political advancement, as well as protection from the warlike Creeks, was dependent upon increased
population, and that good land would draw settlers quicker than
anything else. Georgia therefore made land easily available to
any and all who wanted to settle.

Land allowed under the old headright system was increased in
early 1783 to 200 acres free (except for office and surveying fees)
to heads of families. Up to 1,000 additional acres could be purchased on the basis of 50 acres for each member (white or black)
of the family at the rate of one shilling per acre for the first 100
acres and an increase of six pence per acre for each additional 100
acres. Land courts were to be held by the justices of each county
once a month, at which applications for lands were received and
warrants for survey issued, a duty previously performed by the
executive. After the land was surveyed, the fees paid, and the
grantee had lived on it for six months and improved three acres
out of every 100, the executive made the final grant.[35] The executive recommended that the issuing of warrants for survey be
taken from the county land courts and returned to it, but the
assembly took no action.[36] The land act of 1785 made all headright grants up to 1,000 acres free except for office and surveying
fees.[37]

When the new counties of Franklin and Washington were laid out in 1784, a special land court (composed of the governor and three members of the council) initially issued warrants for survey in these counties. Lands were to be settled within fifteen months of the issuance of the warrants, or the warrants would lapse. No taxes were to be paid for the first three years if the lands were settled and cultivated according to law. The lands between the north and the south forks of the Oconee River up to the temporary Indian line were to be reserved for twelve months for officers, soldiers, and seamen (except refugees and militiamen) who were entitled to bounty grants from Congress or the state. Bounty grants in the military reserve were to be made without any costs except office fees and without requirements as to settlement or cultivation. As an inducement to new settlers, nonresidents were allowed to reserve land for twelve months in these counties before they moved to Georgia.[38]

This special land court met in Augusta on April 6, 1784, and began to receive petitions and issue warrants for survey.[39] Its troubles in issuing 2,000 or more warrants to land-hungry frontiersmen were graphically described by its clerk, David Rees. "Fancy to yourself," Rees wrote to Governor John Houstoun, "my dear sir, the Honorable the President and members of Council, four or five in number, convened on the business of their countrymen, and 1500, or perhaps 2000 men, set on by designing villains, approaching the doors with threats and menaces, crying out aloud, that their warrants they would have at any rate." Finally, the grantees were calmed and persuaded to wait an additional week until all the warrants could be prepared and ready for issue. Then came the day for handing out the warrants. Pandemonium reigned because everybody wanted his warrant immediately. As Rees said, "The general vocification was, why can't I get *my* warrant, as well as another such a one has got his—and by G--d I'll have mine. My office was no longer one at my command; the breach being made—the Torrent soon widened it—and he thought himself the happiest person that could *Grab* the greatest number of them [warrants]. The Alphabetical order that I had observed was soon obliterated, and no trace of regularity or decorum left. They soon had the warrants—from my Table—on the floor—at the door and on the highway—about 4 or 500 were soon missing by this outrage." Many of the missing ones were later returned; duplicates had to be made for the others. "Speculation, as I hinted before, has certainly extinguished in many men, passing for Gentlemen, every spark of Probity and Integrity. Many have sworn that instead of 287½ acres of land, for which their warrants were made, they were entitled to 575 acres, and others, *on second thought* have deposed that they petitioned or meant to petition for the other County, in both of which cases the warrants are taken up, and new ones made out accordingly."[40] Rees, like many residents from the coast, was certain that he did not like frontier democracy in the raw but was helpless in knowing how to combat it. It is no wonder that the coast did not trust the upcountry, which was getting so much political power into its hands.

When the executive met in Augusta in September, 1784, and signed grants for the warrants issued by the special land court in April and May, there is the first evidence of soldier bounty grants being issued.[41] The majority of grants issued in the 1780s were for under 1,000 acres and well within the headright and bounty systems. There were individual grants for as high as 20,000 acres, and many individuals received numerous grants that totaled well into the thousands of acres.[42] Most speculators secured bounty warrants from veterans who needed money at once or who were not interested in the lands—especially from veterans who did not live in Georgia. There were Georgia state and militia officers who signed certificates stating that veterans who had served under them were entitled to bounty lands and then themselves acquired the warrants of survey and the lands when granted.[43] Thomas Carr and Richard Call are examples of Virginians who secured Revolutionary warrants in Virginia, came to Georgia and secured the lands, and settled at Augusta as land speculators. Carr and others brought slaves from Virginia and engaged in farming and slave trading as well as land speculation. Call and other speculators bought lands from the commissioners of confiscated estates; but, since this business took more money than the acquisition of survey warrants, the practice was less common.[44] John Wereat was close to the truth when he said that nothing but land speculation interested Georgians. Lachlan McIntosh complained that the speculators in bounty warrants made agreements with the county surveyors and that veterans found it almost impossible to get their own bounties surveyed.[45]

Because of the frontiersman's desire for the best land and because of the great rush into the back country, there never seemed to be enough land available. There was a continual demand that more land be secured from the Indians and opened to white settlement. Many people pushed over the Indian boundary line and selected and settled upon good lands still belonging to the Indians. Despite the efforts of the government to prevent such action, it could never be stopped. Land laws stated that settlements beyond the Indian boundary were void, but many people must have secured grants to lands they had settled illegally. Indian cessions were settled almost as soon as they were ceded by the Indians and often before they could be surveyed.[46]

The mix-up and destruction of records during the war years created great confusion about land titles. The assembly and executive devoted much time in trying to correct the confusion. The usual procedure in cases of missing or incomplete records was for people to petition that certain lands be confirmed to them because of missing records or incomplete grants. If there were no conflicting claims of ownership, the assembly usually confirmed the titles as requested.[47] Much of the executive's time was taken up in passing land grants and settling disputed cases between individuals who claimed the same lands.

The destruction of markers, the movement of markers by people who wanted to increase the size of their holdings, the general inability to find permanent markers in a new and wild country, and the poor or hurried surveying that often was done all contributed to the confused system of surveying and marking lands. At times it was necessary to compel people to renew their markers or to have their lands resurveyed. There is no doubt that many people received much more land than they were entitled to under the bounty or headright system. The basis for grants was an affidavit by the grantee as to what he was due for bounty or headright purposes. For a bounty grant, a certificate from the ex-commanding officer was also necessary. Land was plentiful, and many people were not too careful what they swore to. In 1788 the surveyor general was ordered to pass no warrants of over 1,000 acres and to stop all abuses of the land laws that came to his knowledge.[48] A final note on land granting was an order by the executive that no grants be passed which included the whole or part of the Broad or Savannah rivers, which should be the common property of all Georgians.[49]

SOCIAL AFFAIRS
1782 - 1789

14

****

IN SOCIAL matters and institutions, during the postwar decade two effects of the Revolution were evident—an attempt to return to prewar conditions, and a turn toward democratization. Georgians soon discovered, with regret, that the war had changed much in their everyday lives and that only in the fields of amusement and poor relief was it possible to return to approximate prewar conditions. The separation from Britain and the general leveling effect of the war generally destroyed any official status of individuals or institutions. The budding aristocracy and the established church were gone. The idea of freedom and opportunity for the common man was perhaps most obvious in the establishment of a public school system and in the changes in religious organizations. In considering life in this period, it is important to realize that Georgia was an area dominated by the frontier viewpoint. Postwar leaders were rougher and more uncouth than the colonial leaders, and the tone of society changed accordingly.

One of the first and most obvious changes in the social field was the disestablishment of the Anglican Church by the state constitution of 1777. Immediately after the British evacuation in 1782, organized religion was at a low ebb. The Anglican and Lutheran clergy had left with the British; and the outstanding dissenting clergy, Zubly and Moses Allen, were dead. Itinerant Baptists had effected little permanent organization in the upcountry. Church buildings were either destroyed or in bad repair, congregations were scattered, and governing bodies were disorganized. The most pressing problem for most Georgians was economic support for the here and now rather than concern for the hereafter.

However, there were Georgians who thought that religion and education should receive official encouragement. Eleven days after the assembly returned to Savannah, a bill was introduced for the establishment of churches and schools, but consideration was postponed.[1] Early in 1783 the executive called upon the inhabitants of each county to meet in their churches to elect vestrymen, church wardens, and other needed officials. On Easter Monday Savannah Anglicans met and chose vestrymen and church wardens, and the trustees of the Presbyterian Meeting House soon called a meeting to consider physical repairs and procurement of a minister.[2] In 1784 bids for repairs on the Presbyterian and Anglican churches and the Anglican parsonage in Savannah were advertised for, and the glebe lands of Christ Church (Anglican) were advertised for rent.[3]

In his opening message to the assembly on July 8, 1783, Governor Lyman Hall, a New Englander by birth and education, recommended that laws be passed to restrain vice and to encourage virtue and that encouragement be given to religion and education. The assembly agreed to a committee report recommending the establishment of churches and schools, but took no further action. The same month a number of inhabitants of Augusta petitioned the assembly that the glebe lands at Augusta be sold and that the money be used to construct a church to replace the one destroyed during the war. The assembly agreed to the sale of lots and directed the erection of a church and seminary of learning with the proceeds. The 1784 assembly considered a bill "for promoting religion and piety" but took no action.[4]

The 1785 assembly passed a religious establishment act that was the transitional step between a single established church and voluntary support of religion. The act declared that a knowledge and practice of the Christian religion tended to make good men and citizens, and that the regular establishment and support of religion were among the most important objects of legislative action. The bill directed heads of families in each county with thirty families to choose a minister, who should "on every Sunday Publickly explain and Inculcate the great doctrines and precepts of the Christian Religion as opportunity shall offer." County ministers' salaries should be paid from state taxes collected in each county. All sects and denominations were to have equal liberty and toleration in the exercise of their religion, and presumably in the choice of county ministers. Religious societies already in existence were confirmed in all usages, rights, immunities, privileges, and public appropriations which they already held.[5]

The only evidence of any application of this church establishment law was a notice for Episcopalians in Chatham County to give in their names to the church wardens so that tax money could be received from the state under the law. In 1786 the Baptist Association remonstrated against the law to the assembly, but the assembly took no action toward repeal.[6] However, there is no evidence and little likelihood that the law ever went into effect. It was invalidated by the constitution of 1798 but never repealed.

The 1785 assembly also passed a new marriage law. In many areas no clergyman was regularly available, and many people had long ignored the colonial requirement that marriages must be performed by a clergyman. The new law legalized all marriages previously performed by a minister or justice of the peace and provided that henceforth all ordained ministers and justices of the peace might perform marriages after eight days' public notice or upon authority of a license issued by the governor or register of probates. This recognized an existing practice that it would have been difficult to change, especially in the back country.[7]

Existing churches all had difficulty securing ministers in the immediate postwar period. The Anglicans in Savannah are known to have had a rector for at least the first three months of 1784 in the person of the Reverend John Holmes, an S. P. G. missionary to St. George's Parish before the Revolution and one of the two Whig Anglican clergymen in Georgia. After the death of Holmes, March 20, 1784, there are indications that there was no regular rector at Christ Church for about two years. The Reverend Edward Lucas kept a grammar school at the parsonage in 1786, and it is assumed that he was rector as well before the arrival of the Reverend William Nixon in July. Nixon remained at Christ Church for about two years, and the Reverend Benjamin Lindsay was rector in June, 1788. Apparently the Episcopalians had no parish organization at Augusta until the summer of 1789.[8]

When the British withdrew from Ebenezer, the Salzburgers began restoration of their damaged town and church. Since the pastor, Christopher F. Triebner, had left with the British, a new pastor was requested from Germany. Temporary pastors sometimes served the Ebenezer and Savannah Lutherans until John Ernest Bergman arrived from Germany in the spring of 1785 to take up pastoral duties at both places. Bergman set about immediately to repair the damages to the Lutheran church organization brought about by the war and the division of its congregations. The next year there appeared Christian Eberhardt Bernhardt, who remained at Ebenezer as schoolmaster for about a year. Bergman remained at Ebenezer and continued his pastoral duties well into the nineteenth century, but the church never regained its former position of dominance in the community. Only one pastor could be employed, as opposed to two or three before the war, because the funds formerly available from the Society for Propagating Christian Knowledge were cut off. The close knit feeling of the Salzburgers broke down with the Revolution. Some Lutherans tended to become Methodists and Baptists; Bergman himself had close relations with the Methodist Bishop, Francis Asbury, who usually visited Bergman during his trips to Georgia.[9]

The Congregationalists at Midway also had trouble in securing and keeping ministers. They had at least two young Yale-trained ministers during the 1780s, Abiel Holmes and Jedediah Morse, each of whom remained a short time.[10] The church organization continued to function, but the building burned by the British in 1778 was not replaced until 1792, when the substantial frame meeting house which still stands was built.

In the last half of the 1780s, the Methodist and Baptists began the growth in the back country that was soon to make them the leading denominations in Georgia. The first Methodist minister came to Georgia in 1785; and the next year two other ministers, John Major and Thomas Humphries, arrived. At the end of a year's toils, they reported 430 Methodists in the state, mainly in upcountry Wilkes County. Work of ordained and lay preachers made Georgia important enough for Bishop Asbury to hold the first Methodist conference at the forks of the Broad River in Wilkes County in 1788. Asbury reported that many who had no religion in Virginia found it upon removal to Georgia and South Carolina, where he was sure the Methodist Church would flourish.[11]

There had been Baptist ministers in Georgia since the early 1770s. Daniel Marshall, the best known early Baptist clergyman, died at his church at Kiokee in November, 1784, after a busy and eventful life. A Georgia Baptist Association was separated from the South Carolina Association in 1784 or 1785, when five churches are known to have existed. Thirty-one churches, a few of them in

South Carolina, were represented at a meeting of the Georgia Association in October, 1788.[12]

Although many of the settlers of the upcountry were Scotch-Irish, the Presbyterian Church never made the effort to minister to this area that the Methodists and Baptists did. There were by 1788 no more than eight or ten Presbyterian churches in upcountry Wilkes and Greene counties. Independent Church, Zubly's old church in Savannah, was repaired; but nothing is known of its operation or activities in the 1780s nor of the Presbyterian Church among the Scots at Darien.[13]

There was probably Jewish worship, at least periodically, in Savannah after 1786, when the Jews are reported to have rented a house to be used for religious services.[14]

Education, the handmaiden of religion, made considerably more progress in postwar Georgia than did religion. The constitution of 1777 provided that "Schools shall be erected in each county, and supported at the general expense of the state. . . ," but nothing was done to carry out this provision until after the fighting stopped. In his July, 1783, assembly message, Governor Lyman Hall recommended that steps be taken to encourage both education and religion. In the field of education Hall recommended that land be granted to endow schools and that property formerly used for the support of education but then in private hands be secured by the state.[15] The assembly passed a bill which directed commissioners to lay out lands at Augusta in acre lots, sell these lots at public auction, and use the income thus secured for the erection of a church and seminary of learning. The public ferry at Augusta and the income from it were put under the control of the commissioners. The commissioners were authorized to procure professors, institute by-laws, and conduct the academy. The same act appointed commissioners to lay out Washington in Wilkes County and Waynesborough in Burke County, sell the lots, and use the income to erect a "free school" and church in Washington and the necessary public buildings in Waynesborough. One thousand acres of land was authorized to each county in the state for the erection of free schools.[16]

When the University of Georgia was chartered in 1785, its governing board was given general oversight over all publicly supported schools in the state and was directed to inspect them and to make general recommendations about schools, their curricula, and instructors. The next year the assembly directed that academies be established in every county, appointed commissioners for each county, and voted £1,000 value of confiscated estates plus vacant lands to support each academy.[17]

Richmond Academy, at Augusta, the oldest public school in the state, began operation on the second Tuesday in April, 1785, in new buildings erected for its use. Its initial rates were four dollars per quarter for children in the first stage (letters, spelling, and reading), five dollars for those in the second stage (English grammar, writing, and arithmetic), and ten dollars for those in the third stage (Latin or Greek and mathematics). By July fees were reduced to two, three, and five dollars per quarter for the three stages. The next year the commissioners were given additional lands for the benefit of the academy, and newspaper publicity indicates that henceforth the academy prospered.[18]

Besides Richmond Academy, Augusta had private schools, which helped to make it the cultural center of the upcountry. A French School was advertised in 1786 and an evening school in January, 1789, where S. Chandler would teach French, arithmetic, bookkeeping, geography, use of globes, mensuration, algebra, trigonometry, heights and distances, astronomy, navigation, surveying, and gauging. An adjunct to public education in Augusta was the Academic Society which held public debates at the academy. The catholic interests of the society are indicated by the subjects announced for debate: "Is it consistent with the policy of the American Republic to establish a Navy?" "Which is the most desirable, a very beautiful and accomplished young lady, with a small, or no fortune, or one of an ordinary person, good sense, large fortune, and advanced in years?" "Is the knowledge of the dead languages a necessary part of education in this country?" "Would universal toleration, in religion, be consistent with good government?"[19]

The academy in Washington began operation in January, 1786, with a rector and one tutor. By November it held an examination before the chief justice, commissioners, and other gentlemen and gave a play in the evening. Rates ranged from two to six dollars per quarter. In 1788 the academy moved one mile out of Washington to Chalybeate Springs, reputed to be a very healthy spot and one where students would be more immediately under the supervision of the rector than in Washington.[20]

Savannah continued its pattern of private day and evening schools at which French, English, ancient languages, reading and

writing, navigation, bookkeeping, needle work, dancing and music, and many other subjects were offered to the public. Schools
were taught by clergymen and laymen, natives and recent immigrants, men and women—in short by as varied a group of instructors as the curriculum which they offered.[21] The assembly on
February 1, 1788, established an academy for Chatham County,
appointed trustees, and set aside vacant lands and confiscated estates for the support of the school.[22] Actual instruction at the
Chatham Academy was delayed for some months beyond its
founding.

The act establishing Chatham Academy confirmed ownership
of the property of Bethesda College to the Countess Dowager of
Huntington, to whom it had been willed by George Whitefield.
Bethesda reopened in June, 1788, under the patronage of the
Countess of Huntington. The Reverend David Phillips, lately
come from England, was superintendent of the school and the
Reverend Benjamin Lindsay, Rector of Christ Church, was classi-
cal tutor. Instruction was to be given in English grammar, writing, use of figures, every branch of mathematics, use of globes,
Latin, Greek, and French. Fees were thirty guineas per year, including board, washing, etc. Bethesda was called a college, but its
instruction was on a par with that of the newly-founded county
academies and the private schools.[23]

The academy for Liberty County was established by law in
Sunbury in 1788, and £1,000 value of confiscated estates was set
aside for its support. At the same time commissioners were appointed to resurvey the town of Brunswick, as nearly as possible
on its original lines, to sell town lots, and to build an academy
for Glynn County at Brunswick.[24] There is no record that the
Liberty and Glynn County academies began operations in the
period of this study.

Besides county academies, Georgians were also interested in a
state university to provide higher education and to coordinate the
educational system. The movement for a university got its beginning from New England-born and Yale-educated men, Governor
Lyman Hall and Abraham Baldwin. As noted above, Hall recommended to the assembly in 1783 that education and religion should
be encouraged in order to restrain vice and encourage virtue.
This message, which was concerned with the entire realm of
government, was referred to a special committee of Joseph Clay,
Edward Telfair, and John Houstoun. The assembly agreed to a

committee report which directed that a reserve of land for the endowment of a college should be laid out in each new county created thereafter.[25] Seven "Trustees for a College" (John Houstoun, James Habersham, William Few, Joseph Clay, Abraham Baldwin, William Houstoun, and Nathan Brownson) were elected on February 24, 1784, and the next day the counties of Franklin and Washington were created with a reserve of 20,000 acres of land in each to serve as an endowment for the college.[26]

Abraham Baldwin's address to the trustees at what was probably their first meeting shows that he was mainly responsible for the organization of the university. He pointed out that there was no university south of Virginia and that it was bad policy to send youth out of the country to be educated in foreign ideas and ideals. He suggested that the proposed university be located in a healthy climate and have sufficient land attached to raise fresh milk and provisions that would provide an adequate and cheap diet for faculty and students, help to support charity students, tend to promote an interest in gardening and agriculture, and prevent student mischief. All that was necessary to begin a university whose main concern was practical education and not the knowledge of the ancients would be a small collection of books for instruction in "the principles and rudiments of language, more particularly of the English; the ready and exact use of numbers; some of the first principles of Geography, History, Mensuration, a Pair of Globes, and some small part of a Philosophical apparatus." After these books and apparatus were collected, students and a tutor could be sought. Once the university began operation it would increase in students, facilities for instruction, and usefulness. Baldwin then proceeded to outline a constitution under which he thought the university should operate. It was so similar to the charter as passed by the assembly in 1785 that it seems obvious that Baldwin wrote the charter, which tradition has long attributed to him.[27]

The charter of the University created a board of visitors of the governor, council, speaker of the assembly, and chief justice to visit the University and to see that the intent of the assembly was carried out. More immediate control was vested in a board of trustees to consist of the seven trustees named in 1784 plus John Habersham, Abiel Holmes, Jenkins Davis, Hugh Lawson, William Glascock, and Benjamin Taliaferro. Both boards, united into one, made up the "Senatus Academicus of the University of Georgia," which made University statutes, subject to disallowance by the assembly. The president was appointed by the Senatus Academicus upon the recommendation of the trustees, who appointed all other faculty members and set salaries, had direct control of University property and funds, prescribed the curriculum, and adopted regulations for the University. Faculty members and officials were required to be Christians, but no student "of any religious denomination, whatsoever," was to be denied full equality and liberty at the University because of his religious beliefs. The president, with the consent of the trustees, was empowered to confer all honors, degrees, and licenses that were usually conferred by colleges and universities.

The Senatus Academicus was directed at its annual meetings to consult and advise upon matters of the University and on other matters, "to remedy the Defects, and advance, the Interests of Literature through the state in general." Its members were to study the schools in their counties so that they could recommend types of schools and curricula needed. The president and trustees were directed to inspect once a year all schools which received public funds, all such schools being considered a part of the University. Thus all public education was put under the Senatus Academicus or trustees who were directed to make recommendations to the assembly for the entire educational system.[28]

Such was the educational system planned for the small but rapidly growing frontier state. Much of the thinking and work came from Abraham Baldwin and Lyman Hall, Yale-educated New England immigrants. Ezra Stiles, the president of Yale, was consulted by Baldwin before the charter was written.[29] The system was a bold dream that could be projected only by a young commonwealth certain of great days ahead. It was helped both by the republican enthusiasm of the eighteenth-century enlightenment and by the successful fight against the political control of England. It was a part of the rise of the common man who was coming into his own in control of state politics, carefully guided by educated leaders who believed in human perfectibility, even of crude frontiersmen. County academies and a state university would insure continued democracy and liberal political institutions. Such was the dream of the Revolutionary generation. The University did not begin operation until 1801, and the entire educational system outlined in its charter was never fully achieved. The vision of a new day to be brought about by an educated and enlightened electorate was disturbed and delayed, but it still lingers in the hearts of many Georgians.

An important adjunct to education, especially in a society that believes in freedom of expression, is the press. James Johnston, Georgia's only colonial newspaper editor, was named in the state act of confiscation and banishment. He was, however, taken off the act in August, 1782, and put on the act of amercement. He reclaimed his printing equipment and in January, 1783, secured a contract as state printer and brought out the first issue of the *Gazette of the State of Georgia* (renamed *Georgia Gazette,* October 23, 1788). Johnston was no more rabid Tory than others who were put on the bill of amercement; his political beliefs never seemed to interfere with his journalistic or printing abilities; and he was undoubtedly the only available editor and printer in Georgia.[30]

The format and contents of Johnston's newspaper continued much like the former ones, but more local news was now included. Account of state marriages and deaths were included. The longest funeral notice went to Samuel Elbert, Revolutionary leader, Continental and Georgia officer, and ex-governor. Elbert's funeral in Savannah was attended by the Cincinnati, Masons, county militia, and many prominent citizens.[31] The announcement that Joseph Clay, the son of the Savannah merchant of the same name, had won a medal at Princeton commencement for the best dissertation on the subject "What are the best means to be adopted by civil government for the promotion of piety and virtue among the people?" was carried with considerable pride.[32] Johnston did not forget former Georgians who had returned to England. The marriage of ex-Lieutenant Governor John Graham's daughter in London was thought worthy of note. The same issue carried an account of the death of "Sir Patrick Houstoun, Bart. of this State, who about 12 months ago went to London. The many amicable qualities of this worthy gentleman having rendered him extremely dear in life, his death cannot but be an event of uncommon concern and regret to his numerous connections and acquaintances."[33] Two other and more important ex-Georgians got shorter notices and no favorable comment. A London dispatch of November 22, 1785, reported, "Yesterday morning died, at his house in Westminster, Sir James Wright, Bart. many years Governor of Georgia." And in the summer of 1786, "General Oglethorpe, died August last, aged 103."[34] Oglethorpe had really died

June 30, 1785, at the age of 89, but his age was commonly reported much greater in the British press.

Augusta got its first newspaper in the summer of 1785 when Greenberg Hughes began publication of the *Augusta Gazette,* which lasted for a year or longer. On September 30, 1786, John Eardman Smith began the publication in Augusta of the *Georgia State Gazette,* or *Independent Register.* On April 4, 1789, the name was changed to *Augusta Chronicle and Gazette of the State.* Through these two newspapers, the present *Augusta Chronicle* claims its birth date to be August 30, 1785. Continuity since September 30, 1786, can be traced, and it seems that there is continuity from the earlier date through the *Augusta Gazette.*[35] Augusta was now the capital, and Smith soon became the state printer. He sold the usual paper, writing supplies, and blank forms and did job printing. To secure greater circulation, Smith frequently announced the fact that he would take indigo or tobacco in payment for subscriptions and requested various prominent citizens throughout the state to act as subscription agents for him.[36]

Another reflection of a society, especially of its social consciousness, is the treatment it gives to unfortunates. Truly the poor are always with us, but after a war there are often more unfortunates than usual. This was true in 1782-83 because of the destruction of the war years and because of the returned refugees who had no means of immediate support. Until a crop could be planted and harvested, the state government found it necessary to procure food and distribute it to the distressed inhabitants. Salt procurement and distribution were especially difficult in the immediate postwar years and took up a great deal of the executive's time.[37]

In 1785 the executive was doubtful if the temporary relief act of 1782 was still in effect, but the next year a comprehensive and permanent poor relief act was passed by the assembly. It provided that a special session of the county justices should be held after the spring term of the superior court in each county to bind out orphans and other children in need and to appoint overseers for the county poor. This court was empowered to levy a tax of not over six pence per £100 property valuation, to be used for poor relief.[38]

Private agencies supplemented governmental relief. The Savannah philanthropic organization, the Union Society, had resumed its prewar activities by 1784. There is a record of at least one meeting every year thereafter except for 1788. Between 1784 and 1789 nineteen children, mostly orphans, were bound to tradesmen or sent to their relations. In 1786 the assembly incorporated the Society with twenty-one members, most of them prominent Savannah Jews and Christians, for the relief of distressed widows and for the schooling and maintaining of poor children.[39]

The lazaretto, or quarantine station on Tybee Island, the subject of so much colonial executive and legislative consideration, lost its prominence in the postwar years. It must have been no longer used or some mention of it would have been discovered. There was little governmental concern with smallpox after the war, in contrast to frequent concern before the war. Once the executive directed the attorney general to investigate a report that a Savannah Negro had smallpox and to have him removed to Tybee Island if he had the disease. In 1786 Governor Edward Telfair issued a proclamation during a smallpox epidemic in Augusta giving permission to all who wished to be inoculated and directing quarantine measures to be taken.[40] The assumption is that the disease remained as serious as it had been in the colonial period but that the government gave up its close medical supervision. Some pretense at keeping up a hospital for sick seamen in Savannah was made after 1784, when port fees were applied to its upkeep. Beginning in 1786 the assembly elected a health officer and surgeon annually to head this hospital.[41]

Little record of doctors living and practicing in Georgia has been discovered, beyond the notices of several doctors beginning practice in Augusta. However, there were undoubtedly doctors in Savannah and throughout the state, and there is no reason to doubt that the state was as well supplied with doctors after the war as before. Bond & Company, the one drug store known to have existed in Savannah, announced its opening in 1786. It would sell medicines and compound physicians' prescriptions, sell medical instruments, garden seed, and painters' colors, and put up medicine boxes for ships and plantations.[42] Medicine continued, as formerly, to be sold by merchants and doctors.

Besides being concerned about the sterner matters of religion and education, and the unfortunate and sick, Georgians were interested in affairs of a lighter nature. There was in Savannah a theater, housed in the filature in 1783 and perhaps later, that was staffed by a local association of gentlemen whose efforts were at intervals supplemented by visiting actors and entertainers. Tragedies and comedies were presented, often with short one-act "entertainments," "farces," or comedies in addition to the main bill and with music between the acts. Plays were presented as commercial enterprises, for the benefit of charity, and for the benefit of certain actors. Prices of admission ordinarily ranged from three to five shillings per seat.

From October, 1783, through June, 1784, nine plays were advertised for presentation in Savannah, seven of them for the benefit of charity, and apparently all by local talent.[43] In April, 1785, twenty-eight inhabitants of Savannah petitioned that Dennis Ryan and his company of comedians be allowed to perform plays in Savannah, but the executive refused the request on the grounds that the petition was signed by too few people to support the players. However, in June a large group secured permission for James Godwin and John Kidd, of Charleston, to perform plays in Savannah for nine nights.[44] They advertised at least eight different plays, including *King Richard III* and *The Taming of the Shrew*, during the summer. In November Godwin and Kidd petitioned for permission to give plays occasionally in order to pay their Savannah debts, an indication that their summer season had not been too profitable.[45]

At the end of 1785 a group of Savannahians were granted permission to open a theater in the town. Soon the *Gazette* carried news of improvement of the theater "by way of Boxes, to accommodate six or eight Persons each." The opening play was Dr. Young's tragedy *Revenge* plus a three-act comedy, *The Mayor of Garratt*. The actors were members of the Charitable Society of Savannah "with the assistance of Messrs. *Godwin* and *Kidd.*" Throughout January and February a play a week was advertised, with benefits for Mrs. Godwin, Mrs. Kidd, and the musicians. Plays continued through June but on a reduced schedule.[46] Visiting actors and other entertainers, usually on the West Indian Circuit, visited Savannah at rather rare intervals. There were also such entertainments as tumbling and posturing feats "by a person who has performed in London"; there were also lectures, and other popular entertainment.[47]

Judging from the number of licenses to sell liquor and to keep houses of entertainment, no Savannahian needed to go thirsty if he desired alcoholic drink. A coffeehouse was opened on the bay in the fall of 1785 that advertised coffee at any minute from seven in the morning until nine at night, as well as at breakfast, dinner, and supper. There was a spacious dining room for dinners, large parties, and private balls; there were private rooms for business and small parties, and a few rooms available to genteel lodgers. A book of ship arrivals and departures was to be kept, and all the principal newspapers were to be procured from the different states.[48] If the advertisement was carried out, no American town as isolated as Savannah could hope to offer more.

Music was not neglected by teachers and performers. A number of people advertised to teach instrumental and vocal music in schools or private homes, during the day or evenings. In 1785 John Hiwell, who declared himself a former inspector of music in the American army, advertised that he would give a concert for his benefit and teach all instruments if he got enough scholars. He met with enough success to remain in Savannah eight months and perhaps longer.[49] Music teachers sometimes also set up in Augusta when they did not get sufficient encouragement in Savannah. Dancing schools were popular. In the fall of 1785 Mr. Godwin, the actor, advertised a dancing school with morning, afternoon, and evening sessions. The next March he announced that he was giving up the stage but would continue to teach dancing. Charles Francis Chevalier advertised a school where he taught dancing and fencing in Savannah in 1783 and in Augusta three years later. Besides these and other teachers who located in Savannah, there were visiting artists (mainly musicians and portrait painters) who stopped in Savannah to display their talents.[50]

Social clubs undoubtedly existed in Savannah as they had formerly, but little record has been found of any. A hunting club was organized in December, 1783, with twenty-one leading citizens as charter members. Other applicants could be admitted to membership if no member voted against them. Every member was to furnish a beagle for the use of the club and to provide a good mount for himself. Bread, beef, or ham, and a case of liquor were to be provided by the club at its meetings, which were to be held every second Saturday.[51]

By the summer of 1785 Augusta was growing rapidly and was taking on a new importance as the upcountry metropolis. The academy was opened. A newspaper and printing office began operation, and regular postal connections with the outside world were established. New houses and stores were built.[52] The next year additional lots were laid out, and Augusta became the capital of the state. Social life in Augusta was similar to that in Savannah but had less elegance and more frontier characteristics. No record of any theatrical performances has been found. Balls and concerts are mentioned frequently, but the races were the main social event. There was a Jockey Club by 1785 which offered purses as high as a hundred guineas. For the December, 1786, races a purse of £100 sterling was offered the first day, £50 the second day, and £30 the third day. In addition prizes of £3 for the best stall-fed beef, 30 shillings for the three best muttons, and 20 shillings for the two best veals were offered. In the evenings after the races, balls were held.[53] At least one celebration of St. Tammany's Day in Augusta was recorded with a hundred gentlemen participating in the festivities—a procession and a dinner with eleven toasts.[54]

Little record of social functions outside Savannah and Augusta has been found. The usual frontier social functions took place, and horse racing was certainly engaged in wherever a sufficient number of people and horses could be collected. Notice of two plays presented in Washington (probably by local actors) have been found.[55] Other plays may have been presented by local actors, but the presence of touring actors or entertainers outside Savannah or Augusta is extremely doubtful.

For Georgians who wished to join, there were fraternal orders that had both a social and civic program. The Masonic order flourished, especially in regions where there were a sizable number of Virginia immigrants, and included many leading citizens in its membership. There were at least six lodges in the state by 1787. An annual meeting of all lodges was held in Savannah every December at which state officers were elected.[56] Besides the annual meeting and meetings of individual lodges, there were usually celebrations of saints' days, especially St. John's Day. Such celebrations usually consisted of a procession to the church, a sermon, a "most excellent" dinner, and the remainder of the day spent in "extreme harmony."[57]

The Georgia Society of the Cincinnati was organized on August 13 and 14, 1783, in response to an invitation from the national society. General Lachlan McIntosh was elected president; Colonel Samuel Elbert, vice president; Captain John Milton, secretary; Lieutenant Colonel John McIntosh, treasurer; and Major John Habersham, assistant treasurer. Most of these officers retained their places until 1789 when General Anthony Wayne was elected president and a new slate of officers installed. The Georgia Society usually held quarterly meetings in Savannah, or in Augusta if the assembly was in session there. At these meetings Society business was transacted, a dinner was served, thirteen toasts were inevitably drunk, and the "day concluded with joy and satisfaction, everyone feeling a soldierly affection for each other." The main business was the election of officers and delegates to the general meeting and the reading of dispatches from the general society. In Georgia, the Society seems to have been a fraternal order entirely. There is no record that it was opposed as "aristocracy" or that it tried to exert any political influence. Its membership was too small to exert much influence upon the state had it tried. At the 1788 and 1789 meetings, toasts were drunk urging Rhode Island and North Carolina to adopt the United States Constitution. Besides the Continental officers, a few French and Georgia state officers were admitted as honorary members. Along with the Georgia State Society, there was a district society at Augusta.[58]

Georgians were especially fond of all days that could be celebrated with liquid refreshment. A pattern for July 4th celebrations developed in Savannah and Augusta, which began with a parade and review of the military (Continental and state troops and militia) and a public dinner for the troops participating. At an "elegant repast" for the military officers, civilian officials, and important guests, thirteen toasts were always drunk. The rest of the day was usually spent in the "utmost good form and patriotic endeavor." There were often addresses by local or visiting officials and sometimes a Cincinnati address or a special church service. Augusta was more likely to end the day with a ball and concert than Savannah and other towns, and all towns might be illuminated at night with candles and bonfires. The account of the Savannah celebration for 1784 reports that plenty of people were drunk but that there was no bad behavior. Accounts have been found of celebrations in Savannah, Augusta, Washington, and Wrightsborough, and by state troops in the field. The toasts drunk at Savannah in 1783 are a good example of July 4th toasts:

1. The state of Georgia
2. The United States in Congress assembled
3. His Most Christian Majesty Louis the 16th, our great ally
4. His Catholic Majesty the King of Spain
5. The Seven United Provinces
6. General Washington and the Patriot Army of America
7. Cavalier de la Luzerne

8. Count Rochambeau and the gallant troops which served under him in America

9. Our Ministers at foreign courts

10. The Navy of the United States

11. The memory of those American Heroes who sealed the Liberty of their Country with their blood

12. May trade and commerce flourish

13. May this Anniversary continue a Festival until the latest posterity.[59]

Toasts changed from year to year to fit the current situation. In 1785 two were concerned with Georgia's relations with the Confederation: "May Georgia never need exertion to comply with her confederal engagements." "May Congress never want support to maintain the liberties of the States."[60]

Only one record has been discovered of the celebration of Washington's birthday in Georgia. This was a dinner for some thirty gentlemen who had served in the war, held at the State Hotel in Savannah on February 11, 1786. The usual thirteen toasts were drunk. The vessels in the river displayed their colors and fired their cannon in honor of the occasion.[61]

Most personal social life must have been of the sort not recorded in the newspapers or personal letters of the day. Certainly there were private parties and drinking bouts, literary and musical sessions for those interested, dinners of all sorts, horse races, and the usual combination of fun and work that went together on the frontier. Though the separation from Britain resulted in the dropping of old days of celebration and the adding of new ones, the pattern of celebration remained the same. The greatest changes in entertainment came from the increased commercial recreation resulting from the increasing population and the increasing predominance of the common man and of the frontier in the state.

INDIAN RELATIONS
1782 - 1789

15

****

THROUGHOUT the war years, many Creeks cooperated with the British in fighting the Whigs, but the Cherokees had given little trouble after their defeat by Georgia and the Carolinas in 1776 and 1777. Georgia's first Indian trouble after the British evacuation in 1782 came that fall when South Carolina and Georgia militia under General Andrew Pickens and Colonel Elijah Clarke went into the Cherokee country to eliminate a troublesome group of Tories. The Tories were driven into Florida, several Indian towns were destroyed, and at Long Swamp in October the Cherokees ceded to Georgia[1] lands south and west of the Tugaloo and Savannah rivers. The next May Georgia commissioners met Cherokees at Augusta to make the first general settlement since the British evacuation. Here the Cherokees confirmed the Treaty of Long Swamp, giving to Georgia all their lands between the Savannah and Keowee rivers on the east and the Oconee River on the west. These lands were on the fringes of the nation and apparently were not highly prized by the Cherokees.[2]

Relations between Georgia and the Creeks were good for a few months after the British evacuation. The British commander at St. Augustine and British Indian Superintendent Thomas Brown said that they tried to keep the Indians quiet, and the Creeks undoubtedly realized that little more British help could be expected. The British Indian Department in the South was closed in the summer of 1783, but Superintendent Brown remained in St. Augustine for several more months.[3]

Georgia negotiated with the Cherokees at Augusta in May, 1783, and tried, unsuccessfully, to negotiate with the Creeks at the same time. Part of the Cherokee cession secured at this time was claimed by the Creeks, and Georgia was anxious to get the Creeks to cede all their lands east of the Oconee River, a strip of land forty to sixty miles in width and some 200 miles in length. The Creeks refused to come to Augusta probably because of promises of help from the British in St. Augustine and the bad treatment they had received from Georgians who violated their lands and stole their horses and cattle.[4]

Another reason why the Creeks refused to treat with Georgia was Alexander McGillivray, who had recently risen to a position of leadership in the Creek Nation. McGillivray was the son of a Savannah Scottish Indian trader and a half-breed Creek woman of a chief's family. His natural ability was polished by education and business experience in Savannah and Charleston before the war. When his loyalist father returned to Britain, Alexander took up residence among the Creeks and nursed his hatred of Georgia and Georgians. His Indian blood and training, his ability, his knowledge of white men and their ways, and his hatred of Georgia and Georgians made him a leader among the Creeks in their bitter struggle with Georgia over the lands east of the Oconee River. McGillivray's power among his people was such that his influence and favor were sought by the British, the Spanish, and the Americans. He at various times held civil and military office under all three governments, sometimes from two at the same time. His influence among the Creeks is undeniable, despite the fact that he was a white in all his personal tastes, lived in a plantation house with Negro slaves in the midst of the Creek Nation, and never addressed a public Creek meeting except through an interpreter. McGillivray revived the old Creek policy of playing Georgia and the United States against Spain and of appealing to both without letting either know what the other had promised in hopes of thus getting more for the Creeks.[5]

In the 1780s the Creek Indians occupied territory that is today approximately the lower half of Alabama and Georgia west of the Oconee River. The nation was divided into two major groups, the Upper and the Lower Creeks. The Lower Creeks' towns were located mostly along the Chattahoochee and Flint rivers with hunting lands as far east as the Oconee. The Upper Creeks were located along the Tombigbee and Alabama rivers with easy access to Mobile and Pensacola. The Lower Creeks, especially some of their chiefs, tended to be friendlier to Georgia than the Upper Creeks and less under the influence of McGillivray, who lived among the Upper Creeks. The Creek government was a loose confederation that could seldom speak for the entire nation unless there was a general meeting of representatives from all the towns. Towns and individual Indians not present at meetings tended to repudiate any action taken that they did not approve.

In August, 1783, when the Georgians renewed their demands for the Creek lands to the Oconee, McGillivray demanded British assistance in return for Creek help during the late war. The British authorities in St. Augustine advised McGillivray not to begin hostilities but gave him some ammunition and told him to apply to the newly arrived Spanish authorities.[6] However, a small group of Creeks, led by Tallasee King and Fat King, met the Georgia commissioners at Augusta in October and signed a treaty on November 1 that confirmed the Cherokee cession of May and ceded the lands east of the Oconee that the Georgians demanded.[7]

No sooner had this treaty been signed than McGillivray and his party denied its validity. McGillivray said the Augusta meeting came at an inconvenient season, that the chiefs who signed the treaty did so only after they had been threatened with instant death if they did not sign, and that the Creek general council "severely censured" the two kings who signed and declared a cession valid only if made by unanimous consent of the entire nation. Fat King and Tallasee King did not repudiate the treaty, but they did maintain that the whites were taking more lands than the treaty allowed.[8]

Georgia was determined to enforce the treaty as valid. The assembly, affirming that the state was acting in good faith in negotiating the treaty and that such small Indian representation was not unusual, voted to purchase gifts for the Indians who signed the treaty, and laid out two counties—Washington and Franklin—from the ceded territory.[9] The same assembly hoped to improve Indian relations by specifying that all Indian trade must be carried on by licensed traders in stores instead of privately in the Indian country and that all private land purchases from the Indians were void.[10] By July, 1784, there were murders of whites by Indians in the disputed Oconee lands, and Colonel Elijah Clarke was ordered to use militia to protect the white settlers.[11]

Georgians had hoped that the removal of the British from the

Georgia-Florida area at the end of the Revolution would result in improved relations with the Creeks. Instead, Georgia-Creek relations were worse during the 1780s than they had ever been before. There were three main reasons: the insistent demand of the frontiersmen for more Indian lands, the excellent leadership of the Creeks by McGillivray and his hatred of Georgia, and the help that the Creeks got from the Spanish authorities and from Panton, Leslie & Company, a British Indian trading firm, which remained in the Floridas after they became Spanish in 1784.

The negotiation of the 1783 Treaty of Augusta and the attitude of both the Creeks and the whites toward it illustrate Georgia-Creek relations for the 1780s. There was always a pro-Georgia party among the Lower Creeks that was willing to negotiate land cessions with Georgia. The Upper Creeks, under the leadership of McGillivray, were always ready to repudiate any cession made, on the grounds that they had not agreed to it. Georgia always insisted that the cessions were valid and allowed whites to settle on the disputed lands. Often some of these whites were murdered by Indians who opposed the cession, and "satisfaction" was taken by frontier militia upon the first Indians that it could find, regardless of their connection with the murdered whites.

Of course, such actions often brought a threat of an all-out Creek war against Georgia, but such a war never came. The belligerence of the Creeks was always directly related to the amount of military supplies they thought they could get from the Spanish. Spanish backing, which came through Panton, Leslie and Company, was enough to encourage the Creeks to worry the Georgians but never enough to allow them to begin the all-out war to drive the whites off the disputed lands. Spain, like the Creeks, tried to play the friend to both the Creeks and the United States to her own advantage. McGillivray played a delaying game of promising future negotiations but refusing to negotiate at the specified time and threatening to fight but failing to do so. He was always trying to see if he could get more Spanish backing, and at the same time trying to find out just what sort of an attitude the United States would take and how much backing it would give to Georgia in Creek-Georgia disputes. He never got the support that he wanted from Spain and never was convinced that the United States was strong enough or was willing to back Georgia until Washington became president. Then he agreed to cede the disputed Oconee lands which Georgia had been claiming since 1783.

Georgia's situation was in several respects similar to that of the Creeks. She wanted the Oconee lands desperately but never felt strong enough to fight the entire Creek Nation to secure them. She kept hoping for help from the United States, from the State of Franklin, from South Carolina, and from her other Indian neighbors—help that never really came in sufficient amount to undertake the war from the Oconee lands. Georgia and the United States never knew how much backing the Creeks were getting from the Spanish and were never prepared for a full-scale war. The only troops available to fight the Creeks without Congressional help, which never came, were Georgia militiamen. Militiamen were good for raids into the Indian country but were undependable for a lengthy war. Hence Georgia always accepted any suggestions, even from McGillivray, to delay hostilities. Georgia was always anxious to negotiate but never could get McGillivray to a treaty session until 1788 and could not hold him then until a treaty was agreed to.

In the summer of 1784 the Spanish negotiated treaties with the Creeks, Choctaws, and Chickasaws at Pensacola by which these Indians acknowledged themselves to be under Spanish protection and promised to exclude from their nations all traders without Spanish licenses. Spain agreed to protect Indian lands that were within her territory. Although Spain was claiming lands as far north as the Tennessee and Ohio rivers, she did not claim the Oconee lands desired by Georgia; and Esteban Miro, the Spanish governor at New Orleans, refused to give the Creeks any official backing in the dispute over these lands.[12]

In the spring of 1785 the Continental Congress appointed commissioners to inform the Southern Indians of the terms of the peace treaty with Britain, to make a general peace with the Indians, and to determine the Indian-white boundary lines.[13] Georgia was trying to survey the Indian-white boundary line agreed upon at Augusta in 1783 before the federal commissioners arrived in Georgia.[14] While the pro-Georgia Creeks were promising to meet the Georgia commissioners, McGillivray was in St. Augustine attempting to get help from the Spanish governor, but he could get no definite promise out of him.[15] When the invitation from the Continental commissioners arrived, before the Creek boundary line had been surveyed, Governor Elbert gave up any hopes of separate state action and informed the Creeks that the Congressional conference would be the occasion for surveying the new boundary line.[16]

Governor Elbert furnished the guard requested by the federal commissioners but informed them that only the assembly could vote the $2,000 they requested. McGillivray said that he was glad the Continental commissioners were finally coming to treat with the Creeks and that he would meet them.[17] When the commissioners arrived at Galphinton on the Ogeechee on October 24 they found but few Indians there. After two weeks' wait, Indians from only two towns had arrived. The commissioners refused to treat with so few Indians, explained the purpose of the meeting, distributed presents, and left to meet the Cherokees.[18]

Various reasons were given why so few Creeks appeared at Galphinton. Governor Elbert's statement that the 1783 boundary lines would be run did not help. McGillivray had said before the meeting that the Creeks could not treat unless the whites removed from the Oconee lands, but after the meeting he did not refer to this condition as a reason for his non-attendance. The commissioners, even though they did not know that the Creeks had just gotten their first large supply of Spanish ammunition, suggested that Spanish intrigue kept the Indians away. Before the arrival of the Spanish ammunition made him change his mind, McGillivray had probably meant to attend. However, non-attendance was consistent with his policy of procrastination and delaying any real settlement until he could see clearer both Spanish and United States policy.[19]

After the Continental commissioners left Galphinton, Georgia's representatives, Elijah Clarke and John Twiggs, signed a treaty with the Indians present on November 12, 1785, confirming the 1783 Treaty of Augusta and making a new Indian cession of all lands between the Altamaha and St. Marys rivers. McGillivray immediately protested that this treaty was no more valid than the one signed at Augusta in 1783.[20]

The Continental commissioners went north from Galphinton to Hopewell on the Keowee River, where they negotiated treaties with the Cherokees in December, 1785, and with the Choctaws and Chickasaws in January, 1786. The Georgia-Cherokee frontier followed the one described in the Cherokee Treaty of Augusta in 1783. North Carolina and Georgia agents objected to the Cherokee treaty, contending that it violated the rights of the states; and North Carolina tried unsuccessfully to prevent Congressional approval of the Hopewell treaties. Both states declared that everything in the treaties conflicting with their territorial and political rights was null and void within their borders.[21]

Georgia accomplished no more by the Treaty of Galphinton than she had by the Treaty of Augusta, for the majority of the Creeks were determined not to abide by either. At a general meeting in in the spring of 1786 the Creeks agreed to use force if necessary to drive Georgians off the disputed Oconee lands. McGillivray went to New Orleans to see what Spanish backing he could get; Creek attacks on white settlements in the disputed Oconee cession resulted in a number of deaths. Georgia's agent to the Creeks believed the majority of the nation favored war, to begin just as soon as the crops were gathered. Many of the settlers in the disputed lands withdrew across the Ogeechee.[22]

Georgia began to prepare for war in earnest. Governor Telfair made application to South Carolina and Virginia for a loan of arms and ammunition, without much success. When the assembly met in July, Telfair recommended both preparations for war and a new peace effort. The assembly authorized the executive and eight special commissioners to hold a treaty to settle all differences with the Creeks. A guard of 1,500 militia was to attend the treaty to convince the Indians that Georgia could begin a war if they refused to agree to a satisfactory treaty. £2,000 for the purchase of arms and ammunition and the impressment of provisions and horses were authorized. The Cherokees, Choctaws, and Chickasaws were asked to side with Georgia or be neutral; and a real attempt was made to coordinate Georgia's war effort with 1,000 troops promised by the State of Franklin to help secure for Franklin certain lands near the Tennessee River. Georgia instructed her delegates to report the matter to Congress and to get approval for her action. Spies in the Creek Nation reported that the Spanish had promised the Creeks sufficient ammunition for the war and that McGillivray had actually secured 100 horseloads at Pensacola.[23]

Preparations for the new Creek treaty went forward also. While the Upper Creeks generally sided with McGillivray, the Lower Creeks were reported to be opposed to the war, and if properly wooed, friendly to Georgia. The Cherokees were said to be generally friendly to Georgia, but not sufficiently so to fight on her side.[24] The Georgia commissioners made preparations to meet the Creeks at Shoulderbone Creek on the Oconee River and pledged that no harm would come to the Indians attending. A special invitation was sent to McGillivray with a denial of the rumor that the state was trying to have him assassinated. McGillivray answered that most of the Creeks desired peace, but added that before any negotiations could take place the whites must withdraw from the Oconee lands. He was sure that if the whites withdrew beyond the Ogeechee there would be peace until a general treaty could be held in April. The desire of the Lower Creeks for peace was responsible for their sending a considerable delegation to Shoulderbone, but McGillivray kept most Upper Creeks away.[25]

Negotiations began at Shoulderbone on October 21, 1786, with a demand of the Georgia commissioners that the Creeks give satisfaction for recent murders of whites, return all stolen property, and adhere to the treaties of Augusta and Galphinton. The Indians replied that they were willing to give satisfaction for the murders, that McGillivray was the main reason for Creek opposition to Georgia but did not speak for the entire nation, and that the lower towns represented wanted peace and would do what they could to preserve it. The demand of the commissioners for five hostages as a guarantee that the treaty would be carried out and the insistence that the new Indian line be marked without delay almost broke up the conference, but in the end the Indians furnished the hostages. On November 3, presents were distributed and the treaty signed. Of the fifteen towns represented, only three were from the Upper Creeks, but the Indians present insisted that they were authorized to speak for the other towns.

In the treaty, the Indians promised that six individuals from the parties that had murdered the six whites would be put to death in the presence of white representatives—the usual method of giving satisfaction for the murder of whites by Indians. All stolen property and all prisoners in the nation would be returned. Whites who attempted to settle on the Indian lands were to be apprehended by the Indians and turned over to the governor for punishment according to law. Indiscriminate retaliation of one race for evils committed by the other would be stopped. The cessions of Augusta and Galphinton were confirmed, and the boundary lines were to be marked as soon as it was convenient for the Indians. Once the boundary line was marked, nobody was to cross it without a special license.[26]

The Georgia agent to the Creeks was instructed to use his influence to have the treaty fully ratified and signed by as many additional headmen as possible and to see to the release of the whites and Negroes held prisoner by the Indians.[27] Georgians now breathed sighs of relief and were sure that a major Creek war had been averted. Governor Telfair informed Congress, Governor Sevier of Franklin, the Cherokees, the Choctaws, and the Chickasaws that the Creek troubles had been terminated and that no further action on their part was necessary.[28]

McGillivray did not intend to abide by the new treaty and used his influence against it. He later reported that force and intimidation were used to secure the treaty, although the minutes of the commissioners do not so indicate. He did not mention that the Creeks at Shoulderbone were from the part of the nation not friendly to him.[29]

While Georgia was preparing for war and trying to preserve peace with the Creeks in the summer and fall of 1786, Congress was also concerned with Indian relations. In the summer it created an Indian Department and appointed superintendents with powers to negotiate directly with all Indian tribes. North Carolina and Georgia sought unsuccessfully to limit the powers of the federal superintendents in dealings with Indians who lived within the boundaries of any state, but they did secure Congressional instructions that negotiations with such Indians should be carried on in conjunction with the states concerned. James White, a former North Carolina delegate to Congress, was elected superintendent of the district south of the Ohio River.[30]

The treaty of Shoulderbone prevented the expected Creek war during the winter of 1786-87 and brought relative peace to the Creek frontier.[15] The 1787 assembly went into Indian relations fully and conferred with Superintendent White, who had just arrived in Georgia. White seemed generally to approve of Georgia's actions toward the Creeks and agreed to be one of the state commissioners for surveying the Indian line agreed upon at Shoulderbone.[32] Then White sent to the Creek Nation to get the other side of the story. In the nation White insisted that both sides must be willing to compromise and said that he thought Georgia had all the territory she would need for settlement for some time to come. He attempted to get a general Creek meeting to confirm the treaties of Augusta, Galphinton, and Shoulderbone; but the Creeks felt sure of Spanish backing and refused to attend such a meeting.[33]

White tried to see both sides of the Georgia-Creek argument and sent a complete report on it to Secretary at War Henry Knox. White said that he secured the release of the Shoulderbone hostages because he thought their remaining prisoners of the whites only created ill-will among the Creeks who tended to be friendly. He blamed the friendship of McGillivray and the Creeks toward Spain on the fact that the United States had waited so long to approach them, and he was sure that the Creeks had delayed fighting Georgia to see what Congress would do. McGillivray proposed to White that a separate state should be created south of the Altamaha for the Indians, who would then give up the Oconee lands that Georgia so ardently desired. McGillivray said he would then take the oath of allegiance to the United States, and apparently hoped to continue his influence among the Creeks in the new state without interference from Georgia. White referred this matter to Congress, not because he thought it would be acted upon favorably, but because he thought consideration of it would help to maintain peace on the Georgia frontier. White did not know it, but McGillivray probably was convinced that he could not get enough help from Spain to drive the Georgians off the Oconee lands.[34]

White listed three main causes of the Creek trouble: (1) the natural reluctance of the Indians to give up their lands; (2) the fact that the cessions so far had been obtained from so few Indians and with some coercion; and (3) the continual encroachments of the whites upon Indian lands. White was sure that much of the Indian trouble was instigated by McGillivray, whose attitude stemmed from his personal resentment against Georgia and his being in the pay of Spain. The Creeks were favorably located for their war against Georgia, because they could retreat into Spanish territory if hard pressed.[35] This report was a good analysis of the Creek situation, but it suggested no solution. It was White's main work as Indian superintendent, and his reputation must rest upon it. He had brought Georgia and the Creeks no closer together but had perhaps delayed hostilities which seemed imminent when he arrived in the state.

By April, 1787, there were renewed reports of Creek outrages and predictions of Indian war for which Governor Mathews urged both Georgia and Congress to prepare. In the summer a number of whites were killed in the disputed Oconee lands.[36] After one Indian raid in which a few whites were killed, militia crossed the Oconee and killed twelve of the first Indians encountered; these were later identified as friendly Lower Creeks who had nothing to do with the murders the whites were trying to avenge. The Lower Creeks resented this indiscriminate "taking of satisfaction" contrary to the Treaty of Shoulderbone, and demanded a white life, including the leader of the militia party, for each of the twelve Indian lives lost—something that no Georgia authorities could agree to.[37]

This uneasy situation and loss of life on both sides continued throughout the summer. Georgia made renewed overtures for help to the Chickasaws and Choctaws, and to Franklin. On the other side, Governor Mathews suggested that if McGillivray would petition for it he could be granted Georgia citizenship and that the confiscated property of his father might be given to him. In September there was more trouble in the Oconee lands, especially in Greene County, and many thought a real Creek war was beginning.[38]

On July 3, 1787, Governor Mathews called the assembly into special session to deal with the Indian situation, but no quorum assembled. On September 20, Mathews tried again and after repeated efforts by the governor and speaker, a quorum assembled in Augusta by October 18. A two-weeks session concerned itself almost entirely with Indian troubles and a South Carolina boundary dispute. A committee reviewed state and federal Indian relations for the previous four years and came to the conclusion that the real cause of the Creek troubles was the too sudden interference of Congress with the state treaties. This interference gave the Indians the opinion that if they fought Georgia she would get no help from Congress and that Congress, rather than Georgia, might make final disposition of the disputed Oconee lands.[39] The militia law was revised, and from 1,500 to 3,000 state troops were authorized to fight the Creeks in the expected war. Land bounties beginning with 640 acres for privates were offered to spur enlistments.[40] A special tax payable in foodstuffs was imposed to obtain provisions for the troops, and needed military supplies were ordered secured.[41] New tries for Choctaw, Chickasaw, and Franklin help were made; and Franklin promised from 1,000 to 1,500 men. The governor, at the direction of the assembly, wrote the Spanish governors at St. Augustine and Pensacola requesting that "agreeable to the Law of Nations" they prevent any munitions going to the Creeks during their fighting with Georgia.[42]

Governor Mathews reported to Congress in November that the Indians had killed thirty-one whites since August and had destroyed the town and courthouse at Greensboro and many houses on the frontier. Mathews asked Congress to provide arms for the state troops recently authorized and suggested that the Congress should protest to Spain against her furnishing arms to the Creeks.[43]

Secretary at War Henry Knox made an able report to Congress on the Southern Indian situation in the summer of 1787. He pointed out the necessity for a decision of who—Congress or the states—had the right to deal with the Indians and suggested that Congress must declare its superiority in this field or get Georgia to cede her western lands to the United States. Knox thought a land cession an easier and better solution. Then Congress itself could deal with the Creeks with no interference from Georgia. Otherwise Knox expected a general Indian war.[44] While this report was being considered in committee, William Few of Georgia made two unsuccessful attempts to have the Indian Superintendent instructed to hold a new treaty with the Creeks that would confirm Georgia's treaties. Congress took no stand on Knox's or Few's suggestions but directed that the three Southern states each appoint a commissioner to act with the Indian Superintendent in negotiating with the Southern Indians.[45]

Throughout the winter of 1787-88 and the spring of 1788, Creek attacks on the Georgia frontiers continued. Most of the raids resulted in cattle and Negro stealing instead of death, but several whites and Indians were killed each month, and the militia and state troops were kept continually on the alert.[46] By spring Indian troubles had increased, and it looked as if a real war was on the way. At any rate, the state again began preparations in earnest. To help recruiting of state troops, a complete suit of clothing was added to the land bounty already audthorized for enlistment.[47]

George Whitefield, an agent of the federal commissioners, and McGillivray toured the Creek country together in April; and McGillivray urged peace, often against the inclination of the Indians. McGillivray even considered making application to Georgia for citizenship and receiving his father's confiscated property, as Governor Mathews had suggested earlier.[48] The Spanish minister to the United States insisted that Spain was trying to persuade the Creeks to maintain peace.[49] Insufficient Spanish backing and the fact that Richard Winn, the new federal Indian Superintendent, had just arrived in Georgia probably accounted for McGillivray's peaceful attitude. By July the Creeks agreed to meet the superintendent and federal commissioners in September, and Georgia ordered all hostilities suspended.[50]

Now, when it seemed that everything was arranged for a treaty, McGillivray demanded as a preliminary to any meeting that all settlers retire from the disputed Oconee lands. Both Georgia and the federal commissioners refused to agree to this, but McGillivray said he was sure the chiefs would not agree to treat otherwise.[51] Governor Handley called the assembly to meet on July 15, but a quorum never assembled. There were insufficient funds for a treaty, and the executive could raise no more. Handley suggested the treaty be postponed and thought that McGillivray might accept, if the impending change in the federal government were given as the reason. McGillivray accepted the postponement and promised a suspension of hostilities if Georgia reciprocated. Handley tried to prevent the whites beginning any trouble, and there were only a few minor reports of trouble in the fall.[52]

The winter of 1788-89 was fairly quiet on the Georgia-Creek frontier. There were a few small raids, but no deaths were reported. Late in March the state was more worried by a mutiny of state troops raised to fight Indians than it was by Indian troubles.[53] Governor George Walton and Superintendent Winn agreed to hold a treaty at Rock Landing on the Oconee (a few miles from the site of the future town of Milledgeville) on June 8.[54]

Just when it seemed that everything was in readiness for the treaty, Indian outrages broke out in Liberty and Wilkes counties. A general council of the Creeks was reported to have decided to resume hostilities and clear the Oconee lands of white settlers, apparently because of new supplies of ammunition from Spain.[55] State militia, state troops, and South Carolina were called upon for help; and the federal commissioners were urged to rush to Georgia to negotiate. No sooner had all this been done than word was received from the Creek country that the treaty would be held as scheduled, and the warlike preparations were cancelled.[56] The commissioners went to Rock Landing, where McGillivray persuaded them to postpone the treaty until September 15, despite the objections of Governor Walton.[57]

By September 15, the new United States government was in operation. President Washington felt that the United States commissioners should not be local men. He therefore appointed new commissioners from New England and Virginia—Benjamin Lincoln, Cyrus Griffin, and David Humphreys—and instructed them to try to get the Creeks to cede the lands included in the treaties of Augusta, Galphinton, and Shoulderbone. Otherwise he was afraid that Georgia would not remain loyal to the new central government. In return for this cession the commissioners were authorized to grant, if necessary, a port of entry into the Creek country below the Altamaha; to bestow gifts of goods and money, and military distinction upon Creek leaders (obviously McGillivray); and to give a promise of United States guarantee of further territorial integrity of the Creek Nation.[58]

The new federal commissioners arrived in Augusta on September 17, dined with Governor Walton, and set out for Rock Landing the next day. After four days of negotiations, a draft treaty was read that confirmed the cessions of Augusta, Galphinton, and Shoulderbone. The Creeks immediately left Rock Landing with the statement that they would not give up their Oconee lands, that their hunting season was at hand, and that the truce would continue until the spring when the matter of a treaty could be considered again.[59] McGillivray later said he was determined to get what he wanted, because he had received a letter from New Orleans with promises of Spanish help just before he went to Rock Landing.[60] The commissioners went to Augusta to write their report, which blamed McGillivray and the rumor of Spanish ammunition for the failure to get a treaty. They further reported that Georgia's three Creek treaties were legitimate land cessions and that the United States should back Georgia fully in her troubles with the Creeks.[61]

President Washington now decided upon a new approach to the Creek problems. He sent Colonel Marinus Willett to the Creek country as a personal representative to invite McGillivray and other chiefs to New York for negotiations. Willett apparently convinced McGillivray that he was dealing with an independent government not subject to influence by Georgia. The two toured the Creek Nation and got approval for the New York negotiations before Willett, McGillivray, and several others chiefs set out for New York in June, 1790. The party received lavish welcome and entertainment en route and in New York while the negotiations were carried on.[62]

As bait for the inevitable demand for a land cession, McGillivray was made a brigadier general in the United States army—the same rank that he held in the Spanish army—given a pension of $1,200 a year, and promised that the Creeks could import goods from the United States duty free if their supplies should be shut off from Florida. McGillivray agreed to the cession of all the lands east of the Oconee (first ceded at Augusta in 1783) but not to the cession of the lands between the Altamaha and St. Marys made at Galphinton and Shoulderbone. The rest of the Creeks' lands were guaranteed to them, and they acknowledged themselves to be under the protection of no nation but the United States—the same agreement that they already had with Spain. The treaty was signed on August 7, approved by the Senate on August 12, and proclaimed by President Washington on August 13. The Creeks did not ratify the treaty immediately, but they had no hopes of retaining the Oconee lands.[63] The disputed Oconee lands had finally been secured, but McGillivray would continue to trouble Georgia until his death in 1793.

Georgia would probably have had better Indian relations had its assembly not been so influenced by the frontier philosophy that the only good Indian was a dead Indian. A few governors tried to restrain the frontiersmen from trespassing upon the Indian lands; but without real legislative backing and with only frontier militia to use in enforcement, restraint of frontiersmen was impossible. Given the conditions that existed in Georgia in the 1780s it is hard to see how there could have been any real difference in the pattern of Indian relations, regardless of how individual incidents may have differed. Georgia frontiersmen and Creeks under the leadership of Alexander McGillivray could not agree! Only an outside force like the United States government could accomplish anything, and the United States never adopted a real policy toward the Creeks until the new government under President Washington took office.

CONTINENTAL, INTERSTATE, AND "FOREIGN" AFFAIRS 1782 - 1789

16

****

IF LEFT to themselves, Georgians would never have rebelled against Great Britain; and they did not desire absolute independence once they joined the Revolution. They wanted a central government strong enough to afford them needed protection against their Creek neighbors. Georgia had a small population and was weak in the 1780s, though she possessed the largest land area of any state after Virginia ceded her lands north of the Ohio River to Congress. Georgians were sure that smallness, weakness, and actual control of much of their territory by Spaniards and Indians were only temporary and that Georgia would soon be a large and powerful state. If Georgians were too optimistic, they were only showing a common frontier characteristic.

Hence Georgians had no desire to curtail the general powers of the central government. If they wanted to limit its powers to negotiate with the Indians within the state, it was because they did not like the way these federal negotiations were carried out and Georgia's interests "ignored." They continued to call upon Congress for financial and military aid to oppose the Creeks, all the while objecting to Congressional Indian negotiations. If the state government did not heed Congress' requests for additional power or amendment of the Articles of Confederation, the reason was because it was too busy with other things or not especially worried about a weak union. If Georgia did not pay its part on federal requisitions or support her Congressional delegates, it was because she had no currency that could be used outside the state.

Generally Georgians wanted to do their part toward the federal government. The fact that these desires were not fulfilled resulted from the troubles of the times—something that most frontiersmen could not understand.

Some indication of a state's interest in the federal government can be derived from its representation in Congress. Georgia's representation was not expecially good in the 1780s. There were two delegates present throughout most of 1782, but for 1783 and the first half of 1784 no delegates were present. Delegates were elected in February, 1783, but for some unknown reason were never furnished credentials for attendance.[1] Throughout most of 1785-1787, Georgia had two delegates present but never the three delegates requested by Congress after 1785. Georgia was last represented on September 18, 1788; Congress itself never had a quorum after October 10.[2] Georgia's most faithful delegate in Congress from 1784 through 1786 was William Houstoun. His regular attendance may be accounted for by a love affair that kept him in New York and which resulted in marriage in 1788.[3]

Two good reasons for this poor attendance were the infrequency with which Georgia's delegates were paid and the distance of Congress from Georgia. Delegates continually complained of small payments for salary and expenses, no payments at all, the difficulties of the journey, and the neglect to their personal business caused by long absences in Congress.[4] Georgia had no especially able delegates, or any who became real leaders in Congress. Abraham Baldwin, William Few, and William Pierce in 1787 and 1788 were more active than most Georgia delegates and were fully accepted by their colleagues as useful working members of Congress.

Not only did Georgia lack delegates in Congress; but, before 1786, the assembly was notorious for ignoring Congressional requests. Twice, in 1781 and in 1783, Congress requested power from the state to levy a five per cent duty on imports, to pay the national debt. The Georgia Assembly took no action on either request, although the first was approved by eleven states. There was some excuse for lack of action in 1781 and 1782 because of the presence of British troops in the state and the disruption that combat caused. Both sessions of the 1783 assembly considered the impost, but took no action on it.[5]

At the 1785 assembly, bills to allow Congress to regulate trade with the West Indies and to impose import duties got

through a second reading.[6] At the March-April, 1785, circuit of
the superior courts, Chief Justice George Walton in his charges
to the grand juries pointed out the inattention of the assembly to
the Congressional request for the five per cent impost and said
that he thought the impost was the best way to uphold the credit
of the United States. Every grand jury presented as a grievance
the fact that the assembly had ignored the impost. At the fall
circuit, Walton recommended that Congress be given the power
to regulate commerce. Every court except the one in Wilkes
County made a presentment in line with Walton's recommendation. Wilkes again recommended that the five per cent impost be
granted.[7]

The 1786 assembly gave Congress power to levy the five per cent
impost, agreed to the proposed amendment to the Eighth Article
of Confederation changing the basis of state contributions to the
federal treasury from land values to population, provided for
payment of back Congressional requisitions, and approved a Congressional recommendation of April 30, 1784, giving Congress
power to prohibit certain types of imports and exports for fifteen
years.[8] The next year the United States was given the same
rights to sue in state courts that the state had, and state officials
were directed to make the necessary presentments and prosecutions. Crimes and frauds against the United States were to receive the same punishment as crimes against the state, and United
States commissioners to settle public accounts were given the
power to call witnesses and to examine them under oath.[9] Georgia had now acted upon all Congressional recommendations except
the one that she cede her western lands to the United States, and
there was sentiment toward making this cession when the boundary
controversy with South Carolina and the state's war accounts
with the United States were settled.[10]

Georgia's popularity in Congress was not increased by her failure to pay her quota on specie requisitions for the support of
the federal government. While the state was occupied by the
British, no federal quotas were assigned to her by Congress; but
the requisition sent to the states in September, 1782, for $1,200,-
000 to pay the interest on the domestic debt, contained $14,400
as Georgia's quota.[11] Throughout the rest of the life of the Confederation, Georgia was assigned the smallest state quota on all
federal requisitions. Georgia took no action to pay her quotas
before 1785, but in 1786 she passed a bill to pay all back requisi-

tions and made other provisions to pay later requisitions. However, all records of payments made to the federal treasury show that Georgia made no payments in specie or indents (a type of paper currency acceptable by Congress). Indents were reported on hand in the state treasury several times and were ordered paid. Specie payments voted were always to be paid out of specie yet to come into the treasury, and it is possible that the specie never materialized. Several of the Georgia acts directed that payments on federal requisitions be made to the Georgia federal loan office, but no records for the loan office have been discovered. It is possible that payments on requisitions were made to the loan office, and the records have been lost. Otherwise it must be assumed that Georgia tried to pay at least a part of her federal requisitions, but that her finances made payment impossible.[12]

Provisions to pay Georgia's portion of the interest and principal of the Continental debts were made when the 1783 assembly directed that the interest paid to the state on £108,889.16. 6 in personal bonds received in payment for confiscated estates be set aside to pay the interest on the state's quota of the Continental debt. The excess in interest due to the state over that due on the federal debt, calculated at £1348. 3. 2 a year, was to be loaned out by the state treasurer to secure funds to pay Georgia's part of the principal on the foreign debt. Any residue after the foreign debt was paid was to be used to pay Georgia's quota on the federal domestic debt.[13] Interest on the bonds in the state treasury was not paid, and there is no indication that anything was accomplished by this law.

To settle the war accounts between Georgia and Congress, Edward Williams was appointed as commissioner to Georgia by Superintendent of Finance Robert Morris on February 3, 1784. Williams resigned the next year, apparently having done little or nothing in his office.[14] He was replaced by Job Sumner, who reported in the summer of 1786 that Georgia had assumed all the claims of her individual citizens against the United States and that state accounts were ready to be presented to the federal commissioner of accounts in the fall for final settlement in the winter,[15] yet there is no indication that any claims were presented or settled. An unidentified "State of Public Accounts of Georgia,"[16] dated 1787, showed the following situation:

Debits

Loans from Congress during the war, reduced to specie scale	$678,964	
Old Continental money reduced by 40 to 1	128,000	
Requisitions of Congress to Nov. 1786	105,038	45/90
Total owed by Georgia to United States	$912,071	45/90

Credits

State charges against the United States	£135,932.	0. 3
Final settlements in the state treasury	16,253.	6. 8¼
A large but unstated expenditure of Georgia during the war for land bounties, galleys, and support of partisan corps of troops.		

The 1787 assembly complained that neither of the federal commissioners for settling accounts had done anything toward the duties of his office, despite the fact that the state auditor had long had his books and charges against the United States ready for examination.[17] When the final settlement of state accounts with the United States was made in 1793, a balance of $19,988 was found due to Georgia by the United States.[18]

Somewhat more satisfactory than her Continental relations were Georgia's relations with South Carolina in the 1780s. In this decade the two states got along as well as they ever had. The one major point of difference between them was a boundary dispute which lasted from 1783 until 1788 but was finally settled amicably. There was a difference of opinion as to where the Savannah River, the accepted boundary between the two states, began; and there was an argument about the ownership of land west of the headwaters of the Altamaha and St. Marys rivers. Both states appointed commissioners early in 1783 to settle this problem, but they took no action.[19] In the summer of 1784 the governors of both states protested that the other was granting lands claimed by both states between the Keowee and the Tugaloo rivers.[20] When the Georgia and South Carolina assemblies met in January, 1785, both decided that if no satisfactory agreement could be reached the matter was to be laid before Congress for determination by a federal court as prescribed in the Articles of Confederation. Georgia offered to negotiate on the northern boundary, but South Carolina insisted that both disputes be negotiated and so referred the matter to Congress for settlement by a federal court.[21]

South Carolina's claim to the northern area was based upon a literal interpretation of her own and Georgia's charters. By the second Carolina charter of 1665, Charles II granted to the Lord Proprietors all the lands between the twenty-ninth degree and the thirty-sixth degree and thirty minutes of north latitude. (Today this includes all territory from Deland, Florida, to just below the northern boundary of North Carolina.) The Georgia charter of 1732 gave to Georgia all land between the Savannah and Altamaha rivers west to the Pacific. South Carolina maintained that the Savannah River began where its tributaries, the Keowee and the Tugaloo, joined. Hence all land between this junction and the North Carolina line west to the Mississippi belonged to South Carolina. Georgia contended, on the other hand, that the source of the Keowee River (the most northern branch of the Savannah, so far as Georgia was concerned) was the head of the Savannah River.

The Proclamation of 1763 annexed to Georgia all lands between the Altamaha and St. Marys rivers. South Carolina maintained that all lands west of the headwaters of these two streams still belonged to her by her charter and had not been annexed to Georgia. Georgia maintained that the tract added by the Proclamation of 1763 extended west to the Mississippi. A new commission of Governor James Wright in 1764 stated that the southern boundary of Georgia was the St. Marys River and a line drawn from its head west to the Mississippi.[22] Apparently nobody in Georgia knew about this commission, though Governor Elbert had written to London to secure copies of charters, deeds, and proclamations that might help Georgia's case.[23] It is doubtful if South Carolina seriously hoped to secure this southern claim, but probably used it to gain an additional bargaining point on the northern claim.

Congress decided in the fall of 1786 that the court to settle these disputes should meet in New York on the third Monday in June, 1787.[24] Georgia and South Carolina now redoubled their efforts to settle the controversy by direct negotiations. Commissioners from both states met at Beaufort, South Carolina, on April 24, 1787, and settled the matter five days later with the signing of the Convention of Beaufort.[25]

This convention contained the following agreements. (1) The

boundary between Georgia and South Carolina was agreed upon as the most northern branch of the Savannah River from the sea to the junction of the Tugaloo and Keowee, from thence the most northern branch of the Tugaloo until it intersected the northern boundary of South Carolina. If the Tugaloo did not extend so far north, then the northern boundary of Georgia was to be a line drawn from the head spring of the Tugaloo directly west to the Mississippi. All the islands in the Savannah and Tugaloo were given to Georgia. (2) Navigation of the Savannah River was to be open and free of all duties and tolls to the citizens of both states. (3) South Carolina ceded all claims of lands to the east, south, southeast, or west of the boundary to Georgia. (The use of the term east of this line is not clear. All of South Carolina is east of this line.) (4) Georgia ceded all claims to lands to the north or northeast of this line to South Carolina. (5) Lands granted by either state between the Tugaloo and the Keowee were to belong to the first grantee. (6) The South Carolina commissioners said the convention did not weaken the 1763 grants made by South Carolina south of the Altamaha, but the Georgia commissioners refused to negotiate on this subject.

The convention was signed by John Habersham and Lachlan McIntosh for Georgia and by Charles Cotesworth Pinckney, Andrew Pickens, and Pierce Butler for South Carolina. John Houstoun, another Georgia commissioner, refused to sign the convention; instead he entered a protest against it. He maintained that the Georgia charter meant the Keowee to be a part of the Savannah and that Georgia had a perfect right to the land between the Keowee and the Tugaloo. The South Carolina claim to the land west of the Altamaha-St. Marys line was so weak as to be of no value. Hence, said Houstoun, Georgia gave up the disputed area between the Tugaloo and the Keowee but got nothing in return. Houstoun said that South Carolina should be allowed to navigate the Savannah River but that since Georgia possessed entire control of the river this navigation should not be guaranteed as a right.[26]

Houstoun's dissent brought forth a statement from Habersham and McIntosh to support their stand. They said that their main objects were to restore harmony with South Carolina, to leave no room for future disputes, and to save the expense of the federal court. They maintained that the Proclamation of 1763 confined all the colonial governments to the area east of the moun-

tains and could not possibly give Georgia lands west of the
source of the St. Marys—a decidedly weak argument. They said
that they accepted the Tugaloo as the main stream of the Savannah when it was proved to them to carry more water than the
Keowee. To have denied South Carolina full navigation rights of
the Savannah would have resulted in no agreement being reached,
they were sure.[27]

Both Georgia and South Carolina ratified the Convention of
Beaufort when their legislatures met in February, 1788.[28] Congress had already ratified it in August, 1787, when she accepted
the narrow strip of land that South Carolina thought she had
won between the Tugaloo and the North Carolina line.[29] (It was
later discovered that the Tugaloo really rose in North Carolina;
so the United States deeded the eastern part of this supposed
cession to Georgia in 1802 when Georgia ceded the present area of
Alabama and Mississippi to the United States.) As soon as the
Convention of Beaufort was known about in Philadelphia, the
federal court was cancelled. Several of its judges had already assembled in New York for the work of the court and made application to Congress for the expenses thus incurred. Congress referred them to South Carolina and Georgia for payment. South
Carolina offered to pay half the expenses incurred; but there is
no record of Georgia ever making a similar offer or paying
anything.[30]

The South Carolina boundary controversy illustrates the tenacity
with which Georgia held to her western territory, despite the
fact that she could derive no immediate benefit from the area
west of the Oconee River. Georgia insited that the western boundary of the United States be the Mississippi and that navigation of
that stream be guaranteed when Congress considered the peace
treaty with Britain in 1782 and when Spanish negotiations were
carried on in 1786-1787.[31]

Georgia could not hope to maintain any real control over that
portion of her western territory which was inhabited by Indians,
but she did try to maintain some sort of control over areas of
white settlement. During the 1780s there were two unsuccessful
attempts to set up counties in these western lands. The first of
these was the so-called Houstoun County in the Muscle Shoals area.
William Blount, on behalf of himself and Richard Caswell, John
Sevier, Joseph Martin, and other land speculators, secured a cession of land from the Cherokees in the Muscle Shoals area, in-

tending to move settlers there from the Holston River in North Carolina. Blount petitioned the Georgia Assembly in 1784 to lay out a county that would include all the territory between the Tennessee River and the North Carolina (present Tennessee) line. The assembly appointed commissioners to investigate the area and to grant land, provided no person received more than 1,000 acres. A committee was appointed to bring in a bill for laying out a county, but no such bill was introduced; and no further action was taken by that assembly.[32]

Twice during 1784 it was reported that Spaniards, accompanied by Delaware Indians, were attempting to settle at Muscle Shoals.[33] The commissioners appointed by the assembly went to Muscle Shoals, carried out their mission, and reported to the executive. They appointed militia officers for the area, and in the spring of 1785 the executive appointed justices of the peace for the "District of the Tennessee."[34] In the summer of 1786 an assembly committee reviewed the matter from the time of Blount's petition, noted that settlers were reported coming into the area rapidly, and recommended that a county be laid out at once. However, the bill to create a county was lost by a vote of 23 to 26. The commissioners who had visited the area and set up a partial local government were voted 5,000 acres of land in reward for their services. A surveyor was elected for the district but ordered to make no surveys until he received further orders from the assembly—orders that never came.[35]

In the fall of 1786 about 100 French from Canada and 100 Delaware Indians were reported settling at the bend of the Tennessee.[36] A bill for laying out a reserve of land there was postponed by the 1787 assembly, probably because of the negotiations with South Carolina over the northern boundary of Georgia. Later that year the assembly provided that the land bounties for Franklin militiamen who were expected to join Georgia in the anticipated Creek war should be located in the bend of the Tennessee.[37] The troubles of Georgia and Franklin with the Creek Indians were undoubtedly connected with the continued delay in creating a county at Muscle Shoals, and the demise of Franklin as a state seems to have caused a further delay. No county was ever created, and finally the matter was allowed to drop.

Georgia's second try at founding a county in its western territory was more fantastic than the Houstoun County attempt. Thomas Green, a resident of the Natchez district on the Mississippi River, petitioned the assembly in 1785 on behalf of the inhabitants of his district praying that Georgia take them under her protection. The assembly, always anxious to extend its effective range and entirely ignorant of the situation in the western part of its domain, obliged by the creation of Bourbon County. The county was to extend along the Mississippi from the Yazoo River south to the thirty-first parallel, east as far as the Indians had ceded lands to the British (limits not known to the assembly), then north along the line of any Indian cession to the Yazoo River, and west along the Yazoo to the point of origin. No land office was to be opened until later, but citizens of the United States and friendly powers were to have preference in acquiring title to lands they already possessed in the county. Thirteen justices of the peace, several of them residents of the area, were named.[38]

The assembly instructed the new justices that, if Spanish officials in the area of Bourbon County objected to the creation of the county, the justices were to ignore any area claimed or occupied by Spain and exercise their authority only in area not so claimed. The justices were specifically told not to enter into any dispute with the Indians or Spaniards about territorial claims or navigation of the Mississippi and were warned that if they did so they could expect no help from Georgia. Any Spanish claims were to be reported to the Georgia government, trade and friendship with the Indians were to be cultivated, and no private purchases of land from the Indians were to be allowed.[39]

Four of the justices (Thomas Green, William Davenport, Nathaniel Christmas, and Nicholas Long) were appointed commissioners to set up the new county government after the model of Georgia's other counties. Green rushed back to Natchez and arrived in June before any of the other commissioners. He immediately informed the Spanish commandant in Natchez of his mission and asked if there were any objections to the creation of the new county government. Before the commandant had time to receive instructions from New Orleans, Green called upon the inhabitants to form a county government under his guidance. Other justices named in the act for creating Bourbon County objected, and a meeting of inhabitants was called to oppose Green's actions and to prevent "the ruin and destruction of this country if it should fall under the government of Georgia." There was talk of forming a separate state and calling upon Congress for recognition.

Some of the inhabitants were British loyalists who objected to the idea of being a part of the United States, especially since they thought they might lose their lands. Some were satisfied with the Spanish government, which left them alone. Some objected to the action of Green and did not trust him or anything done by him. Green appointed himself a militia colonel and did what he could to establish the county government, despite the fact that at least two of the four commissioners were necessary to take any "legal" action. Miro, the Spanish governor at New Orleans, had been warned of Georgia's actions and invited Green to New Orleans to discuss the matter. Instead Green left Natchez immediately for the Indian country, apparently out of fear of the Spanish authorities, and dropped any further attempts at creating Bourbon County.[40]

William Davenport, another commissioner for founding Bourbon County, next arrived in Natchez and tried to repair the damage that Green had done. The Spanish commandant refused to allow him to take any action until permission was received from Governor Miro in New Orleans. Davenport found the people at Natchez divided into a pro-American and an anti-American party. Three men who called a mass meeting to oppose Georgia rule and to petition Congress for separate statehood were imprisoned by the commandant for calling an illegal meeting. Some of the inhabitants were reported to have offered to follow Davenport if he would lead them in an attack on the Spanish fort, but he refused to take any military action. By the end of August the other two Georgia commissioners, Nicholas Long and Nathaniel Christmas, arrived in Natchez and acted in cooperation with Davenport. Governor Miro would make no decision without instructions from Spain, but he did allow the Georgia commissioners to remain at Natchez if they took no further action about organizing Bourbon County.[41]

By this time the Spanish minister to the United States was protesting Georgia's action to Secretary of Foreign Affairs Jay. Congress considered the matter and decided that the United States had a right to this territory but disapproved any attempts of individuals to disturb good relations with Spain and forbade immigrants to the area to molest inhabitants already there. Georgia's delegates to Congress were willing to disallow the action of Green.[42] By the time this information reached Natchez and Georgia, the Spanish had the situation well in hand. Bernardo de Galvey, the Viceroy of New Spain, instructed Miro to have nothing to do with the Georgia claims but to order the commissioners to leave Natchez in fifteen days and to be out of Spanish territory in one month. They left, apparently in the specified time.[43] For a year afterwards there were additional plans of immigrants to go to the Natchez district from the frontier regions of Virginia and North Carolina and requests for Georgia protection for such immigrants.[44]

There is no evidence that Georgia took any further action in regard to Bourbon County. Certainly it did not grant lands to Green and his friends as requested or try to give the Americans in the Natchez district any protection against the Spanish. When Georgia ceded part of its western territory to the United States in 1788, it repealed the act creating Bourbon County, which had really been dead for two years.[45] If Georgia could not settle a county at Muscle Shoals with the help of Franklin, creation of a county on the Mississippi River where Spain was in effective control was certainly impossible. The assembly had not known the situation on the Mississippi when it created Bourbon County, and there was just a remote possibility that the venture might succeed. The whole thing was typical of American frontier communities of the period.

Georgia could have saved herself all the troubles about her western lands by ceding them to the United States as Congress requested in 1780 and 1786. The western area north of the Ohio was ceded soon after the original request of Congress; but neither Georgia nor the Carolinas took any action until after the second Congressional request. A few months before the Convention of Beaufort was negotiated, South Carolina ceded the lands she claimed. The Georgia assembly passed an act of cession on February 1, 1788, which ceded all lands between the thirty-first and thirty-third degrees of north latitude west of the Chattahoochee River—the southern half of Georgia's western lands and that area claimed by both the United States and Spain. The conditions of the cession were that the United States should guarantee to the inhabitants of the ceded lands a republican form of government, that navigation of all rivers in the ceded territory would be free to all United States citizens, that the $171,428 45/90 spent by Georgia to quiet the Indians be allowed as charges against past due or yet to be made specie requisitions of the United States, and that the United States guarantee all remaining Georgia territory.[46]

The Georgia act of cession was laid before Congress on May 29, and Congress considered and agreed to a committee report on this act on July 15.[47] The committee opposed accepting the cession as offered for several reasons. The land ceded was entirely separated from the rest of the United States by the northwestern part of Georgia and was described as being of no immediate value to the United States. The amount due from Georgia on specie requisitions was reported as only a small part of the $171,428 credit she asked, and Georgia was considerably in debt to the United States by loan. A specific guarantee of Georgia's lands such as she asked was considered improper and had not been made to any other state. The committee recommended that Georgia cede all her western lands instead of only the southern half and ask credit for only past due specie requisitions and apply the remainder to repayment of Georgia loans from the United States. Having had what she considered a generous offer turned down by Congress, Georgia did not see fit to make the desired cession until 1802.

Besides troubles with the Spanish on the Mississippi, Georgia had trouble with the Spanish in the Floridas in the 1780s. Spanish officials were welcomed back to the Floridas by the Georgia government with profuse wishes for good relations[48]—wishes that never materialized. By 1789 many Georgians realized that they got along better with the British in East Florida after the Revolution than they did with the Spanish who replaced them. The two biggest items over which Georgians and the Spanish differed were runaway slaves and Indians.

Georgia slaves had always run away to East Florida and the Creek country. From 1763 until 1776 British control of the Floridas made the pursuit and return of fugitive slaves easier than it had ever been before. Almost as soon as the Spanish returned to East Florida, a request was made for help in searching for runaway slaves. The Spanish governor replied that he could not allow the return of slaves because all the pre-1763 regulations for East Florida were in effect. However, he had written to Madrid on this matter. He pointed out the changed conditions since 1763 and hoped to receive permission to return escaped slaves.[49] Throughout the 1780s, Georgians trying to recover slaves from East Florida were always met with the reply that permission for such return had not yet been received from Madrid. Negotiations of the Georgia Congressional delegation and of Congress with the Spanish minister produced no results.[50] All the Spanish governor would ever agree to was the return of stolen slaves.[51] Because it was impossible to secure runaway slaves peacefully, many Georgians went into East Florida to recover their runaway slaves and stolen stock without permission of the Spanish authorities. Sometimes sizable parties of armed Georgians—even militia units—participated in such actions but always without the approval of the Georgia Executive.[52]

The problem of Spanish backing of the Creeks in their opposition to Georgia has been considered in the preceding chapter. Here the Spanish authorities never made a definite statement of their policy but usually insisted that they wanted to do what they could to keep peace between Georgia and the Creeks.[53] It seems unlikely that they ever did very much to keep peace. Creek backing came mainly through the British firm of Panton, Leslie and Company, and there is no doubt that the Spanish knew and approved the actions of this Indian trading house.[54]

There was little cause for friendly contact between Georgia and Spanish East Florida, as there had been with British East Florida before 1776. The Spanish inhabitants were little interested in the plantation economy that had developed in British days, and St. Augustine became mainly a military outpost. A great deal of trouble between Georgia and East Florida was caused by border ruffians living in the St. Marys region who were more interested in personal gain than in loyalty to either side or in good relations between the two. These people, with the help of Indians and escaped Negroes, raided both sides of the border, crossing it with impunity to escape the agents of either government sent to oppose them. Because the area from the St. Marys north to the Altamaha and south to the St. Johns was sparsely settled, most opposition to these ruffians had to come from a considerable distance, and there was much wild territory in which they could live and hide easily.

There was little direct contact between Spanish West Florida and Georgia, because they were separated by several hundred miles of Creek Indian country. Georgians soon discovered that the Floridas in Spanish hands were no friendlier than the Floridas in British hands. Border and Indian troubles continued and certainly helped in the eventual acquisition of Florida by the United States.

GEORGIA
AND THE FEDERAL
CONSTITUTION
1787 - 1789

17

****

GEORGIA'S most important contact with the other states in the 1780's was in the writing of the federal constitution of 1787. Georgia first took up this matter when the assembly considered the report of the Annapolis Convention in January and February of 1787. On February 10 the assembly elected William Few, Abraham Baldwin, William Pierce, George Walton, William Houstoun, and Nathaniel Pendleton, or any two of them as delegates to meet with delegates from the other states to revise the federal constitution.[1] Few and Pierce were then in Congress, meeting in New York, and the other four were well known in Georgia political circles.

Few was in Philadelphia on May 14, the scheduled opening date for the convention, and attended its first session on May 25. Pierce arrived on May 31, and Baldwin and Houstoun first appeared on June 1 and 11, respectively. Thereafter with the exception of July 23 (or 26) through about August 6, Georgia had two delegates present at the convention. Baldwin remained throughout, and Few remained except for July 4 through August 3 when he was absent in Congress. Pierce left about July 1 and Houstoun about July 26.[2]

Baldwin was easily Georgia's outstanding delegate in the constitutional convention, yet he spoke but eight times and was concerned with but two important items. Houstoun spoke seven times, Pierce four times, and Few not at all.[3] Pierce wrote a series of interesting character sketches of the members of the convention that throw some light on how the delegates appeared to their contemporaries. He also kept notes on debates from May 31 through June 6 that add some information to the knowledge of that period. Pierce evidently found note taking a greater chore than he had contemplated, for his notes decrease in length every day before stopping altogether.[4]

Baldwin and Pierce both favored a central government with real powers, but would safeguard the rights and powers of the states because they did not think that Congress could care for local matters adequately. Baldwin thought that the first branch of the legislature should represent the people and the second branch the wealth or property of the country. Pierce favored the election of the first branch of the legislature by the people and the second branch by the states so that both would be represented individually and collectively. He insisted that the government must have direct contact with the people and that the states must give up some of their sovereignty; otherwise there would be no improvement over the existing government. Georgia's delegation usually voted with the "large state" or "stronger central government" group in the convention, as the opinions of Baldwin and Pierce would indicate.[5]

Once the convention split badly over the question of the basis of representation in the upper house and it seemed might even break up over this matter. When a crucial vote was taken on July 2, the Georgia delegation divided its vote and thus caused a tie. A committee was then appointed which brought in the famous Connecticut compromise providing for proportional representation to the lower house and equal representation to the upper house. Some think that without this tie vote and the resulting delay in determining this important question, the convention would have ended before finishing its work. Ordinarily Georgia would have voted with the proportional representation group, but Baldwin voted for equal representation. Neither Baldwin nor Houstoun ever gave any reason for their votes, but Luther Martin of Maryland said that Baldwin voted against proportional representation because he was afraid that if proportional representation carried, the small states would withdraw from the convention. Baldwin was closely associated with the delegates from Connecticut, his former home, and may have been influenced by them. He and Houstoun may have agreed to split Georgia's vote to allow further time to work out a compromise, but there is no proof beyond Martin's statement.[6]

The other matter in which Georgia's delegates showed some positive interest was the foreign slave trade. Baldwin joined Charles Pinckney and Charles Cotesworth Pinckney of South Carolina in arguing that slavery was a local matter which should be left to the states, that Georgia would oppose any attempt to abridge one of her "favorite prerogatives," and that the states still allowing the foreign slave trade probably would abolish it shortly if left alone. Only the Carolinas and Georgia favored further importation, but the other states gave in and allowed importation until 1808, agreeing with Madison that importation was bad but union was better.[7]

Few and Baldwin signed the finished constitution, and Pierce said that he would have signed gladly had he been in Philadelphia at the time of the signing. He did not think the constitution perfect but said that it was perhaps the best that could be got just then. Local circumstances, inequality of the states, and the different interests of the various parts of the union made it impossible to get a better document. There is no reason to suppose that Houstoun would not have signed the constitution if he had been in Philadelphia at the end of the convention.[8]

Pierce and Few returned to Congress and were present when it voted to send the proposed constitution to the states. Pierce sailed for Savannah about a week after Congress' action and brought a copy of the new constitution with him. He arrived in Savannah on October 10, and three days later the constitution was first published in the *Georgia State Gazette*.[9] Within a week the assembly met in Augusta in a special session to consider the Indian troubles and called for the selection of a ratifying convention in the winter election.[10]

The convention began its work on Friday, December 28, with twenty-four delegates present from ten of the state's eleven counties. John Wereat, a former governor and a delegate from Richmond County, became president. Isaac Biggs, who with William Longstreet was to be given patent rights for steam navigation of the Savannah River within a month of the convention's ending, was elected secretary. Governor George Mathews, ex-Governors Edward Telfair and Nathan Brownson, future Governors George Handley and Jared Irwin, Chief Justice Henry Osborne, and long-time Secretary of State John Milton were chosen as delegates. Most of the delegates had been prominent during the Revolution, but there were a few whose only participation in Georgia politics was as members of the convention. The proposed constitution was debated in the convention on Saturday, December 29, and unanimously ratified on Monday morning, December 31. Two days later the formal ratification and signing by the twenty-six delegates present took place. As the last name was signed to the ratification thirteen salutes were fired from two field pieces stationed opposite the state house. On January 5 the convention assembled for its final session, at which it agreed to a letter to the Continental Congress announcing the ratification and ordered its journal published.[11]

The journal of the convention records only formal actions and gives no indication of the debate that took place. The few letters discovered that mention the convention say that everybody was favorable to the constitution.[12] The fact that the debate lasted but one day and that every delegate present signed the ratification bears out this impression. The one located charge of Chief Justice Osborne to a grand jury in the fall of 1787 contains the hope that good would come from the Philadelphia convention.[13] William Few, a member of the Philadelphia convention, was a member of the ratifying convention and obviously worked for the ratification of the constitution. William Pierce, another delegate to Philadelphia, was probably in Georgia when the ratifying convention met. Edward Telfair and Nathan Brownson undoubtedly worked for the ratification. Joseph Habersham, later to be Washington's postmaster general, and George Handley, to be appointed collector of the port of Brunswick in 1789, certainly favored the new constitution. No opponent of the constitution in the ratifying convention is known to have existed. The only located advice against complete adoption of the new constitution is a letter from Lachlan McIntosh to a delegate to the ratifying convention in which he suggests ratification with the proviso that another convention be called to reconsider the constitution at some specified future time so that the interests of the Southern states—which would be in a minority in the new government—might be safeguarded.[14]

The Indian danger in the state for the past two years, with the continued threat of a Creek war, was certainly one of the reasons that Georgia favored the constitution. Georgians realized that they could not protect themselves alone, and appeals to the Continental Congress had brought little help beyond negotiations which possibly delayed actual fighting. Throughout the fall and winter of 1787 Indian trouble was the biggest item of business of both the state executive and assembly. There seems no doubt that the majority of Georgians hoped to get more and better help against the Creeks out of a strengthened central government. Federal help was Georgia's only hope.

Free importation of slaves until 1808 allayed any opposition on the slavery question. The fact that so many Georgians had been born and raised outside the state must have helped to diminish local prejudice and to create a better feeling for the central government. Several important political leaders had recently moved to Georgia from New England, Virginia, and the Carolinas. There was no great internal political split in Georgia—between the coast and the upcountry, between radicals and conservatives, or between rich and poor—to hurt the chances of ratification. Commercial interests in Savannah and the frontiersmen could and did unite in favor of ratification.

Georgia was the fourth state to ratify the constitution after its submission to the states, and it was one of the three to ratify unanimously. Georgia did act very rapidly, considering that the Philadelphia convention had been adjourned for almost a month before a copy of the constitution was received in Georgia. However, the troubles caused by the Creek Indians were responsible for such rapid action. Except for the special session of the assembly to consider the Indian problem, the ratifying convention would have been delayed several months beyond the date it actually met. After ratification of the new constitution, Georgians anxiously awaited news that enough states had ratified and that the new government could go into operation. When word finally came the news was celebrated in Augusta with proper ceremonies.[15]

There had been a few attempts before 1787[16] to amend the Georgia constitution of 1777, but no real action was taken until Georgia had ratified the new federal constitution. The 1788 assembly ignored the amending process specified in the 1777 constitution and provided that a constitutional convention, consisting of three members from each county elected by the assembly, should meet after nine states had adopted the federal constitution, to alter or amend the state constitution. Eighteen of the thirty-three delegates elected by the assembly had been members of the convention that had just ratified the new federal constitution, and twenty of the delegates were members of the assembly that elected them.[17]

After official word was received of the ratification of the new

federal constitution by nine states, the state constitutional convention was called to meet in Augusta on November 4, 1789, and
was in session from November 9 through 24.[18] The constitution
drawn up by the convention was modeled on the new federal
constitution but retained several items from the 1777 state constitution. The constitution was divided into four articles, the first
three of which laid down the organization and duties of the legislative, executive, and judicial departments. The fourth article
contained everything not immediately applicable to these three
departments. No records of the convention and little debate in
the public press or elsewhere about the proposed constitution
have been found. There were arguments that it set up a tyranny
by taking powers away from the immediate representatives of the
people. Others argued that it was superior to the old constitution
because it followed closely the new federal constitution. Instead of
creating tyranny it would abolish anarchy and create efficient
government by giving the governor powers similar to those of the
federal president. Instead of containing minute regulations, it
gave the government broad powers such as any government
needed. The slightly higher property qualification for voting
could be easily acquired by any Georgian worth his salt.[19]

The convention provided, in agreement with the resolution calling it into existence, that each county should elect three delegates
to meet in January, 1789, "vested with full power, and for the sole
purpose of adopting and ratifying, or rejecting" the proposed
constitution. This ratifying convention met on January 5 and, instead of ratifying or rejecting the proposed constitution, suggested eleven amendments. The more important of these reduced
the property qualification of members of both houses of the assembly, reduced the voter qualification to payment of a tax for the
previous year, changed the election of the governor from the
assembly to an electoral college in which each county should have
one vote, and changed the terms of the judges and the attorney
general from seven to three years. The convention then adjourned
until the second Tuesday in June to allow consideration of its
amendments by the people of the state.[20]

Despite the fact that the great majority of the members of this
ratifying convention were also members of the assembly, the assembly directed that a new ratifying convention be elected instead of the old one reassembling. The assembly specified that
the third convention could only consider the proposed constitution

and amendments and should propose no amendments itself. Yet the assembly suggested an additional amendment—that no money be drawn from the treasury except by appropriation.[21]

This third convention met in Augusta on May 4 and was urged by Governor George Walton to take final action and to adopt a constitution that would bring the state and federal governments into harmony. Otherwise, Walton feared the difference in the two constitutions would put the state in an awkward condition. This convention defeated an attempt to consider further amendments, spent only one day in debate, and then adopted a new constitution from the work of the two previous conventions. This constitution was ratified by the convention without further reference to the people and was to go into effect on the first Monday in October, 1789.[22]

Article I specified that there should be a two-house legislature, the General Assembly, consisting of a senate and a house of representatives. Each county had one senator elected every third year, who must be twenty-eight years of age, nine years an inhabitant of the United States, three years a citizen of Georgia, and the owner of 250 acres of land or property worth £250. Members of the house of representatives, elected annually, must be twenty-one years of age, seven years a citizen of the United States, two years an inhabitant of Georgia, and the owner of 200 acres of land or property worth £150. Both senators and representatives must be residents of the county from which they were elected, a practice not always followed under the constitution of 1777; and none could be clergymen or state or federal officials. Counties received from two to five representatives, roughly according to population. There were thirteen for the coastal counties, ten for the lower Savannah River counties, and eleven for the frontier counties. Probably the coast was over-represented, and the frontier under-represented; but the discrepancy was not so glaring as in some other states.[23] Each house had the usual legislative powers over its membership, and members were given the usual legislative immunity while attending sessions. General legislative power was conferred by the statement, "The General Assembly shall have power to make all laws and ordinances which they shall deem necessary and proper for the good of the state, which shall not be repugnant to this constitution."

Article II, concerned with the executive, made several important changes. The executive was to consist of a governor without any council for the first time in Georgia's history. The governor, to be elected for a two-year term of office by the senate from three people chosen by the house of representatives, must be thirty years of age, a citizen of the United States for twelve years, an inhabitant of Georgia for six years, and the owner of 500 acres of land and £1,000 additional property. Several new powers were given to the governor. He could grant reprieves and pardons except in cases of impeachment, treason, or murder, where the assembly retained final power. He was given a legislative veto which could be overridden by a two-thirds vote of both houses. The governor was also directed to issue writs of election to fill legislative vacancies, to give information to the assembly on the state of the republic, and to make recommendations to the assembly. For the first time some real executive leadership might now be possible in state government.

Article III kept the same judicial organization that already existed. Superior courts, the highest courts in the state, were to be held in each county twice each year under such regulations as the legislature specified. Inferior jurisdictions were to be determined by the assembly. Courts merchant were to continue as previously. Judges and the attorney general were to serve for three-year terms.

Article IV specified that electors must be citizens of the state, twenty-one years of age, who had paid a tax the preceding year and had resided within their county for six months. (The voting qualification under the 1777 constitution had been ownership of £10 property or the following of a mechanic's trade.) All state officials were to be elected by the assembly in the same manner as the governor. Freedom of the press and trial by jury were to continue. All persons were declared entitled to the right of *habeas corpus.* The free exercise of religion was guaranteed to all, and nobody was to be forced to support any religion but his own. The former constitutional prohibition against excessive fines and bail was dropped. Estates were not to be entailed, and intestate estates were to be divided equally between the children and the widow unless the widow elected to take her dower. For amendment it was specified that in the election of 1794 three members from each county were to be elected to meet in convention to make any needed amendments to the constitution. No mention was made of local government, subordinate state officials, public education, or many other things that had been included in the constitution of 1777. These things were now taken for granted and were left to the discretion of the assembly.

Georgia was now ready to begin government under new state and federal constitutions. In November, 1788, some confusion was caused by the failure of the assembly to secure a quorum at a session called to provide for the election of presidential electors. The 1789 assembly designated the electors in January just one day before the deadline set by Congress. These electors joined those in the other states in voting unanimously for George Washington as president.[24] William Few and James Gunn were elected federal senators; and George Mathews, Abraham Baldwin, and James Jackson federal representatives.[25] In agreement with the action of the United States Congress, in July all state officials were directed to take an oath to support the constitution of the United States;[26] and the new state constitution went into full effect in November with the meeting of the first assembly organized as it directed.[27] With the new state and federal governments in operation, the limits set for this study are reached.

THE MEANING OF THE
REVOLUTIONARY
PERIOD IN GEORGIA
1763 - 1789

18

****

WHAT were the main changes that six and one-half years of war, three and one-half years of British occupation, complete separation from Britain, and rapid physical and population growth brought to Georgia?

Throughout the period 1763-1789, much of Georgia's thinking and action can be traced directly to the frontier with its warlike Indians, good lands, and frontiersmen's conviction that a better day would soon arrive to compensate for the hard work and small rewards of the present. This frontier optimism can be seen over and over in actions of individual Georgians and of their government.

By 1763 Georgia had outgrown her idealistically impractical infancy and was enjoying a hardy adolescence. She was fast becoming an area of coastal rice plantations and small back-country farms. With the removal of the Spanish from the Floridas, her military security increased greatly. The movement of her boundary south to the St. Marys River and new cessions of Indian land which was opened to white settlement contributed to a rapid physical growth with a pushing back of the frontier that was to continue until the last Indians gave up their Georgia lands to the whites in the 1830s.

Within ten years the 1763 land cession was taken up, and frontiersmen—largely Scotch-Irish direct from Ireland and people from the colonies to the north—were clamoring for more of the rich lands to the north and west of Augusta. Adventurous spirits, people looking for better lands, and the dissatisfied came from as far north as Pennsylvania; but most were from the Carolinas and Virginia. In 1773 a new land cession was secured from the Creeks and the Cherokees that began filling up very rapidly and that helped the back country take on a new importance that was not fully realized by 1775.

Georgia's colonial leadership came from her able royal governor and people of his type. Governor James Wright was an excellent example of eighteenth century conservatism at its best. He believed that everything and everybody had a place and should fall into that place naturally. Political and social leadership under the best of political systems, the British constitution, went naturally to the "better" people. Others should follow their lead without much questioning. Yet Wright was far from being a reactionary who insisted upon keeping everything as it had been. He was too close to the frontier not to know that change was inevitable. He would do his best to direct that change along acceptable lines. He carried out his orders from London, even if he often thought them not the best orders that could be given, and sent his opinions to his superiors in guarded and respectful language. Wright must have regarded Georgia somewhat as does the father of a large and often unruly but basically sound family. He lived with Georgians for fifteen years and was a close enough observer to know by 1775 how they would react.

From 1763 to 1775 the major concern in Georgia was with physical and economic growth, and considerable growth took place. At the same time came the troubles between the colonials and the British government beginning with the Sugar and Stamp acts of 1764-65. While there seems to have been some continuity of personnel in the opposition to the action of the British government, there is no indication that there was a continuing organization, like the popular party in Massachusetts, or that there was sufficient build-up of resentment against the British government to explode into rebellion. Rather it seems that each incident was separate and distinct unless in point of time it was connected with another. But by 1775 there had been enough incidents to build up considerable opposition.

Most of the basic causes of the American War for Independence had little immediate effect in Georgia. There was no extensive trading class to be concerned with the trade regulations and import duties imposed by the revenue laws. Naturally Georgians objected to additional taxes. Who does not? Georgia had few or no land speculators to object to the proclamation line of 1763 beyond which white settlement could not go. The colony had not yet settled far enough for the proclamation line to be an immediate hindrance to westward expansion. Georgia had few influential people who stayed in perpetual debt to British merchants as did the Virginia tobacco planters. The help of the British Indian Department and army against the warlike Creek Indians was certainly needed. The refusal of the British authorities to send troops when Indian war was feared in the 1770s probably hurt the British cause in Georgia and helped to bring on the actual break with England.

The question "Why did Georgia revolt?" is not easily answered. The answer lies in the fact that Georgians considered themselves Americans and were interested in and hurt by the same things that affected the other colonies. They had a sense of belonging that transcended their immediate problems and needs and caught them up in the general program of objection to British policy. They objected to the principles behind such things as the Quebec Act, the Stamp Act, the Townshend Acts, the Intolerable Acts—in short, to the whole attempt of the British government to acquire more power at the expense of the colonials. They were prepared to object in the same way that their fellow colonials did. The fact that Georgia almost always acted after the other colonies did and that her actions usually were similar to those of the other colonies, especially South Carolina, leads to the conclusion that Georgians would not have rebelled had they been left to themselves. To have found so small, weak, and physically exposed a colony in the forefront of revolution would have been most unexpected.

Once the fighting began, Georgia did about what could have been expected from a small, weak state close to the British garrison at St. Augustine and the British-backed Creek Indians. She could never defend herself alone, yet she occupied a frontier position, the protection of which helped the states to her north. The military fiascoes in Georgia were no worse than in other states. Georgians overthrew their colonial government and set up a state government much as did the other rebellious colonies. The state government from its very beginning was much more democratic than the colonial government had been. Effective political power passed immediately into the hands of the majority of the citizens to be used as they saw fit. Voting qualifications were low enough that practically every free man could vote, and the back country received a fairer proportion of representation in the assembly than it did in many of the older states. The fact that Whig military and political activity in Georgia kept that area within the American fold and out of complete British control was of great value to the United States when the peace treaty was written in 1782-83.

British occupation of much of the state during the fighting years limited the area over which the state government could exercise effective power and made the very existence of a state government doubtful for about a year. However, just as soon as there was enough of the state free of the British, a state government reasserted its authority. Most of the colonial political leadership had come from the coast. With the coast under British control for three and one-half years, the upcountry people made up the state government from 1779 through July, 1782, and they gained much political experience which would have been difficult to acquire in any other way.

When the British left Georgia in 1782, many of the old political leaders were dead, gone, or had acquired a Tory taint. The upcountry people did not give up their political importance acquired during the war years. Thus Georgia acquired a much better political balance between the upcountry and the coast than had ever existed before in Georgia and better than existed in older states like South Carolina and Virginia. Though a coast-upcountry political split did exist to some extent in the 1780s and into the nineteenth century, it was not nearly so serious a split as in some other states. With the rapid filling up of the upcountry, there was no chance that the coast could ever acquire real political control again. Upcountry political importance made for more social and economic equality in Georgia than had ever existed before and generally helped to bring more quickly the era of the supremacy of the common man to Georgia. Thus the War of the Revolution and the separation from Britain had a great deal to do with increasing political, economic, and social democracy in Georgia. All Georgians soon realized this changed condition, from which many of them profited.

A comparison of typical leaders in the pre- and postwar years illustrates very well this new importance of the common man. Governor James Wright and James Habersham are good examples of colonial leadership. Wright was a professionally trained lawyer from the English Inns of Court who rose on the ladder of colonial officeholding because of his own ability and not through influence at court. Habersham had come to Georgia in the days of its youth and had grown with it until he became one of the most respected men in the colony. Both men accepted without question the pattern of deference to England and the social stratification so common in the eighteenth century. After the Revolution, Elijah Clarke and George Walton were typical political leaders. Clarke was a North Carolina frontiersman who came to Georgia with almost no material goods but with ability to succeed in the rough-and-tumble society of the frontier. He was a leader in the severe back-country fighting of the war years and a real force in postwar politics. He was usually a member of the assembly, often a member of the council, and a militia brigadier general in the decade after the war. Yet his biographer does not think that he ever learned to write even his own name. Walton was a Virginia orphan who had been apprenticed to a carpenter. He came to Georgia, read law, and began to assume importance during the Revolution. He maintained his position of importance—as governor, chief justice, member of the Continental Congress, member of the Constitutional Convention, and United States senator —by an aggressive leadership that got things done and appealed to frontier voters. He was one of the most popular leaders in Georgia in the 1780s and a real force in state politics. Neither Clarke nor Walton would likely have risen to such important positions so easily in colonial Georgia. Truly, they were products of the Revolution.

Once the British were out of the state, Georgians did not think that anything could hold them back—certainly not "a few Indians." The Creeks had more fighting men than Georgia; they had Spanish backing, and the excellent leadership of Alexander McGillivray. Yet they were never too much for Georgia frontiersmen—that is, until the Creeks were really ready to fight. Then the call for help from Georgia went out to South Carolina, Franklin, Virginia, the United States, or anybody else who might help. Advice from the more conservative Georgians to go slow was almost never heeded, and the frontiersmen usually carried the state government along with them in the effort to secure the lands they wanted from the Creeks. Frontiersmen had that supreme confidence in the right of their position and in their ability to accomplish what they wanted.

Throughout the entire period of 1763-1789, Georgia's physical growth was fairly steady and really quite remarkable. The situation during the war years is difficult to document with any degree of certainty; but there is no doubt that there was growth between 1776 and 1782, especially in the back-country region of Wilkes County. Georgia offered unlimited political and economic opportunity for people of ability who were willing to work for what they wanted. The final removal of the restraining hand of the British government in 1782 and the absence of any other restraints, except the ability of the individual concerned, made for rapid growth in most ways.

Georgia's postwar political democracy has long been known and praised by Georgians. Social and economic democracy, certainly as important, have not received the same amount of emphasis. Religion, education, and ease of land ownership are good examples in these fields. In the colonial period the Anglican church occupied a position of privilege not commensurate with the number of its communicants. With the loss of this favored position during the war, the Anglican church quickly lost its importance to the Methodist and Baptist churches, the churches of the frontiersman and Georgia's leading denominations ever since. The creation of what amounted to a statewide public school system and a state university in the postwar decade was an advance that could hardly have been made in the colonial period. The struggles of George Whitefield to change Bethesda into a college prove this. The public school system did not long continue as envisioned by its creators, but perhaps the state lost its vision of human perfectibility for the common man. Confiscation of Tory estates and the removal of colonial restraints to land granting enabled Georgians to get more land—the economic basis upon which both political and social democracy were built—easier and cheaper than ever before.

Once the storm and dust of battle had cleared away, it was possible to see the changes that had taken place. The majority of Georgians accepted these changes as good. A few of the old privileged group who went along with the separation from England were not so certain. Others, like Governor Wright, must have thought their world was falling apart, as indeed it was. Wright lived to see the fall of the old Georgia that he loved and had done so much to create, but he did not survive long enough to see the new and different Georgia that emerged from the chaos

and ruin of war—a Georgia that he should have been able to pre-
dict in large measure had his knowledge and vision not been dulled
by longings for the old order which would not return. Perhaps it
was just as well that Wright did not live long enough to see the
new Georgia. He might not have understood the possibilities of
the changes any more than Edmund Burke did those of the
French Revolution in 1790. Frontier Georgians did understand
the possibilities and worked hard to take full advantage of them.

APPENDICES

****

APPENDIX A. GEORGIA'S CHIEF EXECUTIVES, 1763-1789

COLONIAL PERIOD

James Wright, appointed Lieutenant Governor, May 30, 1760; assumed duties in Georgia, October 31, 1760.

James Wright, appointed Governor, May 4, 1761; assumed duties in Georgia, January 28, 1762.

James Habersham, President of Council and Acting Governor, July 13, 1771, through February, 1773.

James Wright, resumed duties as Governor, February, 1773; arrested by order of the Provincial Congress, January 18, 1776; fled Georgia, February 11, 1776.

EARLY REVOLUTIONARY

William Ewen, President of the Council of Safety, June 22, 1775.

George Walton, President of the Council of Safety, December 11, 1775.[1]

William Ewen, President of the Council of Safety, February 20, 1776.

RULES AND REGULATIONS OF 1776

Archibald Bulloch, President and Commander-in-Chief, late April, 1776.

Button Gwinnett, President and Commander-in-Chief, March 4, 1777.

CONSTITUTION OF 1777

John Adam Treutlen, Governor, early May, 1777.

John Houstoun, Governor, January 10, 1778.

William Glascock, President of the Executive Council, January 21, 1779.

Seth John Cuthbert, President *pro tempore* of the Supreme Executive Council, July 24, 1779.

John Wereat, President of the Supreme Executive Council, August 6, 1779.

---

1. It is not certain whether Ewen served until Walton was elected in December.

George Walton, Governor by self-styled assembly, November, 1779.[2]
Richard Howley, Governor, January 4, 1780.
Stephen Heard, President of the Executive Council, May 24, 1780.
John Wereat, President of the Supreme Council, August 6, 1779.
Myrick Davies, President of the Executive Council, August, 1780.
Nathan Brownson, Governor, August 17, 1781.
John Martin, Governor, January 2, 1782.

COLONIAL GOVERNMENT DURING THE REVOLUTION

Lieutenant Colonel James Mark Prevost, Lieutenant Governor appointed by the British military commanders, March 4, 1779.
Sir James Wright, Governor, July, 1779, through July, 1782.

CONSTITUTION OF 1777

Lyman Hall, Governor, January 7, 1783.
John Houstoun, Governor, January 8, 1784.
Samuel Elbert, Governor, January 6, 1785.
Edward Telfair, Governor, January 9, 1786.
George Mathews, Governor, January 5, 1787.
James Jackson, Governor, January 7, 1788. Declined to serve.
George Handley, President of the Executive Council, January 16, 1788.
George Handley, Governor, January 24, 1788.
George Walton, Governor, January 6, 1789, through November 4, 1789.

APPENDIX B. ASSEMBLY SESSIONS, 1763-1789
ROYAL ASSEMBLY IN THE COLONIAL PERIOD

Date met		Date session ended	Reason
1763	Jan. 17	April 7	Adjourned
	Nov. 21	Dec. 16	Adjourned
1764	Jan. 10	Feb. 29	Prorogued
	May 26	May 29	Prorogued
	(No actual meeting)	Sept. 4	Dissolved
	Nov. 20	Dec. 20	Adjourned
1765	Jan. 15	March 24	Prorogued
	Oct. 22	Dec. 19	Adjourned
1766	Jan. 14	March 6	Prorogued
	June 16	June 18	Prorogued
	July 15	July 22	Adjourned
	Nov. 10	Dec. 19	Adjourned
1767	Jan. 13	March 26	Prorogued
	Oct. 26	Oct. 30	Adjourned
1768	Jan. 11	April 11	Dissolved
	Nov. 7	Dec. 24	Dissolved

2. Presumably both Wereat and Walton claimed to be the chief executive from November, 1779, until January 4, 1780.

	Date met	Date session ended	Reason
1769	Oct. 31	Dec. 20	Adjourned
1770	Jan. 8	May 10	Prorogued
	Oct. 22	Dec. 21	Adjourned
1771	Jan. 8	Feb. 22	Dissolved
	April 23	April 26	Dissolved
1772	April 21	April 25	Dissolved
	Dec. 9	Dec. 18	Adjourned
1773	Jan. 18	March 13	Adjourned
	June 8	Sept. 16	Adjourned
	Sept. 28	Sept. 29	Prorogued
1774	Jan. 18	March 12	Adjourned
	June 15	June 20	Adjourned
1775	Jan. 17	Feb. 10	Prorogued
	Nov. 7 (No quorum assembled.)		
1776	Jan. 16 (No quorum assembled.)		

PROVINCIAL CONGRESSES

Number[1]	Date Elected	Dates in Session
1st.	Dec., 1774	Jan. 8-25, 1775.
2nd.	June, 1775	July 4-17, 1775. Expired Aug. 20, 1775.
3rd.	Aug.-Sept., 1775	Nov. 16-Dec. 9, 1775. Expired Dec. 31, 1775.
4th.	Jan., 1776	Jan. 20-April 15, 1776.[2] June 4-? Expired Aug. 31, 1776.
5th.[3]	Sept. 1-10, 1776	First Tuesday in Oct.-? Nov. 18, 1776-Feb. 24 (?), 1777.[4]

ASSEMBLIES UNDER CONSTITUTION OF 1777

	Date met	Date session ended
1777	May 7 (?)	June 7
	Aug. 19	Sept. 16
1778	Jan. 10, or earlier	March 1
	April 27 or later	May 4 (Adjourned until first Tuesday in Oct.)
		June 26
	Oct. 8, or earlier	Nov. 15 (?)

1. A new number is assigned after each new election.
2. There were probably adjournments in this period, but insufficient records exist to determine positively.
3. This Congress was usually called a Convention. It carried on the same type of legislative business that other Congresses had done and also wrote the Constitution of 1777.
4. There were probably adjournments in this period, but no proof is available. The date of expiration is unknown, but it was February 24 or a few days earlier.

Date met	*Date session ended*
1779 Jan. 7, or earlier	Jan. 23 still in session, no indication of how long session lasted.
July 4 & 24	(Indications that representatives of some of the counties met as an Assembly in Augusta but did not secure a quorum.)
Nov. 28, or earlier	Walton faction Assembly met. Apparently met no longer than two weeks.
1780 Jan. 4, or earlier	In session Jan. 23. No date of adjournment discovered. Apparently a short session.
1781 Aug. 17	Aug. 22
1782 Jan. 1	Jan. 12
April 17 (Quorum April 20)	May 4
July 3 (Quorum July 13)	Aug. 5
Oct. 21 (Quorum failed to meet.)	

COLONIAL ASSEMBLIES, 1779-1782

1780 May 8 or 9	June 12, adjourned
June 25	July 10, prorogued
Sept. 25	Oct. 7, adjourned
Oct. 17	Oct. 30, adjourned
Nov. 15	Nov. 15, adjourned
Dec. 11	Dec. 19, adjourned

From this date no complete journals are extant. The following dates when the assembly was actually known to have been in session are from the *Royal Georgia Gazette*. Apparently in 1781 and 1782 there were many short sessions and frequent adjournments.

1781 Jan. 15 met.
Feb. 28 bills approved.
March 6 bills approved
April 9 bills approved
April 26 bills approved
May 18 bills approved
May 19 adjourned until June 6
June 6 bill approved. Adjourned until June 26
June 26 met
Aug. 2 bills approved. Adjourned until Jan. 15, 1782
Oct. 2 met
Nov. 29 bill approved

STATE ASSEMBLIES UNDER CONSTITUTION OF 1777, 1783-1789

	Date met	Session ended
1782	Feb. 23 in session	
	May 31 in session	
	June 16 in session	
1783	Jan. 7	Feb. 18 adjourned
	May 1-6 No quorum	
	May 15-26 No quorum	
	July 1 (Quorum July 8)	Aug. 1
1784	Jan. 8	Feb. 26
	July 5-13. No. quorum	
	Oct. 6-14. No quorum	
1785	Jan. 4 (Quorum Jan. 6)	Feb. 22
1786	Jan. 3 (Quorum Jan. 9)	Feb. 14
	July 17 (Quorum July 22)	Aug. 15
1787	Jan. 2 (Quorum Jan. 4)	Feb. 11
	July 3-11. No quorum	
	Sept. 20 (Quorum Oct. 18)	Oct. 31
1788	Jan. 1 (Quorum Jan. 7)	Feb. 1
	July 22-Aug. 6. No quorum	
	Nov. 4-13. No quorum	
1789	Jan. 6	Feb. 4

APPENDIX C. GEORGIA'S DELEGATES IN THE CONTINENTAL CONGRESS, 1775-1788

	Delegate	Dates of Attendance
1775	Lyman Hall	May 13-Aug. 2
	Archibald Bulloch	Sept. 5-Nov. 26 (?)
	John Houstoun	Sept. 5-Dec. 14 (?)
	John Joachim Zubly	Sept. 5-?
	Noble Wimberly Jones	Did not attend
1776	Button Gwinnett	May 20-Aug. 2 (?)
	Lyman Hall	May 20-Nov. 2, Dec. 20-31
	George Walton[1]	June 29-Nov. 2, Dec. 12
	Archibald Bulloch	Did not attend
	John Houstoun	Did not attend
1777	Nathan Brownson	Jan. 3 (or earlier)-May 1
		Aug. 23-Oct. 9
	Lyman Hall	Jan. 1-Feb. 11 (or later)
	George Walton[1]	April 18 (or earlier)-Oct. 9

1. Walton was a member of the committee of three in Philadelphia for the period of Dec. 21, 1776 through March, 1777. This was Congressional business though attendance at Congress is not recorded for this period.

Delegate	Dates of Attendance
1777 Edward Langworthy	Nov. 17-Dec. 31
Joseph Wood	Nov. 17-Dec. 31
Button Gwinnett	Did not attend
John Houstoun	Did not attend
1778 Edward Langworthy	Jan. 1-June 27 (?), Aug. 15-Dec. 26
Joseph Wood	Jan. 1-Feb. 27 (or later)
Edward Telfair	July 13-Nov. 16 (?)
John Walton	July 23-Aug. 4 (or later) Aug. 31 (or later)- Nov. 16 (?)
Joseph Clay	Did not attend
Lyman Hall	Did not attend
George Walton	Did not attend
1779 Edward Langworthy	Jan. 1-April 12 (?)
John Houstoun	Did not attend
Edward Telfair	Did not attend
1780 William Few	May 15-Dec. 31
Edward Telfair	May 15-Sept. 12 (or later)
George Walton	May 15-Sept. 21 (or later) Oct. 20 (or earlier)-Dec. 31
Richard Howley	July 6 to Aug. 24 (or later) Sept. 25 (or earlier)-Dec. 31
Benjamin Andrew	Did not attend
Lyman Hall	Did not attend
1781 William Few	Jan. 1-July 18
Richard Howley	Jan. 1-June 18 (or later) July 7 (or earlier)-Sept. 21
George Walton	Jan. 1-Sept. 27
Edward Telfair	Sept. 17-Dec. 31
Noble Wimberly Jones	Sept. 27-Dec. 31
Samuel Stirk	Did not attend
1782 Noble Wimberly Jones	Jan. 1-Nov. 2
Edward Telfair	Jan. 1-Sept. 10 (or later)
William Few	May 1-Oct. 3 (or later)
1783 Joseph Habersham	Did not attend
William Houston	Did not attend
William Few	Did not attend
Joseph Clay	Did not attend
Nathan Brownson	Did not attend
1784 William Houstoun	June 30-Aug. 13, Nov. 1-Dec. 24
William Gibbons	Nov. 1-Dec. 24
Samuel Elbert	Declined to serve

	Delegate	Dates of Attendance
1784	William Few	Did not attend
	Joseph Habersham	Did not attend
	Lachlan McIntosh	Did not attend
	Edward Telfair	Did not attend
1785	William Houstoun	Jan. 19-Dec. 30
	John Habersham	May 30-Oct. 27
	Abraham Baldwin	May 30-Oct. 13, Nov. 23-Dec. 2
	William Few	Did not attend
	William Gibbons	Did not attend
	Edward Telfair	Did not attend
1786	William Houstoun	Jan. 26-Nov. 3
	William Few	May 8-Dec. 4
	Henry Osborne	Did not attend
1787	William Few	Jan. 17-May 12, July 5-Aug. 3
		Sept. 20-Nov. 7
	William Pierce	Jan. 17-May 24, July 6-Aug. 1,
		Aug. 27-Oct. 1
	Abraham Baldwin	Nov. 5-10
	George Walton	Did not attend
1788	Abraham Baldwin	Jan. 21-Feb. 9, March 31-Sept. 18
	William Few	May 26-Sept. 18
	Edward Telfair	Did not attend
	James Gunn	Did not attend
	George Walton	Did not attend
1789	Abraham Baldwin	May have attended Jan.-March[2]
	Edward Telfair	Did not attend
	James Gunn	Did not attend
	Nathaniel Pendleton	Did not attend
	William O'Bryen	Did not attend

2. Baldwin was in New York, but there is doubt if he presented his credentials or attended Congress in this period.

NOTES

****

CHAPTER I

1. The journal of this congress was printed in Charleston in 1764 and is reproduced in William L. Saunders, Walter Clark, and Stephen B. Weeks, eds., *The Colonial Records of the State of North Carolina* (10 vols., Raleigh, 1886-1890), X, 156-207. (Henceforth cited as *NCCR*.) A complete account of the congress and a copy of its treaty are in Charles G. Jones, Jr., *The History of Georgia* (2 vols., Boston, 1883), II, 43-46.

2. The most complete account of the governmental organization and operation of royal Georgia is Percy Scott Flippin, "The Royal Government in Georgia, 1752-1776," *Georgia Historical Quarterly*, VIII, 1-37, 81-120, 243-291; IX, 187-245; X, 1-25, 251-276; XII, 326-352; XIII, 128-153. (Henceforth cited as *GHQ*.) Shorter accounts are in Albert B. Saye, *A Constitutional History of Georgia, 1732-1945* (Athens, 1948), 47-70, and in any general history of Georgia.

3. See article on Wright by E. Irving Carlyle in *Dictionary of National Biography*, LXIII, 107-109.

4. Wright to the Earl of Hillsborough, May 31, 1768, Allen D. Candler and Lucian Lamar Knight, eds., *The Colonial Records of the State of Georgia* (26 vols., Atlanta, 1904-1916. Vols. 27-39 in manuscript at Georgia Department of Archives and History, Atlanta); Ms. CRG, XXXVII, 311. (Henceforth cited as *CRG* or *Ms. CRG*.)

5. For accounts of Wright's plantations, slaves, crops, etc., see *Collections of the Georgia Historical Society*, VI (Savannah, 1904), 101-121. (Henceforth cited as *Collections*, GHS.)

6. John R. Alden, *John Stuart and the Southern Colonial Frontier* (Ann Arbor, 1944), 232, 294-295; Ms. CRG, XXXVII, 329; *CRG*, X, 576-579; *Georgia Gazette*, Dec. 14, 1768; Wright to Hillsborough, Jan. 14, 1769, Ms. CRG, XXXVII, 391.

7. Wright to Hillsborough, Jan. 5, 1767, Ms. CRG, XXXVII, 154.

8. On the 1773 cession see Alden, *John Stuart*, 301-306; Ms. CRG, XXXVII, 547-655. The treaty is in *ibid.*, XXXIX, 499.

9. The 1773-1774 Creek troubles are treated in Alden, *John Stuart*, 306-311; Jones, *History of Georgia*, II, 132-135; *Georgia Gazette* for the period; and *CRG* and Ms. CRG, *passim*.

10. On land granting see Flippin, "The Land System," *GHQ*, X, 1-25.

11. Council minutes, Oct. 2, 1770, *CRG*, XI, 155; James Habersham to Henry Laurens, June 3, 1771, *Collections*, GHS, VI, 132; Habersham to James Wright, Dec. 29, 1771, *ibid.*, 159.

12. "Report of Sir James Wright on the Conditions of the Province of Georgia, on 20th Sept. 1773," *Collections*, GHS, III, 167. See also Stella H. Sutherland, *Population Distribution in Colonial America* (New York, 1936), 259-260.

13. Wright's report Sept. 20, 1773, *Col-*

lections, GHS, III, 164-165.

14. *Ibid.* and *Georgia Gazette* furnish most of the information about Georgia's trade.

15. The best treatment of religion in colonial and Revolutionary Georgia is Reba Carolyn Strickland, *Religion and the State in Georgia in the Eighteenth Century* (New York, 1939). The information on religion comes from Strickland unless another source is indicated.

16. *CRG,* XVIII, 258-272, summarized in Strickland, *Religion and the State in Ga.,* 104-105.

17. Strickland, *Religion and the State in Ga.,* 130; *CRG,* XII, 20-21, 320.

18. Strickland, *Religion and the State in Ga.,* 110.

19. The best picture of Georgia dissenters at the end of the colonial period is a very interesting "Letter of Rev. John J. Zubly, of Savannah, Georgia," [1773], in *Proceedings of Massachusetts Historical Society,* 1864-1865, pp. 214-219.

20. Strickland, *Religion and the State in Ga.,* 108-109; J. H. Campbell, *Georgia Baptists* (Macon, Ga., 1874), 175-176.

CHAPTER II

1. *CRG,* XVII, 113-114, 131-132, 345-346, 353, 356-358, 696, 763-764; XIV, 459.

2. Assembly resolutions March 25, 1765, in *CRG,* XIV, 252-253; XVII, 199-200. Assembly committee of correspondence to Colonial Agent Knox, April 15, 1765, *Collections,* GHS, VI, 30-33.

3. Committee of correspondence to Knox, April 15, 1765, *Collections,* GHS, VI, 32; James Habersham to Knox, Oct. 27, 1765, *ibid.,* 44-46.

4. Committee of correspondence to Knox, July 18, 1765, *ibid.,* 40-41.

5. See especially *Georgia Gazette,* April 25, May 2, June 27, Aug. 15, 22, Sept. 5, 19, Oct. 3, 10, 17, 24, 1765.

6. *CRG,* XIV, 270-273.

7. *Ibid.,* 270-274. *Georgia Gazette,* Oct. 31, 1765.

8. *Georgia Gazette,* Oct. 31, 1765; Wright to Conway, Jan. 31, 1766, Jones, *History of Georgia,* II, 61.

9. *Georgia Gazette,* Oct. 31, Nov. 14, 1765.

10. Oct. 31, 1765, *CRG,* IX, 435.

11. *Georgia Gazette,* Nov. 7, 1765.

12. *Ibid.*

13. *CRG,* IX, 438-439. Proclamation in *Georgia Gazette,* Nov. 14, 1765.

14. Wright to Conway, Jan. 31, 1766, Jones, *History of Georgia,* II, 61-62.

15. *CRG,* XIV, 300-301, 304-306, 315.

16. Nov. 22, 1765, *ibid.,* IX, 439-440.

17. *Ibid.,* 453-458, 460; Wright to Conway, Jan. 31, 1766, Jones, *History of Georgia,* II, 62.

18. Wright to Board of Trade, Jan. 15, 1766, BT Ga., XXX, 273, quoted in Flippin, *GHQ,* VIII, 91-92; Wright to Conway, Jan. 31, 1766, Jones, *History of Georgia,* II, 62; extract of a letter from Georgia, Jan. 6, 1766, *South Carolina Gazette and Country Journal,* Jan. 21, 1766.

19. Wright to Conway, Jan. 31, 1766, Jones, *History of Georgia,* II, 62; *S. C. Gazette,* Jan. 21, 1766; James Habersham to George Whitefield, Jan. 27, 1766, *Collections,* GHS, VI, 54-55.

20. *S. C. Gazette,* Feb. 25, 1766; Ms. CRG, XXXVII, 121-122.

21. *S. C. Gazette,* Oct. 31, Dec. 17, 1765; Ms. S. C. Council Journal (S. C. Archives Dept., Columbia), 628, 639, 649-650, 701-702, 703-709; William Bull to Conway, Feb. 6, 1766, Ms. Public Records of S. C., XXXI, 22-25; Wright to Conway, Feb. 12, 1766, Ms. CRG, XXXVII, 112.

22. Wright to Conway, Feb. 7, 1766, Jones, *History of Georgia,* II, 64-65.

23. *S. C. Gazette,* April 29, 1766.

24. Wright to Conway, March 10, 1766, Ms. CRG, XXXVII, 116-117.

25. *CRG,* XIV, 300-301, 304-306, 315.

26. *Ibid.,* 358.

27. *Ibid.,* 370-372, 374.

28. *Ibid.,* 377-381. Wright to Conway, July 23, 1766, Ms. CRG, XXXVII, 129-130.

29. Shelburne to Wright, Sept. 22, 1766, Ms. CRG, XXXVII, 126-127.

30. John J. Zubly, "The Stamp Act Repealed." Pamphlet, Rare Book Room, Library of Congress. (Hence-

forth cited as LC.)

31. For a general treatment of the Georgia agent see Flippin, "Royal Government in Georgia," *GHQ,* VIII, 284-291.

32. Committee of correspondence to Knox, July 18, 1765, *Collections,* GHS, VI, 40-41.

33. Habersham to Knox, Oct. 28, 30, 1765, *ibid.,* 44-49.

34. *CRG,* XIV, 293-294; XVII, 224.

35. *CRG,* XIV, 335-336.

36. *CRG,* XVII, 269.

37. *CRG,* XIV, 317-319.

38. *Ibid.,* 387, 458; XVII, 356; Habersham to Samuel Lloyd, Sept. 5, 1767, *Collections,* GHS, VI, 60.

39. *CRG,* XVII, 363-368, 372-373.

40. *Ibid.,* 373-374; Wright to Shelburne, April 6, 1767, Ms. CRG, XXXVII, 183-187.

41. *CRG,* X, 433.

42. *CRG,* XIV, 527, 567, 573-574; XVII, 392, 438; XIX, Part I, 12-14.

43. *Georgia Gazette,* Jan. 26, March 9, 1774; CRG, XVII, 774-786. Franklin's career as Georgia Agent is treated fully in Alfred Owen Aldridge, "Benjamin Franklin as Georgia Agent," *Georgia Review,* VI, 161-173.

44. Wright to Commons House, Jan. 20, 1767, *CRG,* XIV, 412-414.

45. Commons House to Wright, Feb. 18, 1767, *ibid.,* 441; Wright to Shelburne, April 6, 1767, Jones, *History of Georgia,* II, 97-98; Wright to Gage, Feb. 25, 1767, Gage Papers, American Series, William L. Clements Library, University of Michigan. (Henceforth cited as CL.)

46. Commons House to Wright, March 26, 1767, *CRG,* XIV, 474-475; Wright to Gage, April 2, 1767, Gage Papers, Am. Series.

47. *CRG,* XIV, 474-477; Wright to Gage, July 20, 1767, Gage Papers, Am. Series.

48. Gage to Wright, May 16, 1767, Gage Papers, Am. Series; and Ms. CRG, XXXVII, 245-246.

49. Shelburne to Wright, July 18, 1767, Ms. CRG, XXXVII, 214.

50. Wright to both houses of assembly, Oct. 27, 1767, *CRG,* XIV, 479-480, 486; XVII, 380.

51. *Ibid.,* XIX, Part I, 44-45.

52. Gage to Wright, June 12, 24, Aug. 25, 1768, Gage Papers, Am. Series.

53. For the general history of American legislatures' reaction to the Mutiny Act see John C. Miller, *Origins of the American Revolution* (Boston, 1943), 237-240; and George E. Howard, *Preliminaries of the Revolution* (New York, 1905), 175-176, 183-185.

54. Wright to Shelburne, April 6, 1767, Jones, *History of Georgia,* II, 98-99.

55. Act of April 11, 1768, *CRG,* XIX, Part I, 8-9.

56. April 11, 1768, *CRG,* XIV, 584.

57. Alexander Wylly to Speaker of Massachusetts House of Representatives, June 16, 1768, *Georgia Gazette,* Aug. 31, 1768.

58. Hillsborough to Wright, Sept. 15, 1768, Ms. CRG, XXXVII, 332-333.

59. Wright to Hillsborough, May 23, 1768, *ibid.,* 282-283.

60. *CRG,* XVII, 454; XIV, 592-593, 595-596.

61. *Ibid.,* XIV, 643-645.

62. *Ibid.,* 656-659; *Georgia Gazette,* Dec. 28, 1768; Wright to Hillsborough, Dec. 23, 1768, Ms. CRG, XXXVII, 380.

63. Wright to Hillsborough, Aug. 15, 1769, Ms. CRG, XXXVII, 412.

64. *Georgia Gazette,* July 19, 1769.

65. *Ibid.,* Sept. 13, 1769.

66. *Ibid.,* Sept. 20, 1769.

67. *Ibid.;* Allen D. Candler, ed., *The Revolutionary Records of the State of Georgia* (3 vols., Atlanta, 1908), I, 8-11. (Henceforth cited as *RRG.*)

68. Wright to Hillsborough, Sept. 20, 1769, Ms. CRG, XXXVII, 417-418; March 1, 1770, *ibid.,* 436; *Georgia Gazette,* March 21, 1770.

69. Wright to Hillsborough, Aug. 15, 1769, Jones, *History of Georgia,* II, 109-112.

70. *Georgia Gazette,* Sept. 27, Oct. 4, 1769.

71. Wright to Hillsborough, Nov. 8, 1769, March 1, May 10, 1770, Ms. CRG, XXXVII, 423, 436, 441-442; Edward Telfair to Basil Cowper,

Oct. 7, 1767, Telfair Papers, Mss. Division, Duke University Library.

72. Wright to Hillsborough, Nov. 8, 1769, May 10, 1770, Ms. CRG, XXXVII, 423, 441.

73. *S. C. Gazette*, May 10, June 28, Dec. 13, 1770; *Virginia Gazette* (P D), Aug. 16, 1770.

74. March 25, 1765, *CRG*, XVIII, 689-691.

75. Wright to secretary of state, Dec. 26, 1768, PRO, Board of Trade, Ga., XXXI, 231, quoted in Flippin, *GHQ*, VIII, 245.

76. *CRG*, X, 945-946; XV, 46-49, 86-87; Wright to secretary of state, May 11, 1770, Ms. CRG, XXXVII, 450-451.

77. Commons House to Wright, Feb. 20, 1770, *CRG*, XV, 123-124.

78. *Ibid.*, 127-128, 159-160; Council to Wright, March 12, 1770, *Georgia Gazette*, March 14, 1770.

79. *CRG*, XV, 153; XIX, Part I, 170.

80. *Ibid.*, XV, 202, 206-207.

81. Feb. 20, 1771, *ibid.*, 298-299.

82. *Ibid.*, 295-296; XI, 253-257.

83. Feb. 22, *ibid.*, XI, 253-258; XV, 300.

84. Wright to Dartmouth, Aug. 10, 1773, Ms. CRG, XXXVIII, Part I, 83-84; Dartmouth to Wright, Oct. 28, 1773, *ibid.*, 92-93.

85. April 24, 1771, *CRG*, XV, 305-306.

86. *Ibid.*, 311-312.

87. *Ibid.*, XI, 335-336; XVII, 650; XV, 313-314; Wright to Hillsborough, April 30, 1771, Ms. CRG, XXXVII, 535-538.

88. Hillsborough to Habersham, Dec. 4, 1771, Ms. CRG, XXXVII, 552-553; *CRG*, XI, 429.

89. See letters of Habersham to Wright, Hillsborough, Knox, and others in the fall and winter, 1771-1772, Ms. CRG, XXXVII, 550-625; *Collections*, GHS, VI, 150-151, 155-158, 166.

90. Habersham to Wright, March 12, 1772, *Collections*, GHS, VI, 168-169. Only nineteen people in Savannah voted in this election.

91. *CRG*, XV, 320-323; Ms. CRG, XXXVII, 637-647.

92. *CRG*, XV, 324-325, 329-330; XVII, 655-658.

93. *Ibid.*, XV, 330-334; XVII, 663-664;

Habersham to Hillsborough, April 30, 1772, *Collections*, GHS, VI, 174-180.

94. Hillsborough to Habersham, Aug. 7, 1772, Ms. CRG, XXXVIII, Part I, 1-3.

95. *Collections*, GHS, VI, 181, 183-184.

96. John J. Zubly, *Calm and Respectful Thoughts on the Negative of the Crown on a speaker chosen and presented by the Representatives of the People*. Pamphlet, Rare Book Room, LC.

97. *Collections*, GHS, VI, 187-188, 197.

98. *CRG*, XV, 337-338; Habersham to Charles Pryce, Jan. 16, 1773, *Collections*, GHS, VI, 221-222.

99. *Collections*, GHS, VI, 145-223, *passim*.

100. A minute of the court meeting, Jan. 7, 1772, is in Public Record Office (London), Colonial Office, Class 5, Vol. 145, p. 8v. (Henceforth cited PRO, CO 5:.)

101. *Ibid.*, p. 8v, 8r. See memorial of Chief Justice Stokes on these applications in PRO, CO 5:116, 334ff, and Ms. CRG, XXXIV, 35-36.

102. Sept. 10, 1773, *CRG*, XV, 421-427.

103. *Georgia Gazette*, Feb. 2, 1774. This committee consisted of the speaker, Noble Wimberly Jones, Joseph Clay, Samuel Farley, David Zubly, Thomas Nethercliff, Nathaniel Hall, Henry Yonge, John Stirk, or any five of them.

CHAPTER III

1. Wright to Dartmouth, July 25, 1774, *American Archives*, 4 Series (6 vols., Washington, 1837-1846), I, 633-634.

2. *RRG*, I, 11; *American Archives*, 4 Series, I, 549.

3. Wright to Dartmouth, July 25, 1774, *American Archives*, 4 Series, I, 633-634.

4. "A Friend of Georgia" handbill dated July 25, 1774, filed with *Georgia Gazette* in GHS.

5. *Georgia Gazette*, Aug. 3, 1774; George White, *Historical Collections of Georgia* (New York, 1854), 44.

6. *American Archives*, 4 Series, I, 638-639.

7. A copy is in *RRG*, I, 12-13.

8. Aug. 5, 1774, *ibid.*, 14-15; Jones,

History of Georgia, II, 150-151.

9. *Georgia Gazette,* Aug. 17, 1774; *RRG,* I, 15-17.

10. Letter of Sept. 2, 1774, *American Archives,* 4 Series, I, 766-767.

11. Wright to Dartmouth, Aug. 13, 1774, *ibid.,* 708; Aug. 24, 1774, *Collections,* GHS, III, 180-182; Wright to Gage, Aug. 19, 1774, Gage Papers, Am. Series.

12. Apparently this protest was taken to Savannah by someone who did not attend the meeting; it is not clear if he tried to gain admission. The petition is in *RRG,* I, 24-26, and the statement about its non-receipt is in *ibid.,* 22-23.

13. The following petitions have been located: Christ Church Parish, Savannah, 101 signatures; St. Paul's Parish, Kyokee and Broad River settlements, 127 signatures; St. Paul's Parish, Augusta, 38 signatures; St. George's Parish, Wrightsborough, 123 signatures; St. George's Parish, Queensborough (Irish Settlement), 53 signatures; St. George's Parish, 144 signatures; St. Matthew's Parish and Ebenezer, 47 signatures.

These petitions are in *Georgia Gazette,* Sept. 7, 21, 28, and Oct. 12, 1774. All but one are printed in *RRG,* I, 17-34, copied from White, *Hist. Coll. of Ga.,* 48-49, 283-284, 437, 438, 412-413, 603-606, with fewer signatures and other changes.

14. The objections to the objections are in *Georgia Gazette,* Sept. 21, Oct. 19, 26, 1774.

15. The reports of the St. John's meetings are rather indefinite. See a letter from St. John's Parish, Sept. 2, 1774, *American Archives,* 4 Series, I, 766-767, and *Georgia Gazette,* Aug. 24, Sept. 7, 1774.

16. Extract of a letter from Philadelphia, Sept. 3, 1774, *Georgia Gazette,* Sept. 21, 1774.

17. Not all early 1775 records are extant.

18. Wright to Gage, Nov. 4, Dec. 24, 1774, Gage Papers, Am. Series.

19. Wright's proclamation Nov. 11, 1774, *Georgia Gazette,* Nov. 16, 1774.

20. The first time any voting qualifica-

tion other than the ownership of fifty acres of land had been used in Georgia.

21. *Georgia Gazette,* Dec. 7, 14, 21, 28, 1774; Jan. 11, 1775.

22. Extract of a letter from Savannah, Dec. 9, 1774, *American Archives,* 4 Series, I, 1033-1034; Joseph Clay & Co. to Messrs. Bright & Pechin, Dec. 10, 1774, Ms. Letter Book of Joseph Clay & Co., GHS.

23. *Georgia Gazette,* Dec. 14, 1774.

24. *RRG,* I, 37-42; White, *Hist. Coll. of Ga.,* 554-556.

25. Wright to Dartmouth, Dec. 13, 1774, *American Archives,* 4 Series, I, 1040; Dec. 20, Ms. CRG, XXXVIII, Part I, 367-368; Wright to Gage, Dec. 24, 1775, Gage Papers, Am. Series.

26. *Georgia Gazette,* Jan. 25, 1775.

27. *RRG,* I, 54-56; White, *Hist. Coll. of Ga.,* 521-522.

28. *RRG,* I, 43-48; White, *Hist. Coll. of Ga.,* 58-61.

29. Letter of Jones, Bulloch, and Houstoun to Continental Congress, April 6, 1775, *RRG,* I, 63-66; Jones, *History of Georgia,* II, 172-174.

30. Wright to Dartmouth, Feb. 1, 1775, Ms. CRG, XXXVIII, Part I, 371-374. No journal of the congress is known to exist.

31. Council Minutes, Jan. 3 and 9, 1775, *Collections,* GHS, X, 7-10; Wright to Dartmouth, Feb. 1, 1775, Ms. CRG, XXXVIII, Part I, 371-374.

32. *RRG,* I, 34-36; *American Archives,* 4 Series, I, 1152-1153.

33. *RRG,* I, 36-37; *American Archives,* 4 Series, I, 1155-1156.

34. *American Archives,* 4 Series, I, 1154-1155.

35. *Ibid.,* 1153-1154; *Georgia Gazette,* Feb. 1, 1775.

36. *American Archives,* 4 Series, I, 1160; *Georgia Gazette,* Feb. 1, 1775.

37. *RRG,* I, 48-53.

38. Council Minutes, Feb. 10, 1775, *Collections,* GHS, X, 11-12; Feb. 11, 1775, *The Journals of Henry Melchior Muhlenberg* (3 vols., Philadelphia, 1942-1945), II, 682.

39. Jones, Bulloch, and Houstoun to Continental Congress, April 6, 1775,

RRG, I, 63-66; Jones, *History of Georgia,* II, 172-174. This letter is a very good summary from the viewpoint of disgusted Whigs of the situation in Georgia for the first three months of 1775. Jones to Benjamin Franklin, May 6, 1775, Noble W. Jones Papers, Duke University Library.

40. South Carolina action of Feb. 8 and 16, 1775, *S. C. Gazette,* March 6, 1775, and *RRG,* I, 57-58; Pennsylvania, April 27, *American Archives,* 5 Series, II, 421; Maryland, May 3, *ibid.,* 380; New Jersey, May 26, *New Jersey Archives,* X, 597-598; Virginia, June 19, *American Archives,* 4 Series, II, 1221.

41. May 17, 1775, *Journals of the Continental Congress, 1774-1789* (Library of Congress Edition, 34 vols., Washington, 1904-1937), II, 54. (Henceforth cited as *JCC.*)

42. Joseph Clay & Co. to Michael Collins, April 8, 1775, Ms. Letter Book of Joseph Clay & Co., GHS.

43. Andrew Elton Wells to Samuel Adams, March 18, 1775, Samuel Adams Papers, New York Public Library.

44. *RRG,* I, 58-62; *S. C. Gazette,* Feb. 27, 1775; *JCC,* II, 45-47.

45. *JCC,* II, 47. This is probably what Wright meant when he said that the St. John's people no sooner entered the association than they broke it. Wright to Dartmouth, April 24, 1775, White, *Hist. Coll. of Ga.,* 523.

46. *Georgia Gazette,* March 29, 1775; Wright to Dartmouth, April 24, 1775, Ms. CRG, XXXVIII, Part I, 426-427; *American Archives,* 4 Series, II, 1830-1831; *JCC,* II, 44-45, 47-50.

47. Council Minutes, Feb. 21, 1775, *Collections,* GHS, X, 12-14; Wright's proclamation of Feb. 21, 1775, *American Archives,* 4 Series, I, 1253; Wright to Dartmouth, Feb. 24, 1775, and supporting evidence, Ms. CRG, XXXVIII, Part I, 395-417.

48. Dartmouth to Wright, Feb. 1, 1775, Ms. CRG, XXXVIII, Part I, 364.

49. Gage to Major Furlong, April 16, 1775, Gage Papers, Am. Series; Gage to Wright, April 16, 1775, *Collections,* GHS, III, 188.

50. Wright to Gage, June 7, 1775, Gage Papers, Am. Series; Wright to Dartmouth, June 17, 1775, *Collections,* GHS, III, 187-188; council minutes, July 25, 1775, *ibid.,* X, 34.

51. The original and substituted letters are in *American Archives,* 4 Series, I, 1109-1111. See R. W. Gibbs, *Documentary History of the American Revolution* (3 vols., 1853-1857), I, 100; and John Drayton, *Memoirs of the American Revolution* (2 vols., 1821), I, 346-350, 357, for the story of the substitution of the letters. The substituted letter to Gage is in Gage Papers, Am. Series. Wright reported this episode to Dartmouth, Jan. 3, 1776, *Collections,* GHS, III, 230.

52. Lord William Campbell to Gage, July 1, 1775, Gage Papers, Am. Series; Charleston Committee of Intelligence to the Committee at Savannah, July 4, 1775, *American Archives,* 4 Series, II, 1569; *JCC,* II, 185; Wright to Dartmouth, July 10, 1775, *Collections,* GHS, III, 194-195.

53. Council minutes, May 2, 11, 1775, *Collections,* GHS, X, 20-22; Wright's proclamation, *Georgia Gazette,* May 17, 1775.

54. Jones, *History of Georgia,* II, 175-176, says that Noble W. Jones, Joseph Habersham, Edward Telfair, William Gibbons, Joseph Clay, John Milledge, "and some other gentlemen" broke open the magazine. None of the contemporary accounts give any names. Council minutes, May 12, 1775, *Collections,* GHS, X, 22-23; proclamation of Wright, May 12, 1775, *Georgia Gazette,* May 17, 1775; Wright to Dartmouth, May 12, 1775, Ms. CRG, XXXVIII, Part I, 439.

55. *Georgia Gazette,* June 7, 1775. The *Gazette* did an admirable job of reporting these events.

56. Deposition of George Baillie, July 6, 1775, Ms. CRG, XXXVIII, Part I, 533-534; council minutes, July 4, 1775, *Collections,* GHS, X, 28-29; *CRG,* XII, 412-413.

57. Depositions of James Kitching, June 29, and Isaac Antrobus, July 4, 1775, Ms. CRG, XXXVIII, Part I, 482-495. Council minutes, July 4, 1775, *CRG*, XII, 411-412; *Collections*, GHS, X, 28.
58. Wright to Dartmouth, July 8, 10, 18, 1775, *Collections*, GHS, III, 191, 194, 198-199; depositions, Ms. CRG, XXXVIII, Part I, 606-616, 631-634; Jones, *History of Georgia*, II, 180-182; William B. Stevens, *A History of Georgia* . . . (2 vols., Philadelphia, 1847-1859), II, 103-104.
59. Noble W. Jones to Committee for Receiving Donations for the Distressed Inhabitants of Boston, *American Archives*, 4 Series, II, 871-872.
60. Letter from Charleston, June 29, 1775, *ibid.*, 1120; circular from South Carolina Committee, *NCCR*, X, 57.
61. Wright to Dartmouth, June 9, 17, July 10, 1775, Ms. CRG, XXXVIII, Part I, 446-449; *Collections*, GHS, III, 183-186, 195. Tonyn to Gage, July 17, 1775, Gage Papers, Am. Series; Campbell to Gage, July 29, 1775, *ibid.*; Campbell to Dartmouth, July 19, 1775, *Fourteenth Report*, Historical Manuscripts Commission, Part X, 332. (Henceforth cited as HMC.)

CHAPTER IV

1. *RRG*, I, 232-234.
2. *Ibid.*, 252, gives the date as June 5; *Georgia Gazette*, June 21, 1775, gives the date as June 13.
3. *RRG*, I, 252-253; *Georgia Gazette*, June 14, 21, 1775.
4. For notices and resolutions of these meetings see *Georgia Gazette*, June 14, 21, 28, 1775.
5. Jones, *History of Georgia*, II, 177.
6. *RRG*, I, 231. The entire journal of the first meeting of this congress is given in *ibid.*, 229-259, and the material which follows is from that source unless some other source is given.
7. A copy of the sermon, printed by Henry Miller (Philadelphia, 1775), is in the DeRenne Collection, U. of Ga. It is reprinted in *American Archives*, 4 Series, II, 1557-1568. On

Zubly's early Whig activities see Marjorie Daniel, "John Joachim Zubly-Georgia Pamphleteer of the Revolution," *Georgia Historical Quarterly*, XIX, 1-16. (Henceforth cited as *GHQ*).
8. Council minutes, July 7, 1775, *Collections*, GHS, X, 30; Wright to Dartmouth, July 8, 1775, *ibid.*, III, 162. The proclamation of July 10 is in *Georgia Gazette*, July 12, 1775.
9. Action of Congress July 17, 1775, *RRG*, I, 258; council minutes, July 25, 1775, *Collections*, GHS, X, 34-35; Wright to Dartmouth, July 29, 1775, Ms. CRG, XXXVIII, Part I, 523-533.
10. The resolutions are in *RRG*, I, 235-239; Jones, *History of Georgia*, II, 185-188; Stevens, *History of Georgia*, II, 109-114; White, *Hist. Coll. of Ga.*, 67-70.
11. *RRG*, I, 240-241.
12. *Ibid.*, 241, 243.
13. *Ibid.*, 241, 243, 263-267.
14. *Ibid.*, 244-248.
15. July 11, *ibid.*, 249-251.
16. *Ibid.*, 243, 251-252.
17. *Ibid.*, 254-255. The apportionment was as follows:

Christ Church
Savannah 17
Little Ogeechee 3
Vernonburgh 2
Sea Islands 3
Acton 2
St. Matthew 7
Abercorn & Goshen.............. 2
St. George 9
St. Paul 9
St. Philip 7
St. John 12
St. Andrew 9
St. David 3
St. Patrick 2
St. Thomas 2
St. Mary 2
St. James 2
1773 Indian Cession.............. 3
18. *Ibid.*, 257-258.
19. *Ibid.*, 259.
20. *Ibid.*, 260-262.
21. *Ibid.*, 258-259.
22. Bulloch to President of the Continental Congress, July 20, 1775, *JCC*,

II, 192-193.

23. *RRG,* I, 259. There is no indication that the congress reassembled on August 19.

24. Wright to Dartmouth, Aug. 7, 1775, *Collections,* GHS, III, 205. For tactics used to get signatures see this letter of Wright and Tho. Skinner to James Hore, Sept. 18, 1775, PRO, CO 5: 134, f. 140.

25. *JCC,* II, 251-252. Sept. 15, 1775.

26. See happenings in July-Sept., 1775, in *Georgia Gazette* (especially Sept. 20); Ms. Letter Book of Joseph Clay & Co., GHS (especially July 13, 30, Aug. 4, 11, 18, Sept. 16); Wm. Moss to John & Thomas Hodgson, Aug. 17, 1775, PRO, CO 5: 134, f. 14b; Minutes of General Committee, Sept. 14-18, in Ga. Records Misc., Force Transcripts, Mss. Div., LC.

27. *S. C. Gazette,* Sept. 7, 1775.

28. Joseph Clay & Co. to Mr. Stead, Sept. 16, 1775, Ms. Letter Book, GHS; diary of Richard Smith on debates in Congress, Sept. 14, 1775, Edmund C. Burnett, ed., *Letters of Members of the Continental Congress* (8 vols., Washington, 1921-1936), I, 194; John Adams, notes on debates in Congress for Sept. Oct., *JCC,* III, 472-504.

29. See correspondence of Wright throughout this period in Ms. CRG, XXXVIII, Part I, last 200 pages.

30. Charleston Council of Safety to Georgia Council or Congress, Dec. 14, 1775, White, *Hist. Coll. of Ga.,* 86-87, and action of Georgia Council of Safety, Dec. 24, 1775, *RRG,* I, 81.

31. See minutes of the council of safety for Nov., 1775-Feb., 1777, in *RRG,* I, 68-227.

32. *Ibid.,* 105-106.

33. *Ibid.,* 71-72, 80, 82, 100.

34. *Ibid.,* 73, 76.

35. Jan. 16, 1776, *ibid.,* 100.

36. Wright to Dartmouth, Aug. 17, 1775, *Collections,* GHS, III, 207; *Georgia Gazette,* Aug. 16, 1775.

37. Statement of Chief Justice Stokes before royal council, Aug. 15, 1775, *CRG,* XII, 431. Oaths of the Rev. Haddon Smith, Aug. 7, 1775, and John Neidlinger, July 25, and Aug.

16, 1775, in Fulham Palace **Ms.,** N. C., S. C., and Ga., No. 28, pp. 1-11.

38. Ms. CRG, XXXVIII, Part I, 625-626; Wright to Dartmouth, Dec. 19, 1775, *Collections,* GHS, III, 228.

39. *RRG,* I, 256, 71-72; royal council minutes, Aug. 1, 15, 1775, *Collections,* GHS, X, 36-46; Wright to Dartmouth, Aug. 17, 1775, Ms. CRG, XXXVIII, Part I, 562-583.

40. Wright to Dartmouth, Oct. 14, 1775, Ms. CRG, XXXVIII, Part II, 1.

41. Royal council minutes, March 7, 9, June 6, 1775, *Collections,* GHS, X, 14-16, 24-25.

42. Anthony Stokes, *A Narrative of the Official Conduct of Anthony Stokes* (London, 1784), 26.

43. *Ibid.,* 10; memorial of Stokes to Treasury, Jan. 5, 1778, **Ms. CRG,** XXXIX, 38; Wright to Dartmouth, Oct. 14, 1775, *Collections,* GHS, III, 216-217.

44. Memorial of Stokes, Jan. 5, 1778, **Ms.** CRG, XXXIX, 38-44; XXXVIII, Part II, 47-50; *Collections,* GHS, III, 223-224; PRO, CO 5: 115, pp. 219-223; Stokes, *Narrative,* 12-22; *Georgia Gazette,* Dec. 6, 1775.

45. Wright to Dartmouth, Sept. 16, 23, 1775, *Collections,* GHS, III, 209-210; Ms. CRG, XXXVIII, Part I, 617-625; J. Pownall to Wright, Oct. 4, 1775, *ibid.,* 508-510; Dartmouth circular Nov. 8, 1775, *Documents, Relative to the Colonial History of New York* (14 vols., Albany, 1856-1883), VIII, 642.

46. Council minutes, June 6, 1775, *Collections,* GHS, X, 25; depositions in Wright to Dartmouth, June 7, 1775, Ms. CRG, XXXVIII, Part I, 450-465.

47. Wright to Dartmouth, July 29, 1775, *Collections,* GHS, III, 200-203; **Ms.** CRG, XXXVIII, Part I, 536-538; *S. C. Gazette,* Aug. 1, 1775.

48. Memorial of Smith to Bishop of London, April 4, 1776, Fulham Palace Ms., Va., III, No. 46.

49. *Georgia Gazette,* Aug. 30, 1775; White, *Hist. Coll. of Ga.,* 606-607; Wright to Dartmouth, Aug. 17, Sept. 16, 1775, *Collections,* GHS, III, 208-210; Grierson to Wright, Aug. 6,

1775, and council minutes, Aug. 15, 1775, *CRG*, XII, 434-437; Brown to Lord North, June 4, 1783, PRO, CO 5: 82, pp. 761-768; Brown to Cornwallis, July 16, 1780, PRO, Cornwallis Papers, Bundle 2, No. 140.

50. *Georgia Gazette*, Nov. 15, 1775. Governor Chester of West Florida issued a similar proclamation on Nov. 11, 1775, *American Archives*, 4 Series, IV, 341-342.

51. P. LeConte to Jack LeConte, Jan. 1, 1776, Henry Clinton Papers, CL.

52. Joseph Habersham to Philotheos Chiffelle, June 16, 1775, *American Archives*, 4 Series, II, 1007-1008, and letter from Charleston, 1111-1112; Wright to Dartmouth, June 20, 1775, *Collections*, GHS, III, 189-190; Stuart to Gage, July 9, 1775, Gage Papers, Am. Series; Stuart to Charleston Committee of Intelligence, July 18, 1775, *American Archives*, 4 Series, II, 1681-1682.

53. Georgia Council minutes, July 4, 25, 1775, *Collections*, GHS, X, 29, 34-35; Stuart to Gage, July 20, 1775, Gage Papers, Am. Series; Stuart to Gage, Sept. 15, 1775, *American Archives*, 4 Series, III, 714-715; Stuart to Dartmouth, Sept. 17, 1775, PRO, CO 5: 76, f. 351-356.

54. Stuart - Dartmouth correspondence, PRO, CO 5: 76.

55. Wright to Dartmouth, Sept. 23, 1775, *Collections*, GHS, III, 212; Stuart to Major Small, Oct. 2, 1775, *American Archives*, 4 Series, IV, 315; council minutes, Oct. 31, 1775, *Collections*, GHS, X, 46-47.

56. Stuart to Dartmouth, Dec. 17, 1775, *NCCR*, X, 348.

57. Alexander Skinner to General Grant, Sept. 21, 1775, *American Archives*, 4 Series, IV, 329.

58. Gage to Stuart, Sept. 12, 1775, Gage Papers, Am. Series; Stuart to Alexander Cameron, Dec. 16, 1775, PRO, CO 5: 77, f. 55; Lt. Gov. Moultrie of East Florida to General Grant, Oct. 4, 1775, *American Archives*, 4 Series, IV, 336. For a general treatment of Creek affairs in 1775 see Homer Bast, "Creek Indian Affairs," *GHQ*,

XXXIII, 1-10.

59. Jan. 7-16, 1776, *RRG*, I, 86-101.

60. Interview of Jan. 18, 1776, in Ms. Noble W. Jones Papers, GHS; and *American Archives*, 4 Series, IV, 799.

61. *RRG*, I, 101-104; Journal of South Carolina Council of Safety, Jan. 30, 1776, North Carolina State Records, XI, 271 (Henceforth cited as *NCSR*.); Journal of South Carolina Provincial Congress, Feb. 14, 1776, *American Archives*, 4 Series, V, 570.

62. Martin Jollie to Governor Tonyn of East Florida, Feb. 13, 1776; Capt. Andrew Barkley to Sir Henry Clinton, Feb. 23, 1776; Wright to Clinton, Feb. 21, 1776, all in Henry Clinton Papers, CL; Capt. Andrew Barkley to Wright, Feb. 19, 1776, *RRG*, I, 106-107.

63. Wright to council, Feb. 13, 1776, *RRG*, I, 269-272.

64. *Ibid.*, 108, 111-112.

65. March 2, *ibid.*, 110-113.

66. South Carolina Provincial Congress, March 2, 5, 24, *American Archives*, 4 Series, V, 585-586, 588, 607-608; Wm. Ewen, President, Georgia Council of Safety to South Carolina Council of Safety, March 16, 1776, *ibid.*, 599-600.

67. Georgia Council of Safety to South Carolina Provincial Congress, March 4, 16, 1776, *ibid.*, 53-54, 599-603.

68. *S. C. Gazette, March* 20, 27, 1776.

69. Barkley to Clinton, Feb. 23, 1776; Wright to Clinton, Feb. 21, March 3, 10, 29, 1776, Henry Clinton Papers, CL.

70. It is most improbable that the article published in the *Gazette* by the Rev. Haddon Smith, Rector of Christ Church, under the name "Mercurious" was one of the principal reasons why Georgia did not enter the Continental Association earlier than she did, as Smith maintained in his memorial to the Bishop of London. April 4, 1776, Fulham Palace Ms., Va., III, No. 46.

71. In this connection see the opinion of Strickland, *Religion and the State in Georgia*, 118-119.

72. On the Indian situation as a reason

for loyalty see extracts of Georgia letters, Sept. 7 and Dec. 9, 1774, in *American Archives,* 4 Series, I, 773, 1033-1034.

73. For Parliamentary help and influence of royal officials as an aid to loyalty see letter, Sept. 4, 1774, *ibid.,* 773.

74. Dartmouth to Wright, Nov. 2, 1774, Ms. CRG, XXXVIII, Part I, 325. See also Dartmouth to Wright, May 3, 1775, *American Archives,* 4 Series, II, 475.

75. Wright to Hillsborough, Aug. 6, 1768, Ms. CRG, XXXVII, 354-355; Hillsborough to Wright, Dec. 9, 1769, *ibid.,* 421-422.

76. Wright to Dartmouth, Aug. 24, 1774, *Collections,* GHS, III, 181; Feb. 13, 1775, Ms. CRG, XXXVIII, Part I, 392-393.

77. Habersham to Wright, Dec. 4, 1772, *Collections,* GHS, VI, 217.

78. On Johnston's personal beliefs see Anthony Stokes to Johnston, Dec. 16, 1775, Ms. CRG, XXXVIII, Part II, 48-50; Stokes, *Narrative,* 16-19; Johnston to Stokes, Dec. 15, 1775, Ms. CRG, XXXVIII, Part II, 47; Johnston's signature on a loyalist petition, *ibid.,* 19-20.

79. See Wright to Hillsborough, Nov. 18, 1768, cited in Flippin, *GHQ,* XIII, 151.

80. The repeated statements of Wright that the trouble in Georgia was caused by the bad example set by South Carolina and other colonies have been pointed out. Lord William Campbell, Governor of South Carolina, was willing to agree that South Carolina set a bad example for Georgia. Campbell to Dartmouth, Aug. 19, 1775, Dartmouth Mss., HMC, *14 Report,* Part X, 353-355.

CHAPTER V

1. Printed in *RRG,* I, 274-277; Jones, *History of Georgia,* II, 218-220; and White, *Hist. Coll. of Ga.,* 96-98.

2. Georgia Records, Misc., Force Transcripts, Mss. Div., LC.

3. *RRG,* I, 116-119.

4. June 4, 1776, speech and reply in *American Archives,* 4 Series, VI, 718-720. There is no journal of this congress to indicate what it did to carry out Bulloch's recommendations.

5. *RRG,* I, 170-171.

6. *Ibid.,* 147-148.

7. *Ibid.,* 158.

8. *Ibid.,* 208-209.

9. *Ibid.,* 131.

10. *Ibid.,* 167.

11. *Ibid.,* 199.

12. The exact date and circumstances surrounding Bulloch's death are unknown. See Charles F. Jenkins, *Button Gwinnett* (New York, 1926), 122-123.

13. Archibald Bulloch to Geogia delegates, April 5, 1776, *JCC,* IV, 368.

14. John Adams to James Warren, May 20, 1776, Burnett, *Letters,* I, 460-461; General Mercer to President of Congress, June 15, 1776, *American Archives,* 4 Series, VI, 903; General John Armstrong to General Charles Lee, May 8, 1776, *Collections,* New York Historical Society, 1872, p. 11 (Henceforth cited as NYHS.); Henry Laurens to John Laurens, Aug. 14, 1776, *ibid.,* 217-218; New Hampshire delegates to President of New Hampshire, May 28, 1776, Burnett, *Letters,* I, 466.

15. White, *Hist. Coll. of Ga.,* 200-201.

16. May 10, 1776, *JCC,* IV, 342.

17. Bulloch's proclamation is undated but must have been issued between Aug. 8 and 20. *RRG,* I, 280-281.

18. Printed in Albert B. Saye, *New Viewpoints in Georgia History* (Athens, 1943), 169-170; and Jenkins, *Button Grinnett,* 108-110. See also Lachlan McIntosh to George Walton, Dec. 15, 1776, *GHQ,* XXXVIII, 256.

19. The constitution is printed in *RRG,* I, 282-297. This is the source of the analysis in the text unless another source is given.

20. Colonial assemblymen had not always resided in the parish they represented and had been required to own 500 acres of land.

21. It had been possible to qualify in more than one parish under the

colonial property qualification.

22. These counties may be seen on the 1796 map of Georgia from Guthrie's *Geography,* reproduced below pp. ___. All of the original counties have as of today been considerably reduced in size except Glynn, Camden, and Chatham.

23. An illustration of this seal is given in Jenkins, *Button Gwinnett,* 110.

24. Pennsylvania was the only other state with a one-house legislature.

25. Georgia's constitution of 1777 was as democratic a document as was written in the early Revolutionary period. It may be compared with other revolutionary constitutions by consulting Claude H. Van Tyne, *The American Revolution, 1776-1783* (New York, 1905), IX; Allan Nevins, *The American States During and After the Revolution* (New York, 1925); and John R. Alden, *The American Revolution, 1775-1783* (New York, 1954), X.

26. Clay to Messrs. Bright and Pechin, July 2, 1777; Clay to Henry Laurens, Oct. 16, 21, 1777; *Collections,* GHS, VIII, 35, 47-49, 55.

27. Henry Laurens to John Laurens, Aug. 14, 1776, *Collections,* NYHS, 1872, pp. 217-218; resolve of St. Andrew's Parochial Committee, Sept. 10, 1776, Lachlan McIntosh Papers, GHS; council of safety action, June 26, 1776, *RRG,* I, 146-147.

28. Thomas Brown to Governor Tonyn, Nov. 8, 1776, PRO, CO 5: 557, pp. 97-99; Tonyn to Germain, Dec. 7, 1776, *ibid.,* 67-68.

29. Clay to Edward Telfair, Aug. 10, 1777; Clay to Henry Laurens, Oct. 16, 21, 1777, *Collections,* GHS, VIII, 37-38, 46-57.

30. See below, pp. 103-04.

31. For examples see *RRG,* II, 34-36.

32. For examples see *ibid.,* 6-7.

33. The first incident, Feb. 22, 1777, came under the Rules and Regulations; the second, April 16, 1778, under the constitution; Jones, *History of Georgia,* II, 262-264, 285-286; *RRG,* II, 75-76.

34. There are no assembly journals for these years. A list of acts passed and copies of most of these acts do exist.

35. For copies of the laws concerned see *CRG,* XIX, Part II, 45-60, 61-67, 67-70, 87-99, 103-126.

36. June 7, 1777, and Nov. 15, 1778, *ibid.,* 58-60, 128-129.

37. *Ibid.,* 53-58, 72-80.

38. Ms. Index of Georgia Laws, Ga. Dept. of Archives and History, Sept., 1777, and March, 1778 (Henceforth cited as GDAH.); *RRG,* II, 27, 52-53.

39. See tables of such legislation in Claude H. Van Tyne, *The Loyalists in the American Revolution* (New York, 1902), 318-341.

40. March 1, 1778, *RRG,* I, 326-347; amending act Oct. 30, 1778, *CRG,* XIX, Part II, 100-103.

41. Nov. 15, 1778, *CRG,* XIX, Part II, 126-127.

42. See below, pp. 103-04.

43. This fact is obvious from the letter book of McIntosh for the spring of 1777. *GHQ,* XXXVIII, 356-368.

44. McIntosh, as a member of the council of safety, had opposed the recent election of Gwinnett as president and had refused to sign his commission. All evidence in the McIntosh case (Lachlan and George—one case in all practical effects) is highly partisan and conflicting. See Congressional action, Jan. 1, 1777, *JCC,* VII, 8-9; President of Congress to President of Georgia, Jan. 8, 1777, Burnett, *Letters,* II, 209. Much information is in Papers of the Continental Congress, No. 73. (Henceforth cited as PCC.) See especially Tonyn to Germain, July 19, 1776, 35-36; Gwinnett to President of Congress, March 28, 1777, 19-21; minutes of Georgia Council of Safety, March 19, 21, 26, 1777, pp. 108-111. The fullest treatment of George McIntosh's case from his side is his memorial to Congress, Oct. 8, 1777, *ibid.,* No. 41, VI, 33-37.

45. This phase of the George McIntosh case can be followed in his memorial to Congress Oct. 8, 1777 (cited above); extract of journal of House of Assembly, June 5, 1777, PCC, No.

73, pp. 119-120; Governor Treutlen to President of Congress, June 19, 1777, and Aug. 6, 1777, *ibid.*, 43-47, 99-102 (printed in Jenkins, *Button Gwinnett*, 243-250); Georgia Council minutes, June 19, 25, 1777, *GHQ*, XXXIV, 23-26.

46. *JCC*, VIII, 757-758; IX, 764-765, 787-790.

47. In addition to the material cited in notes 44-46 above, the following is useful. Jenkins, *Button Gwinnett*, 135-172, 215-217, gives a pro-Gwinnett account. Edith Duncan Johnston, *The Houstouns of Georgia* (Athens, 1950), 348-365, has a somewhat more pro-McIntosh account. Both sides are given in three contemporary pamphlets, "The Case of George M'Intosh," "Addition to the Case of George M'Intosh," and "Strictures on the Case of George M'Intosh," *Hazard Pamphlets*, Vol. 39, Rare Book Room, LC.

48. On the duel see Lyman Hall to Roger Sherman, June 1, 1777, printed in Jenkins, *Button Gwinnett*, 226-230; Lachlan McIntosh to Colonel John Laurence, May 30, 1777, printed by the American Autograph Shop, 1937; Thomas Gamble, *Savannah Duels and Duellists, 1733-1877* (Savannah, 1923), 11-16.

49. Petition of assembly Sept. 13, 1777, printed in Jenkins, *Button Gwinnett*, 265-266. Petitions from the counties in PCC, No. 73, pp. 51-58, 67-95, 113-114. The argument of these petitions was "guilt by association," that many of the friends of Lachlan and George were Tories.

50. Walton to Washington, Aug. 5, 1777, Burnett, *Letters*, II, 439; Washington to Walton, Aug. 6, 1777, *Writings of Washington* (Washington, 1933), IX, 25-26; *JCC*, VIII, 616; Henry Laurens to Lachlan McIntosh, Aug. 11, 1777, Burnett, *Letters*, II, 444. The Lachlan McIntosh case received a modern scholarly and pro-McIntosh treatment in Alexander A. Lawrence, "General Lachlan McIntosh and His Suspension from Continental Command During the

Revolution," *GHQ*, XXXVIII, 107-118. The McIntosh papers are in *GHQ*, XXXVIII-XL. Those which bear on the duel and suspension from command are in XXXVIII, 356-368; XXXIX, 63-68, 172-180.

51. Drayton to Humphrey Wells, June 8, 1777, White, *Hist. Coll. of Ga.*, 203-205.

52. July 14, 1777, *GHQ*, XXXIV, 31-32. The proclamation is dated July 15, *RRG*, I, 309-310, 314-315.

53. Drayton to Treutlen, Aug. 1, 1777, White, *Hist. Coll. of Ga.*, 207-209.

54. *RRG*, I, 240-241; *JCC*, II, 240-242.

55. Diary of John Adams, Sept. 15, 1775, Burnett, *Letters*, I, 194-195; Diary of Richard Smith, *ibid.*, 192-196; *JCC*, II, 240.

56. Diary of Richard Smith, Sept. 14, 15, 1775, Burnett, *Letters*, I, 194-196; *JCC*, II, 251-252.

57. Joseph Clay to Mr. Stead, Sept. 16, 1775, Joseph Clay & Co., Ms. Letter Book, GHS; John Adams' notes on debates, Sept. 23, Oct. 27, *JCC*, III, 481-482, 491-494, 499-500, 504.

58. *JCC*, III, 472-491.

59. On Zubly's troubles after his return to Georgia, see Eunice Ross Perkins, "John Joachim Zubly, Georgia's Conscientious Objector," *GHQ*, XV, 313-323; on Zubly's attitude toward his banishment and loss of property see "Rev. J. J. Zubly's Appeal to the Grand Jury. Oct. 8, 1777," *ibid.*, I, 161-165.

60. For a detailed treatment of the congressional career of one of these delegates see Edmund C. Burnett, "Edward Langworthy in the Continental Congress," *GHQ*, XII, 211-235.

61. Henry Laurens to Joseph Clay, Aug. 20, 1777, Burnett, *Letters*, II, 458; Clay to Laurens, Oct. 21, 1777, *Collections*, GHS, VIII, 55.

62. Certificate of Colonel William Kennon, 14 May (or Feb.) 1777, *GHQ*, I, 45-49; Treutlen to John Hancock, Aug. 6, 1777, PCC, No. 73, pp. 102-103; *JCC*, VIII, 644-646.

63. Howe to President of Congress, Sept. 12, 1777, PCC, No. 160, pp. 397-398; Laurens to Isaac Motte, Jan. 26, 1778,

Burnett, *Letters,* III, 51; Clay to Howe, Oct. 15, 1777, *Collections,* GHS, VIII, 41-45.

64. Howe to Governor Houstoun, May 3, 1778, PCC, No. 160, pp. 457-458; Clay to Howe, May 19, June 20, 1778, *Collections,* GHS, VIII, 71-73, 86-87; Clay to Laurens, May 30, 1778, *ibid.,* 76-78.

65. Sept. 21, 1778, *JCC,* XII, 937-939.

66. Laurens to Governor Houstoun, June 22, July 18, 1778, Burnett, *Letters,* III, 313, 336-337.

67. Jenkins, *Button Gwinnett,* 76-77.

68. John Adams, notes on debates, July 26, 1776, *JCC,* VI, 1077-1078.

69. Oct. 7, 1777, *JCC,* IX, 779-782.

70. *JCC,* XI, 656.

71. Nathaniel Scudder to Speaker of New Jersey Assembly, July 13, 1778, Burnett, *Letters,* III, 327; Josiah Bartlett to John Langdon, July 13, 1778, *ibid.,* 329; *JCC,* XI, 712-716; Burnett, "Edward Langworthy in the Continental Congress," *GHQ,* XII, 220.

72. *JCC,* XI, 670-671.

CHAPTER VI

1. *JCC,* III, 324-327.

2. A complete list of the original officers is given in White, *Hist. Coll. of Ga.,* 94; and *Georgia Gazette,* Feb. 7, 1776.

3. McIntosh to Washington, Feb. 16, April 28, 1776, White, *Hist. Coll. of Ga.,* 92-94, 97-98; General John Armstrong to President of Congress, May 7, 1776, *American Archives,* 4 Series, V, 1219-1220. These figures agree with those of an undated memorandum of Governor Wright in Ms. CRG, XXXVIII, Part II, 119-120.

4. *JCC,* IV, 172, 180-181; Washington to McIntosh, June 4, 1776, *American Archives,* 4 Series, VI, 709.

5. Committee reports of March 25, May 29, 1776, *JCC,* IV, 235-400; Lee to President of Congress, June 6, 1776, *Collections,* NYHS, 1872, p. 54.

6. McIntosh to Washington, Feb. 16, 1776, White, *Hist. Coll. of Ga.,* 92-93; report of conference of Georgia deputies with General Lee, *Collec-*

tions, NYHS, 1872, pp. 114-117, and *RRG,* I, 150-154; Lee to Board of War, Aug. 27, 1776, *Collections,* NYHS, 1872, pp. 241-245.

7. *Ibid.*

8. Lee to President of Congress, July 2, 1776, *Collections,* NYHS, 1872, pp. 108-110.

9. Lee to Board of War, Aug. 27, 1776, *ibid.,* 241-245.

10. Lee to Armstrong, Aug. 27, 1776, *ibid.,* 246.

11. Lee to Archibald Bulloch, Aug. 23, 24, 1776, *ibid.,* 238, 240-241.

12. McIntosh to Washington, White, *Hist. Coll. of Ga.,* 92-94.

13. Lee to Bulloch, Aug. 28, 1776, *Collections,* NYHS, 1872, pp. 247-248.

14. Resolutions of July 5, 24, and Sept. 16, 1776, *JCC,* V, 521-522, 606-607, 762-763; John Hancock to Convention of Georgia, *RRG,* I, 194-199.

15. Sept. 16, 1776, *JCC,* V, 761.

16. Col. Elbert to John Stirk and Seth John Cuthbert, Oct. 2, 1776, *Collections,* GHS, V, Part II, 6. For North Carolina recruiting see *NCCR,* X, 700, 718, 805; *NCSR,* XI, 409, 445, 446, 708; XII, 23, 35; XXII, 915-916. On Virginia recruiting see *Va. Gazette,* (P) June 14, (D) June 5, (P) Aug. 23, (D) Sept. 27, (P) Dec. 6, 1776; (P) Jan. 17, (P) Feb. 14, 21, Mar. 28, (P) June 13, 27, 1777.

17. McIntosh to Georgia Congressional delegation, Dec. 17, 1776, *GHQ,* XXXVIII, 256-257; Gov. Tonyn of East Florida to Augustine Prevost, Jan. 13, Tonyn to Germain, April 2, 1777, PRO, CO 5: 557, pp. 269-272, 382.

18. Orders of Lee, Sept. 8, 1776, *NCCR,* X, 795-796. See also *ibid.,* 858-859, 880; *NCSR,* XI, 357.

19. *NCSR,* XI, 445, 685-687, 692; XII, 35, 171-172, 339, 348; XIII, 480; *JCC,* IX, 783, 792-793.

20. *RRG,* I, 212.

21. *Ibid.,* 85-86, 130.

22. Sir Basil Keith to Germain, March 27, 1776, PRO, CO 5: 71, pp. 81-83; Capt. Hugh Gromedge to Dartmouth, April 30, 1776, Dartmouth Ms., HMC, *14 Report,* X, 417; *RRG,*

I, 191-193, 208.

23. Tonyn to British naval commander at Savannah River, Aug. 5, 1776, PRO, CO 5: 556, p. 765; *RRG,* I, 175-176, 178, 227-228.

24. John Hancock to the states, Nov. 20, 1776, *American Archives,* 5 Series, III, 776-777; William Kennon to Lee, Dec. 7, 1776, *ibid.,* 1105-1106.

25. *RRG,* I, 193, 210-211.

26. St. Augustine troops returns for Aug., Sept., and Oct., 1775, PCC, No. 51, I, 37-40, 45-48, 171-173; and *American Archives,* 4 Series, IV, 319, 321-326. For St. Augustine fears see *ibid.,* III, 788-789; IV, 319, 336.

27. *JCC,* IV, 15; Richard Smith diary, Jan. 1, 2, 1776, Burnett, *Letters,* I, 293-294.

28. Tonyn to Clinton, Feb. 13, 15, 1776; Martin Jollie to Tonyn, Feb. 13, 1776, Henry Clinton Papers.

29. Georgia Council of Safety, May 14, 16, 1776, *RRG,* I, 123-124, 127-128; Florida Council minutes, May 20, 1776, PRO, CO 5: 571, pp. 197-199; Tonyn to Clinton, May 21, 1776, *ibid.,* 556, pp. 679-682.

30. *RRG,* I, 148; McIntosh to Lee, July 7, 1776, *Collections,* NYHS, 1872, p. 125; Tonyn to Germain, July 18, 1776, PRO, CO 5: 557, pp. 165-172; extract of a letter from Charleston, July 27, 1776, *American Archives,* 4 Series, VI, 1230; McIntosh to Lee, July 29, 1776, *GHQ,* XXXVIII, 159; *Va. Gazette,* (P) Sept. 6, (D) Sept. 7, 14, 1776.

31. *Collections,* NYHS, 1872, pp. 106, 144-160, 171.

32. Lee to President Rutledge of South Carolina, Aug. 1, 3, 6, and Lee to Richard Peters, Aug. 2, 1776, *ibid.,* 186-187, 188-189, 199, 200.

33. Estimated at 1500 by one Charlestonian, Aug. 7, 1776, *American Archives,* 5 Series, I, 805. *Va. Gazette,* (D) Sept. 27, 1776.

34. Tonyn to British vessels in Savannah River, Aug. 5, 1776, PRO, CO 5: 556, pp. 755-756; Tonyn to Germain, Aug. 15, 1776, *ibid.,* pp. 703-740.

35. Extract of a letter from St. Augustine, Aug. 20, 1776, *American Ar-*

chives, 5 Series, I, 1076.

36. *RRG,* I, 179-182; *Collections,* NYHS, 1872, pp. 233-235.

37. Council of safety, Aug. 20-24, *RRG,* I, 183-189.

38. Andrew Turnbull to Arthur Gordon, Sept. 1, 1776, and Tonyn to Germain, Sept. 9, 1776, PRO, CO 5: 556, pp. 767-770, 795-798; Col. Augustine Prevost to Gen. Howe, Sept. 9, 1776, HMC, *Report of American Manuscripts in the Royal Institution of Great Britain* (4 vols., 1904-1909), I, 58.

39. Thomas Brown to John Stuart, Sept. 29, 1776, PRO, CO 5: 78, pp. 69-70; Tonyn to Howe, Oct. 8, 1776, *ibid.,* 94, pp. 73-74; Tonyn to Germain, Oct. 30, 1776, *ibid.,* 557, p. 21; William Ellery to Governor Cooke, Oct. 11, 1776, *American Archives,* II, 990, gives Lee's reasons.

40. Tonyn to Howe, Oct. 8, 1776, PRO, CO 5: 94, pp. 73-74; Tonyn to Germain, Oct. 30, 1776, *ibid.,* 557, pp. 22-24; Georgia Council of Safety, Oct. 7, 1776, *RRG,* I, 205-206; McIntosh letters of Oct. 1, 7, 22, 29, 1776, *GHQ,* XXXVIII, 160, 162, 163, 166.

41. Howe to Germain, Nov. 30, 1776, HMC, *Stopford-Sackville Mss.* (London, 1904-10), II, 50.

42. Tonyn to British vessels in Savannah River, Aug. 5, 1776, PRO, CO 5: 556, pp. 755-756; Capt. George Cooke to Maryland Council of Safety, Oct. 4, 1776, *American Archives,* 5 Series, II, 863.

43. *American Archives,* 5 Series, II, 957; III, 1329.

44. Wm. Howe to A. Prevost, Jan. 15, 1777, HMC, *Royal Institution,* I, 84.

45. *S. C. & American General Gazette,* Feb. 27, 1777; articles of capitulation, PRO, CO 5: 557, pp. 357-360; Thomas Brown to Tonyn, Feb. 20, 1777, *ibid.,* 345-356; Jones, *History of Georgia,* II, 260-263.

46. Council of safety, Feb. 21, 22, 1777, *RRG,* I, 224-225, supplemented by Jenkins, *Button Gwinnett,* 122; Joseph Clay to John Burnley, Feb. 23, 1777, *Collections,* GHS, VIII, 20-

21; Robt. Howe to Moultrie, Feb. 23, 1777, *NCSR,* XI, 706-707.

47. Howe to Moultrie, Feb. 23, 1777, *NCSR,* XI, 706-707; Gwinnett to John Hancock, March 28, 1777, with council of safety minutes of March 4, PCC, No. 73, pp. 21-30; Howe to Washington, May 14, 1777, Jenkins, *Button Gwinnett,* 141-142; Howe to Congress, May 8, 1777, PCC, No. 160, pp. 252-257; L. Van Loon Naisawald, "Major General Howe's Activities in South Carolina and Georgia, 1776-1779," *GHQ,* XXXV, 25, 26-28.

48. McIntosh to Gwinnett, March 28; McIntosh to Howe, April 2, 1777; McIntosh Letter Book, GHS; Lawrence, "General Lachlan McIntosh and His Suspension from Continental Command During the Revolution," *GHQ,* XXXVIII, 111-115.

49. Tonyn to Stuart, April 15, 1777, PRO, CO 5: 557, pp. 597-598; Tonyn to David Tate, April 20, 1777, HMC, *Royal Institution,* I, 105; Joseph Clay to Josiah Smith, undated, *Collections,* GHS, VIII, 70-71.

50. Extract of a letter from Savannah, April 3, 1777, *Va. Gazette,* (P) May 30, 1777; Lyman Hall to Roger Sherman, June 1, 1777, Charles C. Jones, Jr., *Biographical Sketches of the Delegates from Georgia to the Continental Congress* (Boston, 1891), 98-100.

51. The daily course of the expedition can be followed in Col. Elbert's Order Book, *Collections,* GHS, V, Part II, 19-37, 45. The British side is given in Tonyn to Germain, May 5, June 16, 1777, PRO, CO 5: 557, pp. 405-410, 481-488. Jones, *History of Georgia,* II, 264-269; Jenkins, *Button Gwinnett,* 141-149.

52. Executive council minutes, Aug. 5, Oct. 8, 1777, *GHQ,* XXXIV, 109, 123; Tonyn to Stuart, Aug. 31, Tonyn to Germain, Sept. 18, 1777, PRO, CO 5: 557, pp. 708-709, 547-550; Joseph Clay to Henry Laurens, Sept. 29, Oct. 16, 1777, *Collections,* GHS, VIII, 40, 50-51.

53. Council minutes for the summer in *GHQ,* XXXIV; military records in

Collections, GHS, V, Part II, 37-38, 47, 110-113; Joseph Clay to Henry Laurens, Oct. 16, 21, 1777, *ibid.,* VIII, 51, 54.

54. Action of Oct. 18, 1777, *JCC,* IX, 820-821; James Lowell to William Whipple, Nov. 3, 1777, Burnett, *Letters,* II, 540.

55. *JCC,* VIII, 579, 590; Charles Thompson, notes on debates, July 25, 1777, Burnett, *Letters,* II, 422; Laurens to Lachlan McIntosh, Aug. 11 and Laurens to Clay, Aug. 20, 1777, *ibid.,* 443-444, 458.

56. Clay to Howe, June 20, 1778, *Collections,* GHS, VIII, 86-87; Congressional action of Sept. 21, 1778, *JCC,* XII, 937-939.

57. John Wereat to McIntosh, March 13, 1778, Lachlan McIntosh Papers, Duke University Library.

58. *Collections,* GHS, V, Part II, 56.

59. *Ibid.,* 48-85.

60. PCC, No. 73, pp. 141, 161-174.

61. *Ibid.,* 142-146, 178-185.

62. Executive council minutes, March 9, 1778, *RRG,* II, 80.

63. Thomas Brown to Tonyn, Feb. 19, 1778, HMC, *Royal Institution,* I. 195, 197-199; Tonyn to Wm. Howe, Feb. 24, 1778, *ibid.,* 199; Prevost to Wm. Howe, March 18, 1778, *ibid.,* 211-212.

64. Executive council minutes, April 7, 1778, *RRG,* II, 72-73; letters, PCC, No. 160, pp. 442-454; Tonyn to Wm. Howe, April 28, 1778, HMC, *Royal Institution,* I, 240.

65. Undated proclamation in Tonyn to Germain, May 15, 1778, PRO, CO 5: 558, pp. 317-320.

66. April 16, 1778, *RRG,* II, 75-77.

67. Jones, *History of Georgia,* II, 293. British intelligence agreed to this number.

68. *Gazette of the State of S. C.,* July 15, 24, Aug. 5, 1778; *Collections,* GHS, V, Part II, 122-178; PCC, No. 73, pp. 211-214, 218-230; No. 160, pp. 466-476; HMC, *Royal Institution,* I, 259, 261, 266, 269, 271-273, 275-276; PRO, CO 5: 558, pp. 381-384.

69. Assembly and council orders, Aug. 31, 1778, in Ms. Ga. General Assembly Papers, GHS and *RRG,* II, 97;

Joseph Clay to Bright and Pechin, Sept. 2, and to Henry Laurens, Sept. 9, 1778, *Collections*, GHS, VIII, 101-106.

70. Laurens to Governor Houstoun, Aug. 27, 1778, Burnett, *Letters*, III, 384-385; Howe to Congress, Sept. 22, 1778, PCC, No. 160, pp. 483-487; *JCC* for Oct. and Nov., especially Nov. 10, *JCC*, VII, 1116-1121.

71. *Collections*, GHS, V, Part II, 150-152, 161-182.

72. *Ibid.*, 42-43, 167-168.

73. *Ibid.*, 182-185.

74. Howe to Congress, Sept. 12, 1777, PCC, No. 160, pp. 397-398; Clay to Howe, Oct. 15, 1777, *Collections*, GHS, VIII, 55.

75. Clay to Howe, May 19, to Laurens, May 30, Sept. 9, 1778, *Collections*, GHS, VIII, 71-73, 76-78, 103-104.

76. *RRG*, I, 221; II, 47-50, 70-71, 82-84, 96; *GHQ*, XXXIV, 27, 31, 33, 121, 124; Clay to Laurens, Oct. 13, 1776, *Collections*, GHS, VIII, 51; *S. C. and American General Gazette*, March 13, 1777.

77. Extract from minutes of convention, Jan. 30, 1777, and statement by James Habersham and Thos. Stone, Oct. 28, 1783, "Oliver Bowen," Misc. file, GDAH.

78. Journal of the Commissioners of the Navy of South Carolina, May 1, June 30, 1777, pp. 60, 77, Ms. in S. C. Archives Dept.; enclosure in Tonyn to Germain, April 2, 1777, PRO, CO 5; 557, p. 381.

79. *GHQ*, XXXIV, 32; *RRG*, II, 68-70.

80. Council action, Aug. 25, 27, Nov. 15, 1778, *RRG*, II, 78-88, 92, 118-119. All the disabilities of this suspension were removed by the assembly on July 23, 1783. *Ibid.*, III, 340.

81. Elbert to Howe, April 19, 1778, *S. C. & American General Gazette*, April 23, 1778.

82. Marine Committee to Wereat, Nov. 14, 1776, *American Archives*, 5 Series, III, 671.

83. Stuart to Dartmouth, Jan. 19, 1776, PRO, CO 5: 229, pp. 122-124; memorial of James Jackson and Andrew McLean to Governor Wright, Ms.

CRG, XXXVIII, Part II, 91-92, 95-99.

84. *RRG*, I, 89; Stuart to Clinton, March 15, 1776, PRO, CO 5: 77, p. 213.

85. Tonyn to Taitt, April 20, and Taitt to Tonyn, May 3, 1776, in Tonyn to Clinton, June 8, 1776, Henry Clinton Papers.

86. Henry Stuart to frontier inhabitants, May 18, 1776, *American Archives*, 4 Series, VI, 497; Taitt to Stuart, Aug. 26, 1776, PRO, CO 137: 72, pp. 11-13; Galphin to Willie Jones, Oct. 26, 1776, *American Archives*, 5 Series, III, 648-649; *JCC*, V, 616-617; *NCCR*, X, 681; N. C. Delegates to Council of Safety, July 30, 1776, Burnett, *Letters*, II, 30; Robert Rae to Archibald Bulloch, July 3, 1776, *American Archives*, 4 Series, VI, 1228-1230; ms. council minutes, April 17, 1777, GHS.

87. Indian talk from Archibald Bulloch in Timothy Barnard to David Taitt, July 4, 1776, PRO, CO 5: 94, pp. 151-152; petition from frontier inhabitants, July 31, 1776, *Collections*, NYHS, 1872, pp. 181-182; Galphin to Willie Jones, Oct. 26, 1776, *American Archives*, 5 Series, III, 648-651.

88. *Gazette of the State of S. C.*, July 14, 1777; Wm. McIntosh to Alexander Cameron, July 6, 1777, PRO, CO 5: 78, pp. 385-388; Taitt to Stuart, July 12, 1777, *ibid.*, pp. 393-396.

89. Henry Laurens to Galphin, Sept. 16, 1777, Burnett, *Letters*, II, 494; Stuart to Germain, Oct. 6, 1777, PRO, CO 5: 79, pp. 57-67.

90. Howe to Georgia Assembly, Sept. 4, 1777, PCC, No. 73, pp. 7-13; Howe to Congress, Sept. 12, 1777, *ibid.*, No. 160, p. 296; Clay to Laurens, Oct. 16, 21, 1777, *Collections*, GHS, VIII, 51, 54; *JCC*, IV, 823-824.

91. Andrew Pickens to Richard Winn, June 30, 1778, PCC, No. 150, III, 461; council minutes, Aug. 26, Sept. 18, 24, 1778, *RRG*, II, 90-91, 102-105.

CHAPTER VII

1. Germain to Wm. Knox, Oct. 19, 1776, HMC, *Various Collections*, VI, 126.

2. Memorial of Lord William Camp-

bell, Sir James Wright, William Bull, and John Graham, Aug. 29, 1777, Ms. CRG, XXXIX, 4-9.

3. Memorial of Wright and Graham to Germain, July 17, 1778, *ibid.*, 10-15.
4. Germain to Clinton, March 8, 1778, B. F. Stevens, ed., *Facsimiles of Manuscripts in European Archives Relating to America, 1773-1783* (London, 1889-1895), Nos. 396 and 1062; orders of Aug. 5, 1778, HMC, *Stopford-Sackville*, II, 151.
5. Kirkland's plan is in Henry Clinton Papers. See also Prevost to Wm. Howe, March 18, 1778, HMC, *Royal Institution*, I, 211-212; and Prevost to Clinton, Sept. 16, 1778, Henry Clinton Papers.
6. Peace commissioners' "Secret Instructions" to Archibald Campbell, about Nov. 3, 1778, Stevens, *Facsimiles*, No. 1205; peace commissioners to Germain, Nov. 16, 1778, *ibid.*, No. 1216.
7. Henry Laurens to Washington, Sept. 23, 1778, Burnett, *Letters*, III, 422-423; *Gazette of the State of S. C.*, Nov. 11, 25, 1778.
8. Congressional action, Sept. 24, 1778, *JCC*, XII, 949-950; Laurens to governors of Virginia, North Carolina, and Georgia, Burnett, *Letters*, III, 425. For North Carolina action Oct. 30-Nov. 7, 1778, see *NCSR*, XIII, 258-267; XXII, 936-937.
9. *RRG*, II, 119-120.
10. Burnett, *Letters*, III, 487, 494, 500, 548-549. Committee report of Nov. 10, 1778, Edward Telfair Papers (XII-C), Duke U. Library.
11. Burnett, *Letters*, III, 555.
12. See accounts of participating troops in Roy W. Pettengill, *Letters from America, 1776-1779* (Boston, 1924), 197-198; journal of Colonel Stephen Kemble, Nov. 7, 1778, *Collections*, NYHS, 1883, pp. 165-166; unidentified return of troops under Campbell, Jan. 16, 1779, PRO, CO 5: 97, p. 380. Secret instructions of Admiral James Gambier to Captain Hyde Parker, Nov. 2, 1778, Stevens, *Facsimiles*, No. 1203.
13. Clinton to Prevost, Oct. 29, 1778,

HMC, *Royal Institution*, I, 314.
14. *Continental Journal* (Boston), Feb. 18, 1779; unidentified report of expedition, Nov. 21, 1778, PCC, No. 160, pp. 503-504; Tonyn to Germain, Dec. 19, 1778, PRO, CO 5: 559, pp. 77-80; Jones, *History of Georgia*, II, 305-312; *S. C. & American General Gazette*, Nov. 26, Dec. 3, 10, 1778.
15. Congressional action, Sept. 25, 1778, *JCC*, XII, 951; Cornelius Harnett to Governor of North Carolina, Sept. 26, Nov. 28, 1778, Burnett, *Letters*, III, 426, 512; Howe to President of Congress, Nov. 24, 1778, *NCSR*, XIII, 498-499; Howe to Moultrie, Dec. 8, 1778, Jones, *History of Georgia*, II, 312-314.
16. Deposition of William Haslon, Dec. 6, 1778, in Lincoln to Governor of North Carolina, Dec. 22, 1778, *NCSR*, XIII, 332-334.
17. Council minutes, Dec. 17, 22-26, 1778, *RRG*, II, 124-125, 127-129; John Houstoun to Lincoln, Dec. 21, 1778, U. S. Revolution, Misc., 1778-1779, Mss. Div., LC.
18. Pettengill, *Letters from America*, 198-204; Clinton to Germain, Nov. 18, 1778, Stevens, *Facsimiles*, No. 1221; *Gazette of the State of S. C.*, Dec. 30, 1778.
19. American sources for the capture of Savannah are the conflicting testimony of Howe and George Walton at Howe's court martial, *Collections*, NYHS, 1879, pp. 213-311; Howe to ――――, Dec. 30, 1778, PCC, 158, I, 189-195. British sources are Campbell to Germain, Jan. 16, 1779, *Gentleman's Magazine* (London), 1779, pp. 177-181, and Stevens, *Facsimiles*, No. 1247; Alexander Innes to Clinton, Jan. 20, 1779, Henry Clinton Papers; Hyde Parker to Admiral James Grabier, Stevens, *Facsimiles*, No. 1246. A modern account complete and well balanced, using the above sources is Alexander A. Lawrence, "General Robert Howe and the British Capture of Savannah in 1778," *GHQ*, XXXVI, 303-327.
20. Proclamations of Jan. 4, 11, 1779, Stevens, *Facsimiles*, Nos. 1238, 1244.

Loyalty oath in Henry Clinton Papers, CL.

21. Prevost to Clinton, Jan. 19, 1779, PRO, CO 5: 97, 227-229, 281; Lincoln to Congress, Jan. 23, 1779, PCC, No. 158, I, 201.

22. Campbell to Earl of Carlisle, Jan. 19, 1779, Stevens, *Facsimiles*, No. 113.

23. Wm. Moultrie to C. C. Pinckney, Jan. 10, 1779, William Moultrie, *Memoirs of the American Revolution* (New York, 1802), I, 259.

24. Campbell to Clinton, March 4, 1779, PRO, CO 5: 182, pp. 151-155; Prevost to Germain, March 5, 1779, *ibid.*, 139-142; C. C. Jones, Jr., ed., "Memorandum of the Route pursued by Colonel Campbell and his column of invasion, in 1779, from Savannah to Augusta; . . . ," *Magazine of American History*, XVIII, 256-348; John Ashe to Governor of North Carolina, March 17, 1779, *NCSR*, XIV, 39; Lincoln to Congress, Feb. 27, 1779, PCC, No. 158, I, 235-241.

25. Lincoln to Governor of North Carolina, Dec. 31, 1778, *NCSR*, XIII, 342; Lincoln to Congress, Dec. 31, 1778, Jan. 7, Feb. 6, 1779, PCC, No. 158, I, 181-182, 185-186, 197.

26. *S. C. and American General Gazette*, Jan. 28, Feb. 4, 1779; Leonard Marbury to Samuel Elbert, Jan. 27, 1779, Revolutionary Collection, Duke U.; Paul L. Ford, ed., *Proceedings of a Council of War Held at Burke Jail, Georgia, January 14th, 1779, . . .* (Brooklyn, 1890); Prevost to Clinton, Jan. 19, 1779, PRO, CO 5: 97, 229.

27. John Dooly to Samuel Elbert, Feb. 15, 1779, U. S. Revolution, Misc., 1778-1779, Mss. Div., LC; proclamation of Dooly, June 27, 1779, Ms. CRG, XXXVIII, Part II, 202-203.

28. Sources cited in note no. 24 above; *Virginia Gazette*, (D) April 9, 1779; *S. C. & American General Gazette*, Feb. 25, 1779.

29. *Virginia Gazette*, (D) April 2, 1779.

30. For Lincoln's movements Jan. 3-June 6, 1779, see his ms. orderly book, H M 659, Huntington Library.

31. Prevost to Germain, March 5, 1779, *Gentleman's Magazine*, 1779, pp. 213-214; Prevost to Clinton, March 6, 1779, Henry Clinton Papers; *Royal Georgia Gazette*, March 11, 1779; Lincoln to ――――, March 7, 1779, White, *Hist. Coll. of Ga.*, 633; Ashe to Lincoln, March 3, 1779, *NCSR*, XIV, 271; Ashe to Governor Caswell, March 17, 1779, *ibid.*, 39-43; Ashe's court martial, *ibid.*, 275-284; *Gazette of the State of S. C.*, March 10, 18, 1779; Jones, *History of Georgia*, II, 346-353.

32. Proclamation of Prevost, Parker, and Campbell, March 4, 1779, Stevens, *Facsimiles*, No. 1276. *Royal Georgia Gazette*, March 11, 1779, lists the officials appointed.

33. Proclamation of Prevost, March 17, 1779, PRO, CO 5: 182, pp. 225-228; Prevost to Germain, April 14, 1779, *ibid.*, 208-212.

34. Graham and Stokes were ordered back Jan. 19, 1779, and Wright March 8, Ms. CRG, XXXIX, 101-102; XXXVIII, Part II, 154-155; Stokes, *Narrative*, 47-49.

35. Germain to Wright, March 31, 1779, Ms. CRG, XXXVIII, Part II, 155-159.

36. *Ibid.*, 176-179.

37. Wright to Germain, July 31, 1779, *Collections*, GHS, III, 254-255; Wright to Clinton, July 30, 1779, HMC, *Royal Institution*, I, 483.

38. Eighteen questions of Wright to Germain, Germain Papers, undated papers, CL. Germain expressed the opinion that with these beliefs Wright might not be the best governor to send to Georgia. Germain to William Knox, March 12, 1779, HMC, *Various Collections*, VI, 156.

39. *Royal Georgia Gazette*, Feb. 11, 1779.

40. *Gazette of the State of S. C.*, Feb. 17, 1779.

41. Prevost to Clinton, April 16, 1779, and Clinton to Prevost, April 28, 1779, HMC, *Royal Institution*, I, 419, 423; Parker to Gambier, March 12, 1779, and John Henry to Gambier, March 16, 1779, PRO, Admiralty, 1: 489, pp. 403-405, 407-408.

42. Campbell to Clinton, March 9, 1779,

HMC, *Royal Institution,* I, 395-396; Prevost to Clinton, March 15, 1778, *ibid.,* 398-399; Clinton to Germain, April 3, 1779, Henry Clinton Papers; *Royal Georgia Gazette,* March 11, 1779.

43. Joseph Clay to Bright and Pechin, March 23, 1779, *Collections,* GHS, VIII, 130-131; Notes of James Jackson on David Ramsay's *History of the Revolution in South Carolina,* pp. 9-10, *GHQ,* XXXVII, 62-63; Lincoln to Congress, PCC, No. 158, I, 252-253; Jones, *History of Georgia,* II, 354-355.

44. Notes on council of war held at Black Swamp, S. C., April 16, 1779, *NCSR,* XIV, 293.

45. Joseph Clay to Joseph Carleton, June 9, 1779, *Collections,* GHS, VIII, 138-139; John Butler to Governor Caswell, June 17, 1779, *NCSR,* XIV, 119; Tonyn to Clinton, July 13, 1779, HMC, *Royal Institution,* I, 469-470; *S. C. & American General Gazette,* May 29, 1779; *Gazette of the State of S. C.,* July 9, 1779; description of movement of British army April 28-July 9, 1779, F. Shelly, Savannah, Nov. 8, 1779, H M 1528, Huntington Library.

46. Memorial of Savannah to Wright and council, July 22, 1779, asking for more troops, *CRG,* XII, 437-441; Prevost to Clinton and Wright to Clinton, Aug. 7, 1779, HMC, *Royal Institution,* II, 5-6; returns of troops in Georgia July 1, Aug. 1, 1779, Henry Clinton Papers, CL.

47. McIntosh to Lincoln, Aug. 4, 1779, Misc. Mss., CL; Georgia Council to Lincoln and Governor of South Carolina, Aug. 18, 1779, *RRG,* II, 155-159, 162-165; ms. Journal of South Carolina House of Representatives, 1779-1780, Sept. 5, 1779, pp. 7-10, 33-34, 39.

48. Wright to Germain, Aug. 9, 1779, *Collections,* GHS, III, 258-259.

49. Talk of General Prevost in letter of David Taitt, Aug. 6, 1779, PRO, CO 5: 50, pp. 481-484.

50. Taitt to Clinton, June 11, 1779, Henry Clinton Papers; Prevost to Taitt, March 14, 1779, *ibid.;* Prevost to Germain, April 14, 1779, PRO, CO 5: 182, pp. 203-206; Indian commissioners to Germain, May 10, 1779, PRO, CO 5: 80, pp. 376-380.

51. Alexander Cameron and Charles Stuart to Germain, March 26, 1779, PRO, CO 5: 80, pp. 219-220; Germain to Clinton, Thomas Brown, and Cameron, June 25, 1779, Henry Clinton Papers.

52. Committee report, Jan. 25, 1779, Burnett, *Letters,* IV, 41-42.

53. Congressional action of Jan. 30, Feb. 2, March 18, April 10, July 8, 1779, *JCC,* XIII, 125, 132-133, 336, 436; XIV, 807; Henry Laurens to President of South Carolina, Jan. 31, 1779, Burnett, *Letters,* IV, 50-51; message of Governor Caswell, Jan. 19, 1779, *NCSR,* XIII, 629.

54. Congressional actions of Jan. 22, 28, Feb. 5, 7, *JCC,* XIII, 102, 149, 153-154; Burnett, *Letters,* IV, 52-53, 56; Rutledge to d'Estaing, March 23, 1779, Arch. Nat., Marine, B4, vol. 168, f. 164-165, transcripts in Mss. Div., LC.

55. John Rutledge to d'Estaing, Sept. 5, 1779, Arch. Nat., Marine, B4, vol. 168, ff. 169-170.

56. Lincoln to Congress, Sept. 5, 1779, PCC, No. 158, III, 275-276.

57. Council minutes, Sept. 6, 1779, *Collections,* GHS, X, 49-50; Wright to Germain, Nov. 5, 1779, *ibid.,* III, 262-263.

58. Lincoln's diary of the siege of Savannah, Sept. 3-Oct. 19, 1779, Mss. Div., LC.

59. The d'Estaing-Prevost surrender correspondence is in Jones, *History of Georgia,* II, 379-383. The fact that Maitland and his troops got into Savannah caused one of the major points of contention between the French and Americans. On this point see Alexander A. Lawrence, *Storm Over Savannah* (Athens, 1951), 46-53.

60. The bibliography of the siege of Savannah is extensive, including several contemporary accounts by British, French, and American officers. The most recent, most com-

plete, and best secondary treatment is Lawrence, *Storm Over Savannah*, which includes a complete bibliography from American, French, and British sources. See also W. S. Murphy, "The Irish Brigade of France at the Siege of Savannah, 1779," *GHQ*, XXXVIII, 307-321.

61. Action of October 20, 1779, *JCC*, XV, 1191-1193; diary of John Fell, Nov. 10, 1779, Burnett, *Letters*, IV, 513-514; letter from "a gentleman in Jersey," Nov. 25, 1779, *N. J. Archives*, Second Series, IV, 78-83.

62. Council minutes, Oct. 22, 1779, *CRG*, XII, 449-450.

63. Account of ball given Nov. 9, 1779, *Royal Georgia Gazette*, Dec. 23, 1779.

CHAPTER VIII

1. Joseph Clay to Christopher Pechin, Nov. 2, 1779, *Collections*, GHS, VIII, 155; Congressional action, Nov. 20, 26, 1779, *JCC*, XV, 1315, 1331-1332; N. C. action Oct., 1779, *NCSR*, XXIV, 262.

2. Clinton to Germain, Nov. 20, 1779, Henry Clinton Papers, CL.

3. Resolution of South Carolina House of Representatives, Jan. 29, 1780, Ms. Journal, 1779-1780, p. 120.

4. Clinton to Prevost, Feb. 18, 1780, HMC, *Royal Institution*, II, 91-92; Prevost to Clinton, March 2, 1780, *ibid.*, 96; Wright to Clinton, March 18, 1780, *ibid.*, 103-104.

5. Wright to Clinton, Feb. 3, 1780, Ms. CRG, XXXVIII, Part II, 270-272; Wright to General Paterson, Feb. 14, 1780, *ibid.*, 277-278.

6. *Royal Georgia Gazette* for this period; Clinton correspondence in HMC, *Royal Institution*, II, 100-120; Wright correspondence, *Collections*, GHS, III; Georgia Council minutes, *CRG*, XII.

7. *RRG*, II, 208, 243; Wright to Germain, June 9, 1780, *Collections*, GHS, III, 306.

8. Wright to Germain, June 9, 1780, *Collections*, GHS, III, 305-306; Brown to Cornwallis, June 18, 28, 1780, PRO, Gifts and Deposits, Cornwallis Papers, Bundle 2, No. 83 and 100.

9. On the Nancy Hart legend see E. Merton Coulter, "Nancy Hart, Georgia Heroine of the Revolution: The Story of the Growth of a Tradition," *GHQ*, XXXIX, 118-151.

10. Wright to Cornwallis, July 9, 1780, PRO, Cornwallis Papers, Bundle 2, No. 118. Alured Clarke to Cornwallis, July 11, 1780, *ibid.*, No. 124.

11. Cornwallis to Clinton, July 14, 1780, B. F. Stevens, *The Clinton-Cornwallis Controversy* (London, 1888), I, 231-232.

12. Wright to Germain, July 19, 1780, *Collections*, GHS, III, 310-311; Wright to Cornwallis, July 28, 1780, PRO, Cornwallis Papers, Bundle 2, No. 169.

13. This story was first printed in Hugh McCall, *The History of Georgia* (2 vols., Savannah, 1811-1816), II, 326-327, based, says McCall, upon British officers' accounts in his possession. Brown gives an account of the hanging in South Carolina of thirteen Whigs who had taken oath of loyalty to the King and then joined the Whigs and murdered British troops who refused to join them. Brown to David Ramsay, Dec. 25, 1786, White, *Hist. Coll. of Georgia*, 614-619. For Wright's account of the hangings see Wright to Germain, Sept. 22, Oct. 27, 1780, Ms. CRG, XXXVIII, Part II, 435-436, and *Collections*, GHS, III, 321, and a printed account in PRO, CO 5: 82, pp. 329-330.

14. Jones, *History of Georgia*, II, 447-461; Louise F. Hays, *Hero of Hornet's Nest. A Biography of Elijah Clark* (New York, 1946), 78-125; Samuel C. Williams, "Colonel Elijah Clarke in the Tennessee Country," *GHQ*, XXV, 151-158. See also *NCSR*, XV, 135, 242.

15. Wright to Germain, Oct. 27, 1780, *Collections*, GHS, III, 321-322. Graham's list, undated, is in Cruger to Cornwallis, PRO, Cornwallis Papers, Bundle 4, No. 37.

16. Wright to Cornwallis, Nov. 20, 1780, PRO, Cornwallis Papers, Bundle 4, No. 84; Wright to Germain, Jan. 25, 1781, *Collections*, GHS, III, 332-333.

17. Wright to Cornwallis, April 23, 1781, PRO, Cornwallis Papers, Bundle 5, No. 108.
18. Greene to Congress, May 14, 1781, PCC, No. 155, II, 62-63.
19. The capture of Augusta is covered in full in Jones, *History of Georgia,* II, 477-495, and Clara Goldsmith Roe, "Major General Nathanael Greene and the Southern Campaign of the American Revolution, 1780-1783" (unpublished doctoral dissertation, University of Michigan, 1947), 331-334; Greene papers for May and June in the Clements Library and Duke U. Library; Revolutionary Collection, Duke U. Library; PCC, No. 155, 11, 62-146. Surrender correspondence is printed in White, *Hist. Coll. of Ga.,* 611-614. Jones mistakenly puts the murder of Grierson after the capture of the first fort.
20. Roe, "Greene and the Southern Campaign," 326-331; Greene to Capt. Priors, June 15, 1781, Greene Papers, CL; Greene to Congress, June 9, 20, 1781, PCC, No. 155, II, 117-118, 183; Greene to Elijah Clarke, May 29, 1781, Greene Papers, Duke U. Library; Greene to Joseph Clay, June 9, 1781, *ibid.*
21. Wright to Lt. Col. Nisbet Balfour, July 27, Aug. 16, 1781, HMC, *Royal Institution,* II, 306, 315; Wright to Clinton, Oct. 16, 1781, *ibid.,* 342; loyalist petition, Sept. 22, 1781, Sir James Wright 1779-1782 folder, Telamon Cuyler Collection, U. of Ga.; assembly action, Dec. 8, 1781, *Royal Georgia Gazette,* Jan. 3, 1782.
22. Clinton to Leslie, Dec. 20, 1781, Henry Clinton Papers, CL.
23. Council minutes, Aug. 26, Sept. 26, 1781, *RRG,* II, 256, 268; Greene to Governor Brownson, Nov. 6, 1781, Greene Papers, CL; Greene to Twiggs, Dec. 7, 1781, *ibid.;* Greene to Twiggs, Dec. 12, 1781, Greene Papers, Duke U. Library; Greene to Robert Livingston, Dec. 19, 1781, PCC, No. 155, II, 389; Roe, "Greene and the Southern Campaign," 405.
24. Returns of troops under Clinton throughout the period in Henry Clinton Papers, CL. See especially returns of Aug. 15, 1780, Dec. 20, 1781. "State of His Majesty's Forces in North America," PRO, CO 5: 105, p. 480.
25. Fourteen Von Porbeck letters, dated from Feb. 24, 1780, through June 1, 1782, are in the Von Jungkenn Collection, CL. They are vol. 3, nos. 14, 65, 69, 71, 74; vol. 4, nos. 1, 6, 21, 31; vol. 5, nos. 21, 23, 25, 26, and 61. They were translated for me by Mr. H. J. Lacher, of Athens, Ga.
26. Cornwallis to Clinton, Aug. 6, 1780, *NCSR,* XV, 262.
27. Wright to Germain and Cornwallis, April 2, 1781, Ms. CRG, XXXVIII, Part II, 494-496.
28. Wright to William Knox, Feb. 16, 1782, *Collections,* GHS, III, 371.
29. Nisbet Balfour to Cornwallis, Nov. 5, 1780, PRO, Cornwallis Papers, Bundle 4, No. 15, p. 13.
30. Petition of inhabitants of Ebenezer, in Wright to Cornwallis, July 9, 1780, *ibid.,* Bundle 2, Nos. 104 and 118.
31. Council minutes, Nov. 23, Dec. 24, 1779, *Collections,* GHS, X, 67-68, 74.
32. Wright to Clinton, May 10, June 2, 1780, HMC, *Royal Institution,* II, 120, 135; Wright to Cornwallis, July 3, 1780, PRO, Cornwallis Papers, Bundle 2, No. 169.
33. Balfour to Cornwallis, June 27, 1780, PRO, Cornwallis Papers, Bundle 2, No. 97.
34. Clinton's instructions to Major Ferguson, May 22, 1780, Henry Clinton Papers, CL; Cornwallis to Clinton, June 30, 1780, *NCSR,* XV, 249-255; Wright to Cornwallis, July 28, 1780, PRO, Cornwallis Papers, Bundle 2, No. 169.
35. *CRG,* XV, 625-627, 646-647; Wright to Germain, Dec. 1, 1780, *Collections,* GHS, III, 322-323.
36. Wright to Germain, March 5, 1781, *Collections,* GHS, III, 335-338; *Royal Georgia Gazette,* May 3, June 7, 1781; Germain to Wright, June 4, 1781, Stevens, *Clinton-Cornwallis Controversy,* II, 11-12.
37. General Lincoln declared on Decem-

ber 2, 1779, that there was only about one company for the entire four battalions; PCC, No. 158, II, 306. For Congressional and state action see *JCC*, XVI, 26-27, 156; Lincoln to Governor Howley, Feb. 19, 1780, Misc. Mss., CL; *RRG*, II, 57.

38. Assembly action, Aug. 21, 1781, *RRG*, III, 25.

39. On state troops see council minutes for the period, especially *RRG*, II, 272-273, 326, 337-338; III, 64-65, 88-90, 98; *Royal Georgia Gazette*, Nov. 22, 1781; John Twiggs to Greene, Dec. 16, 1782 (misdated for 1781), PCC, No. 155, II, 409-411.

40. Andrew Pickens to Greene, May 25, 1781, Revolutionary Collection, Duke U. Library.

41. Military 1779-1792 folder, Telamon Cuyler Coll., U. of Ga.

42. Greene to Wayne, Jan. 9, 1782, Greene letterbook, Mss. Div., LC.

43. Leslie to Germain, Jan. 3, 1782, HMC, *Royal Institution*, II, 379; Leslie to Clinton, Feb. 18, 1782, PRO, CO 5: 105, pp. 5-6; troop returns in Henry Clinton Papers, CL.

44. Wayne to Greene, Jan. 25, Feb. 1, 1782, Greene Papers, CL.

45. Greene to Martin, Jan. 9, 1782, *ibid.;* Martin to Wayne, Jan. 19, 1782, *ibid.*

46. Statement of Mark King, Jan., 1782, Mark King Papers, GHS; John Graham to Germain, Jan. 31, 1782, Ms. CRG, XXXVIII, Part II, 568-569.

47. Wright's correspondence for 1782 in *Collections*, GHS, III, especially 362-364.

48. Wayne to Greene, Feb. 6, 11, 22, 1782, Greene Papers, CL; Martin to Greene, Feb. 9, 1782, *ibid.;* Leslie-Clinton correspondence, Feb.-March, 1782, HMC, *Royal Institution*, II, 399-418.

49. Wayne to Greene, Feb. 28, 1782, Jones, *History of Georgia*, II, 507. See also Wayne to Greene, Jan. 23, 1782, Greene Papers, CL.

50. Wayne to Martin, Feb. 19, 1782, Georgia council correspondence, Force transcripts, Mss. Div., LC.

51. *RRG*, II, 320. Copy of proclamation in German in Von Jungkenn Mss., Vol. 5, No. 26, CL; in English, HMC, *Royal Institution*, II, 401.

52. Von Porbeck to Von Jungkenn, March 2, 1782, Von Jungkenn Mss., V, No. 25 CL; Leslie to Clinton, March 12, 1782, HMC, *Royal Institution*, II, 418; Clarke to Leslie, April 11, 1782, *ibid.*, 447-448; Wayne to Greene, March 11, 1782, Greene Papers, CL.

53. *NCCR*, VIII, 760.

54. Sources cited in note 52 above.

55. Wayne to Greene, April 28, 1782, Greene Papers, CL; Greene to John Hanson, May 18, 1782, PCC, No. 155, II, 443.

56. "Cessation of Hostilities," special vol. in Greene Papers, CL. The Wayne-Wright correspondence is in HMC, *Royal Institution*, II, 504.

57. Leslie to Clinton, April 17, 27, 1782, HMC, *Royal Institution*, II, 456, 470.

58. Germain to Carleton, April 4, 1782, PRO, CO 5: 106, pp. 1-13; Carleton to Leslie, May 22, 1782, HMC, *Royal Institution*, II, 494.

59. Carleton to Leslie, May 23, 27, 1782, HMC, *Royal Institution*, II, 494-495, 500; address of Wright and assembly to Leslie, June 16, 1782, *CRG*, XV, 662-665; Wright to Carleton, July 6, 1782, HMC, *Royal Institution*, III, 11.

60. Jones, *History of Georgia*, II, 523-527.

61. Carleton to Leslie, May 23, 1782; Wayne to Greene, June 30, 1782, Greene Papers, CL.

62. Wayne stated in different letters that the British evacuated Savannah on both July 10 and 11. July 11 seems to be the correct date. Wayne to Governor Martin, July 10, 1782, Force Transcripts, Ga. Indian, No. 12, Mss. Div., LC; copy of occupation order July 11, *ibid.;* Wayne to Greene, July 12, 1782, PCC, No. 155, II, 503-505; Jones, *History of Georgia*, II, 518; *RRG*, III, 167.

63. Wayne to Greene, July 12, 1782, PCC, No. 155, II, 503-505, 537-550; *RRG*, III, 121, 130-131; *JCC*, XXIII, 834-836.

64. Wayne to Greene, July 12, 1782, PCC, No. 155, II, 503-505.
65. Greene to Wayne, July 13, 1782; Greene to Martin, July 14, 1782; Wayne to Greene, July 17, 1782; Greene to John Habersham, Aug. 2, 1782; Greene to Wayne, Aug. 2, 1782; all in Greene Papers, CL.
66. Carleton to Shelburne, Aug. 15, 1782, PRO, CO 5: 106, pp. 329-336.
67. Wayne to Greene, June 30, 1782, Greene Papers, CL.
68. Tonyn to Carleton, Oct. 11, 1782, HMC, *Royal Institution*, III, 163-164; Tonyn to Shelburne, Sept. 24, Nov. 14, 1782, PRO, CO 5: 560, pp. 465-466, 469-471; compilation of refugees in East Florida by Jno. Winniett, inspector of refugees, Nov. 14, Dec. 23, 1782, *ibid.*, 477, 507; undated return received from Leslie, July 18, 1782, *ibid.*, 805-810; John Simpson to Thomas Townshend, Aug. 19, 1782, John Simpson Papers, Georgia Misc., Duke U.
69. Carleton to Shelburne, Aug. 15, 1782, PRO, CO 5: 106, pp. 329-336; Leslie to Carleton, July 13, 1782, HMC, *Royal Institution*, III, 28-29; Archibald Campbell to William Knox, Sept. 15, 1782, HMC, *Various Collections*, V, 188; return of people embarked from South Carolina and Georgia, Dec. 13, 1782, Winslow Papers, Misc., Mass. Hist. Soc., *Proceedings*, 2 Series, III, 95.
70. "Notes on Ramsay," *GHQ*, XXXVII, 78; Stevens, *History of Georgia*, II, 289.
71. HMC, *Royal Institution*, II-III, *passim; RRG*, III, 127.
72. Undated draft, headed "Negroes," PRO, CO 5: 8, pp. 82-85; Leslie to Carleton, June 27, 1782, HMC, *Royal Institution*, II, 544; Carleton to Leslie, July 15, 1782, *ibid.*, III, 201.
73. PRO, CO 5: 560, pp. 805-810.
74. Assembly resolutions, July 3, 15, 16, 1782, *RRG*, III, 119-120, 127, 130; Joseph Clay to Greene, Aug. 6, 1782, Greene Papers, CL.

CHAPTER IX

1. Wright to Germain, Nov. 6, 1779, *Collections*, GHS, III, 269-270; council minutes, Oct. 22, 1779, *CRG*, XII, 450-451.
2. Charge of Stokes to grand jury, Dec. 14, 1779, *Royal Georgia Gazette*, Dec. 23, 1779; Wright to Germain, Jan. 20, Feb. 20, 1780, *Collections*, GHS, III, 272-273, 276.
3. Council minutes, Feb. 16, March 8, 1780, *Collections*, GHS, X, 89, 91.
4. Henry Clinton Papers, CL.
5. Council minutes, March 24, 1780, *Collections*, GHS, X, 96; Wright to Germain, March 24, 1780, *ibid.*, III, 279-281; Wright to Clinton, March 28, 1780, Ms. CRG, XXXVIII, Part II, 292-294.
6. Council minutes, May 5, 1780, *Collections*, GHS, X, 103.
7. *Ibid.*, 104; *CRG*, XV, 564-565.
8. *CRG*, XV, 548-552, 556-557; XII, 472-475; Ms. CRG, XXXVIII, Part II, 349-352.
9. PRO, CO 5: 685, pp. 1-6, 17-18; *RRG*, I, 348-363.
10. Wright to Germain, July 19, 1780, *Collections*, GHS, III, 310. The journal of the Commons House is in *CRG*, XV, 547-624. No journal of the Upper House has been located. The acts passed are in PRO, CO 5: 685, pp. 1-24.
11. *Royal Georgia Gazette*, June 22, 1780.
12. Council minutes, June 29, Aug. 1, 7, 12, 28, Sept. 8, 1780, *Collections*, GHS, X, 111-112, 115-120.
13. *Collections*, GHS, X, 128; *CRG*, XV, 624-637.
14. Wright to Germain, Dec. 20, 1780, *Collections*, GHS, III, 328.
15. For a record of royal assembly sessions, 1779-1782, see Appendix B.
16. Wright to Board of Trade, Jan. 23, 1782, *Collections*, GHS, III, 364. These thirty-three acts are in PRO, CO 5: 685. Copies of two other acts have been located, and the title of one other is known.
17. Act approved April 26, 1781, PRO, CO 5: 685, pp. 65-67.
18. William Knox to Lt. Col. Mark Prevost, Oct. 25, 1779, PRO, CO 5: 182, pp. 287-290; Ms. CRG, XXXIV, 650-653.

19. Knox to Mr. Cumberland, Feb. 18, 1780, PRO, CO 5: 81, pp. 26-28; Germain to Wright, July 7, 1780, July 4, 1781, Ms. CRG, XXXVIII, Part II, 395-396, 491.
20. *CRG,* XII, 469-472; Wright to Germain, May 19, 1780, Ms. CRG, XXXVIII, Part II, 308-309.
21. *Royal Georgia Gazette,* June 14, Sept. 27, 1781.
22. Germain to Wright, March 31, 1779, Ms. CRG, XXXVIII, Part II, 155-159.
23. Approved March 6, 1781, *Royal Georgia Gazette,* May 24, 1781.
24. Stokes, *Narrative,* 89.
25. Board of Trade to Wright, June 12, 1781, Ms. CRG, XXXIV, 658-659; Germain to Wright, June 4, 1781, *ibid.,* XXXVIII, Part II, 492-493.
26. Memorial of board of police, April 12, 1780, Henry Clinton Papers, CL; instructions of Archibald Campbell to commissioners of claims, March 15, 1779, and report of commissioners, March 15, 1779, Germain Papers, CL.
27. Germain to Wright, July 9, 1779, Ms. CRG, XXXVIII, Part II, 165-166.
28. Wright to Germain, Feb. 10, Dec. 20, 1780, and report of commissioners of claims, April 24, 29, May 20, 1780, *Collections,* GHS, III, 274-275, 288-300, 328-329.
29. *CRG,* XV, 593, 596-597, 600-601. A copy of the bill, listed as "Georgia Treason Act," is in the Mss. Div., LC.
30. Act approved July 1, 1780, *RRG,* I, 348-363; Wright to Germain, Jan. 26, 1781, *Collections,* GHS, III, 333.
31. *RRG,* I, 364-372.
32. Wright to Germain, Aug. 17, 1780, Ms. CRG, XXXVIII, Part II, 384-400; *CRG,* XII, 475-488; Richard Howly to Nathanael Greene, May 20, 1782, Revolutionary Collection, Duke U.; N. Greene to Howley, June 8, 1782, Greene Papers, Duke U.
33. Germain to Wright, Nov. 9, 1780, Ms. CRG, XXXVIII, Part II, 406; council minutes, Sept. 20, 1780, *Collections,* GHS, X, 127-128.

34. *Collections,* GHS, X, 112-115; council minutes, Nov. 13, 1780. "Revolution-British (Wright)" folder, Telamon Cuyler Collection, U. of Ga.
35. *Collections,* GHS, X, 107, 119, 127-128; petitions of Joseph Gibbons, July 2, 1780, and James Alexander, July 11, 1781, in "Revolution-British (Wright)" folder, Telamon Cuyler Coll., U. of Ga.
36. Levi Sheftal, John Sutcliffe, William Stephens, Andrew More, John Martin, and James Gordon.
37. On this see above pp. 137-38.
38. Wright to Germain, Dec. 21, 1780, Jan. 18, 1782, *Collections,* GHS, III, 329, 362.
39. Germain to Wright, Jan. 19, 1780, April 4, June 4, 1781, Ms. CRG, XXXVIII, Part II, 247-252, 467, 492-493.
40. A good picture of Georgia 1779-1782 and Wright's objections to leaving are given in his "concise view of the situation of affairs there [Georgia] for three years past," Sept. 3, 1782, Jones, *History of Georgia,* II, 523-527.
41. *RRG,* II, 129.
42. William Glascock to Congress, July 10, 1779, PCC, No. 73, pp. 240-244.
43. *RRG,* II, 129-130, 135-136.
44. *Ibid.,* 140; Glascock to Congress, July 10, 1779, PCC, No. 73, 240-244.
45. Account of a meeting of Georgians at Black Swamp, South Carolina, April 9-10, 1779, *Gazette of the State of S. C.,* April 28, 1779.
46. *RRG,* II, 141-144; supreme executive council to Lincoln, Aug. 18, 1778, *ibid.,* 155.
47. See statements from Richmond, Wilkes, and Burke counties, *ibid.,* 146, 154, 170.
48. Aug. 6, 1779, *ibid.,* 147-148.
49. *Ibid.,* 144-152, 165-166, 176-179; Wilkes County Court records, 1779, Duke U.
50. Lincoln and Clay to John Wereat, Nov. 2, 1779, *Collections,* GHS, VIII, 160-161.
51. Proclamation in Jones, *History of Georgia,* II, 428.
52. *Collections,* NYHS, 1879, p. 307.

53. *Gazette of the State of S. C.*, Dec. 8, 1779; Walton to Congress, Nov. 29, 1779, PCC, No. 73, p. 246; Glascock to Congress, Nov. 29, 1779, *ibid.*, 254; *RRG*, II, 182-183; Lachlan McIntosh to Benjamin Lincoln, Dec. 11, 1779, Lachlan McIntosh Papers, Duke U.

54. Glascock to Congress, Nov. 20, 1779, PCC, No. 73, p. 254; Samuel Huntington to McIntosh, Feb. 15, 1780, *ibid.*, No. 162, II, pp. 313-314; James Lovell to Samuel Adams, Feb. 16, 1780, Burnett, *Letters*, V, 39; *RRG*, II, 189.

55. Glascock to Congress, May 12, 1780, PCC, No. 73, pp. 266-268.

56. Walton to Congress, Sept. 7, 1780, *ibid.*, 270-272; report of committee and action of Congress, Sept. 25, 1780, *JCC*, XVIII, 861.

57. July 16, 1781, *JCC*, XX, 752-753.

58. Assembly action of Feb. 1, 1783, PCC, No. 162, II, pp. 326-327; imperfect copy in *RRG*, III, 248.

59. Most of the documents are in PCC, No. 162, II, 313-327. A recent and complete account is Alexander A. Lawrence, "General Lachlan McIntosh and His Suspension from the Continental Command during the Revolution," *GHQ*, XXXVIII, 124-141.

60. *RRG*, II, 196-202; Jones, *History of Georgia*, II, 433.

61. Howley to Clay, Feb. 1, 1780, *RRG*, II, 207-208.

62. Act approved, Jan. 23, 1780, *CRG*, XIX, Part II, 130-140; on the land office see *RRG*, II, 226, 237-238.

63. *RRG*, II, 208-209, 212-214, 231.

64. Proclamation of Feb. 2, 1780, *ibid.*, 210-211; see also *ibid.*, 220.

65. *Ibid.*, 213-214, 247; John Armstrong to John Davis, Burnett, *Letters*, V, 250.

66. Henry Lee to Greene, June 4, 1781, Revolutionary Collection, Duke U.; Greene to Elijah Clarke, June 12, 1781, Greene Papers, Duke U.; Greene to John Wilkinson, June 13, 1781, *ibid.*; Greene to Georgia delegates, June 22, 1781, *ibid.*; Joseph Clay to ———, Aug. 9, 1787, *Collec-*

tions, GHS, VIII, 217.

67. Greene to Georgia delegates, July 18, Aug. 25, 1781, Greene Papers, Duke U.; Greene to Clarke, Twiggs, and Few, July 24, 1781, *ibid.*

68. *RRG*, III, 7-8, 11-13, 15-17, 22-23.

69. *Ibid.*, 18-25, 28; *Royal Georgia Gazette*, Aug. 30, 1781.

70. *CRG*, XIX, Part II, 142-144; *Royal Georgia Gazette*, Aug. 30, 1781; *RRG*, III, 12-13, 17; II, 255-256, and *passim* for Aug. and Sept., 1781.

71. *RRG*, III, 11. Proclamation in *Gentleman's Magazine*, 1781, p. 585.

72. Journal of session in *RRG*, III, 7-30.

73. *Ibid.*, II, 254, 268, 270-271, 277, 279-280, 283, 289, 291, 292.

74. *Royal Georgia Gazette*, Sept. 20, 1781; March 14, 1782; Brownson to Greene, Dec. 15, 1781, Revolutionary Collection, Duke U.

75. *RRG*, II, 254, 263, 264, 267, 273, 281, 285-286, 292.

76. *Ibid.*, 283; III, 31-33.

77. *RRG*, III, 34-35, 40.

78. *Ibid.*, 50, 77.

79. *Ibid.*, 44-46, 58.

80. *Ibid.*, 59-60; *CRG*, XIX, Part II, 147-151.

81. *RRG*, II, 315, 327, 337; III, 55.

82. *Ibid.*, III, 79-81.

83. *Ibid.*, 75, 79-80.

84. Journal of this session is in *ibid.*, 31-81.

85. Negotiations of March 12, through May 10, 1782, *ibid.*, 322, 325, 333.

86. Jan. 21, 1782, *RRG*, II, 308.

87. On confiscation and banishment see below pp. ———. The journal of this session is in *RRG*, III, 82-118.

88. *Ibid.*, 118-122.

89. *Ibid.*, 122; II, 340.

90. See Appendix C below, for Congressional attendance.

91. For Walton's activities in Congress see *JCC*, XIX-XXI, Jan.-Oct., 1781.

92. Diary of Thomas Rodney, March 10, 1781, Burnett, *Letters*, VI, 21.

93. George Measam to General Gates, Sept. 21, 1780, *NCSR*, XIV, 634-635.

94. *JCC*, XIV, 598-599, 990-991; XVI, 156.

95. On Georgia's lack of payments see Burnett, *Letters*, IV, 46; V, 54; VI,

260-261, 271-272.

96. *JCC,* XIX, 112-113; *RRG,* III, 79.

97. *JCC,* XIII, 239-244, 340; Burnett, *Letters,* IV, 419-420.

98. *JCC,* XVIII, 901-902, 1070-1071.

99. James Lovell to Samuel Adams, March 17, 1780, Burnett, *Letters,* V, 78-80.

100. Reprinted in White, *Hist. Coll. of Ga.,* 106-110.

CHAPTER X

1. On the adoption of the association see above pp. 45-50, 58, 61-62.

2. Robert Mackay to Mary Mackay, Sept. 25, 1775, Mackay-Stiles Papers, Vol. 44, Sou. Hist. Coll., U. of N. C.; James Cuningham to Earl of Huntington, Feb. 9, 1776, HMC, *Twentieth Report,* III, 170; *S. C. Hist. and Genealogical Magazine,* V, 191; *RRG,* I, 89; papers of Capt. John Alexander, PRO, CO 5: 148, p. 69; Martin Jollie to Gov. Tonyn, Feb. 13, 1776, Henry Clinton Papers, CL.

3. *RRG,* I, 89, 108, 111-112; *American Archives,* 4 Series, V, 571-573, 585; bond of Aaron Milhado and Levi Sheftall, May 29, 1776, Sheftall Papers, Duke U.

4. *RRG,* I, 216-217; II, 26-27, 79-80, 121; *American Archives,* 5 Series, III, 1532-1533.

5. Joseph Clay to Bright and Pechin, Nov. 21, Dec. 7, 17, 18, 1776, *Collections,* GHS, VIII, 13-17, and Ms. Clay Letter Book, GHS.

6. Clay to Bright and Pechin, March 19, April 8, Sept. 29, Dec. 16, 1777, June 2, Sept. 2, 3, 1778, *Collections,* GHS, VIII, 22, 24-25, 39, 61-62, 79, 101-102.

7. Clay to Bright and Pechin, March 19, 1777, *ibid.,* 22; *RRG,* I, 307, 312, 316, 319-320.

8. *RRG,* I, 178-179; II, 12-14; *CRG,* XIX, Part II, 72-80; Howe to Congress, Sept. 12, 1777, and to Governor of Georgia, Jan. 29, 1778, PCC, No. 160, pp. 397-398, 418-424.

9. Lewis C Gray, *History of Agriculture in the Southern United States to 1860* (2 vols., Washington, 1935), II, 1021-1023; *Collections,* GHS, X, 79.

10. See Joseph Clay letters of May 15, June 14, Sept. 29, 1777, Feb. 3, March 12, June 2, Sept. 24, 1778, *Collections,* GHS, VIII, 30, 33-34, 41, 68, 80; and Ms. Joseph Clay Letter Book, GHS; Major Romaine de Lisle to Henry Laurens, Sept. 9, 1778, PCC, No. 78, XIX, 261; Samuel Elbert to Henry Laurens, PCC, No. 78, VIII, 291-292.

11. *RRG,* II, 238, 263.

12. *Royal Georgia Gazette,* March 22, 1781.

13. *RRG,* II, 196; Burnett, *Letters,* V, 54-55; Continental supplies furnished to Georgia militia, April 4, 1781, Greene Papers, CL; *JCC,* XX, 496-497; XXII, 190.

14. Greene to Alexander Martin, Nov. 11, 1781, Greene Papers, CL; Greene-Wayne correspondence, Jan.-July, 1782, *ibid.*

15. *RRG,* II, 264.

16. Proclamations dated Jan. 15, and Feb. 2, 1779, in Henry Clinton Papers, CL; *Royal Georgia Gazette,* March 3, 1779. See also HMC, *Royal Institution,* I, 398.

17. Clinton to Germain, March 30, 1779, Henry Clinton Papers, CL; *N. J. Archives,* 2 Series, III, 536; Treasury action March 16, 1780, PRO, T 28/2, p. 54; Germain to Wright, Sept. 6, 1780, Ms. CRG, XXXIX, 107.

18. Undated petition of Georgia loyalists to Wright, Loyalists Mss., GHS.

19. *Royal Georgia Gazette,* Feb. and March, Nov. 25, 1779, June 7, Nov. 15, 1781; *CRG,* XII, 457-458.

20. *Royal Georgia Gazette,* Nov. 25, 1779; December 13, 1781.

21. *Ibid.,* 1779-1781.

22. On the treatment of refugees see *NCSR,* XXXIV, 351, 372; Wm. W. Hening, *Statutes at Large: A Collection of the Laws of Virginia,* X, 307-308; *Calendar of Virginia State Papers,* III, 241; *Archives of Maryland,* XLV, 311; XLVII, 258.

23. *JCC,* XX, 748-749; XXI, 782-783, 852; *N. J. Archives,* 2nd Series, V, 286; Mass. Hist. Soc., *Proceedings,* 2 Series, IX, 105, 169-172.

24. *RRG,* II, 318.

25. *Ibid.*, 280-290, 310-311, 315, 322, 323, 325, 333, 339, 344; III, 93-95, 97, 102, 111; Joseph Clay to John Banks, Jan. 6, 1782, Ms. Clay Letter Book, GHS, 240; John Martin to General Wayne, Jan. 19, 1782, Greene Papers, CL; report of food issued Jan. 7-13, 1782, "Military 1777-1792" folder, Telamon Cuyler Coll., U. of Ga.

26. *RRG*, I, 319-320; II, 4-6, 14, 17-18, 60, 80, 219, 227, 281, 336, 398.

27. Wright to Germain, April 6, 1780, *Collections*, GHS, III, 284; return of refugees in Georgia, April 15, 1780, Henry Clinton Papers, CL; Clinton to John Graham, March 15, 1781, HMC, *Royal Institution*, II, 252.

28. Wright to Germain, June 14, Sept. 7, 1781, Ms. CRG, XXXVIII, Part I, 542-543, 546; petition of loyalist refugees, 1781-1782, "Revolution-British" folder, Cuyler Coll., U. of Ga.; *Royal Georgia Gazette*, Feb. 11, 1779; Dec. 20, 27, 1781; Jan. 3, 1782.

29. See above pp. _____. Strickland, *Religion and the State in Ga.*, 148.

30. *Ibid.*, 149, 158; Joseph Clay to Lady Huntington and William Piercy, Feb. 16, 1784, *Collections*, GHS, VIII, 196-201.

31. Seymour to Society for the Propagation of the Gospel in Foreign Parts, April 26, 1781; Feb. 14, March 14, 1782; Feb. 14, 1784; SPG transcripts, Mss. Div., LC, film pages 41-50; Ga., 50-52; Fla., 302-305.

32. Lt. Gov. Gambier, Bahamas, to SPG, June 15, 1778, SPG, Series B, VI, No. 52, LC; William O'Bryen to Brown, Oct. 21, 1777, *ibid.*; Brown to SPG, April 15, 1780, Dec. 29, 1781, SPG, Ga., 31-41, 42-45; *CRG*, XV, 604-605; *Collections*, GHS, X, 111; Germain to Wright, May 2, 1781, Ms. CRG, XXXIX, 110.

33. See above pp. _____.

34. Strickland, *Religion and the State in Ga.*, 144-145; *Royal Georgia Gazette*, July 26, Dec. 20, 1781.

35. Strickland, *Religion and the State in Ga.*, 147.

36. White, *Hist. Coll. of Ga.*, 532-533; *RRG*, III, 550.

37. Strickland, *Religion and the State*

in *Ga.*, 118-119, 152-153.

38. *Ibid.*, 156. See Strickland, 139-164, for a treatment of religion in Georgia during the Revolution.

39. *Royal Georgia Gazette*, Jan. 11, Feb. 22, 1781.

40. *Royal Georgia Gazette*, March 15, Sept. 20, Oct. 4, 11, 18, Nov. 29, Dec. 6, 1781; June 6, 1782; *S. C. and Am. Gen. Gazette*, Dec. 23, 1780.

CHAPTER XI

1. *RRG*, III, 122; *ibid.*, II, 340, 342.

2. *Ibid.*, III, 123-124, 132; *ibid.*, II, 345-353.

3. *Ibid.*, III, 122-124, 187.

4. *Ibid.*, 157-159.

5. *Ibid.*, 118-188; *CRG*, XIX, Part II, 167-174, 152-162, 162-166.

6. Assembly action July 28-31, 1782, *RRG*, III, 159, 161-162, 167.

7. Council minutes, Feb. 6 and 15, 1783, *RRG*, II, 439-440, 451.

8. See continual complaints about lack of provisions in Revolutionary and Nathanael Greene Papers, Duke U., July, 1782-June, 1783, especially Greene to Lyman Hall, Jan. 20, 1783, and Samuel Finley to Greene, April 15, 1783; action of governor and assembly is in *RRG*, II, 435, 447.

9. Greene to Lyman Hall and to John Habersham, June 26, 1783, Greene Papers, Duke U.; Wayne to Hall, June 29, 1783, Force Transcripts, "Ga. Indians, Misc. Corr., 1782," No. 27, Mss. Div., LC.

10. Patrick Carr to Gov. Martin, Aug. 11 and 22, 1782, Force Transcripts, "Ga. Indians, Misc. Corr., 1782," No. 13 and 13a, Mss. Div., LC.

11. *RRG*, II, 356, 384-386, 397; Tonyn to Gov. Martin, Aug. 28, 1782, Force Transcripts, "Ga. Council Corr.," 6-8, Mss. Div., LC; Ga. deputies to Martin, Dec. 5, 1782, *ibid.*, 8-9.

12. Proclamation of Tonyn, Oct. 11, 1782, HMC, *Royal Institution*, III, 164; petition of people of St. Marys to Tonyn, Sept. 20, 1782, "E. Fla. Papers," Cuyler Coll., U. of Ga.; Tonyn to Hall, March 20, 1783, "Letters," *ibid.*; Wm. Brown to Tonyn, Feb. 6, 1783, *ibid.*

13. *RRG*, II, *passim* (fall, 1782-spring,

1783); *ibid.,* 420-423; *JCC,* XXVIII, 560; John Rutledge to Greene, Sept. 18, 1782, Burnett, *Letters,* VI, 480-481; Greene to Hall, March 15, 1783, Greene Papers, Duke U.

14. *RRG,* II, 388-89, 443, 468-483; Gov. Tonyn to Gov. Hall, March 20, 1783, "Letters," Cuyler Coll., U. of Ga.

15. Hall to Tonyn, April 21, 1783, *Gazette of the State of Georgia,* May 8, 1785; *ibid.,* March 11, 1784; *RRG,* II, 608-609.

16. *RRG,* II, 625, 630-633.

17. *CRG,* XIX, Part II, 146, 147-151.

18. *RRG,* I, 373-397; III, 115.

19. Gov. John Martin to Wayne, Jan. 19, 1782, Greene Papers, CL; Wayne to Martin, March 15, 1782, Force Transcripts, "Ga. Indians," No. 12, Mss. Div., LC; Wayne to Martin, March 26, 1782, *ibid.,* No. 47.

20. *RRG,* III, 137-138, 145, 176.

21. *Ibid.,* 173-175, 177-179; *CRG,* XIX, Part II, 152-162.

22. Return of refugees from Georgia in East Florida received from General Leslie, July 18, 1782, PRO, CO 5: 560, pp. 805-810; return of people embarked from S. C. and Ga., Charleston, Dec. 13, 1782, Winslow Papers, Mass. Hist. Soc. *Proceedings,* 2 Series, III, 95; Carleton to Shelburne, Aug. 15, 1782, PRO, CO 5: 106, pp. 329-335.

23. Georgia loyalists in the Bahamas have been located through Wilbur Henry Siebert, *Loyalists in East Florida 1774 to 1782* (Deland, Fla., 1929, 2 vols.) and through the courtesy of the late Mrs. Maxfield Parrish, Windsor, Vermont, and St. Simons Island, Georgia, who was engaged in research on loyalists in the Bahamas.

24. *RRG,* II, 348, 361-363.

25. See *Gazette of the State of Georgia* throughout the fall of 1783.

26. Ms. GDAH.

27. *Gazette of the State of Georgia,* June 30, 1785; *RRG,* I, 413-601, gives accounts of sales, apparently incomplete.

28. See act of July 29, 1782, *CRG,* XIX, Part II, 216-236.

29. *RRG,* III, 339. Seth John Cuthbert to Samuel Elbert, July 9, 1785, "*Letters,*" Cuyler Coll., U. of Ga.; *Georgia State Gazette,* July 21, 28, Aug. 4, 11, 1787.

30. Act of Feb. 13, 1786, *Acts of the General Assembly,* 1786.

31. Militia act, Aug. 20, 1781, Watkins, *Digest,* 238; resolve of Aug. 19, 1781, Force Transcripts, "Ga. Indians," No. 42, Mss. Div., LC; Stevens, *History of Georgia,* II, 358. Full workings of the land bounty system are given in Alex M. Hitz, "Georgia Bounty Land Grants," *GHQ,* XXXVIII, 337-348.

32. *RRG,* II, 587; Ms. Assembly Journal, 1784-86, p. 257 (Feb. 16, 1785).

33. *RRG,* II, 580-581, 594; III, 155, 160-161, 561; I, 602-607. Ms. Assembly Journal, 1784-86, pp. 499-500; *ibid.,* 1787-88, p. 403.

34. *RRG,* III, 108-109, 115, 171, 228; Ms. Assembly Journal, 1784-86, pp. 514-516; Wayne to Greene, June 15, 1782, Greene Papers, CL.

35. *RRG,* III, 107-109.

36. *Ibid.,* 21, 116, 165-166, 438-439; Ms. Assembly Journal, 1784-86, pp. 264-265; *RRG,* II, 639-640; *CRG,* XIX, Part II, 449-450.

37. *RRG,* III, 524-525, 543, 545, 550-551; II, 724; *JCC,* XXI, 978-979; Burnett, *Letters,* VI, 225.

38. Act of Jan. 10, 1782, "Council, Governor, Secretary of State folder," Cuyler Coll., U. of Ga.; resolution of Aug. 1, 1783, *RRG,* III, 413.

39. Act of Feb. 13, 1786, *CRG,* XIX, Part II, 518-522.

40. Ms. Assembly Journal, 1784-86, pp. 150-151, 267; Ms. Council Minutes, June 13, 1785, p. 121; act of Aug. 14, 1786, Marbury and Crawford, *Digest,* 203-204.

CHAPTER XII

1. See table of assembly sessions in Appendix B below.

2. *RRG,* III, 204-206.

3. *Ibid.,* 276.

4. *Ibid.,* 224.

5. *Ibid.,* II, 509-514.

6. *CRG,* XIX, Part II, 243-248, 290-

292.

7. Ms. Assembly Journal, 1785, *passim*.
8. *Ibid.*, 1784-1786, pp. 135-136, 283, 284. Rules for other assemblies are in their journals early in the session.
9. *RRG*, II, 596-597.
10. *Ibid.*, III, 300-302; *CRG*, XIX, Part II, 312-340.
11. Ms. Assembly Journal and Ms. Council Minutes, Jan. 7-25, 1788; Thomas U. P. Charlton, *The Life of Major General James Jackson* (Augusta, 1809), reprint (n.p., n.d. [Atlanta, 1896]), 53-56. In 1798 Jackson was elected governor, accepted, and served.
12. Act of March 1, 1778, contemporary copy, DeRenne Coll., U. of Ga.; later acts, *CRG*, XIX, Part II, 450-452, 547-551.
13. *CRG*, XIX, Part II, 288-290.
14. Presentments, *Gazette of the State of Georgia*, March 13, Oct. 16, 1783; council action, *RRG*, II, 471-472, 513.
15. W. Stephens to Seaborn Jones, Jan. 12, 1787, C. C. Jones Papers, Duke U.
16. *Gazette of the State of Georgia*, Dec. 2, 1784; *Georgia State Gazette*, Oct. 20, 1787; *S. C. State Gazette and General Advertiser*, March 6, Nov. 9, 1784; *Charleston City Gazette*, Nov. 7, 1787, Dec. 12, 1788.
17. *CRG*, XIX, Part II, 284-287, 452-454.
18. Ms. Assembly Journal, 1784-86, pp. 493-494; *GHQ*, II, 198-224. *Gazette of the State of Georgia*, April 27, 1786.
19. *RRG*, III, 529; *CRG*, XIX, Part II, 455-457; act of Feb. 8, 1787, to explain Article XLIX of the constitution, Ms. GDAH.
20. *RRG*, II, 730; the law in question is in *CRG*, Part II, 288-290.
21. *Gazette of the State of Georgia*, April 27, 1786.
22. *Acts of the General Assembly of the State of Georgia, 1786*, p. 4.
23. *RRG*, II, 527-529; act of Feb. 13, 1786, Ms. GDAH; Ms. Assembly Journal, 1784-1786, pp. 227-228.
24. Ms. Executive Council Minutes, 1789, p. 106.
25. *RRG*, III, 411-412; *Acts of the Gen-eral Assembly of the State of Georgia, 1786*, p. 4.
26. *CRG*, XIX, Part II, 471-474, 534-540; acts of Feb. 13, 1786, and Jan. 22, 1787, Ms. GDAH.
27. *Gazette of the State of Georgia*, Nov. 17, 1785.
28. Ms. Assembly Journal, 1789, pp. 141-142.
29. *Georgia State Gazette*, Nov. 11, 1786, and June 2, 1787.
30. Ms. Assembly Journal, 1784-86, pp. 374-376.
31. *CRG*, XIX, Part II, 550-551.
32. *RRG*, III, 326; *CRG*, XIX, Part II, 419-433; *Gazette of the State of Georgia*, May 5, 1785.
33. Ms. Assembly Journal, 1784-86, pp. 520-521.
34. *CRG*, XIX, Part II, 563-568.
35. *Ibid.*, 533.
36. *Ibid.*, 560-561.
37. Index to Georgia Laws, p. 88, GDAH.
38. *CRG*, XIX, Part II, 466-468; Ms. Assembly Journal, 1784-86, pp. 285, 289, 292-293, 297, 301, 305-306; Ms. Council Minutes, 1789, pp. 93-94.
39. William Harden, "A Neglected Period of Georgia History," *GHQ*, II, 198-224; Ms. Assembly Journal, 1784-86, pp. 410-411; Isaac Biggs to Joseph Thomas, undated, *GHQ* XII, 178-179.
40. *RRG*, II, 519-605; III, 334-335, 563; *Gazette of the State of Georgia*, June 10, 1784; Ms. Assembly Journal, 1784-86, p. 212.
41. *CRG*, XIX, Part II, 162-166.
42. *Ibid.*, 562-563; *Acts of the General Assembly of the State of Georgia*, Jan.-Feb., 1788, pp. 15-16.
43. *Gazette of the State of Georgia*, Feb. 13, 1783.
44. Petition of Ralph and Jacob De-Pass, "Petitions, 1784," Cuyler Coll., U. of Ga.; Ms. Assembly Journal, 1784-86, pp. 233, 239; *CRG*, XIX, Part II, 379.
45. *CRG*, XIX, Part II, 375-378.
46. *Ibid.*, 449-450; Watkins, *Digest*, 340, 379.
47. *RRG*, II, 511-512; *CRG*, XIX, Part II, 237-242, 263-279.

48. Ms. Index of Georgia Laws, 67, GDAH.
49. *CRG,* XIX, Part II, 216-225.
50. *Ibid.,* 183-200.
51. *Ibid.,* 442-443.
52. Seth J. Cuthbert, to Speaker of the Assembly (?), Jan. 5, 1786, "Letters, 1786," Cuyler Coll., U. of Ga.
53. Ms. Assembly Journal, 1784-86, pp. 350-351.
54. *Ibid.,* 405-408.
55. *Ibid.,* 441-447; *Acts of the General Assembly,* August, 1786, pp. 5-7.
56. Ms. "State of Public Accounts of Georgia," GHS; Ms. Assembly Journal, 1787-88, pp. 162, 189; Mathews to Wm. Few and Wm. Pierce, March 23, 1787, Ms. Governor's Letter Book, 1787-89, p. 36; Ms. Council Minutes, 1786-88, pp. 216, 229-231.
57. Ms. Assembly Journal, 1787-88, pp. 275-277, 312-313, 349-350, 428.
58. Salaries as voted by the assembly are in *RRG,* III, 244, 440; Ms. Assembly Journal, 1784-86, pp. 159-160, 254, 325; 1787-88, pp. 51, 91, 178-189, 355-357; 1789, 57-59.
59. Ms. Assembly Journal, 1789, 57-59.
60. *RRG,* III, 483; II, 657; Ms. Assembly Journal, 1784-86, pp. 375, 529.
61. *CRG,* XIX, Part II, 263-279; *RRG,* II, 526-527; III, 354-355.
62. *CRG,* XIX, Part II, 398-416.
63. *Acts of the General Assembly,* 1787, pp. 1-8; *Georgia State Gazette,* March 15, 1788.
64. Treasurer John Meals to Governor George Handley, March 14, 1788, "Letters, 1788," Cuyler Coll., U. of Ga.
65. Ms. Assembly Journal, 1787-88, pp. 47-48; 1789, pp. 162-172.
66. Ms. copy of act of Oct. 31, 1787, GDAH; Ms. Assembly Journal, 1789, pp. 84-85, 91-92, 105; Ms. Council Minutes, 1789, pp. 191-192; *Georgia State Gazette,* Feb. 21 and March 14, 1789.
67. *CRG,* XIX, Part I, 406-414, 439-449; Part II, 145, 237-242; Joseph Clay to John Wright Standley, Jan. 24, 1783, *Collections,* GHS, VIII, 168.
68. *CRG,* XIX, Part II, 244; *RRG,* II, 549.
69. *RRG,* III, 501, 573-574; Ms. Index of Ga. Laws, 67, GDAH; Ms. Assembly Journal, 1784-86, p. 244.
70. Feb. 13, 1786, *CRG,* XIX, Part II, 498-515; Feb. 10, 1787, Ms. GDAH; Feb. 3, 1789, *Georgia State Gazette,* Feb. 14, 1789.
71. Seth J. Cuthbert to Speaker of the Assembly, Jan. 5, 1786, "Letters, 1786," Cuyler Coll., U. of Ga.
72. *Ibid.;* Ms. Assembly Journal, 1789, pp. 48-49.

CHAPTER XIII

1. Joseph Clay to various correspondents, Jan. 24, Feb. 5, April 23, 1782, *Collections,* GHS, VIII, 167, 175, 190-191; J. Anthony to James Clark, Sept. 23, 1782, Clarke Papers, Duke U.
2. Thomas Burke to Gov. Thomas Burke, Sept. 20, 1782, *NCSR,* XVI, 656.
3. Clay to Joachim N. Fanning, April 23, 1783; *Collections,* GHS, VIII, 190; Clay to _____, Feb. 23, 1783, *ibid.,* 177-181; Clay to Messrs. Graham and Clark, April 27, 1783, Ms. Clay Letter Book, GHS, 236.
4. Executive action, May 13, 1783, *RRG,* II, 501-502.
5. Clay to various correspondents, Jan.-May, 1783, *Collections,* GHS, VIII, 167-168, 186-188, 191-193; Ms. Clay Letter Book, GHS, 254, 269-270; *RRG,* II, 389-390, 401-402, 464-465, 498-499; Edward Telfair Papers for Oct.-Dec., 1783, Duke U.
6. Clay to Joachim N. Fanning, April 3, 1784, *Collections,* GHS, VIII, 207-208.
7. *JCC,* XXV, 544; XXVI, 79; XXVIII, 285-345; XXIX, 532-533; *Gazette of the State of Georgia,* Nov. 10, 1785; *Georgia State Gazette,* June 2, 1787; April 5, 1788; Ms. Council Minutes, 1788-89, pp. 150-151.
8. *Gazette of the State of Georgia,* Feb. 12, 1784; June 23, 1785.
9. See ship arrivals and departures in Georgia newspapers.
10. See protest of Aug. 25, 1785, in *Gazette of the State of Georgia,* Sept. 1, 1785; James Habersham to "My Dear Brother," Sept. 19, 1785, John

& Joseph Habersham Papers, Duke U.

11. Ms. Council Minutes, 1785, pp. 85B-86B; Ms. Assembly Journal, 1784-86, p. 362; 1787-88, pp. 178-179.

12. *Georgia State Gazette* for the period concerned.

13. Joseph Clay to James Seagrove, April 22, 1783, Ms. Clay Letter Book, GHS, 282; council minutes, May 5, 1783, *RRG,* II, 497; *Gazette of the State of Georgia,* July 22, 1784; Jan. 20, 1785.

14. Eben Prescott in *Georgia State Gazette,* Sept. 8, 1787.

15. Memo. between Coxe & Frazier of Philadelphia on behalf of Clay, Telfair & Co. of Savannah and Jeremiah Fox of Philadelphia, tobacco and snuff maker, Sept. 9, 1785, Edward Telfair Papers, Duke U.

16. *Georgia State Gazette,* June 7, 1788.

17. Ms. Assembly Journal, 1784-86, pp. 376-377; 1787-88, pp. 59-60; Ms. Council Minutes, 1786-88, pp. 137-138.

18. Law passed Feb. 21, 1785, *CRG,* XIX, Part II, 417-418.

19. *Acts of the General Assembly,* Aug., 1786, pp. 5-7; Ms. Assembly Journal, 1787-88, pp. 73, 79.

20. *Gazette of the State of Georgia,* Sept. 21, Oct. 12, 1786, *et passim; Georgia State Gazette,* Dec. 9, 1786.

21. Ms. Assembly Journal, 1787-88, p. 56.

22. *Georgia State Gazette,* Jan.-March, 1787, *passim;* Wm. Spotswood to Rev. Jeremy Belknap, Oct. 9, 1788, *Mass. Hist. Collections,* 6 Series, IV, 421; Ms. Assembly Journal, 1789, pp. 73-74, 93, 109-110; *Augusta Chronicle,* April 18, 1789.

23. For a general treatment of Southern agricultural conditions and changes in the 1780s see Gray, *History of Agriculture in the Southern U. S.,* II, Chapter XXVI.

24. James Armstrong to Thomas Burke, Aug. 25, 1782, *NCSR,* XVI, 646; Joseph Clay to various correspondents, 1783-1785, *Collections,* GHS, VIII, 175, 194-195; March 22, 1787, Ms. Clay Letter Book, GHS; Clay to ⸺⸺, Dec. 6, 1785, Ed. Telfair Papers, Duke U.; James Belcher to

John Scott, April 10, 1787, Page Papers, U. of N. C.

25. Clay to John Wolcock, April 22, 1784, *Collections,* GHS, VIII, 211.

26, *RRG,* III, 394-397; *CRG,* XIX, Part II, 380-394; Eliza A. Bowen, *The Story of Wilkes County, Georgia* (Marietta, Georgia, 1950), 86-87.

27. *Gazette of the State of Georgia,* April 20, 1786; *Georgia State Gazette,* Jan. 20, 1786, April 5 and May 10, 1788; Gray, *History of Agriculture in the Southern U. S.,* II, 610-611; *GHQ,* I, 41; Savannah custom records, 1789, Record Group I. G. 36, National Archives.

28. Gray, *History of Agriculture in the Southern U. S.,* II, 673-681; "The Beginning of Cotton Cultivation in Georgia," *GHQ,* I, 39-45; Charleston, *City Gazette,* April 12, 1788.

29. Charleston, *City Gazette,* Dec. 24, 1788.

30. *Georgia State Gazette,* Nov. 22, 1788.

31. *RRG,* II, 480. On cattle raising see John H. Goff, "Cow Punching in Old Georgia," *Georgia Review,* III, 341-348.

32. *Gazette of the State of Georgia,* Sept. 29, 1785.

33. For Oct., 1782, sale of coastal lands, see Ms. *CRG,* XXXIX, 289-290. Joseph Clay to John W. Stanley, Jan. 24, 1783, *Collections,* GHS, VIII, 169; Clay to J. T. Sterling, April 24, 1790, *ibid.,* 223-224.

34. *RRG,* II, 496-497, 549-551, 567, *et passim.*

35. *CRG,* XIX, Part II, 201-215, 280-284; *RRG,* II, 450-453; Joseph Clay to John W. Stanley, Jan. 24, 1783, *Collections,* GHS, VIII, 167.

36. *RRG,* II, 525-526.

37. *CRG,* XIX, Part II, 434-441.

38. *Ibid.,* 292-304.

39. *RRG,* II, 789-799; John Habersham to ⸺⸺, April 10, 1784, Ms. John Habersham Papers, GHS; *Gazette of the State of Georgia,* April 15, 1784.

40. David Rees to John Houstoun, June 2, 1784, John Houstoun Papers, GHS; Stevens, *History of Georgia,* II, 355-358, prints part of this letter.

41. *RRG,* II, 696-730.

42. See council minutes, *RRG*, II, and ms. in GDAH.

43. On the bounty system and speculation see Alex M. Hitz, "Georgia Bounty Land Grants," *GHQ*, XXXVIII, 337-348, George Ogg Papers, Duke U.; Minis Collection, U. of N. C.

44. On the activities of Carr and Call see Ms. Carr Collection, U. of Ga.; *Gazette of the State of Georgia*, Aug. 2, 1785.

·45. John Wereat to McIntosh, July 30, 1784, "Ga. Indians," Force Transcripts, Mss. Div., LC; McIntosh to the executive, Sept. 1, 1784, Lachlan McIntosh Papers, Duke U.

46. *Gazette of the State of Georgia*, March 8, 1784; June 24, 1786; *CRG*, Part II, 516-517; Ms. Assembly Journal, 1787-88, p. 123. For a fuller treatment of the effect of land hunger on Indian relations see Chapter XV below.

47. See for example Ms. Assembly Journal, 1784-86, pp. 217-220, *et passim*.

48. Ms. Council Minutes, 1788-89, pp. 204-205.

49. *Ibid.*, 1789, p. 121.

CHAPTER XIV

1. *RRG*, III, 141, 155-156.

2. *Ibid.*, II, 467-468; *Gazette of the State of Georgia*, April 24 and May 1, 1783.

3. *Ibid.*, April 22 and May 20, 1784.

4. *RRG*, II, 512; III, 381, 389, 404, 456; Ms. Assembly Journal, 1784-86, pp. 9, 11, 19, 53-54; *CRG*, XIX, Part II, 248-256.

5. *CRG*, XIX, Part II, 395-398.

6. *Gazette of the State of Georgia*, Jan. 26, 1786; Ms. Assembly Journal, 1784-86, pp. 291, 298-299.

7. *CRG*, XIX, Part II, 458; Strickland, *Religion and the State in Georgia*, 123.

8. *RRG*, III, 460; *Gazette of the State of Georgia*, April 1 and Nov. 11, 1784; Feb. 2 and July 20, 1786; *Georgia State Gazette*, June 7, 1788; Strickland, *Religion and the State in Georgia*, 167-170.

9. P. A. Strobel, *The Salzburgers* (Baltimore, 1855), 211-226. Bernhardt's

removal is noted in *NCCR*, VIII, 765.

10. H. B. Folsom, "Midway Congregational Church," 13-15, Thomas Gamble Scrap Book, Midway Church & Sunbury, 115-117, Savannah Public Library.

11. Strickland, *Religion and the State in Georgia*, 162-173; Bowen, *The Story of Wilkes County*, 118-121; George G. Smith, *The History of Georgia Methodism from 1786 to 1866* (Atlanta, 1913), Chapter III; Francis Asbury, *Journal* (3 vols., New York, 1821), II, 29-30, 44-45, 67.

12. Strickland, *Religion and the State in Georgia*, 162; Bowen, *Story of Wilkes County*, 109-111; J. H. Campbell, *Georgia Baptists: Historical and Biographical* (Second edition, Macon, Ga., 1874), 55-59.

13. Bowen, *Story of Wilkes County*, 146-149; James Stacy, *A History of the Presbyterian Church in Georgia* (n.p., n.d.), 8-9.

14. White, *Statistics of Georgia*, 101-102. The best treatment of religion in Georgia in the 1780s is Strickland, *Religion and the State in Georgia*, 161-182.

15. *RRG*, II, 512-513.

16. *Ibid.*, III, 324; *CRG*, XIX, Part II, 248-256.

17. *CRG*, XIX, Part II, 369-370; Ms. Assembly Journal, 1784-86, pp. 397-399.

18. *Gazette of the State of Georgia*, April 7 and Aug. 11, 1785, *CRG*, XIX, Part II, 560-561.

19. *Georgia State Gazette*, Oct. 28, 1786; Aug. 9, Sept. 6, 13, and 20, 1788; Jan. 17, 1789.

20. *Ibid.*, Nov. 25, 1786; Aug. 4, 1787; March 8, 1788; Bowen *Story of Wilkes County*, 58-63, 167-169; Ms. Minutes of Board of Commissioners of Academy at Washington, Georgia, 1784-1789, Duke U.

21. *Gazette of the State of Georgia*, March 27 and Nov. 27, 1783; Feb. 26, 1784; April 14 and Sept. 8, 1785; Feb. 2 and Aug. 17, 1786.

22. Ms. law, GDAH.

23. *Georgia State Gazette*, June 7, 1788;

Minutes of the Union Society; Being an Abstract of Existing Records from 1750 to 1858 (Savannah, 1860), "Bethesda," 14.
24. Watkins, *Digest*, 380-381.
25. *RRG*, II, 512-513; III, 389.
26. *Ibid.*, III, 557, 563-564; II, 607-610; Ms. Assembly Journal, 1784-86, p. 266; *CRG*, XIX, Part II, 300-301.
27. *GHQ*, X, 326-334.
28. The charter, dated Jan. 27, 1785, is in *CRG*, XIX, Part II, 363-371; Watkins, *Digest;* and other compilations of Georgia laws.
29. Ezra Stiles, *The Literary Diary of Ezra Stiles* (3 vols., New York, 1901), III, 118-127, 165-166.
30. On Johnston and his newspaper see Douglas C. McMurtrie, "Pioneer Printing in Georgia," *GHQ*, XVI, 103-106; Louis Turner Griffith and John Erwin Talmadge, *Georgia Journalism, 1763-1950* (Athens, 1951), 8-10; Alexander A. Lawrence, *James Johnston, Georgia's First Printer* (Savannah, 1956).
31. *Georgia State Gazette*, Nov. 8, 1788.
32. *Gazette of the State of Georgia*, Oct. 21, 1784.
33. *Ibid.*, Aug. 11, 1785.
34. *Ibid.*, Feb. 23 and June 8, 1786.
35. McMurtrie, "Pioneer Printing in Georgia," *GHQ*, XVI, 106-108; Griffith and Talmadge, *Georgia Journalism*, 10-13.
36. *Georgia State Gazette*, Oct. 14, 1786; *Augusta Chronicle*, May 23 and 30, 1789.
37. On relief activities for the last half of 1782 and the first few months in 1783, see *RRG*, II, III *passim*. Especially II, 344, 353, 356, 363, 372-3, 376, 389, 438, 440.
38. Minutes of council, Feb. 24, 1785, "Gov., Council, Sec. of State, etc.," Cuyler Coll., U. of Ga. No copy of the 1782 act has been found. *CRG*, XIX, Part II, 547-551 for the 1786 act.
39. *Minutes of the Union Society*, 23, and appendices following p. 206; Watkins, *Digest*, 344.
40. Ms. Council Minutes, 1785, p. 124; proclamation of Telfair, April 1,

1786, Edward Telfair, Misc. file, GDAH.
41. *RRG*, III, 534; Ms. Assembly Journal for annual election of surgeon.
42. *Gazette of the State of Georgia*, Sept. 14, 1786.
43. *Ibid., passim.*
44. Ms. Council Minutes, 1785, pp. 81-82, 110.
45. *Ibid.*, 195, 201; *Gazette of the State of Georgia, passim.*
46. Ms. Council Minutes, 1785, p. 214; *Gazette of the State of Georgia*, Dec. 22, 1785-June 1, 1786, *passim.*
47. *Gazette of the State of Georgia*, June 10, 1784, *et passim; City Gazette* (Charleston), July 17, 1788.
48. *Gazette of the State of Georgia*, Nov. 17, 1785.
49. *Ibid.*, Feb. 10 and Sept. 29, 1785.
50. *Gazette of the State of Georgia, Georgia State Gazette, passim.*
51. *Gazette of the State of Georgia*, Dec. 17, 1783.
52. *S. C. Gazette and Public Advertiser* (Charleston), Aug. 30, 1785.
53. *Georgia State Gazette*, Oct. 21, Dec. 16, 1786.
54. *Augusta Chronicle*, May 9, 1789.
55. *Georgia State Gazette*, Nov. 25, 1786; Sept. 27, 1788.
56. *Ibid.*, Jan. 13, 1787; Dec. 15, 1787; Dec. 20, 1788.
57. *Ibid.*, and *Gazette of the State of Georgia*, 1786-1789, *passim.*
58. Francis Apthorp Foster, *Materials Relating to the History of the Society of the Cincinnati in the State of Georgia from 1783 to its Dissolution* (1934); *Georgia State Gazette*, April 28, 1787; rules of the Georgia Society, Georgia Indians, Misc. "Correspondence, 1782," No. 20, Force Transcripts, Mss. Div., LC.
59. *Gazette of the State of Georgia*, July 10, 1783.
60. *Ibid.*, July 7, 1785. Accounts of July 4 celebrations for 1783 through 1789 have been found in Savannah, Augusta, and Charleston newspapers.
61. *Ibid.*, Feb. 16, 1786.

CHAPTER XV
1. Stevens, *History of Georgia*, II, 410-414.

2. *RRG,* III, 207, 231; II, 423; *CRG,* XXXIX, 500-502. For talks delivered at the treaty see "Indian Treaty Book, 1773-1796," GDAH.

3. Brown to Shelburne, Sept. 25, 1782, PRO, CO 5: 82, pp. 687-694; Brown to Townshend, June 1, 1783, *ibid.,* 735-743; Townshend to Brown, Feb. 14, 1783, HMC, *Royal Institution,* III, 358.

4. McGillivray to Brown, April 10, 1783, PRO, CO 5: 82, pp. 749-753; Wm. McIntosh to Brown, April 14, 1783, *ibid.,* 757-759; Archibald McArthur to Carleton, July 5, 1783, HMC, *Royal Institution,* IV, 203; *RRG,* II, 510-511.

5. On McGillivray see John Walton Caughey, *McGillivray of the Creeks,* (Norman, Okla., 1938); and Arthur P. Whitaker, "Alexander McGillivray," *N. C. Hist. Rev.,* V, 181-203, 289-311.

6. McGillivray to Brown, Aug. 30, 1783, PRO, CO 5: 82, pp. 811-812; Brown to Lord North, Oct. 24, 1783, *ibid.,* 807-808.

7. *Gazette of the State of Georgia,* Nov. 13, 1782; *CRG,* XXXIX, 503-505; Indian talks of April 5, 9, Sept. 20 and 22, 1784, see Indian treaties and troubles, GDAH.

8. McGillivray to John Houstoun, June 30, 1784, cited in Randolph C. Downes, "Creek-American Relations," *GHQ,* XXI, 145-146; McGillivray to James White, *American State Papers, Indian Affairs* (Washington, 1832), I, 18-19 (Cited hereafter as *ASP, IA);* McGillivray to Thomas Pinckney, Feb. 26, 1789, *ibid.,* 19-20; talks of Fat King and Tallassee King, April 5 and Sept. 22, 1784, "Indian Relations," GDAH.

9. *RRG,* III, 540, 565; II, 624; *CRG,* XIX, Part II, 292-304.

10. *CRG,* XIX, Part II, 305-311.

11. *RRG,* II, 655-656, 669-670.

12. On Spanish Indian dealings see Caughey, *McGillivray,* 25; Jane M. Berry, "The Indian Policy of Spain in the Southwest, 1783-1795," *MVHR,* III, 462-477; Arthur P. Whitaker, *The Spanish-American*

Frontier; 1783-1795 (New York, 1927), 60-61, *passim;* Walter H. Mohr, *Federal Indian Relations, 1774-1788* (Philadelphia, 1933), 143-146. On the place of Panton, Leslie and Company in these negotiations see D. C. Corbitt, "Papers Relating to the Georgia-Florida Frontier, 1784-1800," *GHQ,* XX-XXV.

13. *JCC,* XXVII, 457-464; XXVIII, 118-120, 136-139, 159-162, 183-184, 362.

14. *Collections,* GHS, V, Part II, 196-198; Ms. Assembly Journal, 1784-85, p. 270.

15. Vincente de Zespedes to ———, June 12, 1785, "Florida," Brooks Transcripts, 1749-1810, Mss. Div., LC.

16. *Collections,* GHS, V, Part II, 207-211, 215.

17. *Ibid.,* 212, 216; Ms. Council Journal, 1785, p. 150; McGillivray to Andrew Pickens, Sept. 5, 1785, *ASP, IA,* I, 17-18.

18. Ms. Council Journal, 1785, pp. 150, 192-193; *ASP, IA,* I, 16, 26, 49; Wm. Blount to Gov. Caswell, Nov. 11, 1788, *NCSR,* XVIII, 566-567.

19. Whitaker, *Spanish-American Frontier,* 58; McGillivray to Gov. Thomas Pinckney, Feb. 26, 1789, *ASP, IA,* I, 20; Caughey, *McGillivray,* 102-103, 107.

20. *ASP, IA,* I, 17; Whitaker, "Alexander McGillivray," *N. C. Hist. Rev.,* V, 195-198.

21. H. W. Wagstaff, *The Papers of John Steele* (2 vols., Raleigh, 1924), I, 21-22; *ASP, IA,* I, 17; Kenneth Coleman, "Federal Indian Relations in the South, 1781-1789," in *The Chronicles of Oklahoma,* XXXV, 439-446.

22. McGillivray to a friend in New Providence, Nassau, Jan. 20, 1787, in *Georgia State Gazette,* May 19, 1787; Caughey, *McGillivray,* 29-31; Berry, "Spanish Indian Policy," *MVHR,* III, 465-466; assembly action Aug. 3, 1786, PCC, No. 73, pp. 323-331; Ms. "Indian Relations," GDAH.

23. Telfair to various correspondents, May-Aug., 1786, *GHQ,* I, 145-150, and Ga. Council Corr., 64-70, 79-80,

Force Transcripts, Mss. Div., LC. Ms. Assembly Journal, 1784-86, pp. 408-410, 412, 461-463, 470-484, 500-501, 513-514; Wm. Davenport to John Sevier, July 28, 1786, and extract of a letter from Tugaloo, Oct. 16, 1786, in *Georgia State Gazette,* Oct. 21, 1786; George Elhorn to Telfair, Sept. 20, 1786, "Letters, 1786," Cuyler Coll., U. of Ga.

24. "Unpublished Letters of Timothy Barnard, 1784-1820," Ms. in GDAH, pp. 51-64; 1786 correspondence of Joseph Martin to Telfair, "Joseph Martin," misc. file, GDAH.

25. Preliminaries and negotiations at Shoulderbone are in a ms. volume of Shoulderbone Minutes, GDAH. On preliminaries see the first sixty-five pages and John Habersham to Edward Telfair, Oct. 19, 1786, Habersham Ms., Duke U.

26. The Treaty of Shoulderbone is in Shoulderbone Minutes, 92-99, and *CRG,* XXXIX, 524-529.

27. Shoulderbone Minutes, 101-104.

28. Letters of Nov. 15 and 28, 1786, Ms. Governor's Letter Book, 1786-89, pp. 6-15.

29. McGillivray to John Habersham, Nov. 28, 1786, "Letters, 1786," Cuyler Coll., U. of Ga.; McGillivray to friend in Nassau, Jan. 20, 1787, *Georgia State Gazette,* May 19, 1787; McGillivray to James White, April 8, 1787, *ASP, IA,* I, 18; McGillivray to Thomas Pinckney, Feb. 26, 1789, *ibid.,* 20.

30. *JCC,* XXX, 418-419, 420-421, 424; XXXI, 485, 488-489, 490, 747.

31. Mathews to Wm. Few and Wm. Pierce, March 23, 1787, Ms. Governor's Letter Book, 1787-89, p. 36.

32. Ms. Assembly Journal, 1787-88, pp. 140-141, 142-143, 157-158; *Acts of the General Assembly,* 1787, pp. 42-43.

33. White to McGillivray, April 4, 1787, and meeting of Lower Creeks, April 10, 1787, *ASP, IA,* I, 21-23.

34. On this point see Caughey, *McGillivray,* 34-35.

35. White to Knox, May 24, 1787, *ASP, IA,* I, 20-21; White to George Mathews, April 23, 1787, "James

White," misc. file, GDAH.

36. *Georgia State Gazette,* April-July, 1787, especially April 21, 28, and May 19; Mathews to various correspondents, April, 1787, Ms. Governor's Letter Book, 1787-89, pp. 44-46, 54-55, 56-57.

37. *Georgia State Gazette,* Dec. 1, 1787; Indian talks, and Georgia action, July-Aug., 1787, *ASP, IA,* I, 31-33.

38. Mathews to various correspondents, Aug.-Oct, 1787, Ms. Governor's Letter Book, 1787-89, pp. 66-72, 102; Ms. Council Minutes, 1786-88, pp. 234-239; *Georgia State Gazette,* Sept. 15, 22, and 29, 1787.

39. *ASP, IA,* I, 23-24.

40. Watkins, *Digest,* 365-367.

41. Act to raise military supplies, Oct. 31, 1787, ms. GDAH.

42. Ms. Assembly Journal, 1787-88, p. 247; Mathews to governors of the Floridas, to James Seagrove, and to John Sevier, Nov. 6-12, Ms. Governor's Letter Book, 1787-89, pp. 121-123, 125, 127.

43. Mathews to Congress, Nov. 15, 1787, *ASP, IA,* I, 23.

44. Report of July 18, 1787, *JCC,* XXXII, 367-369.

45. *JCC,* XXXIII, 407-408, 454-455, 462-463, 530-531, 707-711.

46. *Georgia State Gazette;* Ms. Council Minutes and Ms. Governor's Letter Book; "Letters, 1786," Cuyler Coll., U. of Ga.

47. Watkins, *Digest,* 375; George Handley to various correspondents, Ms. Governor's Letter Book, 1787-89, pp. 134-136, 137-141, 165-171.

48. *City Gazette* (Charleston), April 18 and Oct. 9, 1788; White, *Hist. Coll. of Ga.,* 157-159.

49. Abraham Baldwin to Joseph Clay, March 31, 1788, Burnett, *Letters,* VIII, 712.

50. *Georgia State Gazette,* Aug. 2 and Oct. 17, 1788.

51. Commissioners to McGillivray, July 16, and McGillivray to Commissioners, Aug. 12, 1788, *ASP, IA,* I, 29.

52. *Ibid.,* 28-29; *City Gazette* (Charleston), Dec. 3, 1788; *Georgia State Gazette, passim;* Ms. Governor's

Letter Book, 1787-89, pp. 204-205.

53. *GHQ,* XXXV, 82-89.

54. Walton to Richard Winn, April 2, 1789, Ms. Governor's Letter Book, 1787-89, pp. 230-233.

55. Information of George Galphin, *ASP, IA,* I, 30-35, 36.

56. Ms. Council Minutes, 1789, pp. 52-55, 63-64; Ms. Governor's Letter Book, 1787-89, 257-265; 1789, 1-3, 6-11.

57. White, *Hist. Coll. of Ga.,* 158-159; *John Steele Papers,* I, 51.

58. *ASP, IA,* I, 65-66.

59. *Augusta Chronicle,* Sept. 19, 1789; *ASP, IA,* I, 72-75; Whitaker, "Alexander McGillivray," *N. C. Hist. Rev.,* V, 291-93; Andrew Pickens to Joseph Martin, Oct. 12, 1789, Draper Mss., XX, 31, U. of Wisc.

60. Caughey, *McGillivray,* 39-40.

61. *ASP, IA,* I, 76-78.

62. William M. Willett, *A Narrative of the Military Actions of Col. Marinus Willett, Taken Chiefly from his own Manuscript* (New York, 1831), extracted in Stevens, *History of Georgia,* II, 438-443.

63. Downes, "Creek-American Relations, 1782-1790," *GHQ,* XXI, 181-184; Stevens, *History of Georgia,* II, 437-446.

CHAPTER XVI

1. *RRG,* III, 426, 449-450, 469-470, 540.

2. Secretary of Congress to Georgia, Aug. 9, 1785, Burnett, *Letters,* VIII, 176-177. On Georgia attendance in Congress see Appendix C below.

3. John Habersham to William Gibbons, Oct. 10, 1785, Burnett, *Letters,* VIII, 233; Johnston, *The Houstouns of Georgia,* 333-335.

4. William Houstoun to Samuel Elbert, April 3, 1785, Burnett, *Letters,* VIII, 81-83; Ms. Council Minutes, March 30, 1789, p. 160 B; statement of Robert Forsyth, April 20, 1789, in *Augusta Chronicle,* July 25, 1789.

5. *RRG,* III, 274, 385-386.

6. Ms. Assembly Journal, 1784-86, p. 215.

7. *Gazette of the State of Georgia,* March 10, 24, April 7, 14, 21, Oct. 6, Nov. 3, 24, Dec. 1, 8, 1785; Burnett, *Letters,* VIII, 101; White, *Statistics of Georgia,* 611-612.

8. *CRG,* XIX, Part II, 492-498, 541-543, 552-553, 554-556.

9. Act of Feb. 10, 1787, Ms. GDAH.

10. Abraham Baldwin to Charles Thomson, Feb. 14, 1786, *Collections,* NYHS, 1878, p. 203.

11. *JCC,* XXIII, 564, 570-571.

12. On Georgia action directing payment see Ms. Assembly Journal, 1784-86, pp. 255, 381-382, 522-523; 1787-88, pp. 188-189, 425; *CRG,* XIX, Part II, 552-553; *GHQ,* I, 152-153; *JCC,* XXX, 361-364.

On nonpayment of requisitions see *JCC,* XXVIII, 450; XXIX, 556; XXX, 45-46; XXXI, 751; XXXIII, 572; XXXIV, 557-558, 567, 569; Burnett, *Letters,* VII, 460; PCC, No. 141, I, pp. 75-75a; *NCSR,* XVI, 929.

13. *RRG,* III, 353-354; *CRG,* XIX, Part II, 226-228.

14. *RRG,* II, 740-741; Ms. Assembly Journal, 1785, p. 186; *JCC,* XXVIII, 243, 246; PCC, No. 141, I, 87a-88.

15. *GHQ,* I, 141; Ms. Assembly Journal, 1784-86, p. 324; PCC, No. 138, II, 425-426.

16. "State of Public Accounts of Georgia," Jan. 1, 1787, GHS.

17. Ms. Assembly Journal, 1787-88, pp. 146-148.

18. *Calendar of Virginia State Papers,* VII, 52-53.

19. *RRG,* III, 276, 282-285; Ms. Journal of S. C. House of Representatives, 1783, pp. 87-88, 107-108, 366-367.

20. Gov. Ben. Guerard, of S. C. to Gov. John Houstoun, of Ga., June 9, 1784, Ms. Journal of S. C. Privy Council; Houstoun to Guerard, June 18, 1784, S. C.-Ga. Interstate Relations, S. C. Archives Dept.

21. Ms. Ga. Assembly Journal, 1785, pp. 191, 225, 257-259; Samuel Elbert to Gov. of S. C., Feb. 12, 1785, *Collections,* GHS, V, Part II, 200; Ms. Journal of S. C. House of Rep., 1785, pp. 65-66, 146, 163-164.

22. Commission of Jan. 20, 1764, *CRG,* IX, 215.

23. Elbert to James Jackson, London merchant, Aug. 5, 1785, *Collections,*

GHS, V, Part II, 214; Ms. Council Journal, 1785, p. 140.

24. *JCC,* XXVIII, 408-410; XXXI, 622-629, 642, 650-654; Burnett, *Letters,* VIII, 468; Charles Thomson to Gov. of Ga., June 2, 1785, "Boundaries Georgia-South Carolina," GDAH.

25. Edward Telfair to Wm. Moultrie, Oct. 20, 1786, Ms. Ga. Governor's Letter Book, 1786-89, pp. 1-2; Watkins, *Digest,* 356. The negotiations and convention at Beaufort are in ms. "Journal of the Commissioners for the Treaty of Beaufort," GDAH. The original signed and sealed convention is also in GDAH.

26. Printed in Johnston, *The Houstouns of Georgia,* 269-270.

27. McIntosh and Habersham to Ga. Executive, May 1, 1787, Journal of the Treaty of Beaufort.

28. Watkins, *Digest,* 378; Ms. Journal of S. C. House of Rep., 1788, pp. 61-62, 283, 293, 297; *City Gazette* (Charleston), March 3, 1788.

29. *JCC,* XXXIII, 467-476.

30. *JCC,* XXXIII, 440, 744; XXXIV, 42-43, 79-80; Burnett, *Letters,* VIII, 602-603, 686.

31. Charles Thomson's notes on debates, Aug. 8, 1782, Burnett, *Letters,* VI, 437; Timothy Bloodworth to N. C. Assembly, Dec. 16, 1786, *ibid.,* VIII, 521; JCC, XXXII, 152, 288-290.

32. *RRG,* III, 525-526, 536.

33. *NCSR,* XVII, 13-14; *RRG,* II, 655-656; *Gazette of the State of S. C.,* Feb. 17, 1785.

34. *RRG,* II, 738-739; Ms. Council Minutes, 1785, p. 46.

35. Ms. Assembly Journal, 1784-86, pp. 456-458, 524-525, 540.

36. *Georgia State Gazette,* Oct. 21, 1786.

37. Ms. Assembly Journal, 1787-88, p. 77; Watkins, *Digest,* 366-368.

38. Ms. Assembly Journal, 1785, pp. 174-175; *CRG,* XIX, Part II, 371-375.

39. Ms. Assembly Journal, 1784-86, pp. 221-224; Edmund C. Burnett, "Papers Relating to Bourbon County, Georgia, 1785-1786," *AHR,* XV, 71-73.

40. Burnett, *AHR,* XV, 73-74, 76-77, 95-97, 105; Joseph B. Lockey, *East*

Florida, 1783-1785 (Berkeley and Los Angeles, 1949), 490, 561.

41. Burnett, *AHR,* XV, 100-101, 105, 303, 305-306, 336-337; Miro to Long, Christmas, and Davenport, Sept. 7 [5?], 1785, "Military, 1777-1792," Cuyler Coll., U. of Ga.

42. *JCC,* XXXIX, 774-775, 829-830.

43. Burnett, *AHR,* XV, 350-353.

44. *JCC,* XXXII, 195-196.

45. Watkins, *Digest,* 370, 371.

46. Ms. Assembly Journal, 1787-88, pp. 77-78, 135, 280, 335-336; Watkins, *Digest,* 370.

47. *JCC,* XXXIV, 188.

48. Gov. John Houstoun to Vincente Manuel de Zespedes, Aug. 10, 1784, and reply of Zespedes, Aug. 25, 1784, Lockey, *East Florida,* 250-251, 260-261.

49. John Houstoun to Gov. Zespedes, Oct. 27, 1784; Zespedes to Houstoun, Nov. 28, 1784, *ibid.,* 301, 316.

50. Ms. Assembly Journal, 1787-88, pp. 397-398; Ms. Council Minutes, 1789, p. 131; *JCC,* XXXIV, 188-444.

51. Carlos Howard to Henry O'Neill, May 23, 1785, Lockey, *East Florida,* 548.

52. James Jackson to Major Carter, Nov. 17, 1787, "Letters, 1787," Cuyler Coll., U. of Ga.; Jackson to governor, June 2, 1788, "Letters, 1788," *ibid.*

53. Zespedes to Gov. Mathews, Dec. 10, 1787, "East Florida Papers, 1782-1795," Cuyler Coll., U. of Ga.

54. On Panton, Leslie and Company see D. C. Corbitt, "Papers Relating to the Georgia-Florida Frontier, 1784-1800," *GHQ,* XX-XXV.

CHAPTER XVII

1. Ms. Assembly Journal, 1787-88, pp. 76-77, 129; Watkins, *Digest,* 363; Max Farrand, *The Records of the Federal Convention of 1787* (3 vols., New Haven, 1911), III, 576-577.

2. Farrand, *Records of the Federal Convention,* III, 587-589; *Georgia State Gazette,* June 30, 1787.

3. Saye, *Constitutional History of Georgia,* 127.

4. Farrand, *Records of the Federal Convention,* III, 78-97; *AHR,* III,

325-334.

5. Farrand, *Records of the Federal Convention,* I, 59, 137, 469-470, 474, 475.
6. See Martin's "Genuine Information" to the Maryland legislature in *ibid.,* III, 188.
7. *Ibid.,* II, 371-372.
8. *Ibid.,* III, 100-101; *AHR,* III, 313-314.
9. *AHR,* III, 311ff; *Georgia State Gazette,* Oct. 13, 1787.
10. Resolution of Oct. 26, 1787, Ms. Assembly Journal, 1787-88, pp. 239-240.
11. E. Merton Coulter, ed., "Minutes of the Georgia Convention Ratifying the Federal Constitution," *GHQ,* X, 223-227; *Georgia State Gazette,* Jan. 5, 1788. No copy of the printed journal is known to exist.
12. Joseph Habersham to his wife, Dec. 30, 1787, *GHQ,* X, 157.
13. *Georgia State Gazette,* Nov. 3, 1787.
14. Lachlan McIntosh to Jno. ——————, Dec. 17, 1787, Lachlan McIntosh Papers, GHS.
15. *Georgia State Gazette,* Oct. 11, 1788.
16. *Gazette of the State of Georgia,* Jan. 22, 29, Feb. 4, 12, 19, 1784; *Georgia State Gazette,* Feb. 3, June 2, 1787; Ms. Assembly Journal, 1787-88, pp. 122, 300.
17. *Georgia State Gazette,* Feb. 2, Aug. 30, 1788; Ms. Assembly Journal, 1787-88, pp. 393-396, 409-411.
18. *Georgia State Gazette,* Oct. 11, Nov. 15, 29, 1788; Ms. Minutes of Executive Council, 1788-89, pp. 305-338.
19. "Hotspur" and "Casca" in *Georgia State Gazette,* Jan. 10, 1789.
20. Ms. constitution and minutes of convention in GDAH; constitution printed in *Georgia State Gazette,* Jan. 24, 1789.
21. Ms. Assembly Journal, 1789, pp. 160-162; *Georgia State Gazette,* Feb. 7, 1789.
22. *Georgia State Gazette,* March 7, 1789; *Augusta Chronicle,* April 11, 18, May 2, 9, 1789; Walton to President of the Convention, May 5, 1789, Ms. Governor's Letter Book, 1787-89, pp. 249-250. Ms. minutes of the convention are in the GDAH. The constitution is in Watkins, *Digest,* 25-30.
23. On this point see Lucien E. Roberts, "Sectional Problems in Georgia, during the Formative Period, 1776-1789," *GHQ,* XVIII, 213-215.
24. Executive action Oct. 17, 1788, Ms. Executive Council Minutes, 1788-89, p. 314; speaker and members of assembly to Governor Handley, Nov. 13, 1788, *Georgia State Gazette,* Nov. 15, 1788; *ibid.,* Jan. 10, Feb. 7, 1789; Ms. Assembly Journal, 1789, pp. 9-10.
25. Ms. Assembly Journal, 1789, pp. 28, 32-35, 50, 53, 68; Ms. Executive Council Minutes, 1789, pp. 96-99, 103, 104-109, 111-114, 117-120, 128-131; *Georgia State Gazette,* Jan. 31, Feb. 7, 14, 21, 28, March 7, 14, 1789.
26. Proclamation of Governor Walton July 22, 1789, *Augusta Chronicle,* July 25, 1789.
27. *Ibid.,* Oct. 10, 24, 1789; Ms. Senate Journal, 1789-1790, pp. 19-21; Stevens, *History of Georgia,* II, 391-392.

BIBLIOGRAPHY

****

I. BASIC COLONIAL AND STATE RECORDS

Candler, Allen D. and Lucian Lamar Knight, eds. *The Colonial Records of the State of Georgia.* 26 vols. Atlanta: Various state printers, 1904-1916. Vols. 27-39 unpublished in manuscript at Georgia Department of Archives and History and on microfilm at Microfilm Reading Room, Library of Congress. (Mainly transcripts from PRO, CO 5: 636-712. Legislative and Executive records, laws, reports, and correspondence.)

Hawes, Mrs. Lilla M., ed. "The Proceedings and Minutes of the Governor and Council of Georgia, October 4, 1774 through November 7, 1775 and September 6, 1779 through September 20, 1780." *GHQ,* XXXIV-XXXV (1950-1951). Reprinted in *Collections* of the Georgia Historical Society, X (Savannah: the Society, 1952).

Candler, Allen D., ed. *The Revolutionary Records of the State of Georgia.* 3 vols. Atlanta: The Franklin-Turner Co., 1908. (Legislative and Executive journals and miscellaneous documents.)

"Minutes of the Executive Council, May 7 through October 14, 1777." *GHQ,* XXXIII-XXXIV (1949-1950.)

Mss. Assembly Journals, Council Minutes, and Executive Corespondence for the 1780s to supplement Candler, *Revolutionary Records,* in Ga. Dept. of Archives and History.

Georgia Council Minutes, Orders and Proceedings of the Executive Council. Jan. 19-May 18, Oct. 23-November 23, 1786. Revolutionary Collection, Duke U.

"Some Official Letters of Governor Edward Telfair." *GHQ,* I (1917), 141-154.

"Official Letters of Governor John Martin." *GHQ,* I (1917), 281-335.

Index to Georgia Laws, 1761-1813. (Ms. list laws by title only inchronological order.) Ga. Dept. of Archives and History.

Acts Passed by the General Assembly of Georgia. 1755-1789. (Printed either individually or as a collection for each Assembly session by the state printer. Savannah and Augusta. Collections are in the

DeRenne Collection, U. of Ga. Library, GHS, and the Library of Congress. In 1905-1906 the Statute Law Book Company, of Washington, D. C., made facsimile reproductions of all known such acts through 1770.)

Watkins, Robert and George. *Digest of the Laws of the State of Georgia . . . to 1798.* Philadelphia: R. Aitken, 1800.

Marbury, Horatio and William Harris Crawford. *Digest of the Laws of the State of Georgia from its Settlement . . . in 1775 to . . . 1800. . . .* Savannah: Seymour, Woolhopter and Stebbins, 1802.

Acts Passed by the General Assembly of Georgia, 1755-1774. Wormsloe, Ga.: Privately printed, 1881. (Contains acts not known to be printed in the above three items.)

Ms. laws in the Ga. Dept. of Archives and History.

II. MANUSCRIPTS

A. *Georgia Department of Archives and History, Atlanta*

Indian Treaty Book. 1773-1796. (Typescript from treaties filed in Dept.)

Indian Relations. (Typescript from materials filed in Dept.)

Shoulderbone [Treaty] Minutes. 1786 ms. vol.

Boundaries, Georgia-South Carolina. Ms. collection.

Journal of the Commissioners for the Treaty of Beaufort. Ms. vol.

Record of the Court of Land Commissioners, appointed by Governor Wright to grant the Indian cession of 1773. Incomplete typescript and ms. fragments.

Minutes of the three constitutional conventions, 1788-1789, that wrote and adopted Georgia's Constitution of 1789. Also copies of the constitutions.

Miscellaneous papers, correspondence, etc., filed under subject and name of author.

B. *Georgia Historical Society, Savannah*

Clay, Joseph. Ms. Letter Book.

Clay, Joseph & Company. Ms. Letter Book.

Habersham, John. Papers.

Houstoun, John. Papers.

Jackson, James. Ms. notes on David Ramsay, *History of the Revolution in South Carolina.*

Jackson, James. Collection. (Miscellaneous personal papers and letter book.)

Jones, Noble Wimberly. Papers.

McIntosh, Lachlan. Papers and Letter Book.

Stevens, W. B. Papers. (Copies of documents collected by Stevens for use in his *History of Georgia.*)

C. *University of Georgia Library*

Carr Papers. (Collection of personal and business papers of the Carr family from 1780 through 1878.)

Cuyler, Telamon. Collection. (Miscellaneous items from the state archives from the colonial period through the Civil War.)

D. *Manuscripts Division, Library of Congress*

Force Transcripts of Georgia Records.
    Indian Affairs 1751-1825. (Contains much more than Indian Affairs.)
    Council correspondence, 1782 [1785]—1789.
Proclamation of Governors, Oct. 31, 1754-Jan. 29, 1778.
    Miscellaneous items.
U. S. Revolution, Miscellaneous.
Miscellaneous personal papers.
British Public Records Office.
    Colonial Office Class 5: America and West Indies.
        Indian Superintendent correspondence, military correspondence, and Treasury papers.
    Treasury Papers 28: vols. 1 & 2.
    Cornwallis Papers.
        (On PRO transcripts in the Library of Congress see Grace Gardner Griffin, *A Guide to Manuscripts Relating to American History in British Depositories Reproduced for the Division of Manuscripts of the Library of Congress.* The Library of Congress, 1946. There are numerous ms. indexes and calendars for these papers in the Mss. Div. By far the most valuable is B. F. Stevens, "Catalogue Index of Manuscripts in the Archives of England, France, Holland, and Spain, relating to America, 1763-1783." 180 ms. vols.)
Fulham Palace Mss. (Archives of the Bishop of London.)
    North Carolina, South Carolina, and Georgia, 1712-1770.
    Virginia, 1695-1776.
Brooks Transcripts. (Florida material.)

E. *National Archives*

Papers of the Continental Congress (Georgia-Continental Relations).

F. *William L. Clements Library, University of Michigan*

Sir Henry Clinton Papers. (Army correspondence.)
Thomas Gage Papers. (Army correspondence.)
Second Earl of Shelburne (First Marquess of Lansdowne) Papers. Calendared in the *Third* (London, 1872), *Fifth* (1876), and *Sixth* (1877) *Reports* of the Historical Manuscripts Commission as Lansdowne Papers. (Vols. 43-88 are concerned with Shelburne's period in the Colonial Office and the Peace of 1783.)

Lord George Germain Papers. Calendared in "Report on the Manuscripts of Mrs. Stopford-Sackville of Drayton House, Northamptonshire." *Ninth Report,* Historical Manuscripts Commission, Appendix III. London, 1884. (Issued separately. 2 vols. London, 1904-1910.)
Strachey Papers.
Von Jungkenn Mss. (Letters of Lt. Col. Friedrich von Porbeck about conditions in Savannah 1780-1782 in vols. 3-5.)
Nathanael Greene Papers. (Mainly war materials.)
Miscellaneous papers.

G. *Duke University Library*

Minutes of Board of Commissioners of the Academy at Washington, Georgia, 1784-1808.
Wilkes County, Georgia, Court Papers, 1779-1827.
Revolutionary Collection.
Nathanael Greene Papers.
Samuel Elbert Papers.
James Jackson Letters.
Edward Telfair Papers.
George Walton Papers.
Many small collections of Georgians for the period, mainly in the papers purchased from Mrs. Marmaduke Floyd, of Savannah.

H. *University of North Carolina Library, Southern Historical Collection*

Mackey Stiles Papers, Vol. 42. Microfilm.

I. *Henry E. Huntington Library*

Orderly Book of General Benjamin Lincoln, Dec. 6, 1778-June 27, 1779.
Orderly Book of Georgia Militia Regiment commanded by Ely Kershaw, Jan. 2-April 23, 1779.
Report of F. Skelly on the movements of the British Army, Savannah, Nov. 8, 1779.
Minutes concerning the fortifications of Savannah. Board of General British Officers, Jan. 6, 1782.

J. *South Carolina Archives Department, Columbia*

Ms. assembly and executive minutes, executive files on topics of special concern to Georgia.

K. *New York Public Library*

Loyalists Transcripts, as concerned with Georgia loyalists.

III. PRINTED SOURCE MATERIALS

A. *American*

American Archives, 4th Series (ed. Peter Force). 6 vols. Washington: M. St. Clair and Peter Force, 1837-1846. 5th Series. 3 vols. Washington: M. St. Clair and Peter Force, 1848-1853.

American State Papers, Indian Affairs. 2 vols. Washington: Gales and Seaton, 1832.

Andrews, Charles M. "List of the Commissions and Instructions Issued to the Governors and Lieutenant Governors of the American and West Indian Colonies from 1690 to 1784." *Report of the American Historical Association for 1911.* Vol. I.

Asbury, Francis. *The Journal of the Rev. Francis Asbury, Bishop of the Methodist Episcopal Church.* . . . 3 vols. New York: N. Bangs and T. Mason, 1821. Vol. II.

Bland, Julia M. *Georgia and the Federal Constitution.* Washington: Government Printing Office, 1937.

Burnett, Edmund C., ed. *Letters of Members of the Continental Congress.* 8 vols. Washington: The Carnegie Institution of Washington, 1921-1936.

Burnett, Edmund C. "Papers Relative to Bourbon County, Georgia, 1785-1786." *AHR,* XV (Oct., 1909; Jan., 1910), 66-111, 297-353.

Corbitt, D. C. "Papers Relating to the Georgia-Florida Frontier, 1784-1800." *GHQ,* XX-XXV.

Corbitt, D. C. "Some Papers Relating to Bourbon County, Georgia," *GHQ,* XIX, 251-263.

Coulter, E. M., ed. "Minutes of the Georgia Convention Ratifying the Federal Constitution." *GHQ,* X (1926), 223-237.

Farrand, Max. *The Records of the Federal Convention of 1787.* 3 vols. New Haven: Yale University Press, 1911.

Fitzpatrick, John C., ed. *The Writings of George Washington.* 37 vols. Washington: Government Printing Office, 1931-1940.

Ford, Paul L. *Proceedings of a Council of War Held at Burke Jail, Georgia, January 14th, 1779.* . . . Brooklyn, 1890.

Foster, Francis A. *Materials Relating to the History of the Society of the Cincinnati in the State of Georgia from 1783 to Its Dissolution.* [Savannah, Georgia] 1934.

Georgia Historical Society, *Collections.* Published by the Society.

    III. ". . . Letters from Governor Sir James Wright to the . . . Secretaries of State for America, August 24, 1774, to February 16, 1782." Savannah, 1873.

    V, Part I. "Proceedings of the Georgia Provincial Congress, July 4-8, 1775; Proceedings of the Georgia Council of Safety, 3rd November, 1775, to 17th February, 1777; Account of the Siege of Savannah, from a British Source." Savannah, 1901.

    V, Part II. "Order Book of Samuel Elbert, Colonel and Brigadier

General in the Continental Army, October, 1776, to November, 1778; Letter Book of Governor Samuel Elbert, from January, 1785, to November, 1785." Savannah, 1902.

VI. "The Letters of the Honorable James Habersham, 1756-1775." Savannah, 1904.

VIII. "Letters of Joseph Clay, Merchant of Savannah, 1776-1793." Savannah, 1913.

X. "The Proceedings and Minutes of the Governor and Council of Georgia, October 4, 1774, through November 7, 1775, and September 6, 1779, through September 20, 1780." Savannah, 1952.

Gibbes, Robert Wilson. *Documentary History of the American Revolution,* . . . 3 vols. New York: D. Appleton and Co., 1855-1857 (vols. I and II); Columbia, S. C.: 1883 (vol. III).

Hawes, Lilla M., ed. "Papers of James Jackson, 1781-1798." *GHQ,* XXXVIII, 54-80, 147-160, 220-249, 299-329.

Hawes, Lilla M., ed. "The Papers of Lachlan McIntosh, 1774-1799." *GHQ,* XXXVIII-XL.

Hening, William W. *Statutes at Large: A Collection of the Laws of Virginia.* 13 vols. Richmond & Philadelphia: various publishers, 1819-1823.

Jones, C. C., Jr., ed. "Memorandum of the Route pursued by Colonel Campbell and his column of invasion, in 1779, from Savannah to Augusta; . . ." *Magazine of American History,* XVIII (July-Dec., 1887), 256-348.

Labaree, Leonard W. *Royal Instructions to British Governors.* New York: Appleton-Century, 1935.

Library of Congress. *Journals of the Continental Congress, 1774-1789.* 34 vols. Washington: Government Printing Office, 1904-1937.

Lockey, Joseph B. Edited by John Walton Caughey. *East Florida, 1783-1785: A File of Documents Assembled, and Many of them Translated.* Berkeley and Los Angeles: University of California Press, 1949.

McIntosh, George. *The Case of George M'Intosh.* [1777.]

McIntosh, George. *Addition to the Case of George M'Intosh.* [1777.]

McIntosh, George. *Strictures on the Case of George M'Intosh.* [1777.] All three in *Hazard Pamphlets,* XXXIX, Rare Book Room, LC.

Massachusetts Historical Society, *Proceedings.* Published by the Society, Boston. 2 Series, III. "Winslow Papers."

Muhlenberg, Henry M. *The Journals of Henry Melchior Muhlenberg.* 3 vols. Philadelphia: The Muhlenberg Press, 1942-1945.

New York Historical Society, *Collections.* Published by the Society, New York.

1871-1874. "Charles Lee Papers."

1878. "Charles Thomson Papers."

1879. "Proceedings of a General Court Martial Held in Philadelphia

... for the Trial of Major General Howe, Dec. 7, 1781." Reprinted from the original pamphlet, Philadelphia, 1782. Pp. 213-311. 1883. "Journal of Col. Stephen Kemble."

Documents Relative to the Colonial History of New York. 14 vols. Albany: State Printers, 1856-1883.

Palmer, William P. & others, eds. *Calendar of Virginia State Papers.* 11 vols. Richmond: state printer, 1874-1893.

Pettengill, Roy W., ed. and translator. *Letters from America, 1776-1779.* Boston: Houghton Mifflin, 1924. (Letters from German officers who fought with the British Army during the Revolution.)

Phillips, U. B., ed. "Some Letters of Joseph Habersham. 1775-1790." *GHQ,* X, 144-163.

Saunders, William L., Walter Clark, and Stephen B. Weeks, eds. *The Colonial Records of the State of North Carolina.* 10 vols. Various state printers, 1886-1890. *The State Records of North Carolina.* 20 vols. (Vols. 11-30). Various state printers, 1895-1914.

Saye, Albert B., ed. "The Commission and Instructions of Governor John Reynolds." *GHQ,* XXX (1946), 125-162.

Stiles, Ezra. Franklin B. Dexter, ed. *The Literary Diary of Ezra Stiles.* 3 vols. New York: Charles Scribner's Sons, 1901.

Wagstaff, Henry W. *The Papers of John Steele.* 2 vols. Raleigh, N. C.: Edward & Broughton Printing Co., 1924.

White, George. *Historical Collections of Georgia.* New York: Pudney and Russell, 1854.

White, George. *Statistics of the State of Georgia.* Savannah: W. Thorne Williams, 1849.

Minutes of the Union Society: Being an Abstract of Existing Records from 1750 to 1858. Savannah: John M. Cooper, 1860.

Zubly, John J. *Calm and Respectful Thoughts on the Negative of the Crown on a Speaker Chosen and Presented by the Representatives of the People.* 1772. Rare Book Room, LC.

Zubly, John J. *The Law of Liberty: A Sermon Preached at the Opening of the Provisional Congress of Georgia.* Philadelphia: Henry Miller, 1775.

Zubly, John J. "Letter of Rev. John J. Zubly, of Savannah, Georgia, 1773." Massachusetts Historical Society, *Proceedings,* 1864-1865. Published by the Society, Boston, 1866.

Zubly, John J. *The Stamp Act Repealed.* Rare Book Room, LC.

Zubly, John J. "Rev. J. J. Zubly's Appeal to the Grand Jury. Oct. 8, 1777." *GHQ,* I, 161-165.

B. *British*

Acts of the Privy Council, Colonial Series, 1613-1783. Vols. 4-6. Hereford: H. M. Stationery Office, 1911-1912.

Historical Manuscripts Commission. Published for H. M. Stationery Office.

Report of American Manuscripts in the Royal Institution of Great Britain. 4 vols. London, Dublin, and Hereford, 1904-1909.

"Manuscripts of the Earl of Carlisle." *Fifteenth Report,* appendix, Part VI, 1897.

"Manuscripts of the Earl of Dartmouth." 3 vols. *Eleventh Report,* Appendix, Part V, 1887. *Fourteenth Report,* Appendix, Part X, 1895. *Fifteenth Report,* Appendix, Part I, 1896.

"Papers of William Knox." *Report of Various Collections,* Vol VI, 1908.

"Report on the Manuscripts of Mrs. Stopford-Sackville, of Drayton House, Northamptonshire." Ninth Report, Appendix III. London, 1884.

Stevens, B. F., ed. *An Extract Reprint of Six Rare Pamphlets on the Clinton-Cornwallis Controversy.* . . . 2 vols. London: Privately printed, 1888.

Stevens, B. F. *Facsimiles of Manuscripts in European Archives Relating to America,* 1773-1783. London: Malby and Sons, 1889-1895.

IV. NEWSPAPERS AND MAGAZINES

Augusta Chronicle.
City Gazette (Charleston).
Columbian Herald (Charleston).
Charleston Evening Gazette.
Gazette of the State of South Carolina (Charleston).
Charleston Morning Post.
Royal Gazette (Charleston).
Royal South Carolina Gazette (Charleston).
South Carolina and American General Gazette (Charleston).
South Carolina Gazette and Country Journal (Charleston).
South Carolina Gazette and General Advertiser (Charleston).
State Gazette of South Carolina (Charleston).
Continental Journal (Boston).
Gazette of the State of Georgia.
Georgia Gazette.
Georgia State Gazette.
Royal Georgia Gazette.
Gentleman's Magazine (London). 1779-1782.
Virginia Gazette (Williamsburg).

V. SECONDARY MATERIAL

A. *Georgia.*

Abrahams, Edmund H. "Early History of the Sheftalls of Georgia." American Jewish Historical Society, *Publication*, No. 17, 167-186.

Aldridge, Alfred Owen. "Benjamin Franklin as Georgia Agent." *Georgia Review*, VI (Summer, 1952), 161-173.

Ashmore, Otis and C. H. Olmstead. "The Battles of Kettle Creek and Brier Creek." *GHQ*, X, 85-125.

Bast, Homer. "Creek Indian Affairs, 1775-1778." *GHQ*, XXXIII, 1-25.

Benedict, David. *A General History of the Baptist Denomination in America and Other Parts of the World.* 2 vols. Boston: Lincoln and Edwards (vol. I), Manning and Loring (vol. II), 1813.

Bowen, Eliza A. *The Story of Wilkes County, Georgia.* Marietta, Ga.: Continental Book Company, 1950.

Campbell, J. H. *Georgia Baptists: Historical and Biographical.* 2nd ed. Macon, Ga.: J. W. Burke & Co., 1874.

Carlyle, E. Irving. "Sir James Wright." *Dictionary of National Biography.*

Catalogue of the Wymberley Jones DeRenne Georgia Library. 3 vols. Wormsloe, Ga.: Privately printed, 1931.

Charlton, Thomas U. P. *The Life of Major General James Jackson.* Augusta, 1809. (Reprint, n.p., n.d. [Atlanta, 1896].)

Coleman, Kenneth. "Restored Colonial Georgia, 1779-1782." *GHQ*, XL (1956), 1-20.

Corry, John Pitts. "Procedure in the Commons House of Assembly in Georgia." *GHQ*, XIII (1929), 110-127.

Coulter, E. M. *A Short History of Georgia.* Chapel Hill: University of North Carolina Press, 1933. (Revised ed., 1947.)

Coulter, E. Merton. "Nancy Hart, Georgia Heroine of the Revolution: The Story of the Growth of a Tradition." *GHQ*, XXXIX (1955), 118-151.

Coulter, E. Merton. "Edward Telfair." *GHQ*, XX, 99-124.

Daniel, Marjorie. "Anglicans and Dissenters in Georgia, 1758-1777." *Church History*, VII (1938), 247-262.

Daniel, Marjorie. "John Joachim Zubly—Georgia Pamphleteer of the Revolution." *GHQ*, XIX, 1-16.

Daniel, Marjorie L. "The Revolutionary Movement in Georgia, 1763-1777." Unpublished doctoral dissertation, University of Chicago, 1935.

DeBrahm, John Gerar William. *History of the Province of Georgia.* Wormsloe, Ga.: Privately printed, 1849.

Downes, Randolph C. "Creek-American Relations, 1782-1790." *GHQ*, XXII (1937), 142-184.

Flippin, Percy Scott. "Royal Government in Georgia, 1752-1776." *GHQ*, VIII-XIII (1924-1929).

Ford, Joseph H. "John J. Zubly, Opponent of British and American Oppression, 1724-1781." Unpublished master's thesis, Emory University, 1941.

Foster, William Owen. "James Jackson in the American Revolution." *GHQ*, XXXI (1947), 249-281.

Foster, William Owen. "James Jackson, Militant Georgia Statesman, 1757-1806." Unpublished doctoral dissertation, University of North Carolina, 1952.

Gamble, Thomas. *Savannah Duels and Duellists, 1733-1877*. Savannah: Review Publishing Company, 1923.

Gamble, Thomas. Personal Scrap Books. Savannah Public Library. (Contain newspaper clippings, pamphlets, letters, and other material collected through a lifetime of interest in Savannah and Georgia history.)

Goff, John H. "Cow Punching in Old Georgia," *Georgia Review*, III (Fall, 1949), 341-348.

Griffith, Louis T. and John E. Talmadge. *Georgia Journalism, 1763-1950*. Athens: University of Georgia Press, 1951.

The Particular Case of the Georgia Loyalists. . . . London (?): G. Wilkie(?), 1783.

Grice, Warren. "Georgia Appointments by President Washington." *GHQ*, VII, 181-212.

Harden, William. "Basil Cowper's Remarkable Career in Georgia." *GHQ*, I, 24-35.

Hays, Louise F. *Hero of Hornet's Nest. A Biography of Elijah Clark*. New York: Stratford House, 1946.

Hitz, Alex M. "Georgia Bounty Land Grants." *GHQ*, XXXVIII, 337-348.

Hubner, Leon. "The Jews of Georgia from the Outbreak of the American Revolution to the Close of the 18th Century." American Jewish Historical Society, *Publications*, XVII (1909), 89-108.

Jenkins, Charles F. *Button Gwinnett*. New York: Doubleday, Page and Company, 1926.

Johnston, Edith Duncan. *The Houstouns of Georgia*. Athens: University of Georgia Press, 1950.

Jones, Charles C., Jr. *Biographical Sketches of the Delegates from Georgia to the Continental Congress*. Boston: Houghton, Mifflin Company, 1891.

Jones, Charles C., Jr. *History of Georgia*. 2 vols. Boston: Houghton, Mifflin Company, 1883.

La Farge, Laurence, Wythe Cooke, Arthur Keith and Marius R. Campbell. *Physical Geography of Georgia* (Geological Survey of Georgia Bulletin No. 42). Atlanta: Stein Printing Company, state printers,

1925.

Lawrence, Alexander A. "James Jackson: Passionate Patriot." *GHQ,* XXXIV, 75-86.

Lawrence, Alexander A. "General Robert Howe and the British Capture of Savannah in 1778." *GHQ,* XXXVI, 303-327.

Lawrence, Alexander A. "General Lachlan McIntosh and His Suspension from the Continental Command During the Revolution." *GHQ,* XXXVIII, 101-141.

Lawrence, Alexander A. *James Johnston, Georgia's First Printer.* Savannah: Pigeonhole Press, 1956.

Lawrence, Alexander A. *Storm Over Savannah: The Story of Count d'Estaing and the Siege of the Town in 1779.* Athens: University of Georgia Press, 1951.

McCain, James Ross. *Georgia as a Proprietary Province.* Boston: Richard G. Badger, 1917.

McCall, Hugh. *The History of Georgia.* 2 vols. Savannah: Seymour and Williams, 1811-1816.

McLendon, S. G. *History of the Public Domain of Georgia.* Atlanta: Privately printed, 1924.

Mercer, Jesse. *History of the Georgia Baptist Association.* Washington, Ga.: Privately printed, 1836.

McMurtrie, Douglas C. "Pioneer Printing in Georgia." *GHQ,* XVI, 77-113.

Murphy, W. S. "The Irish Brigade of France at the Siege of Savannah, 1779." *GHQ,* XXXVIII (1954), 307-321.

Naisawald, L. Van Loan. "Major General Howe's Activities in South Carolina and Georgia, 1776-1779." *GHQ,* XXXV, 23-30.

Perkins, Eunice Ross. "John Joachim Zubly, Georgia's Conscientious Objector." *GHQ,* XV, 313-323.

Roberts, Lucien E. "Sectional Problems in Georgia During the Formative Period, 1776-1789." *GHQ,* XVIII, 207-227.

Saye, Albert B. *A Constitutional History of Georgia.* Athens: University of Georgia Press, 1948.

Saye, Albert B. "Georgia's Delegates to the Federal Convention of 1787. Who They Were and What They Did." Unpublished master's thesis, University of Georgia, 1935.

Saye, Albert B. *New Viewpoints in Georgia History.* Athens: University of Georgia Press, 1943.

Scarborough, Ruth. *The Opposition to Slavery in Georgia Prior to 1860.* Nashville, 1933: (George Peabody College of Teachers, Contributions to Education No. 97.)

Shpall, Leo. "The Sheftalls of Georgia." *GHQ,* XXVII, 339-349.

Simms, James M. *The First Colored Baptist Church in North America. Constituted at Savannah, Georgia, January 20, 1788.* Philadelphia: J. B. Lippincott, 1888.

Smith, George C. *The History of Georgia Methodism from 1786 to 1886.* Atlanta: A. B. Caldwell, Publishers, 1913.

Stacy, James. *A History of the Presbyterian Church in Georgia.* N.p., n.d. (Privately printed.)

Stevens, William B. *A History of Georgia,* . . . 2 vols. Philadelphia: D. Appleton & Co., 1847-1859.

Stokes, Anthony. *A Narrative of the Official Conduct of Anthony Stokes.* London: Privately printed, 1784.

Strickland, Reba Carolyn. *Religion and the State in Georgia in the Eighteenth Century.* New York: Columbia University Press, 1939.

Strobel, P. A. *The Salzburgers and Their Descendants.* Baltimore: T. Newton Kurtz, 1855. (Reprinted Athens: University of Georgia Press, 1953).

White, Henry C. *Abraham Baldwin.* Athens: The McGregor Company, 1926.

Williams, Samuel C. "Colonel Elijah Clarke in the Tennessee Country." *GHQ,* XXV, 151-158.

Zornow, William Frank. "Georgia Tariff Policies, 1775 to 1789," *GHQ,* XXXVIII (1954), 1-10.

B. *The South.*

Alden, John R. *John Stuart and the Southern Colonial Frontier.* Ann Arbor: University of Michigan Press, 1944.

Berry, Jane M. "The Indian Policy of Spain in the Southwest, 1783-1795." *MVHR,* III (1917), 462-477.

Caughey, John Walton. *McGillivray of the Creeks.* Norman: University of Oklahoma Press, 1938.

Cotterill, R. S. "The South Carolina Land Cession." *MVHR,* XII (1926), 376-384.

Crane, Verner W. *The Southern Frontier, 1670-1732.* Durham: Duke University Press, 1928.

Davidson, Philip. "The Southern Backcountry on the Eve of the Revolution." Avery Craven, ed. *Essays in Honor of William E. Dodd.* Chicago: University of Chicago Press, 1935.

Drayton, John. *Memoirs of the American Revolution.* 2 vols. Charleston: A. E. Miller, 1821.

Gray, Lewis Cecil. *History of Agriculture in the Southern United States to 1860.* 2 vols. Washington: Carnegie Institution of Washington, 1935.

Johnson, Cecil. *British West Florida 1763-1783.* New Haven: Yale University Press, 1943.

McCrady, Edward. *South Carolina Under the Royal Government, 1719-1776* (Vol. II); *South Carolina in the Revolution, 1775-1780* (Vol. III); *South Carolina in the Revolution, 1780-1783* (Vol. IV). New York: Macmillan, 1899-1902.

Meriwether, Robert L. *The Expansion of South Carolina 1729-1765.* Kingsport, Tenn.: Southern Publishers, 1940.

Moultrie, William. *Memoirs of the American Revolution.* 2 vols. New York: D. Longworth, 1802.

Pound, Merritt B. *Benjamin Hawkins: Indian Agent.* Athens: University of Georgia Press, 1951.

Ramsey, J. G. M., *The Annals of Tennessee to the End of the Eighteenth Century: . . . .* Charleston: J. Russell, 1853.

Roe, Clara Goldsmith. "Major General Nathanael Greene and the Southern Campaign of the American Revolution, 1780-1783." Unpublished doctoral dissertation, University of Michigan, 1947.

Siebert, Wilbur Henry. *Loyalists in East Florida 1774-1785.* 2 vols. Deland: Florida State Historical Society, 1929.

Siebert, Wilbur Henry. "The Loyalists in West Florida and the Natchez District." *MVHR*, II (1916), 465-483.

Smith, William R. *South Carolina as a Royal Province, 1719-1776.* New York: Macmillan, 1903.

Uhlendorf, Bernard A., ed. & translator. *The Siege of Charleston . . . .* Ann Arbor: University of Michigan Press, 1938.

Wallace, David D. *The History of South Carolina.* 4 vols. New York: The American Historical Society, Inc., 1934.

Wallace, David D. *South Carolina. A Short History, 1520-1948.* Chapel Hill: University of North Carolina Press, 1951.

Whitaker, Arthur P. "Alexander McGillivray." *North Carolina Historical Review*, V (1928), 181-203, 289-311.

Whitaker, Arthur P. "The Muscle Shoals Speculation, 1783-1789." *MVHR*, XIII (1926-1927), 365-386.

Whitaker, Arthur P. *The Spanish-American Frontier, 1783-1796.* New York: Houghton Mifflin Co., 1927.

INDEX

****